THE
INSIDER'S
ESSENTIAL GUIDE
TO

SAT
CRITICAL
READING
AND
VOCABULARY

LARRY KRIEGER
WITH CONTRIBUTIONS BY
CHRISTIAN HEATH

The Insider's Essential Guide To
SAT CRITICAL READING
AND VOCABULARY

LARRY KRIEGER
WITH CONTRIBUTIONS BY
CHRISTIAN HEATH

ISBN: 978-0-9852912-2-8

An INSIDER TEST PREP publication of Larry Prep LLC

Art Direction & Design by Station16 Creative (Station16 LLC)

For more Insider resources visit
www.InsiderTestPrep.com

TABLE OF CONTENTS

PART I   1

THE ESSENTIAL 600 WORDS

PART III   243

THE ESSENTIAL GUIDE TO CRITICAL READING

ABOUT THE INSIDER'S ESSENTIAL GUIDE TO SAT CRITICAL READING AND VOCABULARY

NO WIND FAVORS A SHIP WITHOUT A DESTINATION

When I was your age, my guidance counselor asked me to describe my goals. When I said that I didn't know, my counselor admonished me by saying, "Larry, no wind favors a ship without a destination." My counselor was right—goals are important. So I'd like to begin by asking you an important question: What score are you trying to achieve on the Critical Reading portion of the SAT? As you think about your answer, keep in mind that the average Critical Reading score is 500, and that only about ten percent of all test-takers score above a 650.

I'm guessing that the overwhelming majority of you are striving for a score above a 600. Congratulations! *The Insider's Guide to SAT Critical Reading and Vocabulary* is designed to help you achieve your goal.

FIVE LEVELS OF QUESTIONS
IT IS VERY IMPORTANT TO UNDERSTAND THAT SAT TEST QUESTIONS ARE DIVIDED INTO THE FOLLOWING FIVE LEVELS OF DIFFICULTY:

LEVEL 1: These questions are easy. About eighty percent of all test-takers correctly answer the Level 1 questions. If you answer all of the Level 1 questions correctly, your score will be about a 340.

LEVEL 2: These questions are a bit more challenging. About 65 percent of all test-takers correctly answer Level 2 questions. If you answer all of the Level 2 questions correctly, your score will be about a 440.

LEVEL 3: These questions are average to above average in difficulty. About fifty percent of all test-takers correctly answer Level 3 questions. If you answer all of the Level 3 questions correctly, your score will be about a 580.

LEVEL 4: These questions are challenging. Only about 35 percent of all test-takers correctly answer Level 4 questions. If you answer all of the Level 4 questions correctly, your score will be about a 680.

LEVEL 5: These questions are very challenging. Only about twnety percent of all students correctly answer Level 5 questions. If you answer all of the Level 5 questions correctly your score will soar into the 700s!

VOCABULARY! VOCABULARY!! VOCABULARY!!!

Answering Level 4 and Level 5 questions correctly is crucial to achieving a Critical Reading score above a 600. My students often ask me, "What can we do to correctly answer the Level 4 and Level 5 questions?" I always respond with a simple answer: "Vocabulary! Vocabulary!! Vocabulary!!!"

It is important to understand that challenging vocabulary words are the defining characteristic of most Level 4 and Level 5 questions. This brings us to an important paradox: the hard questions are actually easy if you know the words. You read correctly. The most challenging Level 5 questions can usually be answered very quickly if you have a strong SAT vocabulary.

WHY THE ESSENTIAL GUIDE TO SAT CRITICAL READING AND VOCABULARY IS THE BEST SAT PREP BOOK

There are a number of vocabulary books all claiming to be the best. So why is *The Essential* the best SAT prep book for Critical Reading and vocabulary?

- Essential's vocabulary section contains 600 words. Each of these words has been the answer to a real SAT question. Each SAT is a link in an overlapping chain of tests stretching back over half a century. As a result, test-writers continually repeat key words. Essential takes advantage of this often neglected fact by focusing on words that have been repeatedly used on real SATs.
- Essential's vocabulary section is divided into fifteen chapters based upon types of SAT questions. For example, Critical Reading questions often test your ability to identify an author's tone and spot rhetorical devices such as metaphor and personification. Essential devotes a full chapter to thirty attitude, tone, and mood words and a full chapter to twenty rhetorical device words.
- Essential focuses particular attention on the Level 4 and 5 words you will need to score above a 600. We define and illustrate 110 Level 5 words and 110 Level 4 words.
- Essential's 600 words are all illustrated by vivid examples designed to promote your ability to recall and use the words. The examples are drawn from an eclectic range of topics. You will find examples from popular songs and movies, from AP courses, from current events, from the experiences of my students, and even from my own life and teaching career. In addition, many of my examples focus on topics such as the college admission process that are relevant to your life.
- Many of Essential's words include a heading labeled "Insider Info." These sections are designed to share my knowledge of how a word has typically been used in real SAT questions.
- Essential is more than just a vocabulary book. In order to achieve a high score on the SAT it is not enough to simply learn vocabulary words. You must also know how to apply them to sentence completion and passage-based questions. Chapters 16–22 provide a detailed discussion of the key types of sentence completion questions. These chapters contain almost 300 practice sentence completions.
- Essential concludes with ten chapters devoted to Critical Reading and passage-based questions. Chapters 23–32 help you identify the characteristics of both right and wrong answers. They also show you how the rhetorical device and attitude words you learned

in the vocabulary section are used in passage-based questions. Our Critical Reading section concludes with a detailed examination of short and long paired passages. These ten Critical Reading chapters include almost 100 practice examples.

- The Essential 500 Words includes a special Appendix that identifies the Top Thirty SAT Roots and defines 94 key words derived from these roots.

I hope you enjoy using *The Insider's Essential Guide to SAT Critical Reading and Vocabulary*. Be sure to check out InsiderTestPrep.com for additional insights and materials! Good luck!

ABOUT LARRY KRIEGER

Larry Krieger was born and raised in western North Carolina. He earned his Bachelor of Arts and Master of Arts in Teaching from the University of North Carolina at Chapel Hill and his Master of Arts degree in Sociology from Wake Forest University.

Larry's teaching career began in 1970 at Olympic High School in Charlotte, North Carolina. During the next 35 years Larry taught urban, rural, and suburban students in North Carolina and New Jersey. Larry taught a variety of AP subjects, including American History, World History, European History, American Government, and Art History. His popular courses were renowned for their energetic presentations, commitment to scholarship, and dedication to excellence. All of Larry's AP students scored above a 3, with most scoring a 4 or a 5. In 2004 and 2005, the College Board recognized Larry as one of the nation's foremost AP teachers.

Larry is also widely known as one of America's top SAT coaches. In 2005 Larry led Montgomery High School to a Number 1 ranking in New Jersey. His students achieved a public school record national average score of 629 on the Critical Reading section of the SAT. Larry has conducted SAT workshops across the United States in a variety of cities including Denver, Louisville, Atlanta, and Minneapolis.

Larry's success has extended far beyond the classroom. He is the author of widely known Sociology, American History, and World History textbooks and a number of AP and SAT prep books. Larry founded InsiderTestPrep.com to share his SAT and AP materials with students around the world. *The Insider's Essential Guide to SAT Critical Reading and Vocabulary* joins the *AP US History: The Essential Content* as the company's second major book. Insider Test Prep expects to publish a series of innovative SAT and AP books and eBooks in the near future.

ABOUT CHRISTIAN HEATH

Christian was born and raised in Austin, Texas. As a teenager growing up in the '90s Christian enjoyed reading books, playing video games, and hiking outdoors. He excelled as a student and aced the SAT. Christian left Austin and earned his B.A. in classical piano performance at Pomona College. He fondly remembers long days enjoying the California sun, followed by long nights practicing classical piano pieces.

After graduation, Christian returned to Austin. He promptly got a job working with College Forward to help low-income teenagers at Lehman High School. Christian loved teaching and audaciously decided to found his own test prep company.

Christian's company is a favorite with local families. He has written several SAT prep books and created his own online prep blog at www.eSATPrepTips.com. Larry discovered Christian's blog and within a short time they agreed to work together on this book.

When he is not teaching his students and writing blogs, Christian loves to ride his motorcycles, Thumper and Geraldine. He continues to play his guitar and piano and has an album bubbling in the back of his mind. You can read more about Christian by reading Words 56, 93, 94, 105, 131, 132, 434, 493, 497, 504, and 516.

ACKNOWLEDGEMENTS

Books do not write themselves. They require the help of a number of dedicated and creative people.

First and foremost, I would like to thank my wife Susan. Every chapter benefited from Susan's "close reads." Susan and I also had a lot of fun recalling anecdotes about the students we taught at Jordan-Matthews High School in North Carolina.

I would also like to thank Jan Altman for her help and encouragement. Jan is a tireless researcher and an inspiring SAT and ACT tutor.

I have been blessed with an exceptional number of outstanding students who have made significant contributions to this book. I would like to thank Akash Bagaria and Abha Kulkarni for suggesting a number of outstanding popular culture examples. I would also like to thank Sanjana Mehta for her close reads, Dhara Patel for her great examples, Nikita Kachroo for spontaneously creating the first of the popular "Meet My Students" examples, Anid Laoui for suggesting that I take a look at the film *Ratatouille*, Emily Cai for being a great host and superb writer, Nicole Lorenzi for encouraging me to add a feature on K-Stew and R-Pattz, and Kavin, Nishant, Vikram, Zoee, Rohan, Yash, Varun, Russell, Sahib, and Pranay for being great critical readers. And finally, special thanks to the parents of all my students. We have all benefited from your support and encouragement.

I would like to thank the creative team at Station16 in Atlanta for their hard work and dedication to producing a quality product. I would especially like to thank Annie Smith for her meticulous editing and fine eye for details.

Creating a book requires a great deal of technical support. I would like to thank Joe Mastrull, Kathy Kilgore, and Stephen Grzeszkiewicz at Printech for their fast and efficient support. I would also like to thank my Apple Certified Consultant, Keith M. Sedor for his invaluable help.

THE PERFECT SCORE CLUB

The materials in this book have helped my students achieve outstanding PSAT and SAT scores. Several dozen students have achieved an 800 on Critical Reading and overall scores above a 2300. I would especially like to recognize the following members of our Perfect Score Club. These students achieved either a 2400 on the SAT or a 240 on the PSAT:

VINAY BHASKARA	2400 SAT
ROBBIE BHATTACHARJEE	2400 SAT
HRID BISWAS	2400 SAT
LINDSAY EPSTEIN	240 PSAT
RISHI KANERIYA	2400 SAT
PRANAY NADELLA	2400 SAT
KEVIN SHEN	2400 SAT
CODY SHENG	240 PSAT
ZACK PERKINS	2400 SAT
JOHAN ZHANG	2400 SAT

BOARD OF STUDENT ADVISORS

LINDSAY EPSTEIN

DAVID FAN

RYAN FAN

MORGAN FOWLIE

KEVIN GAN

NISHANT GANDHI

ALEX GONG

RYAN GORMAN

CHRISTIN HONG

ISAAC HONG

RUSSELL HORN

VIVIAN HU

NIKKI JADAV

RISHAB JAIN

MEGHA JOSHI

ARCHANA KANNAN

SRISHTI KARAKOTI

GUNEET KAUR

KARLEE KUC

BRENNA KUGAN

GAURAV KUMAR

REVATHY KUMAR

SALONI LAD

ANID LAOUI

SUSAN LIU

NICOLE LORENZI

WESLYN LU

ROSHNI LULLA

EMILY MA

SRUTI MADHUSUDHAN

TIFFANY MAGENTIREN

DEVAM MALAVIYA

CHARITA MANTORA

CAROLINE MCDONALD

MEGAN MCDONALD

SANJANA MEHTA

SAI OLETI

POOJITA PAIDIPALLI

PRIYAL PARIKH

VIKRAM PASUMARTI

DHARA PATEL

AKHIL PATIL

VARUN PITTA

AVINASH POOLA

RAHUL RAMESH

ASHISH REDDY

MICHAEL REININGER

MITCHELL RESNICK

ANKIT SHAH

PALLAVI SAMBASIVAN

KEVIN SHEN

ANIRUDH SILAI

SAHIB SINGH

YASH SINGH

KAVINAYAN SIVAKUMAR

TYLER SUDOL

KASH TARE

TIFFANY TSENG

ANDY TSAI

REBECCA TU

KEYUR VED

SUDHIR VEL

DANIEL VONARBURG

HIMALI VYAS

ASHLEY YAO

NICK YOUMANS

EMMA YOUNG

RISHI YERRAM

(cont...)

BOARD OF STUDENT ADVISORS (cont...)

PART I
THE ESSENTIAL 600 WORDS

CHAPTER 1
THE TOP TWENTY WORDS

Each SAT is a link in an overlapping chain of tests that stretches back over half a century. As a result, test writers use key vocabulary words repeatedly. This chapter defines and illustrates the twenty most frequently used words on the SAT. You'll find other high-frequency words such as *ANECDOTE*, *SKEPTICAL*, and *AMBIVALENT* in our chapters on Rhetorical Devices (Chapter 2) and the Author's Tone (Chapter 4).

PART 1

1. AESTHETIC
- *characterized by a sensitivity to beauty in art and taste*

INSIDER INFO
AESTHETIC is the Number 1 word on the SAT. There is a fifty percent chance you will see it on your test. Be alert for sentence completion questions that contrast *AESTHETIC*, meaning "beauty," with *UTILITARIAN*, meaning "useful or functional." Of course, it is possible for an object to be both AESTHETICALLY pleasing and functional. For example, Steve Jobs and his Apple design team created iPhones and iMac computers that are praised for their AESTHETIC design and also for their UTILITARIAN features.

2. CONVENTIONAL
- *customary; conforming to established practices*

INSIDER INFO
The CONVENTIONAL approach to critical reading is first to read the entire passage and then to answer all the questions. I advocate a new and UNCONVENTIONAL approach. It is important to remember that almost all critical reading questions are anchored in a specific paragraph. So use a back-and-forth strategy in which you read a paragraph and then answer all the questions that pertain to that paragraph.

3. MITIGATE

• *to make less severe or harsh; to moderate; to lessen; to relieve*

INSIDER INFO

MITIGATE is one of the most frequently used correct answers for sentence completion questions. For example, Arctic animals use fur, feathers, and blubber to MITIGATE or lessen the effects of bitterly cold weather. *MITIGATE* is part of a very important synonym cluster that includes *ASSUAGE, MOLLIFY, ALLEVIATE, and PALLIATE.* All of these words mean "to lessen or make less severe."

4. PRAGMATIC

• *practical; realistic; down to earth*

IN YOUR LIFE

A PRAGMATIC person is a realist who does what is practical and what works best. In contrast, an IDEALISTIC person dreams of perfection. For example, let's say that you are a top math student who made a single careless mistake on your first SAT. Most students would be EUPHORIC (jubilant) to score a 770. But your goal is to score an 800. Should you take the SAT again? A PRAGMATIC student would realize that few if any colleges would reject a student for missing just one math question. An IDEALISTIC student, however, would strive for perfection. What would you do? Would you be a PRAGMATIST or an IDEALIST?

5. ALTRUISTIC

• *characterized by unselfish concern for the welfare of others; not egotistical*

POP CULTURE

In the movie *The Hunger Games*, Katniss and Prim Everdeen are sisters who are both eligible to become tributes in the 74th annual Hunger Games, a gruesome fight to the death on live TV. Prim is a sweet and innocent girl who is just twelve years old. Although the odds are seemingly in her favor, Effie Trinket unexpectedly draws Prim's name out of a huge glass bowl. Stunned by what has happened, Katniss pushes through the crowd of onlookers and shouts, "I volunteer! I volunteer as tribute!" Katniss's ALTRUISTIC act saves Prim's life but places Katniss in mortal danger.

6. DIFFIDENT

• *timid; lacking self-confidence; shy and reserved,*
  especially in social gatherings; SELF-EFFACING

INSIDER INFO

The Latin root *fid*, meaning "faith or trust," is central to the meaning of the SAT word *DIFFIDENT*. People who are DIFFIDENT lack faith in themselves. So a DIFFIDENT person would almost certainly not aspire to be a talk-show host. On SAT sentence completion questions, DIFFIDENT people are often mistaken for being ALOOF and therefore distant and detached.

7. FRANK

- *open and honest; CANDID*

MEET LARRY'S STUDENTS: MEGHA

FRANK is a very tricky word. Most students associate it with a common male name. Megha recently found a clever way to help everyone remember the SAT meaning of *FRANK*. She pointed out that Frank Ocean is a popular hip hop singer and song writer. Ocean recently released a statement acknowledging that he is gay. His FRANK admission enabled Ocean to declare openly, "Now I don't have any secrets." As noted by Megha, "Frank was FRANK."

8. REVERE

- *to show great respect for a person, idea, or symbol; to VENERATE*

IN MY LIFE

When I travel around the country, I always ask my students to name a REVERED local figure. In Charlottesville, Virginia, the students named Thomas Jefferson; in Louisville the students named Muhammad Ali; and in New Jersey the students named Bruce Springsteen. When I asked students in Boston to name a REVERED local figure they cleverly replied "Paul Revere, of course!"

9. SUBTLE

- *gradual and therefore not obvious*

IN YOUR LIFE

The signs that a relationship is in trouble can sometimes be very SUBTLE. For example, a decrease in the number of text messages and the use of last-minute excuses to change long-planned activities can be SUBTLE signs that your boyfriend or girlfriend is beginning to lose interest in the relationship. So be vigilant and look out for SUBTLE changes that seem innocent at first but PORTEND (indicate) future problems.

10. RETICENT

- *reluctant to publicly discuss one's thoughts, feelings, and personal affairs; restrained and RESERVED in style; not outspoken*

INSIDER INFO

RETICENT is a high-frequency word that is often used as an answer in Level 5 sentence completion questions. Test writers typically use *RETICENT* in contrast sentences that include key antonyms such as *outspoken*, *talkative*, and *FLAMBOYANT*. For example, the acclaimed novelist Harper Lee is privately engaging but publicly RETICENT to express her views. Despite the success of *To Kill a Mockingbird*, Lee has granted just one interview in the last forty years.

PART 2

11. **ANTITHETICAL**
- *characterized by an extreme contrast or POLAR opposites*

POP CULTURE
In her song "You Belong with Me," Taylor Swift draws a sharp contrast between herself and her rival. According to Taylor, "She wears high heels, I wear sneakers. She's Cheer Captain and I'm on the bleachers." And to make the contrast even greater, her rival wears short skirts, and Taylor wears t-shirts. In short, the two girls have totally ANTITHETICAL personalities. They are POLAR opposites.

12. **PRESCIENT**
- *perceiving the significance of events before they occur; showing foresight*

AP U.S. HISTORY
The Missouri Compromise of 1820 temporarily defused the political crisis over the expansion of slavery; however, the settlement foreshadowed the increasingly bitter sectional struggles that lay ahead. Thomas Jefferson sensed the future peril when he PRESCIENTLY wrote, "This momentous question, like a fire bell in the night, awakened and filled me with terror … It is hushed for the moment, but this is a reprieve only."

13. **NOSTALGIA**
- *a bittersweet longing for something in the past*

INSIDER INFO
SAT critical reading sections often include passages in which a person revisits a childhood home. The visit inevitably triggers feelings of NOSTALGIA for home-cooked meals and beloved childhood pets. Feelings of NOSTALGIA are not limited to adults revisiting their childhood homes. Over the years I have noticed that many of my graduating seniors become very NOSTALGIC when they view pictures and video clips of themselves and their friends performing in elementary school plays.

14. **BEGUILE**
- *to trick or captivate someone, either with deception or with irresistible charm*

POP CULTURE
In his classic song "She Looks Like an Angel," Elvis Presley fell for a girl who looked, walked, and talked like an angel. BEGUILED by this seemingly perfect girl, Elvis briefly thought that he was in heaven. But Elvis finally got wise and realized that his girlfriend was actually a BEGUILING "devil in disguise" who cheated, schemed, and fooled him with her irresistible charm. Don't expect College Board test writers to BEGUILE you with lyrics from a pop song. Instead, be prepared to see *BEGUILE* in Level 5 sentence completion questions. For example, on a recent test rebellious intellectuals were BEGUILED by provocative political doctrines.

15. OMINOUS

- *menacing and threatening; foreshadowing ill-fortune*

INSIDER INFO

The word *OMINOUS* has become a very popular wrong answer choice. Many students incorrectly believe that *OMINOUS* means "all," because they confuse the letters *omin* with the prefix *omni*, which does mean "all." Don't make this mistake! *OMINOUS* refers to something that is menacing and threatens danger. For example, in the *Harry Potter* saga the Dark Mark is an OMINOUS symbol of the danger posed by Lord Voldemort and his Death Eaters.

16. SUCCINCT

- *brief and to the point; concise*

INSIDER INFO

SUCCINCT is a very popular answer for Level 4 and 5 sentence completion questions. Test writers typically use the phrases "remarkably few words," "notably brief," and "an economy of means" to signal that *SUCCINCT* is the correct answer. It is also important to remember that *RAMBLING* means "long and disjointed" and is thus an antonym of *SUCCINCT*. A writer who is known for a RAMBLING prose style would not be SUCCINCT.

17. DISCERNING

- *demonstrating keen insight and good judgment; able to distinguish good from bad*

POP CULTURE

In the movie *Ratatouille*, Anton Ego is an arrogant but also very DISCERNING French food critic. The haughty Ego has often expressed great DISDAIN (contempt) for Chef Gusteau's famous motto, "Anyone can cook." Ego changes his mind, however, after eating an unforgettable stew prepared by Remy, an ANTHROPOMORPHIC (attributing human characteristics to other animals) rat who is a gifted chef. The DISCERNING critic recognizes that the dish was "an extraordinary meal from a singularly unexpected source." Ego now understands that while "not everyone can become a great artist, a great artist can come from anywhere."

18. BELIE

- *to give a false impression; to misrepresent*

MEET LARRY'S STUDENTS: BRENNA

Brenna has a MULTIFACETED (many-sided) personality. In my SAT class he is RESERVED (shy) and studious; however, his shy demeanor BELIES another far more outgoing side of his personality. It turns out that Brenna is an excellent musician, talented singer, and an amazing break dancer. You can see Brenna perform by going to YouTube and searching for the Lemon Brownie Krew. I promise you won't be disappointed.

19. ANOMALY

- *a deviation from a common pattern; a departure from the norm; something that is ATYPICAL and thus ABERRANT*

POP CULTURE

Everybody knows that rappers are predominantly African Americans who often grew up in the mean streets of an urban hood. Well, not always. Macklemore is best described as an ANOMALY. The white used-fur-coat-wearing rapper hails from the not-so-mean streets of Seattle, Washington. Macklemore is also ATYPICAL in that his songs often combine his raps with a featured black singer.

20. PEREMPTORY

- *an order or command that does not allow discussion or refusal; an arbitrary order*

INSIDER INFO

PEREMPTORY has recently become a very popular answer for Level 5 sentence completion questions. Test writers use BRUSQUE (abrupt) officials, overbearing business partners, and stern teachers to signal a PEREMPTORY manner. Fans of *The Hunger Games* will recall how the Gamesmakers made sudden and PEREMPTORY announcements that arbitrarily changed the course of the contest.

CHAPTER 2
THE TOP TWENTY RHETORICAL DEVICE WORDS

Most SATs now include a question directing you to specific lines in a passage and asking you to identify the rhetorical device used by the author. RHETORIC is the art of speaking or writing. Effective writers employ a variety of rhetorical devices in order to convey meanings in fresh, unexpected ways. This chapter defines and illustrates the twenty most frequently tested rhetorical devices on the SAT.

PART 1

21. ANECDOTE

- *a short story told to illustrate a point*

INSIDER INFO

Many SATs ask you to read a passage and identify an ANECDOTE. Always remember two key points: First, SAT ANECDOTES are short and are never longer than a paragraph. And second, an SAT ANECDOTE illustrates a key point in the passage. For example, John Mercer Langston was a black leader from Virginia who was elected to Congress during the late 19th century. One author used the following ANECDOTE to illustrate that Langston was a fierce defender of equal rights who did not believe in barriers: "During his years in Congress, John Langston rode from his residence near Howard University to the Capitol by a route passing through a particular white neighborhood where residents objected to his twice-daily trips along the street. One day Langston found a wooden barricade there, blocking his passage. The next day, Langston stopped off at a hardware store on Pennsylvania Avenue, where he purchased an ax. When his carriage arrived at the barrier he took the ax and proceeded to chop it down." It is important to note that if the length of an ANECDOTE continues beyond a paragraph, test writers will call it an EXTENDED ANECDOTE.

22. VIGNETTE
 • *a brief literary sketch*

INSIDER INFO
Do not confuse a literary VIGNETTE with an SAT ANECDOTE. While SAT ANECDOTES are less than a paragraph in length, a VIGNETTE is a sketch that is typically several paragraphs long. Test writers rarely use the word *VIGNETTE* in critical reading passage questions. Instead, they typically use VIGNETTES in sentence completion questions as a contrast with SAGAS. It is important to remember that a SAGA is a long epic story.

23. SIMILE
 • *a figure of speech in which two essentially unlike things are compared, often in a phrase introduced by "like" or "as"*

POP CULTURE
SIMILES are all around us. We use them in everyday speech, read them in novels, and hear them in popular songs. Here are three examples:
 • "I love you like a love song, baby." –Selena Gomez, "Love You Like a Love Song"
 • "Uhmma's hands are as old as sand." –An Na, "A Step From Heaven"
 • "Look into my eyes and I'll own you with the moves like Jagger. I got the moves like Jagger." –Maroon 5, "Moves Like Jagger"

24. METAPHOR
 • *a figure of speech in which two unrelated objects are compared*

POP CULTURE
Like SIMILES, METAPHORS are all around us; however, unlike a SIMILE, a METAPHOR does not use either *like* or *as*. It is important to remember that SIMILES and METAPHORS are both figures of speech and are thus examples of FIGURATIVE LANGUAGE. Here are three METAPHORS:
 • "Life is a beach. I'm just playin' in the sand." –Lil Wayne
 • "My heart's a stereo. It beats for you, so listen close." –Gym Class Heroes
 • "Shot me out of the sky. You're my Kryptonite. You keep making me weak." – One Direction, "One Thing"

25. PERSONIFICATION
 • *a figure of speech in which inanimate objects are endowed with human characteristics*

INSIDER INFO
Many tests now include a question asking you to identify a rhetorical device used in a paragraph or specific set of lines. In order for *PERSONIFICATION* to be the correct answer, the lines must meet two tests. First, there must be a specific inanimate object. And second, the object must be given human qualities. For example, in *Darjeeling: A Novel*, the author Bharti Kirschner uses PERSONIFICATION to describe a stack of "final divorce papers" that "stared accusingly from the top of Aloka Gupta's writing desk." This example meets our two criteria because the divorce papers are inanimate objects that have been given the human quality of staring accusingly.

26. PARADOX - CRITICAL READING

• *a seemingly contradictory statement that may nonetheless be true*

INSIDER INFO

A PARADOX always indicates the presence of a contradiction. For example, in their song "What Makes You Beautiful," the boys of One Direction have fallen for a girl who doesn't know she's beautiful. Of course, PARADOXICALLY, that's what makes her so beautiful! Don't expect to see cool lyrics from a One Direction song on your SAT. Instead, expect to see BLAND (colorless, dull) but straightforward PARADOXES in the critical reading passages. For example, in one passage a daughter wrote that at a family reunion her uncle "stood out because he did not stand out."

27. PARADOX - SENTENCE COMPLETIONS

• *a seemingly contradictory statement that may nonetheless be true*

INSIDER INFO

Uses of PARADOX are not limited to critical reading questions. Test writers sometimes begin a sentence completion question with the word *PARADOXICALLY* to signal that the sentence will require contrasting answers. For example, PARADOXICALLY, the poet was outgoing and even GREGARIOUS (sociable) at public readings but reserved and even RETICENT (withdrawn and retiring) in the privacy of her home.

28. VERBAL IRONY

• *saying one thing and implying something else, usually the opposite of the expressed meaning*

INSIDER INFO

SAT test writers focus on VERBAL IRONY, in which the intended meaning of a statement differs from the apparent meaning of the words. For example, in one passage Lewis is a rugged outdoorsman who holds "real estate people" in contempt. He urges his fellow hikers to see a PRISTINE (unspoiled) wilderness area "before the real estate people get hold of it and make it over into one of their heavens." Lewis' use of the word "heavens" is deliberately IRONIC. He actually believes that the realtors will "develop" and therefore ruin the wilderness area.

29. SITUATIONAL IRONY

• *an inconsistency between what is expected or intended and what actually occurs*

INSIDER INFO

Authors use SITUATIONAL IRONY when there is an inconsistency between what is expected or intended and what actually happens. For example, in one recent SAT passage a mother gives her young daughter three gifts—a doll, a doll house, and a book, *The Arabian Nights*. The mother expects that her daughter will treasure the doll and the doll house while ignoring the book. Instead, the daughter is indifferent towards the doll and doll house and prizes the book. This illustrates a SITUATIONAL IRONY since the young girl was influenced most by the gift least valued by her mother.

30. PARALLEL STRUCTURE

- *the repetition of words, phrases, or sentences that are similar in meaning and structure*

INSIDER INFO

PARALLEL STRUCTURE is a rhetorical device that is tested in both the Writing and Critical Reading sections. PARALLEL STRUCTURE is easy to spot in a critical reading passage. For example, in the novel *The Namesake*, Jhumpa Lahiri uses PARALLEL STRUCTURE when she writes, "It is as Nikhil, that first semester, that he grows a goatee and discovers musicians like Brian Eno and Elvis Costello and Charlie Parker. It is as Nikhil that he takes the train into Manhattan with Jonathan. It is as Nikhil that he introduces himself to people he meets." The repetition of the phrase "It is as Nikhil that," in three straight sentences is a particularly vivid example of PARALLEL STRUCTURE. It is important to note that College Board test writers also use the term *REPETITION* to describe PARALLEL STRUCTURE.

PART 2

31. UNDERSTATEMENT

- *a figure of speech in which a writer or speaker deliberately makes a situation seem less important or serious than it is*

AP U.S. HISTORY

Apollo 13 was the seventh manned mission in the American space program and the third intended to land on the Moon. The mission began uneventfully on April 11, 1970; however, two days later an oxygen tank exploded, crippling the service module. In what is now recognized as a classic UNDERSTATEMENT, Commander James Lovell reported the emergency to the Houston command center by calmly saying, "Houston, we have a problem." The crew returned safely home after successfully overcoming the loss of cabin heat, a shortage of potable water, and a disruption of the carbon dioxide removal system.

32. HYPERBOLE

- *the use of exaggerated language for the purpose of emphasis or heightened effect*

INSIDER INFO

HYPERBOLE begins with the root word *hyper*, which means "over." So a HYPERBOLE literally means "to overstate a point or go too far." We frequently use HYPERBOLES in everyday speech to dramatize or exaggerate feelings. For example, students often express dissatisfaction with a TEDIOUS (long and boring) lesson by complaining that "This class is lasting forever." It is interesting to note that *HYPERBOLE* is often used as an incorrect answer in rhetorical device questions.

33. ALLUSION

- *a reference to a person, place, or thing, historical or literary, that adds to the reader's understanding of the subject*

POP CULTURE

Taylor Swift is well known for writing songs that include ALLUSIONS to her former boyfriends. For example, in "Dear John," she accused an older ex-boyfriend of being a manipulative liar who deliberately "messed with the girl in the dress who cried the whole way home." This is a pointed ALLUSION to the then-32-year-old singer John Mayer, whom Taylor bitterly accused of breaking her heart. Stung by Taylor's thinly veiled ALLUSIONS, Mayer retaliated with a song entitled "Paper Doll" that asked, "Was it just too far to fall for a little paper doll?" The "paper doll" is an ALLUSION to Taylor's youth (she was 21) and inability to handle a mature relationship.

34. PARENTHETICAL EXPRESSION

- *an expression inserted into the flow of thought and set off by parentheses*

INSIDER INFO

On the SAT, PARENTHETICAL EXPRESSIONS are typically used to extend the meaning of a word, phrase, or theme. For example, in one passage an author argued that the popularity of texting is promoting poor writing habits. The author contended that "the usual litany of acronyms and abbreviations (such as "2" for *to* or *two*, or "btw" for *by the way*) is seeping into everyday writing" and "eroding a public sense that the quality of writing matters." In this example, the author's PARENTHETICAL comment provides specific examples that illustrate his point.

35. QUALIFY

- *to limit, modify, or restrict*

INSIDER INFO

QUALIFY is a tricky word with two distinct meanings. Most people assume that *QUALIFY* means "to become eligible for something." For example, athletes QUALIFY for a team, and workers QUALIFY for a promotion. *QUALIFY* can also be used as a rhetorical device meaning "to limit, modify, or restrict." SAT test writers frequently use this secondary meaning of the word when they ask students to recognize how an author QUALIFIES a key point. For example, one historian wrote, "In his discovery of the law of the pendulum, Galileo used—if legend can be believed—his own pulse beat as a test." The phrase "if legend can be believed" serves to QUALIFY, or limit, the author's assertion that Galileo used "his own pulse beat as a test."

36. ANALOGY

- *a comparison of an unfamiliar idea or object to a familiar one*

INSIDER INFO

College Board test writers often write critical reading questions asking students to recognize an ANALOGY. For example, what do small oily fish called *menhaden* have in common with the human liver? On first glance, nothing. But looks are deceiving. The menhaden are filter feeders that consume vast quantities of phytoplankton, thus preventing algae blooms that can devastate coastal fisheries. Similarly, the human liver filters out harmful substances from the blood. So we can make an ANALOGY by saying that menhaden are to a bay as the liver is to the human body. Both filter out harmful substances!

37. ANALOGOUS

- *characterized by a parallel similarity that permits the drawing of an ANALOGY*

INSIDER INFO

Most SATs now include a question asking you to read several lines and then identify a situation that is "most ANALOGOUS" to the one described in the passage. Don't be confused by the phrase "most ANALOGOUS to." It simply means to identify a situation that is "most similar" to the one described in the passage.

38. LAMPOON

- *to ridicule with SATIRE*

POP CULTURE

What do *The Colbert Report*, *The Daily Show with Jon Stewart*, and *Saturday Night Live* have in common? They all feature witty skits that LAMPOON the mannerisms of politicians and the antics of celebrities. For example, in 2008, *Saturday Night Live* used Tina Fey to LAMPOON the speech and manner of vice presidential candidate Sarah Palin. The art of LAMPOONING is not limited to television skits. YouTube features a large number of clever PARODIES (funny imitations) of popular videos. For example, both the Key of Awesome and thecomputernerd01 have posted very funny PARODIES of Macklemore's hit video "Thrift Shop."

39. EULOGIZE

- *to praise with eloquent words*

AP WORLD HISTORY

Socrates was both LAMPOONED (ridiculed) for his lofty philosophy and EULOGIZED for his personal integrity. The philosopher Plato deeply mourned Socrates' death. He EULOGIZED his beloved teacher by writing, "of all the men of his time whom I have known, he was the wisest, the justest, and the best."

40. EUPHEMISM

- *a mild or innocuous expression, substituted for one thought to be offensive or unpleasant*

IN MY LIFE

In modern society, we often use EUPHEMISMS to describe things we find distasteful. When my father died, my brother, sister, and I spent several days in North Carolina working on the funeral arrangements and settling his estate. During this time I noticed that no one ever used the word death. Instead, friends, neighbors, and the funeral director all used EUPHEMISMS such as "I am sorry to hear that your father passed away," or "I understand that your dad is no longer with us." One well-meaning neighbor even said, "Your father has been called to a higher service." While these EUPHEMISMS did not change the reality of what happened, they did seem to console my mother.

CHAPTER 3
THE TOP TEN WORDS USED TO EVALUATE ARGUMENTS

Each SAT includes a long dual passage and a short dual passage. The authors of these passages typically disagree about an idea or issue. As a result, it is very common for test writers to pose questions that ask you to evaluate and compare each author's argument. This chapter defines and illustrates ten words that are frequently used in questions asking you to evaluate arguments.

41. POSTULATE

- *a statement that is presented as an established rule or presupposition that is taken for granted*

INSIDER INFO

POSTULATE recently appeared as the answer to a difficult Level 5 sentence completion question. It is important to remember that a POSTULATE is an essential rule that is taken for granted. For example, Euclid POSTULATED that all right angles are congruent; Einstein POSTULATED that the speed of light is unvarying; and Locke POSTULATED that that all people are born with natural rights. Don't confuse a POSTULATE with a COROLLARY. A COROLLARY is a logical extension that follows from a POSTULATE. For example, Theodore Roosevelt's famous COROLLARY was a logical extension of the Monroe Doctrine.

42. CONCEDE

- *to acknowledge or admit; to make concessions* (but...)

INSIDER INFO

SAT authors often CONCEDE or acknowledge a contrary point. For example, one author argued that nuclear power is America's best hope for ending our dependence on imported oil. The author CONCEDED, however, that nuclear power plants do have some risks, such as waste disposal and radiation containment.

43. REBUT

- *to attempt to prove that an accusation or theory is false*

POP CULTURE

According to the movie *Anonymous*, the plays and sonnets attributed to William Shakespeare were actually written by Edward de Vere, the Earl of Oxford. Needless to say, Shakespeare's legion of outraged supporters have vigorously attempted to REBUT this theory. They point out that de Vere wrote undistinguished and often PEDESTRIAN (commonplace) verse that never approaches the eloquence and insights found in Shakespeare's plays.

44. REFUTE

- *to disprove an accusation or theory*

AP EUROPEAN HISTORY

For centuries most people believed that the Earth was the unmoving center of the universe; however, Copernicus and Galileo successfully REFUTED this theory by providing IRREFUTABLE evidence that the Earth is in fact a planet orbiting the sun.

45. UNDERMINE   → overthrow; downfall; corrupt

- *to weaken; subvert; HINDER*

AP U.S. HISTORY

Look closely at the word *UNDERMINE*. It literally means "to dig under a mine and therefore to weaken it." So when an author undermines an argument or position, he or she weakens or subverts it. For example, the Declaration of Independence was intended to UNDERMINE or weaken belief in the divine right of kings.

46. UNDERSCORE

- *to emphasize; to draw special attention to a fact, idea, or situation*

INSIDER INFO

Has one of your teachers ever written a key term on the board and then EMPHATICALLY drawn a line under it? If so, you have witnessed a dramatic and hopefully effective illustration of the word *UNDERSCORE*. It is important to note that although SAT passages rarely include an underlined word or phrase, they often include italicized words and phrases. Pay close attention to italicized words and to rhetorical questions. They are both often used to UNDERSCORE a key fact or idea.

47. COHERENT

- *marked by an orderly, logical, and clear relationship*

POP CULTURE

In the movie *Clueless*, Mr. Hall asks Cher to present a COHERENT two-minute speech answering this question: "Should all oppressed people be allowed refuge in America?" Cher begins by CONCEDING (admitting) that allowing more refugees to enter America will put a "strain on our resources." She then compares allowing refugees to enter America to allowing more guests to attend a garden party for her father's birthday.

Cher ordered more food and the party was a success. Cher therefore concludes that America can certainly make more room for refugees. A clearly confused Mr. Hall believes that Cher's speech lacks COHERENCE, and he gives her a low grade.

48. BIAS

- *a mental tendency or inclination; especially an unfair preference for a person or group; not objective and therefore PARTISAN*

IN YOUR LIFE
Everyone has BIASES. For example, we cheer for our favorite sports teams and vote for our favorite political leaders. It is important to remember always that a BIASED person is not OBJECTIVE.

49. CRITERION

- *a standard of judging something*

INSIDER INFO
Students often ask, "Will I receive a low SAT essay score if the readers don't like my examples?" The answer is that the reader's personal BIASES are not a factor in how they score your essay. Instead, SAT readers follow a scoring guide that contains a set of six clearly defined CRITERIA that are used to evaluate your essay. If you use well-developed examples that illustrate your thesis, you will receive a good score.

50. CONJECTURE

- *a hypothesis formed from incomplete evidence; a deduction*

IN MY LIFE
When I take the SAT, I never speak to the students; however, I broke this rule once, when just before the test began a student discovered that his calculator wouldn't work. Seeing his despair, I offered him my calculator. He turned down my offer saying, "I can't do that. You are a Vietnam veteran who served our country. It wouldn't be right of me to hurt your chance of going back to college and turning your life around." The student made an incorrect CONJECTURE about my life story based upon my age. He assumed that an older looking adult male must be a war veteran taking the SAT to go to college. While I am an older adult, I am not a Vietnam veteran and have several college degrees. So I insisted that he use my calculator. He did and profusely thanked me after the test.

CHAPTER 4
THE TOP THIRTY ATTITUDE, MOOD, AND TONE WORDS

Interpreting a person's mood requires good human relations skills. Interpreting an author's mood requires a good vocabulary and good critical reading skills. Each author has an attitude, or state of mind, toward the subject he or she is writing about. While authors cannot literally frown or smile at the reader, they can reveal their attitudes by the descriptive phrases and examples they use. This chapter defines and illustrates thirty of the most frequently used words in attitude, tone and mood questions.

POSITIVE WORDS

51. SANGUINE
- *confidently optimistic and cheerful*

POP CULTURE
In the movie *The Avengers*, the power-hungry Norse god Loki plans to subjugate Earth and rule the planet as a king. Feeling SANGUINE about the prospect of his success, Loki confidently boasts to Tony Stark (Iron Man), "I have an army." But the surprisingly SANGUINE Stark is not intimidated. He feels supremely confident when he reminds Loki, "We have a Hulk."

52. EXUBERANT
- *really happy and enthusiastic; joyously unrestrained*

MEET LARRY'S STUDENTS: PALLAVI
One day after class I asked Pallavi to describe the happiest day of her life. "That's easy!" Pallavi exclaimed. "The happiest day of my life was two months ago when my friends and I saw Drake perform at an outdoor concert. It rained the entire evening but we didn't care. Drake was awesome! I was ECSTATIC, ELATED, and very EXUBERANT!"

53. DIDACTIC

- *designed or intended to teach and instruct; serving to enlighten and inform*

INSIDER INFO

Your parents, teachers, coaches and religious leaders are often DIDACTIC because they want to teach and instruct. SAT critical reading authors are also frequently DIDACTIC. For example, in one passage an experienced fiction writer adopted a DIDACTIC tone when she offered her daughter the following advice: "Do not try to puzzle your reader unnecessarily; a puzzled reader is an antagonistic reader."

54. EMPHATIC

- *marked by great conviction; forceful and clear; UNAMBIGUOUS*

INSIDER INFO

Don't be confused by the word *EMPHATIC*. It is simply another form of the familiar word *emphasis*. An EMPHATIC statement is neither neutral nor guarded. It is instead assertive and made with great conviction. SAT test writers often ask you to recognize a statement with an EMPHATIC tone. Here are two examples:
- "Ashoka was classical India's greatest ruler," Abha declared with great conviction.
- Fusion of home and work will bring an end to weekends.

55. EARNEST

- *marked by deep sincerity and serious intent*

POP CULTURE

In his song "Watcha Say," Jason Derulo sadly CONCEDES (admits) to his girlfriend that he "was so wrong for so long." He readily acknowledges that he should have treated her better. Derulo then EARNESTLY begs his girl to "give me another chance to really be your man."

56. FERVENT

- *very enthusiastic; having or showing great intensity of spirit*

MEET CHRISTIAN

My FERVENT admiration of composer Ludwig van Beethoven goes far beyond what most people regard as "normal." As a FERVENT admirer of this great man, I consider him history's most important musician. Why, you may ask, do I respect him so deeply? Everyone agrees that Beethoven wrote some of the greatest symphonies of all time. He also advanced the piano as an instrument and was an ICONOCLAST (breaker of rules and traditions) who promoted the idea that a "creative genius" with no social ranking was in fact the equal of princes and kings. I am not alone in my FERVENT adoration of Beethoven. To this day, many composers still REVERE (deeply respect) him as a godlike figure.

57. JOVIAL

- *describes people who display high-spirited merriment; full of joy; JOCULAR*

POP CULTURE

In the *Harry Potter* saga, Fred and George Weasley are JOVIAL pranksters who were both born on April Fools' Day. When they attended Hogwarts, the JOVIAL twins were renowned for such high-spirited pranks as turning a hall into a swamp and transforming unsuspecting students into canaries. After leaving Hogwarts the twins opened Weasley's Wizard Wheezes, a shop that sold magical joke items. J. K. Rowling has said that the JOVIAL brothers are among her favorite characters.

58. SCHOLARLY

- *describes a tone that is academic, learned, and studious*

INSIDER INFO

College Board test writers frequently use *SCHOLARLY* as a tempting but incorrect answer on both sentence completions and critical reading questions. It is important to remember that *SCHOLARLY* is characteristic of a SCHOLAR, who devotes himself or herself to serious academic study. A SCHOLARLY passage would be serious, objective, and filled with well-documented facts and quotations. One way to remember *SCHOLARLY* is to recall that academic SCHOLARSHIPS are awarded to students who study hard and achieve high scores on their SATs.

59. LIGHTHEARTED

- *describes an attitude or mood that is carefree and cheerful*

POP CULTURE

In the movie *The Avengers*, Tony Stark is famous for his LIGHTHEARTED quips. For example, when Hawkeye urgently tells him that Thor is engaged in a desperate fight with an enemy squadron, Stark LIGHTHEARTEDLY quips, "And he didn't invite me."

60. EXHILARATED

- *filled with excitement and enthusiasm; thrilled*

MEET LARRY'S STUDENTS: NIKKI

"I'm so EXHILARATED!" Nikki excitedly exclaimed. "I've got a great example for EXHILARATED." Nikki is a member of the Montgomery High School marching band. The band was invited to perform for the Philadelphia Phillies at their Citizens Bank Park stadium. As Nikki and the band settled into their upper deck seats, she had a great idea. Why not start a human wave? At first, the wave fizzled and was a flop. But Nikki and her friends were persistent. After several attempts the wave caught on as 40,000 cheering fans joined the MHS band in an epic mass wave. Needless to say, Nikki and the entire band were totally EXHILARATED!

NEGATIVE WORDS

61. INDIGNANT

- *characterized by outrage caused by something perceived as unjust or wrong*

POP CULTURE

In her song "Take a Bow," Rihanna is INDIGNANT because she has discovered that her boyfriend has been cheating on her. "Don't tell me you're sorry, because you're not," Rihanna INDIGNANTLY insists. "You're only sorry you got caught." Don't expect SAT passages to be quite as direct as Rihanna's song. Even so, INDIGNANT SAT authors do use forceful words to signal their outrage. For example, one author DECRIED (strongly disapproved) chocolate factories as places that "pump out pollution and provide an indulgence that is unconscionable." The key word *unconscionable* signals the author's attitude of INDIGNATION.

62. SARDONIC

prude; disrespectful

- *very sarcastic; scornful, MOCKING, and DERISIVE*

INSIDER INFO

For many years I used the following famous exchange between Bessie Braddock and Winston Churchill to illustrate the adjective *SARDONIC*:
Bessie Braddock: "Winston, you are drunk!"
Winston Churchill: "Madame, you are ugly. But tomorrow morning, I'll be sober, and you'll still be ugly."
This example never failed to amuse my students. I therefore happily concluded that I had done a good job of teaching *SARDONIC*. But had I? Although my students could define *SARDONIC*, they failed to recognize it in SAT critical reading passages and questions. SAT test writers typically expect students to recognize much more subtle uses of *SARDONIC* than the exchange between Bessie Braddock and Winston Churchill. For example, in one passage a young pianist pretended to have difficulty practicing her scales. When it came time for her to perform, however, the author tells us, "And what do you know—Chopin's waltzes just spring out of her fingertips. A regular prodigy." The author's SUBTLY DERISIVE tone is best described as SARDONIC.

63. FLIPPANT

- *characterized by a casual disrespectful attitude, especially in situations that call for a serious response*

INSIDER INFO

In the movie *The Avengers*, Tony Stark (Iron Man) is famous for his FLIPPANT remarks. For example, when Nick Fury asks Stark to become part of the Avengers Initiative, he FLIPPANTLY replies, "I thought I didn't qualify. I was considered, what was it… VOLATILE, self-centered, and I don't play well with others." While a FLIPPANT remark is easy to spot in a movie, it can be much harder to recognize in an SAT critical reading passage. The key is to recognize when a person responds to a serious question with a disrespectful or FLIPPANT answer. For example, in one passage a reporter asked an archaeologist why she endured the rigors of a demanding dig. The archaeologist FLIPPANTLY replied, "I'm crazy."

64. SKEPTICAL AND SKEPTICISM

• *characterized by an attitude of doubt and distrust; DUBIOUS; CYNICAL*

INSIDER INFO

The words *SKEPTICAL* and *SKEPTICISM* are among the most frequently used words on the SAT. Although they do occasionally appear in sentence completion questions, they appear most frequently in critical reading questions that ask about an author's tone or attitude. *SKEPTICAL* or *SKEPTICISM* will be the answer if the author raises doubts and questions an accepted truth. For example, in one passage a SKEPTICAL author questions the corporate use of comedy consultants by asking, "But how exactly are funnier employees better for business?"

65. NONCHALANT

• *marked by an air of casual unconcern*

POP CULTURE

In *The Hunger Games* each tribute is given a mentor for guidance and support. When Katniss asks her mentor, Haymitch Abernathy, for advice, he NONCHALANTLY tells her to enjoy a bite to eat and accept the fact that she will soon die. Katniss is justifiably enraged by Haymitch's NONCHALANT attitude towards death and the imminent peril she faces.

66. DISDAIN

• *a feeling of intense dislike and great scorn; contempt*

AP U.S. HISTORY

Between 1890 and 1920 a massive wave of "new immigrants" from southern and eastern Europe entered the United States. The new immigrants spoke unfamiliar languages, practiced different religions, and worked for low wages. Alarmed nativists accused the new immigrants of being a threat to their jobs and way of life. Francis A. Walker, president of Massachusetts Institute of Technology, expressed the nativists' DISDAIN for the newcomers when he described them as "beaten men from beaten races; representing the worst failures in the struggle for existence."

67. VEHEMENT
  • *characterized by strong emotions or convictions; very EMPHATIC*

IN MY LIFE
I first invited my mother to meet my future wife Susan at Anderson's, our favorite restaurant in Charlotte, North Carolina. Everything was going really well until Susan asked mom if she would mind if she smoked a cigarette. Mom VEHEMENTLY declared, "I certainly do. Smoking is a filthy, dirty, rotten habit. My son will never marry a woman who smokes!" My mom's VEHEMENT objection stunned Susan. To my surprise and relief Susan said "OK" and never smoked another cigarette. To this day, she and my mother are the best of friends. Don't expect SAT authors to be quite as VEHEMENT as my mother. The key point to remember is that a VEHEMENT statement is characterized by a strongly worded conviction.

68. CAUSTIC
  • *characterized by a critical tone and biting words that cause hurt feelings*

INSIDER INFO
On a recent SAT, many students confused a VEHEMENT tone with a CAUSTIC tone. It is important to remember that a VEHEMENT tone expresses a strong conviction. In contrast, a CAUSTIC tone uses cutting words that can cause hurt feelings. For example, in the television show *Hell's Kitchen*, Gordon Ramsay is a hot-tempered chef who is famous for shouting CAUSTIC barbs at contestants who fail to meet his standards of culinary excellence. In a recent episode, Ramsay CAUSTICALLY mocked one contestant as "Mr. Inconsistency," scornfully told another "You're toast!" and critically asked a third, "Is this your attempt at sabotage?"

69. WARY
  • *marked by caution; a watchful concern that is alert to danger or deception*

POP CULTURE
In the movie *The Dark Knight Rises*, Alfred Pennyworth is Bruce Wayne's trusted butler and confidant. Concerned about Bruce's desire to revive his Batman persona, Alfred warns him to be WARY of the grave risks he would be taking. But Bruce ignores Alfred's warning, forcing his WARY butler to resign from his post. The danger that soon unfolds proves that Alfred's WARINESS was more than justified.

70. POMPOUS
  • *characterized by an excessive and elevated sense of self-importance; arrogant and PRETENTIOUS*

POP CULTURE
In the television show *How I Met Your Mother*, Barney Stinson is proud, boastful, and conceited. In short, he is a POMPOUS person with an inflated sense of his own self-worth. Barney's POMPOUS nature is constantly on display. In one episode he POMPOUSLY proclaims, "I have rediscovered how awesome my life is. I'm awesome." In another episode, Barney hurts his girlfriend's feelings and then POMPOUSLY declares, "In my body, where the shame gland should be, there is a second awesome gland. True story."

NEUTRAL WORDS

71. AMBIVALENT

• *characterized by mixed feelings about a person, object, or course of action*

INSIDER INFO

AMBIVALENT appears on about four of every ten SATs. But watch out! *AMBIVALENT* is often a wrong answer in critical reading questions that ask you to determine an author's attitude or tone. For *AMBIVALENT* to be the correct answer, there must be a clear indication of mixed feelings. For example, if you were chosen to give a commencement address at your high school graduation, you would be proud of the honor but at the same time feel a sense of anxiety about speaking in front of so many people.

72. INDIFFERENT

• *characterized by a lack of interest or concern; APATHETIC*

IN MY LIFE

Many years ago I taught in Siler City, North Carolina, a small town about forty miles from Chapel Hill. I once asked a student named Junior Hicks if he was worried about the threat to global peace posed by nuclear proliferation. Junior promptly responded, "Mr. Krieger, it don't make me no difference." Junior was INDIFFERENT to say the least! Fortunately for Junior, the SAT did not include a writing section at that time!

73. WISTFUL

• *sadly thoughtful; pensively REFLECTIVE*

IN MY LIFE

A few years ago I was sitting on a park bench next to an older woman. As a happy young couple walked by, the older woman looked at me and sadly said, "Once I looked like her. I had long, beautiful hair and a boyfriend who adored me." The older woman's mood was WISTFUL, or sadly thoughtful, as she yearned for a past now gone.

74. WHIMSICAL

• *spontaneously fanciful or playful; given to chance or whims*

POP CULTURE

The 1966 song "Feelin' Groovy" perfectly captures the hippie movement's carefree, WHIMSICAL attitude toward enjoying life. Written by Paul Simon, the song encourages listeners to "slow down" and "make the morning last." Instead of going to a boring job, Simon advises people to spend untroubled days "looking for fun," watching flowers grow, and "feelin' groovy." While College Board test writers will not encourage you to be groovy, they will expect you to know the difference between feeling WHIMSICAL and feeling WISTFUL. Remember, *WHIMSICAL* refers to spontaneous, carefree behavior, while *WISTFUL* refers to a nostalgic mood that is sadly thoughtful.

75. EVENHANDED
 * *marked by impartiality; fair to all sides*

INSIDER INFO
SAT dual passages compare and contrast the views of two authors. Recent tests have included Level 5 questions asking students to recognize which author's argument is more or less EVENHANDED. For example, in a dual passage on the electoral college, one author discussed several weaknesses in the current political system. The second author was more EVENHANDED because he talked about both the electoral college's weaknesses and its strengths.

76. PRUDENT
 * *characterized by a watchful and careful consideration of all potential consequences; cautious and sensible; CIRCUMSPECT*

MEET LARRY'S STUDENTS: MADISON
Would you allow your home to be the site of a party while your parents were out of town? Madison recently faced this problem. She admits that hosting a party would have been "a very cool and popular thing to do." But even a small party would have betrayed her parents' trust. So Madison adopted a PRUDENT attitude, and after weighing all the potential consequences, decided to say no. Madison is now glad that she decided to be PRUDENT. One of her friends was grounded for YIELDING to peer pressure by holding a party that "totally spun out of control."

77. REFLECTIVE
 * *taking time to think carefully about things; thoughtful*

INSIDER INFO
In her song "The One Who Got Away," Katy Perry laments the loss of a boyfriend who once meant everything to her. Her tone is REFLECTIVE as she sadly notes, "In another life, I would be your girl." Don't expect SAT test writers to use lyrics from a Katy Perry song to illustrate a REFLECTIVE tone. Critical reading passages instead often feature an author's REFLECTIONS on an academic topic. In one recent passage, a prominent literary critic adopted a REFLECTIVE tone as he offered his thoughts on how art can represent either the concrete external world or the abstract world of art itself.

78. CONVERSATIONAL
 * *an informal exchange or presentation of thoughts and feelings*

INSIDER INFO
During a typical day most teenagers participate in conversations with their friends and family members. A CONVERSATIONAL tone describes an informal exchange of thoughts and feelings. SAT authors adopt a CONVERSATIONAL tone when they are informal and chatty. For example, in one passage the famous baseball pitcher Satchel Paige adopts a CONVERSATIONAL tone when he opens a paragraph by writing, "After I hit the top, every couple of months just about I got my name in the papers when those writers played guessing games about when I was born."

79. OBJECTIVE

- *looking at issues in a detached and impartial manner*

INSIDER INFO

College Board test writers deliberately avoid using critical reading passages that present CONTENTIOUS (controversial) topics such as abortion, gay rights, or health care. Instead, they typically select passages that present an OBJECTIVE view on neutral topics such as string theory in physics, prehistoric cave paintings, and the origins of traffic rules. The tone of these passages is best described as OBJECTIVE because the authors present events and facts in a detached and impartial manner.

80. MEASURED

- *the quality of being calm and restrained; unhurried and deliberate* → careful; considered; studied; slow

AP U.S. HISTORY

When students hear the word *MEASURE*, they usually think of using rulers and yardsticks to determine the length of something; however, *MEASURE* can also describe a carefully thought out response that employs a calm and restrained tone. For example, on March 4, 1861, Americans nervously waited to hear how Abraham Lincoln would respond to the secession of seven southern states. His inaugural address adopted a carefully MEASURED tone that was both firm and CONCILIATORY (willing to lessen conflict). While insisting that the "Union of the United States is perpetual," Lincoln also pledged that "the government will not assail you. You can have no conflict without being yourselves the aggressors."

→ attack; criticism; undertake mastering; to make impact on

→ continuing; lasting; infinite

CHAPTER 5
THE TOP THIRTY PEOPLE

SAT questions often ask you to identify specific types of people. Chapter 5 will introduce you to the Top Thirty People you might encounter on your SAT. For example, you will meet HEDONISTS who seek pleasure, SAGES who dispense wisdom, and BENEFACTORS who support a cause.

PART 1

81. HEDONIST

- *a person who is devoted to seeking sensual pleasure*

POP CULTURE

The first known HEDONISTS were ancient Greeks and Romans who devoted themselves to carefree lives of pleasure. They would no doubt agree with the philosophy of partying now advocated by LMFAO in their hit song "Party Rock Anthem." The LMFAO duo are modern HEDONISTS who proudly announce that "party rock is in the house tonight." Like true HEDONISTS, they invite everyone to "just have a good time."

82. REPROBATE

- *a person who is depraved, unprincipled, and wicked*

POP CULTURE

Who do you think are the most wicked male and female movie REPROBATES, or villains, of all time? My candidate for the number one male REPROBATE is Batman's archenemy the Joker. The Joker is a MISANTHROPE (hater of humankind) and master criminal who kills rival gangsters and innocent citizens without COMPUNCTION (regret). My candidate for the number one female REPROBATE is Lord Voldemort's fanatical follower Bellatrix Lestrange. Bellatrix is an IMPLACABLE (can't be appeased) enemy of Harry Potter who boasts about killing Sirius Black while taking great pleasure in acts of torture and cruelty.

83. INTERLOPER

- *a person who intrudes where he or she is not wanted; an uninvited guest*

AP U.S. HISTORY

Southerners bitterly resented the Reconstruction governments imposed by the Radical Republicans. White Southerners reserved their greatest scorn for Northern INTERLOPERS, DERISIVELY called "carpetbaggers." These much-despised INTERLOPERS supposedly packed their belongings into carpetbags and then headed south to take advantage of defeated Southerners by meddling in local politics and buying land at depressed prices.

84. ACOLYTE

- *a person who is a devoted fan or follower of someone famous*

POP CULTURE

Lady Gaga is currently one of the world's best known and most popular entertainers. Her music and fashion have attracted millions of ACOLYTES who buy her songs, attend her concerts, and imitate her fashions. Lady Gaga affectionately refers to her ACOLYTES as "Little Monsters."

85. ICONOCLAST

- *a person who attacks cherished ideas, traditions, and institutions*

AP ART HISTORY

Impressionist paintings are now among the world's most admired and valuable works of art. But this was not always the case. At first, outraged critics denounced the Impressionists as ICONOCLASTS who violated SACROSANCT (long-cherished) artistic traditions. For example, the Impressionists rejected the idealized figures, balanced compositions, and polished surfaces advocated by conservative members of the then all-powerful French Academy. Instead, the young Impressionist ICONOCLASTS used quick brush strokes to capture slices or impressions of contemporary life. As Western art's first ICONOCLASTS in five centuries, the Impressionists above all wanted UNFETTERED (unrestrained) freedom of expression.

86. MENTOR

- *a person who acts as a wise and trusted advisor*

POP CULTURE

Justin Bieber was a young and unknown Canadian singer when he first auditioned for the well-known singer Usher; however, Usher immediately recognized Justin's potential star quality and quickly became his musical MENTOR. Usher proved to be a particularly ASTUTE (shrewd) MENTOR. He taught Bieber how to command the stage, perform smooth dance moves, and adopt a confident "swagger." Under Usher's expert TUTELAGE (instruction), Bieber quickly developed from a promising up-and-comer to a full-fledged global pop superstar.

87. BENEFACTOR

- *a person who helps people or institutions*

DID YOU KNOW?

Phil Knight is the co-founder of Nike and one of the world's wealthiest people. He is also a generous BENEFACTOR who has donated over $300 million to his alma mater, the University of Oregon. As the university's most important BENEFACTOR, Knight enjoys a number of special privileges and honors. In addition to using "the best seats in the house" for any university sports event, Knight has an athletic building named for him, a library named for his wife, a law school named for his father, and a basketball arena named for his son.

88. INNOVATOR

- *a person who creates new inventions, ideas, or ways of doing things*

INSIDER INFO

Students usually associate the word *INNOVATOR* with famous inventors such as Thomas Edison, Alexander Graham Bell, and Steve Jobs. It is important to keep in mind that College Board test writers often construct sentence completion questions in which the INNOVATOR is an author who utilizes new writing techniques. For example, James Joyce was an INNOVATIVE novelist who pioneered and perfected the use of stream-of-consciousness writing.

89. PROPONENT

- *a person who fights for a cause, idea, or movement; a CHAMPION*

IN THE NEWS

Dr. Daphne Sheldrick has dedicated her life to being a PROPONENT for wildlife conservation in Kenya. Poachers kill elephants for their valuable ivory tusks. As a result, the elephant population in Kenya has plummeted from 100,000 in 1980 to just 25,000 today. As a dedicated PROPONENT of saving endangered African wildlife, Dr. Sheldrick runs an elephant orphanage and works tirelessly to raise public awareness of the threat to an irreplaceable global treasure. You can learn more about Dr. Sheldrick and her work by visiting her website: www.sheldrickwildlifetrust.org.

90. SAGE

- *a person who is renowned for his or her wisdom and SAGACITY*

AP WORLD HISTORY

The two wisest SAGES of ancient India and China lived at the same time but never heard of each other. The highest, most formidable mountain barrier in the world—the Himalayas—separated their two civilizations. Yet by an odd coincidence, these two SAGES both sought to find wisdom and to know the truth about life. For Buddha, wisdom lay in giving up all selfish desires so that one's soul might escape the pain of life and death. For Confucius, wisdom lay in respecting one's elders and rulers so that families and kingdoms could live in harmony.

PART 2

91. PHILANTHROPIST

- *a person who gives money or gifts to charities; a wealthy person with a generous nature and concern for human welfare*

IN THE NEWS

Bill Gates is the richest person in America and one of the wealthiest individuals in the world. Although he began his career as the RUTHLESS (merciless) founder of Microsoft, Gates has transformed himself into one of the world's foremost PHILANTHROPISTS. The Bill and Melinda Gates Foundation has given away almost $28 billion over the last two decades. The foundation's donations have helped fund INNOVATIVE education programs, medical research, and a MYRIAD (a large number) of other worthwhile PHILANTHROPIC projects.

92. MISANTHROPE

- *a person who distrusts and is contemptuous of other people; MISANTHROPY is thus a general hatred of humankind*

POP CULTURE

What do the Joker in *The Dark Knight* and Lord Voldemort in the *Harry Potter* series have in common? Both are MISANTHROPES who have contempt for other people. Heath Ledger described the MISANTHROPIC Joker as a "psychopathic, mass-murdering schizophrenic clown with zero empathy." J. K. Rowling used similar language when she described the MISANTHROPIC Lord Voldemort as "a raging psychopath, devoid of the normal human responses to other people's suffering."

93. CONNOISSEUR

- *a person who, through study and interest, has a fine appreciation for something*

MEET CHRISTIAN

I became a CONNOISSEUR of classical music in college. While many of my peers were out partying, my best friend Rafa and I found a quiet spot in the music library where we listened to rare vinyl recordings of lesser-known composers and long-forgotten performers such as the sons of the famous J.S. Bach. There are many rewards to being a CONNOISSEUR of classical music. It always thrills me to listen to so-called "difficult" music that requires diligent study and effort to understand and appreciate. As a dedicated CONNOISSEUR I often visually follow along with the music by reading the sheet music as I attempt to squeeze every possible bit of appreciation out of my favorite scores!

94. NEOPHYTE

- *a person who is new at an occupation or task; a beginner; a NOVICE*

MEET CHRISTIAN

Since I work with high school students, I love to share my knowledge of classical music with any young NEOPHYTE who wants to learn more about this under-appreciated art form. Unfortunately, most of my NEOPHYTES associate "classical music" with a few famous pieces such as "Für Elise" or Beethoven's 5th Symphony. Although these pieces certainly make for fun listening, my NEOPHYTES still have much to learn about the incredibly rich variety of classical composers and styles. I, too, was once a NEOPHYTE and only learned my way around by constantly exposing myself to unfamiliar and new music, until I finally became a CONNOISSEUR (See Word 93 above).

95. DILETTANTE

- *an amateur who "dilly-dallies" or engages in an activity without serious intentions; a dabbler*

INSIDER INFO

Students frequently confuse the word *DILETTANTE* with *CONNOISSEUR* (see Word 93). Both DILETTANTES and CONNOISSEURS are amateurs. While a DILETTANTE shows SUPERFICIAL (shallow) interest in a topic or activity, a CONNOISSEUR displays a solid appreciation for the subject he or she is studying. Although Christian sometimes feels like a DILETTANTE when he compares himself to the great masters, he is in fact a CONNOISSEUR who has been playing the piano for fifteen years.

96. DEMAGOGUE

- *a political leader who inflames popular emotions and passions*

AP U.S. HISTORY

During the early 1950s Senator Joseph McCarthy of Wisconsin was a DEMAGOGUE who exploited the Cold War climate of paranoia. On February 9, 1950, McCarthy told an audience in Wheeling, West Virginia that America's foreign policy failures could be linked to Communist infiltration of the State Department. Although McCarthy failed to uncover a single Communist agent, his DEMAGOGIC campaign of INNUENDO (veiled accusations) and half-truths made him one of the most powerful and feared politicians in America.

97. PUNDIT

- *a knowledgeable commentator who offers informed opinions on a topic*

MEET LARRY'S STUDENTS: DAVID

David was born to be a political PUNDIT. His insights into current political events were so great that I always reserved two minutes at the end of each AP Government class for David to offer his opinions on a key concept or controversial issue. My students had so much respect for David that they affectionately nicknamed him "The Pundito." Needless to say, David scored a five on his AP Government exam and went on to have a distinguished academic record at the University of Virginia. He is currently a political analyst for the prestigious Cook Political Report and has even appeared as a PUNDIT on NBC News. I am very proud of David and fondly remember the days when our "Pundito" concluded our AP Government classes with his famous two-minute commentaries.

98. HERETIC

- *a person who opposes accepted and established beliefs*

AP U.S. HISTORY

Anne Hutchinson and Roger Williams are the best known HERETICS in the AP U.S. History curriculum. Both challenged the ORTHODOX (accepted and established) teachings and authority of the Puritan magistrates. Outraged by their HERETICAL views, the Massachusetts authorities banished Hutchinson and Williams to Rhode Island. PARADOXICALLY, religious intolerance in Massachusetts promoted religious tolerance in Rhode Island.

99. PROGENITOR

- *a person who was an originator or major contributor to an artistic style or trend*

INSIDER INFO

A PROGENITOR can be the originator or major contributor to any musical, artistic, or literary style. College Board test writers, however, seem to have a PREDILECTION (preference) for modern jazz drummers. For example, Tony Williams was a PROGENITOR because he "paved the way for later jazz-fusion musicians." Similarly, Max Roach was a PROGENITOR because he was "one of the first artists to exploit the melodic possibilities of the drum."

100. ZEALOT

- *a person who is full of enthusiasm and zeal for a cause*

IN MY LIFE

I have always been a ZEALOT for learning new vocabulary words. When I was your age I kept a list of vocabulary words that I called the "Word Herd." I am still a vocabulary ZEALOT. Now I am committed to AUGMENTING (increasing) your SAT LEXICON (special vocabulary) of Level 3, 4, and 5 words. My motto is and always will be: "Vocabulary! Vocabulary!! Vocabulary!!!"

PART 3

101. RENEGADE

- *a person who defies established conventions; a defector; a deserter*

AP ART HISTORY

Gustave Courbet was a 19th-century French artist who defied established artistic conventions by painting realistic portraits of everyday people. His UNCONVENTIONAL paintings of villagers and common laborers outraged members of the prestigious French Academy who branded Courbet a RENEGADE and refused to display his works. Like a true RENEGADE, Courbet refused to comply with established academic standards. Instead, he AUDACIOUSLY (boldly) displayed his painting in a one-person exhibit he named "The Pavilion of Realism." Courbet's work inspired Mary Cassatt and other Impressionist artists who were also labeled RENEGADES by their conservative peers.

102. CURMUDGEON

- *a person who is CANTANKEROUS; an ill-tempered cranky person who grumbles from habit*

IN MY LIFE

Students and teachers all agreed that Mr. T was a CURMUDGEON. Better known as "Hank the Crank," Mr. T constantly complained about his students and strictly enforced rigid classroom rules. For example, he carefully placed strips of packing tape one foot from each of the four walls in his classroom. Like a true CURMUDGEON, Mr. T sternly assigned detention to any student who stepped across his INVIOLABLE (can't be violated) lines. Years later I met Mr. T at a retirement party. Now retired himself, Mr. T was surprisingly AFFABLE (friendly) as he described his new lifestyle traveling to new places. I now believe that being a CURMUDGEON was a classroom role Mr. T played to enforce strict discipline.

103. POLYMATH

- *a person of great learning in several fields of study*

INSIDER INFO

The October 2009 SAT contained a challenging Level 4 sentence completion question that puzzled many of my students. The question described Ben Franklin as a POLYMATH or PEDANT who excelled in a number of diverse fields. My students all knew that the prefix *poly-* means "many." However, the root word *math* tricked them into concluding that a POLYMATH must be good in a number of different mathematical areas. So after crossing out *POLYMATH* many students ERRONEOUSLY (incorrectly) chose *PEDANT* (a person who likes to show off his or her knowledge of obscure topics). It turns out that *math* is actually derived from the Greek word *manthanein*, meaning "to learn." So a POLYMATH is literally a person who has learned many different fields. I am happy to report that when the College Board tested *POLYMATH* again on the October 2012 exam, all of my students crushed the Level 5 question.

104. NEMESIS

• *a person who is a source of great suffering and distress; a rival*

POP CULTURE

What do President Snow in the *Hunger Games* saga and General Zod in the *Man of Steel* movie have in common? Both embody the chief characteristics of a NEMESIS. Snow is the UNSCRUPULOUS (unprincipled) leader of Panem who attempts to destroy Katniss Everdeen's credibility and suppress the rebellion against the Capitol. General Zod is a RUTHLESS (merciless) warrior chieftain who tries to capture Superman and transform Earth into a new Krypton.

105. PURIST

• *a person who insists on great precision and correctness*

MEET CHRISTIAN

As a dedicated motorcyclist, I have to admit that it can be difficult to tell the difference between the PURISTS and the mentally insane! A PURIST is willing to sacrifice anything, even luxury, in pursuit of his or her goal. In the motorcycle world, this often relates to issues of speed versus comfort. Want to go faster? Be prepared to lose weight, sacrifice seat padding, and even give up having rear-view mirrors. Everything EXTRANEOUS (unnecessary) must be abandoned in the relentless pursuit of a high-velocity machine. A PURIST will endure almost any discomfort for INEFFABLE (can't be put into words) moments when nothing seems real except the rush of speed and the howl of a happy engine.

106. PRODIGY

• *a person who is unusually gifted or intelligent at a young age;*
  someone whose youthful talents excite wonder and admiration

IN THE NEWS

Jack Andraka is a teenage PRODIGY who invented a new technique to detect pancreatic, ovarian, and lung cancers. Jack's GROUNDBREAKING (pioneering) technique is faster, cheaper, and more reliable than existing procedures. With the help of Dr. Anirba Maitra, Professor of Oncology at the Johns Hopkins School of Medicine, Jack won the prestigious 2012 Intel Science Fair grand prize. President Obama recently recognized Jack as one of America's great young inventors. Dr. Maitra proudly predicts that Jack is a PRODIGY who is "the Edison of our time. There are going to be a lot of light bulbs coming from him."

107. AUTOMATON

• *a person who acts in a programmed robotic fashion*

INSIDER INFO

The recent popularity of zombie movies and books has highlighted the behavior of AUTOMATONS who totally lack independent judgment. Don't expect to find zombie-like AUTOMATONS on your SAT. Instead, College Board test writers are keenly aware of new scientific findings that many animals once thought to be AUTOMATONS display feelings such as grief and are also capable of changing their behavioral patterns in response to external stimuli.

108. UNDERDOG

- *a person or team that must overcome great odds to win*

POP CULTURE

Do you believe in UNDERDOGS? On February 22, 1980, a group of untested American college and amateur ice hockey players pulled off the greatest upset in sports history when they defeated the heavily favored Soviet national team in the semifinals of the 1980 Winter Olympics. Although they were overwhelming UNDERDOGS, the American players were INDEFATIGABLE (tireless) and INDOMITABLE (resolute) as they defeated the Soviets, four goals to three. Known as "The Miracle on Ice," the victory has inspired UNDERDOGS by proving that nothing is impossible.

109. CHARLATAN

- *a person who is exposed as a fraud or pretender*

POP CULTURE

What do the Wizard of Oz and Gilderoy Lockhart have in common? Both are CHARLATANS whose seemingly honest and open demeanor was in fact a DISENGENUOUS (dishonest) way of fooling unsuspecting victims. In *The Wizard of Oz*, the people of Oz REVERE (deeply respect) their wizard as a "great and powerful" ruler. However, at the end of the movie, the wizard is exposed as a CHARLATAN who is really a small-town magician from Kansas. In *Harry Potter and the Chamber of Secrets*, Gilderoy Lockhart is a celebrity who authors many books breathlessly describing his dangerous encounters with dark creatures. However, at the end of the movie, Lockhart is exposed as a CHARLATAN who never performed the amazing feats documented in his books.

110. BUNGLER

- *a person who is clumsy and inept and thus botches a task*

INSIDER INFO

College Board test writers frequently use *BUNGLER* as a wrong answer in sentence completion questions about people. I have been surprised by how many students ask me to give them an example of a BUNGLER. I have found that almost all of my students can relate to the Three Stooges. These BUNGLERS almost always found a way to botch up a task or scheme.

CHAPTER 6
THE TOP THIRTY WORDS WITH PREFIXES

A prefix is a word part found at the beginning of a word. This chapter focuses on thirty commonly tested words that begin with prefixes such as "de-," "un-," and "mal-." Knowing these prefixes can help you unlock the meaning of many SAT vocabulary words.

"DE–" MEANS "DOWN"

111. DELETERIOUS
- *harmful; dangerous; destructive*

IN YOUR LIFE

Smoking cigarettes is a DELETERIOUS habit that can cause lung cancer and a number of heart diseases. The DELETERIOUS effects of smoking are not confined to the smoker. Nonsmokers are also affected by inhaling the cigarette smoke of others.

112. DEMISE
- *the end of existence or activity; death*

POP CULTURE

The last few years have witnessed the DEMISE of a number of famous American companies. For example, the Internet helped cause the DEMISE of Blockbuster and Borders Books. At the same time, the demand for healthy foods contributed to the DEMISE of Hostess Brands, the makers of Twinkies and other popular but nutritionless snack foods.

113. DESPONDENT
- *feeling downcast and disheartened*

POP CULTURE
In her song "Back to December," Taylor Swift is feeling DESPONDENT because of the CALLOUS (insensitive) way she broke up with her boyfriend. On a fateful day in December he gave Taylor roses and she "left them there to die." Taylor remembers "all the beautiful times" they shared during the summer and now misses his "sweet smile" and how he held her in his arms. These memories make Taylor feel even sadder and more DESPONDENT. Taylor knows she can't turn back time, so her song is a plea for forgiveness.

114. DEBASED
- *characterized by a lowering in value, quality, or character*

INSIDER INFO
DEBASED is often used to describe how success and greed can corrupt a person's character. It is important to remember that *DEBASED* can also be used to describe how success and constant overuse can DEBASE an architectural style. For example, modern architecture was originally a bold response to new building materials, technological advances, and the skyrocketing cost of land. Soon sleek glass and steel office buildings dominated the skylines of cities around the world. However, critics argued that these monotonous rectangular boxes DEBASED the original modernist style. They called for a new postmodern style that would energize modern architecture with an ECLECTIC (varied) range of designs and ornamental features.

"EX–" MEANS "OUT"

115. EXONERATE
- *to free from accusation or blame; to EXCULPATE*

INSIDER INFO
SAT test writers often link *EXONERATE* with the word *COMPLICITY* to create tricky sentence completion questions. *COMPLICITY* means "to be linked to a crime." So if evidence establishes a defendant's COMPLICITY, then that person would not be EXONERATED from the charge of committing a crime. On the other hand, if the evidence fails to establish COMPLICITY, then the defendant would be EXONERATED and freed from blame.

116. EXORBITANT
- *unreasonably expensive; inordinately priced; literally out of orbit*

IN YOUR LIFE
Some of America's most prestigious private colleges now cost almost $60,000 a year for tuition, fees, room and board. As a result, many parents and students are now

beginning to question what they say is the EXORBITANT cost of attending an elite college.

"RE–" MEANS "BACK"

117. RECIPROCATE

- *to return in kind or degree; to give or take mutually*

POP CULTURE

In his hit song "Grenade," Bruno Mars is deeply in love with an unnamed woman. Bruno promises to do anything for his true love, including saving her life by jumping in front of a train or even catching a grenade. Unfortunately, the woman does not RECIPROCATE Bruno's feelings. She tosses his love in the trash and leaves him alone and heartbroken.

118. RESILIENT

- *able to bounce back from adversity*

IN THE NEWS

On May 31, 1985, Apple's board of directors stripped Steve Jobs of all authority at the company he cofounded. At first Jobs was devastated and didn't know what to do. But Jobs proved to be RESILIENT; he soon started both NeXT and Pixar. In 1997 the RESILIENT Jobs made his triumphant return to Apple.

119. RESURGENCE

- *surging back to prominence; rising again*

IN THE NEWS

Apple faced a seemingly bleak future when Steve Jobs returned to the company in 1997. At that time Apple was worth $3 billion and its stock sold for just $4 a share. Michael Dell and other tech leaders predicted that Apple would soon collapse. Jobs chose to ignore Dell's dire prediction. Instead, he launched a series of revolutionary products that sparked a RESURGENCE in Apple's popularity and profits. Today, with its stock worth over $400.00 a share, Apple is one of the most valuable companies in the world!

120. REVITALIZE

- *to restore vitality and life; to REINVIGORATE*

POP CULTURE

What do the movie *Man of Steel* and urban renewal projects have in common? Both illustrate the word *REVITALIZE*. The goal of *Man of Steel* is to REVITALIZE the Superman franchise. The goal of urban renewal projects is to REVITALIZE deteriorating downtown areas.

"UN-" MEANS "NOT"

121. UNCOUTH

- *displaying deplorable manners that are CRUDE, rude, and BOORISH*

POP CULTURE

Teenagers have a well-known PENCHANT (liking) for movies that feature the antics of UNCOUTH but lovable characters who delight in exhibiting deplorable manners. For example, in *Superbad*, Seth and Evan attend a party where they outdo themselves in their display of UNCOUTH behavior. In one particularly outrageous scene, a drunken Seth accidentally head-butts Jules, leaving her with a black eye.

122. UNFETTERED

- *free from restraint or restriction; free and open*

DID YOU KNOW?

Fetters are leg irons that are used to physically restrain the feet and thus prevent running or kicking. Interestingly, the term *fetter* shares a root with the word *foot*. Since fetters restrain movement, the word UNFETTERED means to be free from restrictions or limitations. On the SAT, UNFETTERED is usually used to indicate free and open inquiry or free and open artistic expression.

123. UNCORROBORATED

- *unsupported by other evidence; unsubstantiated*

IN THE NEWS

Scientists have long speculated that water once flowed on Mars' surface, but their speculations were UNCORROBORATED by actual evidence. Pictures from the Curiosity rover now provide evidence that CORROBORATES (supports) the conclusion that Mars was once home to moving bodies of water.

124. UNNERVED

- *filled with apprehension; deprived of courage and strength*

IN MY LIFE

Have you ever wanted something so badly that it was all you thought about? I was consumed with wanting to make our high school varsity basketball team. Knowing that the first practice was a crucial audition, I mentally rehearsed my game plan. Then I suddenly spotted a DISQUIETING (disturbing; causing anxiety) sight. A procession of trash-talking seniors confidently strode into the gym. Their arrival totally UNNERVED me. I completely missed my first shots as I unsuccessfully struggled to maintain my composure. Needless to say, I couldn't overcome my nerves and didn't make the team.

125. UNDAUNTED

- *not discouraged or disheartened; resolutely courageous; INTREPID*

AP EUROPEAN HISTORY

In 1434, no European had ever sailed beyond Cape Bojador, a treacherous cape located 1,000 miles south of Portugal. Superstitious Europeans believed that boiling seas filled with monsters awaited any mariner foolish enough to venture into these waters. While fainthearted sea captains preferred to avoid the dangerous seas near Cape Bojador, Portugal's Prince Henry the Navigator remained UNDAUNTED. In 1434, Prince Henry ordered Captain Gil Eannes to "strain every nerve" to pass Cape Bojador. Like Prince Henry, Eannes was UNDAUNTED by the mission's psychological and geographical challenges. His successful voyage marked the beginning of a golden age of Portuguese exploration and commercial expansion.

126. UNSAVORY

- *distasteful or disagreeable; morally offensive*

INSIDER INFO

UNSAVORY was originally used to describe foods that are not (*un*) SAVORY (tasty). UNSAVORY, however, is now often used to describe people or actions that are morally offensive and thus leave a bad taste in one's mouth. SAT test writers typically use UNSAVORY to describe questionable business tactics and corrupt politicians.

127. UNFAILING

- *the quality of being sure and certain; constant*

AP PSYCHOLOGY

Noam Chomsky is a renowned linguist who argues that young children possess an innate capacity to learn and produce speech. Chomsky notes that children in widely different cultures UNFAILINGLY progress through the same stages of language development. For example, infants UNFAILINGLY begin to babble sounds in their native language at around nine months of age. Somewhere near their first birthday, infants delight their parents by UNFAILINGLY saying "mama" and "dada."

128. UNAFFECTED

- *the quality of being emotionally unmoved by outside events*

IN THE NEWS

Scientists now believe that unless the world's nations radically curb emissions of greenhouse gases, the planet's temperature will rise by several degrees Fahrenheit before the end of the century. Although the planet may be warming, public interest in the problem is cooling. A significant number of political leaders remain UNAFFECTED by the dire warnings of melting polar ice caps and rising sea levels.

129. UNSCRUPULOUS

- *the quality of being unprincipled; lacking standards of what is right or honorable*

AP U.S. HISTORY

During the early 1900s, journalists known as *muckrakers* exposed the UNSCRUPULOUS activities of corrupt business and political leaders. For example, Ida Tarbell wrote a devastating exposé of the UNSCRUPULOUS practices John D. Rockefeller used to eliminate competitors and build the Standard Oil Company into the "Mother of Trusts." Another muckraker, David Graham Philips, published an essay entitled "The Treason of the Senate," which charged that most U.S. Senators were puppets controlled by UNSCRUPULOUS corporate robber barons.

130. UNPRETENTIOUS

- *characterized by a modest and natural manner; not STILTED or unnatural*

IN MY LIFE

During my career as an SAT and AP teacher I have had the opportunity to teach the children and close relatives of Nobel Prize winners, corporate executives, and even national political leaders. Although a handful of the students were POMPOUS (self-important) and boastful, most were surprisingly hardworking and UNPRETENTIOUS.

131. UNALLOYED

- *pure; free of EXTRANEOUS elements of any kind*

MEET CHRISTIAN

Riding a powerful motorcycle is as close as any motor vehicle can bring you to a feeling of UNALLOYED freedom. No glass and steel cage interferes with the feeling of limitless possibility as I pilot my machine at high speed across open spaces in Texas. No text message or phone call is permitted to intrude, thus freeing me from the constant demands of "real life." So UNALLOYED is this blissful state of freedom that I sometimes catch myself with my mind DEVOID (completely empty) of all thoughts but one—"I'm free…I'm free…I'm free!"

132. UNERRING

- *infallible; incapable of error*

MEET CHRISTIAN

My motorcycle racing hero is Valentino Rossi. Known as G.O.A.T., or "Greatest of All Time," by his MYRIAD (countless) fans, Rossi has an UNERRING precision that only comes from riding motorcycles since he was old enough to stand. Rossi is the first to admit that his phenomenal success on the race track ultimately depends on the UNERRING skill of his talented crew of mechanics and technicians. Without their invaluable support, even the great Rossi could make a critical mistake and crash out.

133. UNWARRANTED

- *uncalled for; unjustified*

IN MY LIFE

As a young first-year teacher, I was initially surprisingly confident in my abilities. I was therefore shocked when my principal called me to his office for "a little chat." Mr. Newman tried to be diplomatic when he told me that I had lots of talent but needed to be better organized. At first I resisted Mr. Newman's suggestion as an UNWARRANTED intrusion into my academic freedom. After some thought, however, I decided that his suggestion was WARRANTED. It turned out that Mr. Newman was right. Well-organized whiteboard outlines soon became my trademark. Over time, these outlines became detailed notes that evolved into my first textbooks. In fact, this very book is descended from outlines I used in my first SAT classes twenty years ago.

"IN-" MEANS "NOT"

134. INSURMOUNTABLE

- *characterized by a barrier or obstacle that cannot be SURMOUNTED or overcome*

POP CULTURE

In her song "Just Give Me a Reason," Pink insists that her relationship with Nate is not DEFUNCT (something that used to exist but is now gone). No obstacle is INSURMOUNTABLE. Pink believes that their love is "not broken, just bent." She and Nate will SURMOUNT (overcome) their problems and "learn to love again."

135. INFINITE

- *having no boundaries in time, space, magnitude, or extent*

DID YOU KNOW?

Have you ever watched a snowfall and wondered if the saying that "no two snowflakes are alike" is really true? Studies indicate that in fact there really are an INFINITE variety of snowflakes. Each snowflake is formed by a UNIQUE (one of a kind) combination of ever-changing air currents, humidity, and temperature. As a result, there is an INFINITE multitude of magnificent crystalline masterpieces, each as different from the next as one person is from another.

136. INCESSANT

- *never stopping; relentlessly and often annoyingly repetitious*

INSIDER INFO

In Latin, *cessare* means "to stop." By attaching the negative prefix *in-*, we derive the SAT word *INCESSANT*, meaning "never stopping." *INCESSANT* is almost always used to describe something negative, like the INCESSANT crying of a baby in a restaurant. Even INCESSANT compliments could become annoying.

137. INDISCERNIBLE
- *difficult or impossible to see or DISCERN*

DID YOU KNOW?
Bacteria were among the first life forms to appear on Earth. Bacteria are UBIQUITIOUS and can be found in enormous numbers almost anywhere on Earth. For example, there are typically 40 million bacterial cells in one gram of soil and a million bacterial cells in one milliliter of fresh water. Despite their UBIQUITY, bacteria are INDISCERNIBLE to the human eye and can only be seen with a microscope.

138. INTEMPERATE
- *given to excessive indulgence of bodily appetites*

IN YOUR LIFE
Doctors agree that INTEMPERATE habits are INIMICAL (very harmful) to your health. Although INTEMPERATE habits can include many forms of behavior, they typically apply to overindulgence in sugary foods and alcoholic beverages. So avoid INTEMPERATE habits and strive to be moderate in all things—except of course when studying your Essential vocabulary words!

"MAL–" MEANS "BAD"

139. MALAISE
- *a feeling of mental, moral, or spiritual unease*

AP U.S. HISTORY
Americans seemed gripped by a powerful feeling of MALAISE during the summer of 1979. Earlier that year militant Muslim fundamentalists overthrew the pro-American Shah of Iran and promptly cut the flow of oil to the United States and its allies. As gasoline prices soared, Americans reluctantly came to realize that the era of cheap energy prices had ended forever. President Carter then perplexed an already uneasy public by chiding his fellow citizens for "falling into a moral and spiritual crisis." Instead of inspiring the country, Carter's "MALAISE" speech worsened the mood of social and economic uncertainty. The feeling of MALAISE finally lifted when President Reagan won election in 1980 and promised a "new morning in America."

140. MALICIOUS

• *having or showing a desire to cause harm*

IN MY LIFE

The seniors at a high school where I taught had a long tradition of doing clever pranks at the end of the school year. For example, one year the seniors filled the vice-principal's office with helium balloons. The prank wasn't MALICIOUS and the vice-principal was a good sport. However, at a nearby high school the pranks got out of hand when a group of seniors let the air out of the tires of the district's entire fleet of buses. The MALICIOUS prank had a number of consequences. The school day had to be cancelled and everyone had to attend a Saturday make-up day. School officials caught the seniors and banned them from attending the prom and graduation.

CHAPTER 7
THE TOP TWENTY WORDS WITH A HISTORY

...s often have fascinating histories. SAT test writers have a long-standing practice of ..."historic words" in sentence completion questions. These questions are a clever ...f testing both your vocabulary and your knowledge of history. This chapter focuses ...enty words that have deep historic roots.

PART 1

141. MYRIAD
- *many; a large number*

DID YOU KNOW?
MYRIAD is actually an ancient Greek word meaning "ten thousand." The largest number the ancient Greeks could conceive of was MYRIAD MYRIAD, or 10,000 times 10,000! It is interesting to note that both centipedes and millipedes are arthropods that have a large, or MYRIAD, number of legs. That is why they belong to the subphylum *Myriapoda!*

142. NARCISSISTIC
- *characterized by excessive self-absorption, especially about one's personal appearance*

POP CULTURE
In Greek mythology, Narcissus was a strikingly handsome youth who saw an image of himself reflected in a pool of water. The more he looked, the deeper he fell in love with his own image. Narcissus would probably be pleased to know that NARCISSISM is alive and well in the modern world. For example, in his hit song "Sexy and I Know It," LMFAO's Redfoo proudly boasts, "When I walk in the spot, this is what I see. Everybody stops and they staring at me." According to the NARCISSISTIC Redfoo, girls look at his sexy body because he supposedly works out.

143. MORIBUND

- *approaching death; on the verge of becoming OBSOLETE*

DID YOU KNOW?

In Roman mythology, Mors was the cold and merciless god of death who cast spells causing eternal sleep. Mors' name continues to live in the SAT word *MORIBUND*. Any product or company that is MORIBUND has been visited by Mors and is on the verge of dying. For example, more and more people are choosing to watch streaming videos of movies and television shows on the Internet. As a result, the DVD is fast becoming a MORIBUND medium.

144. VOLUPTUOUS

- *full of delight or pleasure; having a shapely and pleasing appearance*

DID YOU KNOW?

In ancient Roman mythology, Cupid, the handsome son of Venus, used golden arrows to inspire romantic love in those they struck. Cupid accidentally struck himself with a golden arrow and promptly fell in love with the beautiful maiden Psyche. The two lovers finally overcame Venus' opposition and married. They had a daughter, Voluptas, who was of course very beautiful. Voluptas gave her name to the modern word *VOLUPTUOUS*, meaning "full of delight or pleasure." It is interesting to note that *VOLUPTUOUS* can also refer to a woman's shapely appearance.

145. PROTEAN

- *capable of assuming many different shapes and forms; extremely variable*

INSIDER INFO

Proteus was a sea-god who could change his shape at will. The modern adjective *PROTEAN* refers to this unique ability to change forms. *PROTEAN* often appears in Level 4 and 5 sentence completion questions where it is used to describe a rapidly changing virus that ELUDES (evades) the body's immune system.

146. SOPHISTRY

- *the deliberate use of SUBTLY deceptive and misleading arguments*

INSIDER INFO

SOPHISTRY was originally used to describe the techniques taught by a group of respected RHETORIC teachers in ancient Greece. Today, *SOPHISTRY* is a negative term used to describe the clever use of misleading arguments. By juggling words, a skilled SOPHIST can make bad seem good, and good seem bad. Thus far, SAT test writers have confined *SOPHISTRY* and *SOPHISTIC* to Level 5 sentence completion questions. Be alert for lawyers and debaters who are notorious for being SUBTLY deceptive.

147. LACONIC

- *marked by few words; very brief and to the point; SUCCINCT*

AP WORLD HISTORY

The ancient Spartans were warriors who lived in a region of Greece called Laconia. Unlike the Athenian SOPHISTS, the Spartans valued deeds far more than words. The Spartans were famous for their concise, or LACONIC, diplomatic messages. When the powerful conqueror Philip of Macedon invaded Greece, he sent the Spartans a message asking if they wanted him to come as a friend or foe. The Spartans upheld their reputation for LACONIC replies when they returned the one-word answer, "Neither!"

148. TRIVIAL

- *of little worth or importance; TRIFLING; insignificant; characterized by MINUTIAE*

DID YOU KNOW?

TRIVIAL derives from the Latin words *tri*, meaning "three," and *via*, meaning "road." In ancient Rome, TRIVIAL literally referred to a place where three roads met. Remember, the ancient Romans did not have cars or motorcycles. Most people traveled on foot. At three-way intersections people often paused to exchange small talk about their everyday lives. *TRIVIAL* thus came to mean "of little importance, insignificant."

149. QUIXOTIC

- *characterized by an IDEALISTIC but impractical quest*

IN MY LIFE

I always enjoy teaching my students about Miguel de Cervantes' great novel *Don Quixote*. Cervantes described the adventures of a would-be knight determined to undo the wrongs of the world. Although he failed to fulfill his romantic dreams, Don Quixote did bequeath us the SAT word *QUIXOTIC*, meaning "IDEALISTIC but impractical."

150. HUBRIS

- *OVERBEARING pride and arrogance*

AP EUROPEAN HISTORY

Mary Shelley's novel *Frankenstein* focuses on the tragic consequences of Dr. Victor Frankenstein's HUBRIS. In ancient Greek literature, HUBRIS is a flaw leading one to overestimate one's abilities and take actions that produce tragic consequences. Dr. Frankenstein thought that he was furthering the cause of science by creating a living being from dead flesh. The monster then wreaked terrible vengeance upon Frankenstein for the HUBRIS that made him believe he could USURP (encroach upon) nature.

PART 2

151. CAVALIER
- *characterized by a haughty disregard for others; arrogant and OVERBEARING*

AP EUROPEAN HISTORY

During the mid-1660s in England, the term *CAVALIER* referred to a gallant gentleman who supported King Charles I in his struggle with Parliament. The term continues to have a positive association as the nickname of the University of Virginia and the Cleveland NBA basketball team, but don't be fooled by these positive associations. To their opponents, the CAVALIERS were haughty and arrogant aristocrats. SAT test writers now use *CAVALIER* as a negative adjective to describe people who display an arrogant disregard for others.

152. ANTEDILUVIAN
- *ridiculously old and out-of-date; ARCHAIC; ANTIQUATED*

DID YOU KNOW?

In Christian religious writings, *ANTEDILUVIAN* refers to events that occurred before (*ante*) the biblical flood (*diluvian*) described in the Book of Genesis. Today *ANTEDILUVIAN* is used to describe anything that is extremely old and thus out of date. For example, many high schools have computers that are ANTEDILUVIAN and need to be replaced.

153. INDOMITABLE
- *cannot be tamed or subdued; unconquerable*

IN YOUR LIFE

The Latin word *domitare* means "to tame" and gives us the word *domesticate*. A domesticated animal is one that can be tamed or subdued. An animal or person who is INDOMITABLE, however, cannot be tamed and is thus unconquerable. I have always taught my students that developing an INDOMITABLE will is one of the keys to achieving a high SAT score. As you take the test, remain focused and INDOMITABLE. Above all, never give up!

154. CATHARSIS
- *an experience that cleanses the spirit and leaves a person feeling emotionally refreshed*

AP WORLD HISTORY

CATHARSIS stems from a Greek verb meaning "to purify or purge." As conceived by Aristotle, tragic drama produces a cleansing effect or emotional release in the audience. Today, *CATHARSIS* can be used to describe any emotional release. SAT test writers have used physical exercise and writing a novel as examples of CATHARTIC experiences, since they both release emotional tension and refresh the spirit.

155. DRACONIAN

- *describes laws, rules, and punishments that are very harsh and severe*

POP CULTURE

Draco was an ancient Greek ruler whose code of laws called for very severe or DRACONIAN penalties for even the smallest offense. Draco would no doubt approve of the harsh DRACONIAN laws imposed by President Snow to control the citizens of Panem. In *Catching Fire*, for example, Gale is almost whipped to death for illegally hunting outside the District 12 fence.

156. NEFARIOUS

- *describes people and actions that are extremely wicked and evil; VILE*

POP CULTURE

Wicked people have unfortunately been a part of society since the dawn of history. In ancient Rome, the Latin word *nefarius* referred to a criminal. The word NEFARIOUS is now used to describe a person who is extremely evil. The Wicked Witch of the West (*The Wizard of Oz*), Bellatrix Lestrange (the *Harry Potter* series), and Talia al Ghul (*The Dark Knight Rises*) form a TRIUMVIRATE (group of three) of particularly NEFARIOUS female villains.

157. PROLIFIC

- *very productive; fruitful*

DID YOU KNOW?

In ancient Rome the proletariat formed a social class of citizens who owned little or no property. The proletariat did, however, produce an abundant supply of *proles*, or children. The modern word PROLIFIC is derived from the Latin word *prole*. PROLIFIC still retains its original meaning of "being fruitful and productive." SAT test writers typically use PROLIFIC to describe authors who write numerous books and essays.

158. MERCURIAL

- *unpredictable and given to constantly shifting moods*

DID YOU KNOW?

In ancient mythology, Mercury was the messenger of the gods who flew with the aid of his winged sandals. Mercury was active, swift, and above all changeable. Today MERCURIAL is used to describe a person who is born under the planet Mercury and is thus unpredictable and given to rapidly shifting moods. For example, a MERCURIAL person would be AFFABLE (friendly) one moment and ALOOF (distant, detached) the next.

159. MAUDLIN

- *excessively sentimental; emotional and tearful*

DID YOU KNOW?

MAUDLIN originally referred to Mary Magdalene, a New Testament figure whom artists typically depicted weeping or having red, swollen eyes. In English, *Magdalene* was pronounced "maudlin." The word soon came to mean "excessively emotional and sentimental." For example, *Titanic*, *The Notebook*, and *Bambi* are movies that feature heartbreaking scenes that brought MAUDLIN audiences to tears.

160. ERUDITE

- *learned and SCHOLARLY*

IN MY LIFE

ERUDITE is a frequently used SAT word that has a surprising origin. It comes from the Latin word *erudire*, meaning "to free from rudeness (*rudis*)." *ERUDITE* thus describes a person who is learned and SCHOLARLY and therefore no longer rude. When I was in high school I compiled a list of vocabulary words that I called the "Word Herd" to help me prepare for the SAT. The more words I learned, the more ERUDITE I became. *The Essential Guide to SAT Critical Reading and Vocabulary* is thus an updated "Word Herd," designed to help you become an ERUDITE SCHOLAR who will ace the critical reading sections of the SAT!

CHAPTER 8
THE TOP TWENTY SYNONYM PAIRS

A synonym pair is a set of two words that share the same definition. Learning synonym pairs is an efficient way to AUGMENT your vocabulary rapidly. This chapter is devoted to defining and illustrating the top twenty synonym pairs.

PART 1

161. CAPRICIOUS &
162. FICKLE
- *both words mean "very changeable and impulsive"*

POP CULTURE
In the video "Baby," Justin Bieber falls for a VIVACIOUS (full of life) girl played by Jasmine Villegas. Justin eagerly looks forward to a romance in which he and Jasmine "will never ever-ever be apart." But Justin is shocked when he learns that Jasmine says they are "just friends." Blindsided by the news, a visibly distressed Justin asks, "What are you sayin'?" Sorry to break it to you, Justin, but Jasmine is CAPRICIOUS and thus given to shifting moods. As you might guess, the break-up proves to be very brief. By the end of the video, Justin and the FICKLE Jasmine are back together again.

163. ENMITY &
164. ANIMUS

- *both words mean "a feeling of intense dislike and ANIMOSITY; ANTIPATHY"*

POP CULTURE

In the movie *Harry Potter and the Sorcerer's Stone*, Draco Malfoy arrogantly advises Harry, "You'll soon find that some wizarding families are much better than others, Potter. You don't want to go making friends with the wrong sort. I can help you there." Offended by Draco's DISDAINFUL attitude, Harry rejects his advice, thus creating an ENMITY that lasts through the rest of their years at Hogwarts.

165. ADAMANT &
166. INTRANSIGENT

- *both words describe behavior that is unyielding and inflexible; OBSTINATE, RECALCITRANT, OBDURATE, and INTRACTABLE are other frequently used synonyms*

POP CULTURE

In her song "We Are Never Ever Getting Back Together," Taylor Swift admits that she once believed that she and her boyfriend "were forever." However, all that has changed now. Taylor ADAMANTLY insists that their relationship is totally over. Although the guy says that he still loves her, Taylor remains INTRANSIGENT as she EMPHATICALLY proclaims, "We are never ever ever getting back together."

167. PAINSTAKING &
168. METICULOUS

- *both words mean "very careful and precise; EXACTING"*

IN THE NEWS

Steve Jobs was the legendary co-founder of Apple. Jobs was a PERFECTIONIST who was renowned for his PAINSTAKING attention to detail and his relentlessly high standards. For example, architects and designers spent a year building a model Apple Store in a secret warehouse near the company's headquarters. Jobs' search for the perfect layout was so METICULOUS that he rejected the model and ordered his designers to start over. Jobs' PAINSTAKING work paid off. Today there are more than 400 Apple Stores worldwide.

169. LOQUACIOUS &
170. GARRULOUS

- *both words mean "very talkative"*

IN MY LIFE

As an SAT "guru" I am frequently invited to visit classes and talk about the importance of building a strong vocabulary. On one memorable occasion a third-grade class proudly informed me that they knew the meaning of the "big" SAT word *GARRULOUS*. When

I asked how they knew this difficult Level 5 SAT word, the children all made a honking sound to imitate the GARRULOUS geese in *Charlotte's Web*. Too bad *Charlotte's Web* did not also include LOQUACIOUS ladybugs!

171. TENDENTIOUS &
172. PARTISAN

- *both words describe strong and biased views on controversial issues*

INSIDER INFO

Each SAT contains a dual passage comparing and contrasting the views of two authors on a topic. The topics rarely feature TENDENTIOUS views on a controversial topic. However, the October 2011 SAT did include a dual passage in which two PARTISAN authors debated the merits of investing in nuclear power or coal power. Unlike most bland SAT critical reading passages, both authors EMPHATICALLY expressed their BIASES in a TENDENTIOUS manner.

173. CASTIGATE &
174. EXCORIATE

- *both words mean "to express very strong and harsh SCATHING disapproval"*

POP CULTURE

The MTV Video Music Awards program is notorious for producing controversial moments. Miley Cyrus' 2013 performance may take the Moonman for the show's most deliberately outrageous exhibition ever. The former Disney star shocked viewers by gyrating and twerking her way through a risqué "Blurred Lines" duet with Robin Thicke. Twitter promptly exploded with over 300,000 tweets per minute as critics CASTIGATED Miley's antics. The Parents Television Council called Miley's performance "unacceptable," while other critics EXCORIATED Miley as the "Queen of Obscene." Pop culture critic Prachi Gupta wrote a SCATHING review in which she speculated that if an alien race stumbled across footage of Miley's performance, they would conclude that the human race is depraved and then destroy Earth. The heated controversy left Miley with a major career QUANDARY (dilemma): Should she attempt to restore her good-girl Hannah Montana image or continue to shock her fans?

175. DEXTEROUS &
176. ADROIT

- *both words mean "skillful"*

DID YOU KNOW?

The Latin word *dexter* means "right hand." Since the ancient Romans believed that right-handed people had more manual skill than left-handed people, the word *DEXTEROUS* came to mean "very skillful." Similarly, *ADROIT* is a French word meaning "to the right." Like the Romans, the French believed that right-handed people were the most skillful. These long-standing linguistic BIASES can still be seen in the SAT words *DEXTEROUS* and *ADROIT*. Both words are used to describe people who are skilled with their hands.

177. HISTRIONIC &
178. OVERWROUGHT

- *both words describe an exaggerated and theatrical display of emotion; MAWKISH*

POP CULTURE

The reality TV series *Keeping Up with the Kardashians* thrives on showing viewers the HISTRIONIC reactions of members of the Kardashian family to the problems and rumors surrounding their lives. The level of OVERWROUGHT emotions reached a new high (or low) immediately following the much-hyped marriage between Kim Kardashian and Kris Humphries. Within weeks celebrity magazines reported that (gasp!) their marriage was falling apart. The rumors proved to be true when Kim divorced Kris just 72 days after saying "I do."

179. ESOTERIC &
180. RECONDITE

- *both words describe knowledge that is obscure and hard for non-specialists to understand; ARCANE*

MEET LARRY'S STUDENTS: VINAY

Vinay is a CONNOISSEUR (knowledgeable amateur) of aviation. He can spout tons of ESOTERIC aviation knowledge at the drop of a hat. For example, Vinay can quickly tell you that a Boeing 787-8 burns 17% less fuel than an Airbus A330-200 on a 5,000-mile flight because it is made of carbon fiber-reinforced plastic as opposed to the aluminum-based used by the A330. Unfortunately, unlike little known details about movies, celebrities, and rappers, Vinay's RECONDITE aviation knowledge isn't of much use at parties. However, his more than 1,000 Twitter followers eagerly look forward to Vinay's impressive array of ARCANE aviation tweets.

PART 2

181. BRUSQUE &
182. CURT

- *both words describe behavior that is rude, blunt, and PEREMPTORY in manner*

AP U.S. HISTORY

On December 1, 1955, a then-unknown African American seamstress named Rosa Parks boarded a Montgomery city bus to ride home from work. Tired from a long day, Rosa took a seat in a row reserved for "colored people." When the bus unexpectedly filled up, the white driver BRUSQUELY demanded that Rosa give up her seat to a white passenger. Although she was exhausted, Rosa was even more tired of enduring the daily humiliations imposed by Jim Crow segregation laws. When Rosa did not respond, the driver CURTLY asked, "Are you going to stand up?" Rosa refused, saying just one fateful word, "No." Her historic act of defiance mobilized Montgomery's African American community and led to the successful Montgomery Bus Boycott.

183. UNORTHODOX &
184. UNCONVENTIONAL

- *both words refer to ways of doing something that break with established practices or customary procedures*

POP CULTURE

The music industry does not encourage the development and promotion of self-made artists. Normally, aspiring musicians must sign with a major label. In contrast, Macklemore is a Seattle-based rapper who has followed a very UNCONVENTIONAL path to fame and fortune. Macklemore and his producer Ryan Lewis have successfully written, created, and promoted their own songs and videos. Their UNORTHODOX approach has given them financial success, artistic freedom, and professional AUTONOMY (independence).

185. INEPT &
186. MALADROIT

- *both words describe behavior that lacks grace and is thus clumsy and ineffective*

IN MY LIFE

I have a confession to make. I have always wanted to be a skilled dancer. In my favorite fantasy I ADROITLY (skillfully) moonwalk across the classroom while simultaneously teaching Level 5 vocabulary words. Unfortunately, I am a very INEPT dancer. My most MALADROIT performance occurred at a school talent show when I completely bungled a line dance from the Gladys Knight song "Midnight Train to Georgia." The audience (which included my wife) roared with laughter as I fell out of synch with the other dancers. Some people even thought my INEPT performance was a deliberate attempt to be funny. It wasn't!

187. PLATITUDINOUS &
188. HACKNEYED

- *both words describe TRITE, often-repeated statements presented as if they were significant and original*

POP CULTURE

It is characteristic of popular culture to take a word or phrase and use it with such regularity that it becomes PLATITUDINOUS and HACKNEYED. For example, "amazing," "awesome," and "life is a journey" have all become TRITE (clichéd) from overuse. If you have become tired of hearing "amazing" used to describe everything from a new prom dress to a new smartphone, don't worry. The fad for "amazing" will soon pass, and a new word will become PLATITUDINOUS and HACKNEYED.

189. FLAMBOYANT &
190. THEATRICAL

- *both words describe fashions that are exaggerated, showy, and intended to attract attention; OSTENTATIOUS*

POP CULTURE

In the movie The Hunger Games, the residents of the Capitol are portrayed as particularly vain and FLAMBOYANT people who love to adorn themselves with THEATRICAL fashions. The women of the Capitol covet ultra-white skin, long false lashes and bright eye shadow. For example, Venia is a member of Katniss's prep team who is well known for her aqua colored hair and gold facial tattoos. The Capitol's men are equally FLAMBOYANT and THEATRICAL. For example, Flavius loves to dye his hair orange and wear purple lipstick.

191. IMPERTURBABLE &
192. UNFLAPPABLE

- *both words describe people who are calm and composed, especially under great duress*

MEET LARRY'S STUDENTS: RISHI

On March 26, 2011, East Coast students opened their SAT test booklets and read the following essay question: "Do people benefit from forms of entertainment that show so-called reality, or are such forms of entertainment harmful?" The question shocked and flustered students unfamiliar with reality TV programs. While many confused students panicked, Rishi remained IMPERTURBABLE. Rishi later told me that at first he wasn't sure what to do. Although under great duress, he calmly wrote down the names of the only three reality shows he could think of—*American Idol, The Biggest Loser*, and *Dancing With the Stars*. Even though he had never seen *The Biggest Loser*, Rishi understood the show's basic premise and quickly made up an imaginary contestant who benefited from the show by losing over 100 pounds. By remaining UNFLAPPABLE, Rishi successfully completed his essay and later received a 12!

193. WRY &
194. DROLL

- *both words refer to a dry sense of humor, often with a touch of sarcasm*

INSIDER INFO

WRY and *DROLL* have the distinction of being the two most frequently used correct answers on critical reading questions. Many students have told me that they are misled by the answer choices "a WRY sense of humor," or a "DROLL sense of humor." After all, students rarely find anything remotely funny in an SAT critical reading passage. It is important to understand that *WRY* and *DROLL* do not refer to the type of slapstick humor in a scene from one of the *Hangover* movies. Both WRY and DROLL humor are "dry" because they appeal to your intellect. SAT passages that illustrate WRY and DROLL humor always have a touch of sarcasm. For example, when a modern archaeologist was asked to compare ancient and modern garbage, he WRYLY replied, "Modern waste is fresher."

195. PENCHANT &
196. PREDILECTION

- *both words describe a strong liking or preference for something*

MEET LARRY'S STUDENTS: SANJANA

Sanjana has a PENCHANT for ice cream. She loves to go with her friends to nearby Princeton where she can buy mango or cookies 'n' cream at the Bent Spoon. In addition, Sanjana has a special PREDILECTION for a flavor known as Rocky Road that includes nuts and marshmallows mixed with chocolate ice cream. Yum—that does sound like a very SAVORY (tasty) treat!

197. HAUGHTY &
198. IMPERIOUS

- *both words describe an attitude that conveys arrogance, superiority, and pride; SUPERCILIOUS*

AP EUROPEAN HISTORY

Louis XIV was an absolute monarch who ruled France from 1643 to 1715. Unlike the English king, Louis XIV did not share his power with a parliament. The HAUGHTY self-proclaimed "Sun King" believed that he and France were one and the same. Louis IMPERIOUSLY boasted, "*L'etat, c'est moi*," meaning, "I am the state."

199. THWART &
200. STYMIE

- *both refer to obstacles that HAMPER, HINDER, or hold back progress and movement*

POP CULTURE

The plot of action adventure movies often involves the story of how a superhero THWARTS the plan of a NEFARIOUS (evil) villain. For example, in Marvel's *The Avengers*, Iron Man, The Incredible Hulk, Thor, Captain America, Hawkeye, and Black Widow join forces to STYMIE Loki's plan to conquer Earth. In *The Dark Knight Rises*, Batman and Catwoman defeat Bane and Talia al Ghoul and STYMIE their plan to destroy Gotham City.

CHAPTER 9
THE TOP TEN ANTONYM PAIRS

An antonym pair is a set of two words that have contrasting definitions. Learning antonym pairs is an efficient way to AUGMENT your vocabulary rapidly and prepare for contrast sentence completion questions. This chapter is devoted to defining and illustrating the top ten antonym pairs.

201. **MAGNANIMOUS** VERSUS
202. **VINDICTIVE**

- *MAGNANIMOUS is used to describe people who are noble, tolerant and generous in spirit. In contrast, VINDICTIVE is used to describe people who are vengeful and unforgiving.*

AP EUROPEAN HISTORY

When World War I finally ended, President Wilson MAGNANIMOUSLY called for a just and lasting peace based upon the ideals expressed in his Fourteen Points. But the Allies, led by France and Great Britain, were in no mood to be MAGNANIMOUS victors. They demanded that Germany pay for the immense suffering inflicted by the war. The Versailles Treaty reflected the Allies' VINDICTIVE attitude toward Germany. The treaty forced Germany to accept full responsibility for starting World War I and to pay reparations later set at $33 billion. These VINDICTIVE terms humiliated Germany and played a key role in Adolf Hitler's subsequent rise to power.

203. NAÏVE VERSUS
204. SAVVY

- *NAÏVE describes a person who is innocent, GULLIBLE, and guileless. In contrast, SAVVY describes a person who is perceptive and SHREWD.*

POP CULTURE

In the movie *The Wizard of Oz*, Dorothy is a young Kansas farm girl who is suddenly swept by a powerful tornado to the beautiful but mysterious land of Oz. Dorothy's main concern is returning home. She NAÏVELY believes that all she needs to do is travel to the Emerald City, where the all-powerful Wizard of Oz will magically return her to Kansas. As Dorothy travels along the Yellow Brick Road she meets the Scarecrow, Tin Man, and Cowardly Lion. During their journey to the Emerald City, Dorothy gradually becomes a SAVVY judge of the true strengths of her new friends. By the end of the movie, Dorothy is no longer a NAÏVE and helpless little girl. Aided by Glinda, the SAVVY Good Witch of the North, Dorothy taps the heels of her ruby slippers together and returns home to Kansas.

205. PLACATE VERSUS
206. INFLAME

- *PLACATE describes actions intended to calm angry feelings, often by making concessions. In contrast, INFLAME describes actions that arouse passionate feelings.*

AP U.S. HISTORY

Fannie Lou Hamer was a Black civil rights activist in Mississippi during the early 1960s. In 1964 an all-white and anti-civil rights delegation represented Mississippi at the Democratic National Convention. As Vice-Chair of the rival Mississippi Freedom Democratic Party (MFDP), Hamer challenged the credentials of the regular delegation on the grounds that it did not represent all citizens of the state. Democratic Party leaders attempted to PLACATE the MFDP by offering the delegation two non-voting seats. This concession, however, further INFLAMED Hamer and her supporters. Hamer defiantly rejected the compromise by declaring, "We didn't come all the way up here to compromise…Nobody's free until everybody's free."

207. RUTHLESS VERSUS
208. COMPASSIONATE

- *RUTHLESS describes behavior that lacks mercy or pity. In contrast, COMPASSIONATE describes behavior that shows sympathy for another's suffering.*

AP WORLD HISTORY

Ashoka ruled the Mauryan Empire in India from about 270 B.C.E. to 231 B.C.E. At first Ashoka was a RUTHLESS ruler who rejoiced when his army conquered Kalinga in a battle that claimed over 100,000 lives. As he toured the battlefield, however, Ashoka saw the mangled bodies of the dead and heard the agonized pleas of the living. "What have

I done?" Ashoka cried out. "If this is victory, what's a defeat?" Filled with REMORSE (great regret), Ashoka rejected violence, adopted Buddhism, and devoted the rest of his reign to becoming a COMPASSIONATE ruler. Ashoka even employed "officials of righteousness" to look out for the welfare of all the people in his empire.

209. CAJOLE VERSUS
210. COERCE

- *CAJOLE means "to persuade or coax by using flattery and compliments." In contrast, COERCE means "to compel by using force and power."*

POP CULTURE

In Marvel's movie *The Avengers*, Nick Fury, the Director of S.H.I.E.L.D., sends Natasha Romanoff (the Black Widow) to India to find and CAJOLE Dr. Bruce Banner (the Hulk) into joining the Avenger Initiative to THWART (block) the villainous Loki. In contrast, Loki relies upon force as he attempts to conquer Earth and COERCE all humans into accepting him as their king.

211. BREVITY VERSUS
212. PROLONGED

- *BREVITY describes situations or forms of communication that are short or FLEETING. In contrast, PROLONGED describes situations or forms of communication that are stretched out and long.*

POP CULTURE

In their music video "We Owned the Night," Lady Antebellum remembers a perfect night spent with a girl who was "the purest beauty." Although their relationship only lasted for a night, its BREVITY did not detract from its intensity. For a brief romantic moment the couple "owned the night" and "made the world stand still." Lady Antebellum acknowledges that the relationship could not be PROLONGED and that "we'd never speak again." Still, despite the evening's BREVITY, the couple created a cherished memory that would last forever.

213. ELITIST VERSUS
214. EGALITARIAN

- *ELITIST beliefs stress giving privileges only to a select group. In contrast, EGALITARIAN beliefs stress the political equality of all people.*

AP EUROPEAN HISTORY

The French Revolution began as a revolt against the ELITIST privileges of the Old Regime. For example, although the nobles made up less than two percent of the French population, they owned twenty percent of the land, paid no taxes, and held the highest offices in the church, army, and government. EGALITARIAN leaders attempted to REDRESS (remedy) these inequities by proclaiming a new society based upon the ideals of "Liberty, Equality, Fraternity" as they abolished the Old Regime's special privileges. PARADOXICALLY, many of the revolutionary leaders who espoused EGALITARIAN slogans also engaged in ELITIST practices that repressed freedom in the name of public safety.

215. REVERENT VERSUS
216. IRREVERENT

- *REVERENT describes behavior and attitudes characterized by great respect. In contrast, IRREVERENT describes behavior and attitudes characterized by an often SATIRICAL lack of respect.*

POP CULTURE

Most college marching bands perform CONVENTIONAL shows that display REVERENCE for their school's traditions. In contrast, the Leland Stanford Junior University Marching Band (LSJUMB) of Stanford University is renowned for its IRREVERENT performances. The band plays at sporting events, student activities, and "anywhere there is fun and merriment." The LSJUMB members don't play traditional marching band music or wear CONVENTIONAL uniforms. Instead their shows are famous for making IRREVERENT fun of other universities. For example, the LSJUMB was banned from visiting Notre Dame after a halftime show at Stanford in which the drum major dressed as a nun and conducted the band using a wooden cross as a baton.

217. THEORETICAL VERSUS
218. EMPIRICAL

- *THEORETICAL knowledge is based upon speculation rather than experiment or observation. In contrast, EMPIRICAL knowledge is based upon experiment or observation rather than speculation.*

IN THE NEWS

Which air-breathing animal is the sea's deepest diver? For years, marine biologists were forced to rely upon THEORETICAL guesswork. But now new time-depth radio tags are enabling scientists to gather EMPIRICAL evidence about the diving ability of bottlenose whales. For example, northern bottlenose whales swimming in a submarine canyon off Novia Scotia dove 4,767 feet in dives that lasted an incredible seventy minutes.

219. INNOCUOUS VERSUS
220. INSIDIOUS

- *INNOCUOUS describes behavior or actions that are harmless and inoffensive. In contrast, INSIDIOUS describes behaviors or actions that spread in a hidden and usually harmful manner.*

IN YOUR LIFE

Have you ever posted an embarrassing photo of yourself on Facebook or tweeted an off-color joke to a friend? Like most Internet users, you probably believed that no one outside of your circle of friends would ever see your INNOCUOUS posts. But seemingly INNOCUOUS pictures and jokes can live forever on the Internet and come back to haunt you when you apply for a job. Companies can now assemble all of your so-called INNOCUOUS Internet chatter and pictures into a dossier for a prospective employer. So what seems INNOCUOUS today could have INSIDIOUS consequences when you are older.

CHAPTER 10
THE TOP 110 LEVEL 5 WORDS

The SAT rates each question on a five-point scale of difficulty. Level 5 questions are the most challenging questions on the test. At least eighty percent of all test-takers miss a Level 5 question. What makes these questions so difficult? In most cases, the questions call for a knowledge of little-known and often misunderstood vocabulary words. This chapter will define and illustrate 110 Level 5 vocabulary words. It is important to remember that the Level 5 questions are actually very easy if you know the words!

PART 1

221. APLOMB
- *poise under pressure; coolness under strain*

IN MY LIFE

During my first year of teaching, my pants ripped when I bent over to pick up a paper. The students burst into laughter as my face turned bright red. But I kept my cool by laughing with the class at my embarrassing misfortune. Everyone agreed that I had handled the situation with APLOMB.

222. ECLECTIC
- *composed of elements drawn from various sources and styles; diverse; heterogeneous; MULTIFARIOUS*

INSIDER INFO

ECLECTIC is one of the SAT's most frequently used correct sentence completion answers. Be especially alert for a sentence completion question that includes a variety of different genres or stylistic elements. For example, Peruvian folklore is ECLECTIC because it includes songs, legends, and parables drawn from the nation's Incan and Spanish heritage. Recent tests have used *MULTIFARIOUS* as a synonym for *ECLECTIC*. Don't let the length of this word fool you. The prefix *multi*, meaning "many," tells you that *MULTIFARIOUS* means "very diverse."

223. BOMBASTIC
- *marked by PRETENTIOUS writing or speech that is STILTED or unnatural.*

DID YOU KNOW?
BOMBAST was originally a 16th-century name given to cotton padding or stuffing. *BOMBASTIC* gradually evolved into an adjective used to describe writing or speech that is overly padded, in the sense of being wordy and PRETENTIOUS. Here is an example of BOMBASTIC writing taken from an SAT essay written by one of my students: "The day began with a PLETHORA of OMINOUS clouds, which, compounded by a seemingly infinite bus ride, only AUGMENTED the pressure I felt." Try to avoid stuffing too many "big SAT words" into one sentence! SAT readers will not reward BOMBASTIC writing that is overly padded, wordy, and PRETENTIOUS.

224. CREDULOUS
- *disposed to believe reports and stories based upon little evidence; disposed to be overly GULLIBLE*

AP U.S. HISTORY
On Sunday evening, October 30, 1938, about six million Americans turned their radio dials to CBS. Shocked listeners soon heard a frantic announcer describing a terrifying creature with a *V*-shaped mouth, "saliva dripping from its rimless lips that seem to quiver and pulsate." The shaken announcer then grimly informed listeners that the fearsome creatures were "the VANGUARD of an invading army from the planet Mars." Soon CREDULOUS people all across America panicked as weeping families clung to one another for comfort and terrified people ran blindly into streets and fields. A subsequent Princeton University study found that the fictional broadcast deceived about one-third of the listeners. Today, we are INCREDULOUS that so many people were so CREDULOUS!

225. NUANCE
- *a very small difference in color, meaning, or feeling; a delicate shade of difference; a SUBTLE hint of feeling*

POP CULTURE
When the *Harry Potter* saga begins, Severus Snape is a malicious potions teacher with undisguised ANIMOSITY (dislike) towards Harry Potter. As the story unfolds, however, Snape's character becomes more complex and NUANCED. For example, what are Snape's true relationships with Lord Voldemort, Professor Dumbledore, and Harry Potter? J. K. Rowling deliberately creates a NUANCED character whose conflicting loyalties and motives are not revealed until the end of the final book.

226. DICHOTOMY
- *characterized by a division into two parts*

IN THE NEWS
Steve Jobs was known and feared as a person who had little tolerance for mediocre people. The Apple CEO used a strict DICHOTOMY to ARBITRARILY (based upon

personal judgement) categorize everyone he met into two camps. You were either "enlightened" and thus deserving of respect or a "bozo" and thus deserving to be dismissed.

227. VITUPERATIVE

- *marked by harshly abusive criticism; SCATHING*

POP CULTURE

Reality TV celebrity Kim Kardashian stunned her fans by filing for a divorce just 72 days after her televised wedding to Kris Humphries. Kim didn't anticipate the public's swift and highly critical reaction to her decision. One VITUPERATIVE critic bluntly called Kim "a fame-addicted, money-hungry monster." Another offered this VITUPERATIVE observation: "She will only wear what she's being paid to wear. She has incorporated getting paid into every aspect of her life."

228. INNUENDO

- *an indirect and usually negative reference; an insinuation*

POP CULTURE

In an interview with a celebrity magazine, Mariah Carey discussed her new twins, exercise program, and marriage to Nick Cannon. Mariah couldn't resist making a sly INNUENDO directed at Kim Kardashian when she told the reporter: "Sometimes Nick and I make each other mad. But we always talk through our problems. That's why we aren't divorced after less than three months." Note that, rather than making a direct reference to Kim Kardashian's sudden divorce, Mariah relied instead on the much SUBTLER weapon of an INNUENDO.

229. EFFUSIVE

- *gushing with unrestrained enthusiasm*

POP CULTURE

The Bugatti Veyron is the fastest street-legal production car in the world. Owners and automotive writers EFFUSIVELY praise the Bugatti as a perfect blend of art and technology. For example, one noted commentator EFFUSIVELY described the Bugatti as "utterly, stunningly, mind-blowingly, jaw-droppingly brilliant!"

230. VENAL

- *marked by corrupt dealings; open to bribery*

IN THE NEWS

Samuel Eshaghoff was a bright but VENAL student at Emory University who saw a way to make some extra money. According to investigators, six Great Neck North high school students paid Eshaghoff between $1,500 and $2,500 to take the SAT in their place. The VENAL Eshaghoff took their money and delivered higher test scores. His unethical and VENAL action, however, also delivered criminal charges, a probe into cheating at other Long Island high schools, and a new College Board rule requiring all test-takers to provide a photo ID.

PART 2

231. CHICANERY

- *deception by artful trickery; subterfuge*

INSIDER INFO

CHICANERY is one of the most frequently used correct answers for Level 5 sentence completion questions. It is important to remember that *CHICANERY* is a negative word that is used to describe actions that are dishonest and tricky. The Trojan Horse in the *Iliad* is a famous example of a cunning plan based on CHICANERY. College Board test writers often use *CHICANERY* as an answer in double-blank questions in which *WRONGHEADED* is the first answer.

232. ANACHRONISM

- *an error in chronology that occurs when a person, event, or object is chronologically out of place*

POP CULTURE

Hollywood movies often contain ANACHRONISMS that embarrass their directors but amuse eagle-eyed fans. For example, in the hit movie *Titanic*, Jack tells Rose that "when I was a kid me and my father were ice-fishing out on Lake Wissota." In reality, Lake Wissota is a man-made reservoir that wasn't created until five years after the *Titanic* sank. Even *The Godfather* was not immune to the problem of ANACHRONISMS. In one scene set in the 1950s, two long-haired bearded hippies from the early 1970s can be seen in the lobby of a Las Vegas hotel.

233. IDIOSYNCRASY

- *a behavior that is distinctive and peculiar to an individual; an ECCENTRICITY*

MEET LARRY'S STUDENTS: KAJEN

Although *idio* seems like it means "stupid," it is really Latin for "one's own." IDIOSYNCRASIES are thus one's own, usually odd, behavior. For example, when I asked Kajen to name a personal IDIOSYNCRASY, he admitted to taking showers that last up to two hours. Needless to say, I was INCREDULOUS (in a state of disbelief). However, it turns out that several of my top-scoring students have IDIOSYNCRASIES that involve taking a shower. For example, Pranay confessed that he has actually fallen asleep in the shower! Interestingly, both Kajen and Pranay scored an 800 on Critical Reading. I wonder if their shower IDIOSYNCRASIES are somehow connected to their CR scores!

234. OBSTREPEROUS

- *characterized by loud, unruly behavior and noisy, stubborn defiance*

IN MY LIFE

OBSTREPEROUS young children are the BANE (ruin) of air travel. Several years ago I used my hard-earned frequent flier miles to upgrade to a business class seat. I was so excited! But my excitement proved to be short-lived. A mother and her three OBSTREPEROUS young children sat behind and across from me. They cried, screamed, and repeatedly kicked the back of my seat. I finally gave up and moved to what turned out to be a quiet coach seat.

235. COPIOUS

- *large in quantity; plentiful; abundant; VOLUMINOUS*

POP CULTURE

In the movie *Harry Potter and the Half-Blood Prince*, Harry obtains a copy of a potions book that was once owned by a mysterious "Half-Blood Prince." The Half-Blood Prince wrote COPIOUS notes in the margins that enabled Harry to excel in class. At the end of the movie, Snape reveals that he is the Half-Blood Prince and thus the author of the COPIOUS notes.

236. WATERSHED

- *a historic turning point that marks a momentous change of course*

POP CULTURE

On January 9, 2007, Steve Jobs unveiled the iPhone to a cheering audience at the MacWorld convention in San Francisco. Jobs dramatically proclaimed, "Every once in a while a revolutionary product comes along that changes everything … Today Apple is going to reinvent the phone." Jobs was right. The iPhone was indeed a revolutionary new product that marked a WATERSHED in the history of personal communications by ushering in a new era of smart and easy-to-use mobile phones.

237. UBIQUITOUS

- *characterized by being everywhere at the same time; PERVASIVE*

POP CULTURE

Cell phones are now UBIQUITOUS. You can see teenagers using them in malls and passengers using them in airport terminals. Recently, as my wife and I were walking across a nearby college campus, we were struck by the UBIQUITY of cell phones. Almost every student we saw was either talking on a cell phone, reading a text message, or sending a text message.

238. LICENTIOUS

- *characterized by a lack of moral discipline,*
  especially in sexual conduct; DISSOLUTE

POP CULTURE

In 2010, Charlie Sheen was the highest paid actor on television. He earned an astounding $1.8 million per episode of *Two and a Half Men*. However, Sheen's LICENTIOUS conduct in his personal life soon made headlines around the world. Sheen's LICENTIOUS behavior included alcohol and drug use, allegations of domestic violence, and DISSOLUTE (lacking moral restraint) parties with porn stars. Public outrage at Sheen's LICENTIOUS behavior finally forced CBS and Warner Bros. to fire him from his role in *Two and a Half Men*.

239. RECTITUDE
- *the quality of great moral integrity and honesty, PROBITY*

POP CULTURE
In the novel *To Kill a Mockingbird*, Atticus Finch is a lawyer in a small town in Mississippi, where he is known for his personal RECTITUDE. Unlike the rest of the white majority, Atticus believes that race should have nothing to do with a person's guilt or innocence. Atticus therefore decides to accept the responsibility for defending Tom Robinson, a 25-year-old black man accused of assaulting and raping a white woman. Despite Atticus' best efforts, a BIASED (partisan, prejudiced) all-white jury finds Tom guilty. Although he suffers a legal defeat, Atticus wins a moral victory by demonstrating great personal and professional RECTITUDE.

240. SPATE
- *a large number or amount of something*

POP CULTURE
SPATE is used to describe a large number of something. For example, Hollywood studios release a SPATE of action-adventure movies each summer. The summer of 2013 featured a SPATE of action-adventure movies including *Iron Man 3*, *Superman: Man of Steel*, *World War Z*, *Fast & Furious 6*, and *Star Trek Into Darkness*.

PART 3

241. SOPORIFIC
- *causing or tending to cause feelings of drowsiness or sleepiness*

MEET LARRY'S STUDENTS: NIKITA
My students often have amusing stories to illustrate the word *SOPORIFIC*. For example, Nikita told our class about her SOPORIFIC history teacher. The teacher loves to tell long-winded stories about what their high school was like in the early 1970s. His seemingly endless stories were so SOPORIFIC that Nikita could barely keep her eyes open. Fearing that she would fall asleep in class Nikita asked to go to the bathroom. Once there she promptly fell asleep and missed the rest of the class! Don't expect to see SAT sentence completion questions that feature a SOPORIFIC teacher. It is important to remember that lectures, medicines, and even foods can be SOPORIFIC.

242. PRODIGIOUS
- *extraordinarily large in size, amount, or extent*

IN THE NEWS
The devastating tsunami that hit Japan in March 2011 created a PRODIGIOUS amount of debris. Boats, cars, appliances, tires, and even homes were all washed out to sea. A PRODIGIOUS debris field is now drifting across the Pacific Ocean. The leading edge of the debris is now reaching the west coast of the United States, where it is beginning to create a PRODIGIOUS mess!

243. INCONGRUOUS

- *lacking harmony; inconsistent or incompatible with something else*

IN MY LIFE

I have a favorite New York Yankees baseball hat and a favorite Boston Red Sox jacket. I like to wear the combination on brisk Fall days. This INCONGRUOUS combination often confuses people. How can I be a Yankees fan and a Red Sox fan? The two teams are in fact bitter rivals. I usually explain that I bought the two items on business trips and don't care that the combination—"Boston Yankees"—is INCONGRUOUS. The hat and jacket are comfortable, and that is all that matters to me.

244. MYOPIC

- *shortsighted; lacking foresight*

IN MY LIFE

I once had a very bright student who wanted to drop her AP U.S. History class because she didn't like her teacher. I cautioned Natalie not to be so MYOPIC. I pointed out that the Ivy League colleges she was applying to would expect to see AP U.S. History on her high school transcript. But Natalie was ADAMANT (stubborn and unyielding) and switched to a regular U.S. History class. Her MYOPIC decision proved to be costly. Although she had outstanding SAT scores, excellent grades, and an impressive record of community service, Ivy League colleges turned down Natalie's application. The moral of this story is clear: don't be MYOPIC. Keep your eyes on your long-term goals!

245. APOPLECTIC

- *filled with rage; IRATE*

AP U.S. HISTORY

On February 16, 1898, Americans awoke to the shocking news that a mysterious explosion sank the U.S.S. *Maine* in Havana Harbor. Theodore Roosevelt, then the Assistant Secretary of the Navy, was APOPLECTIC. "The *Maine*," he angrily wrote, "was sunk by an act of dirty treachery on the part of the Spaniards." TR became even more APOPLECTIC as he contemptuously watched President McKinley's diplomatic efforts to avoid a conflict with Spain. The BELLICOSE (warlike) Roosevelt exploded in anger and exclaimed, "McKinley has no more backbone than has a chocolate éclair."

246. EDIFY

- *to instruct and enlighten*

AP WORLD HISTORY

The ancient Chinese SAGE (wise person) Confucius used proverbs to EDIFY his disciples. For example, one proverb that he used to teach his unique vision of an ordered society was, "Our greatest glory is not in never falling, but in getting up every time we do." Although it is 2,500 years old, modern teachers could still use this proverb to EDIFY today's students about PERSEVERANCE.

247. ACERBIC

- *characterized by a bitter, cutting tone, CAUSTIC*

POP CULTURE

Simon Cowell is a talent judge on the television show *The X Factor*. He is best known for using his ACERBIC wit to berate contestants he deems INEPT and annoying. For example, Simon unleashed his ACERBIC wit by telling one off-key contestant, "If you sang like this two thousand years ago, people would have stoned you to death."

248. BALEFUL

- *PORTENDING evil and harm; SINISTER and forbidding*

POP CULTURE

In the movie *The Lion King*, Scar is a fearsome and treacherous lion who kills his own brother Mufasa to seize the throne as King of the Jungle. With his coal-black mane, SINISTER smile, and terrifying roar, it is little wonder that Scar's BALEFUL appearance fills the other animals in the jungle with TREPIDATION (fear).

249. EPITOMIZE

- *to embody the essential characteristics of a trait; to typify*

POP CULTURE

The Bugatti Veyron has always fascinated my students. First manufactured in 1900, the Bugatti is universally viewed as the EPITOME of automotive exclusivity, luxury, elegance, and design. Priced at $1.7 million, the Bugatti is the fastest street-legal production car in the world. The Bugatti's 1,200-horsepower engine EPITOMIZES power as the car can reach a top speed of 268 miles per hour.

250. EPHEMERAL

- *very brief; short-lived; FLEETING*

DID YOU KNOW?

EPHEMERAL is both a beautiful and a sad word. It is derived from the Greek word *hemera*, meaning "a day." *EPHEMERAL* reminds us that we should "seize the day" and treasure the beautiful moments of our lives. For example, rainbows are both beautiful and EPHEMERAL. While the unique combination of rain and sunshine creates a wondrous effect, you can only enjoy a rainbow for a few moments before it dissipates.

PART 4

251. IGNOMINIOUS

- *a condition of great public shame, dishonor, and humiliation*

AP WORLD HISTORY

What do Benito Mussolini and Colonel Quaddafi have in common? Both were dictators who suffered IGNOMINIOUS deaths. As World War II ended, Italian resistance forces captured and executed Mussolini. They then hung the body of their former leader upside down from the roof of a Milan gas station. On October 20, 2011, jubilant Libyan rebels found Colonel Quaddafi hiding IGNOMINIOUSLY in an abandoned drainage pipe. They then shot their deposed leader and displayed his body in a cold meat locker.

252. DISINGENUOUS

- *characterized by giving a false appearance of honesty; deceptive and therefore not straightforward, candid, or FRANK*

POP CULTURE

Major online dating sites receive almost 600 million visits a month. The online daters have a strong tendency to write DISINGENUOUS profiles about themselves. About 81 percent of all online daters deliberately misrepresent their height, weight, or age. For example, women DISINGENUOUSLY describe themselves as being 8.5 pounds thinner than they really are. Researchers explain that online daters are DISINGENUOUS because of a desire to create idealized profiles that will make them more attractive to others.

253. INDELIBLE

- *impossible to remove, erase, or wash away; memorable*

AP U.S. HISTORY

On July 20, 1969, millions of people all over the world watched on their television sets as Neil Armstrong, an American astronaut, climbed slowly down the ladder of his lunar landing vehicle and stepped onto the surface of the moon. Pictures of Armstrong's historic lunar footprint have created an INDELIBLE image of human triumph and achievement. Since the moon does not have an atmosphere, there is no wind. As a result, Armstrong's footprint will remain INDELIBLE and can only be erased by a random meteor. I hope my vocabulary examples, like Armstrong's footprint, are leaving an equally INDELIBLE impression on your minds!

254. EQUANIMITY

- *emotional calmness and composure in times of stress*

AP U.S. HISTORY

On the morning of September 11, 2001, President George W. Bush visited a second grade class in Sarasota, Florida. As the excited students proudly read a story entitled *The Pet Goat*, the President's Chief of Staff Andrew Card unexpectedly entered the classroom. Card walked over to the President and whispered in his ear, "America is under attack." Despite the alarming news, Bush maintained his EQUANIMITY. He remained with the students for another seven minutes and attentively listened to them complete their lesson. While some later criticized Bush for not immediately leaving the room, most Americans praised the president for his display of EQUANIMITY. One of the second graders later perceptively noted, "If he wanted the country to stay calm, he needed to show that he was calm."

255. MELLIFLUOUS

- *a sound that is full and sweet and thus pleasing to hear*

DID YOU KNOW?

The modern Level 5 word *MELLIFLUOUS* actually has ancient roots. It is derived from the Latin word *mel*, meaning "honey." Since the root *fluus* means "to flow," *MELLIFLUOUS* literally means "honey-flowing." *MELLIFLUOUS* almost always refers to singers who have voices that are full and sweet. For example, Justin Bieber has a MELLIFLUOUS voice in his Christmas ballad "Under the Mistletoe."

256. ETHEREAL

- *very delicate; airy and light; exquisitely refined*

POP CULTURE

Taylor Swift's video "Love Story"contains a scene in which Taylor and her "Prince Charming" dance in a romantic candlelit castle ballroom. The beautiful aristocratic ladies all wear ETHEREAL gowns made of fine silk. Of course, Taylor's ETHEREAL grace captures the heart of her true love.

257. BASTION

- *a stronghold or fortification; a group or place that defends a way of life*

IN THE NEWS

The South has always prided itself on being a BASTION of good manners. GENTEEL (polite and refined) southern gentlemen are famous for opening doors for their girlfriends and saying "Yes, sir" or "No, ma'am" to adults. But many sociologists believe that digital communications and recent immigration trends are combining to erode southern manners. They predict that the South's status as America's last BASTION of CIVILITY (politeness) may be changing forever.

258. AMALGAM

- *a blend of different elements; a mixture; a SYNTHESIS*

AP U.S. HISTORY

In his famous *Letters from an American Farmer* (1782), the French-born essayist J. Hector St. Jean de Crevecoeur perceptively wrote that America featured a unique AMALGAM of immigrants, "which you will find in no other country." Over two centuries later, America continues to be an AMALGAM, or "melting pot," that includes millions of immigrants from all over the world.

259. ENTRENCHED

- *solidly established, dug in; strongly ingrained*

AP U.S. HISTORY

As the 1950s began, the long-established system of Jim Crow racial segregation remained deeply ENTRENCHED in the American South. For example, at the start of the 1953–1954 school year, 2.5 million African American children attended all-black schools in seventeen Southern states and the District of Columbia. However, on May 17, 1954, the United States Supreme Court issued a landmark decision in *Brown v. Board of Education*, striking down the ENTRENCHED doctrine of "separate but equal."

260. CUPIDITY

• *extreme greed for material wealth; characterized by AVARICE*

IN THE NEWS

In the hit movie *Wall Street*, Gordon Gekko is an UNSCRUPULOUS (unprincipled) investment banker who proudly proclaims, "Greed is good. Greed works." Today, many Americans wonder if Gekko was right. Many critics argue, for example, that the reckless CUPIDITY of Wall Street bankers caused the recent Great Recession.

PART 5

261. INEFFABLE

• *something that is hard to express and difficult to put into words*

POP CULTURE

In the movie *Titanic*, Rose secretly meets Jack near the bow of the ship. Jack asks Rose to hold his hand, close her eyes, and step up to the railing. When she opens her eyes Jack holds her arms as she extends them out into the ocean breeze and gasps, "I'm flying!" Jack and Rose then share an INEFFABLE moment as they kiss for the first time and unknowingly witness the Titanic's final sunset.

262. CHARISMATIC

• *full of personal charm and magnetism*

POP CULTURE

CHARISMA is similar to the contemporary word *swagger*. A person with CHARISMA exudes a natural charm that enables him or her to move with confidence and own any room. For example, former presidents John F. Kennedy and Ronald Reagan were both very CHARISMATIC. In his song "6 Foot 7 Foot," Lil Wayne summed up the modern meaning of *CHARISMA* when he described it as "vodka with spritzer."

263. LUGUBRIOUS

- *expressing the grief and sorrow associated with an irreparable loss; mournful and gloomy*

POP CULTURE

The final fifteen minutes of the movie *A Walk to Remember* features one of the most POIGNANT (touching) and LUGUBRIOUS scenes in film history. The movie, based upon a Nicholas Sparks novel, tells the love story of Landon and Jamie, played by Shane West and Mandy Moore. At the beginning of the movie, Landon is a SURLY (ill-tempered and rude) teenager who is the ANTITHESIS (opposite) of the bookish and religious Jamie. But an accident brings them together, and they soon fall in love. However, just as Landon realizes that he wants to do something with his life, Jamie reveals that she has terminal leukemia and will die before she turns eighteen. In the movie's final LUGUBRIOUS scenes, Jamie and Landon marry just before her tragic death.

264. ELUCIDATE

- *to make clear by explanation; clarify*

AP BIOLOGY

On April 25, 1953, James Watson and Francis Crick published a groundbreaking ELUCIDATION of the double-helix structure of DNA, the molecule essential for passing on our genes and "the secrets of life." Unknown to the public, their ELUCIDATION actually depended upon the pioneering work of another biologist, Rosalind Franklin. Her X-ray image, "Photo 51," proved to be a vital clue in Watson and Crick's decoding of the double helix. While Watson and Crick went on to win a Nobel Prize in 1962 for their ELUCIDATION of DNA's structure, Franklin never received adequate recognition for her discovery. She died in 1958 at age 37 from ovarian cancer.

265. CONUNDRUM

- *a puzzling question or problem that is difficult to resolve*

AP PSYCHOLOGY

Lawrence Kohlberg was an American psychologist who created a series of hypothetical ethical CONUNDRUMS in order to study moral reasoning. In one of his CONUNDRUMS, a woman faced a PROLONGED (extended) period of suffering from a rare form of cancer that could only be cured by a drug just discovered by a local pharmacist, who charged ten times what the medicine cost to produce. The sick woman's husband could only raise about $1,000, or half the price. Explaining that his wife was suffering and could die, the husband begged the druggist to reduce the price. But the pharmacist refused, saying, "I discovered the drug, and I deserve to make a profit." The DISTRAUGHT husband now faced an excruciating CONUNDRUM. Should he steal the medicine, because his wife's right to life superseded the druggist's right to private property? Or should he obey the law and allow his wife to suffer and die?

266. PERNICIOUS

- *causing harm in a hidden and injurious way*

IN MY LIFE

Jody was my first official girlfriend. I was a NAÏVE (innocent) ninth-grader who trusted everyone, including Jody's best friend Paula. Little did I realize that Paula was actually a PERNICIOUS person who secretly spread lies about me to Jody. For example, PERNICIOUS Paula told Jody that I was flirting with other girls at a party. To find out what happened, see Word 267 below.

267. INCREDULOUS

- *not willing to believe; unbelieving*

IN MY LIFE

PERNICIOUS (quietly harmful) Paula's campaign of lies worked (see Word 246 above). I'll never forget what happened next. On April Fools' Day, Paula came to me and said, "Jody doesn't want to go out with you anymore." I was stunned and INCREDULOUS. At first I refused to believe Paula. But it was true. My first girlfriend broke up with me on April Fools' Day. I learned the hard way that "the first cut is the deepest."

268. PANTHEON

- *a select group of illustrious people who have done the same thing*

DID YOU KNOW?

PANTHEON is a Level 5 SAT word that would have been known by all citizens of ancient Rome. The Roman PANTHEON was a famous temple dedicated by Emperor Hadrian to all (*pan*) of the gods (*theoi*). The modern word *PANTHEON* still retains the ancient temple's sense of exclusivity. Today, a *PANTHEON* refers to a select group of notable people who do the same thing. For example, Henry Ford, Walt Disney, and Steve Jobs form a PANTHEON of great American inventors and entrepreneurs.

269. CHAGRIN

- *strong feelings of embarrassment and mortification caused by a failure or keen disappointment*

INSIDER INFO

Sentence completion questions using *CHAGRIN* often provide an example of an embarrassing blunder that mortifies a person. For example, a tailor would be CHAGRINED if he first misplaced an order to alter a prom dress and then, when he found the gown, accidentally spilled coffee on it.

270. INIMICAL
- *injurious or harmful in effect*

IN YOUR LIFE
INIMICAL comes from the Latin word *inimicus*, meaning "enemy." Doctors and public health officials would all agree that smoking is an enemy that is INIMICAL to your health. Smoking can cause lung cancer and a number of heart diseases. The INIMICAL effects of smoking are not confined to the smoker. Nonsmokers are also affected by inhaling the cigarette smoke of others. So let me be EMPHATIC (forceful and clear) and REITERATE (repeat) this earnest ADMONITION (warning): Don't smoke—it's INIMICAL to you and to your friends!

PART 6

271. REFRACTORY
- *obstinately resistant to authority or control; unmanageable and unruly*

IN MY LIFE
My greatest teaching challenge occurred during my first year when my soaring ideals collided with the reality of teaching 39 REFRACTORY first-period "Basics." The Basics were assigned to me because they were all unruly students who had failed U.S. History the previous year. When I asked my department chair for advice, he replied, "They're Basics. They resist authority and are almost impossible to control. Be flexible and try anything. Good luck." To find out what happened next, see Word 272.

272. DISCONCERTED
- *describes a condition of being unsettled and thrown into a state of confusion*

IN MY LIFE
On the first day of class I calmly and confidently handed the Basics a thick U.S. History textbook and assigned Chapter 1 for homework. The Basics were INCREDULOUS (in a state of disbelief). They promptly lived up to their reputation for being REFRACTORY by loudly protesting, "We're the Basics. We don't do homework!" Needless to say, their loud and EMPHATIC protest left me totally DISCONCERTED. Unsettled by a class of 39 rebellious Basics, I didn't know what to say or do. To find out what happened next, see Word 273.

273. CONCILIATORY
- *describes an approach that is flexible and YIELDING;*
  willing to make CONCESSIONS to restore harmony

IN MY LIFE
The Basics' CATEGORICAL (absolute) opposition to doing any homework left me totally DISCONCERTED (unsettled). Faced with 39 REFRACTORY Basics, I chose a PRAGMATIC (practical) and CONCILIATORY approach. I sternly reminded the Basics that they had to pass U.S. History to graduate. But I also told them that I wanted

them to enjoy history and relate it to their lives. My CONCILIATORY approach worked. Instead of beginning with a chapter on European explorers, we began with a unit on contemporary problems in American society.

274. PRECIPITATE

• *to cause to happen especially suddenly or prematurely*

AP U.S. HISTORY

On June 25, 1950, the North Korean army suddenly attacked South Korea. The attack stunned the United States and PRECIPITATED the Korean War. President Truman saw the invasion as a test of containment and an opportunity to prove that Democrats were not "soft" on Communism.

275. CONFLUENCE

• *a merger or coming together of several factors; flowing together*

AP PSYCHOLOGY

Schizophrenia affects approximately one percent of the U.S. population. Its symptoms include delusional beliefs, hallucinations, and fragmented thinking. Psychologists agree that schizophrenia does not have a single cause. Instead, it is PRECIPITATED (caused) by a CONFLUENCE of several factors, including stress, overactive dopamine neurons, and genetic inheritance.

276. PHLEGMATIC

• *sluggish, lethargic and thus not easily aroused into action*

INSIDER INFO

What words do you associate with Basset hounds? Most people would probably list *friendly*, *loyal*, *social*, and *sleepy* as prime characteristics. Of course, College Board test writers are not most people. Their list of traits would feature *PHLEGMATIC*, since Basset hounds are "not easily aroused into action." You can remember *PHLEGMATIC* by associating it with phlegm, the thick, slow-moving liquid secreted by the mucous membrane during a cold or respiratory infection.

277. SEMINAL

• *highly influential in an original way*

AP U.S. HISTORY

What do Edgar Allen Poe's detective story "The Murders in the Rue Morgue" and Jack Kerouac's novel *On the Road* have in common? Both were SEMINAL works in American literature. Poe's short story marked the beginning of modern detective fiction. Kerouac's novel marked the defining expression of the Beat Generation's philosophy of rebelling against mindless conformity by living spontaneously.

278. CONTENTIOUS

- *always ready to argue or provoke a dispute; quarrelsome*

MEET LARRY'S STUDENTS: KARLEE

CONTENTIOUS is a very tricky word. In one of my SAT classes many students saw the root word *content* and mistakenly believed that *CONTENTIOUS* means "full of contentment." When I pointed out that in a debate a contention is a point of argument, many students still seemed confused. At this point, Karlee offered a clever way to remember the meaning of *CONTENTIOUS*. She reminded everyone of a *Hannah Montana* episode ("Ooh, Ooh, Itchy Woman") that featured a class overnight camping trip. Mr. Picker assigned Hannah and Lilly to share a tent with their archrivals Amber and Ashley. Predictably, the four girls proceeded to have a CONTENTIOUS argument over who put up the tent. Karlee's tip worked, and all of my students now remember that *CONTENTIOUS* means "argumentative."

279. RUMINATE

- *to think deeply about a subject; to REFLECT; to contemplate*

POP CULTURE

In his song "Somebody That I Used to Know," Gotye RUMINATES about the times when he and his former girlfriend were together. Gotye cannot erase the memory of when they were a couple. His feelings for her remain "an ache" he cannot forget. Filled with a sadness that won't go away, Gotye reluctantly concludes, "Now you're just somebody that I used to know."

280. HARBINGER

- *a precursor or forerunner; an indicator that someone or something is approaching*

INSIDER INFO

In recent years environmentalists, the public, and College Board test writers have become increasingly concerned with the problems posed by global warming. Recent tests have focused upon the HARBINGERS or indicators of global warming. For example, melting icebergs, rising sea levels, and declining populations of polar bears and penguins are all HARBINGERS of rising temperatures.

PART 7

281. TRUNCATE

- *to cut short; to abbreviate*

INSIDER INFO

The five-paragraph, three-example essay is a very popular SAT format. If done properly, it usually generates a double-digit score. The format does have problems, however. Many students devote too much space to their first and second examples and are then forced to TRUNCATE both their third example and conclusion. The imbalance can result in a lower score. Practice will help you write three evenly balanced examples and avoid the problem of being forced to TRUNCATE an example.

282. INDEFATIGABLE

- *tireless; filled with an inexhaustible supply of energy*

INSIDER INFO

Many of my students choose to write personal essays describing their athletic teams. The essays often feature a performance in a big game. *INDEFATIGABLE* can be a very useful descriptive word in this type of essay. For example, one of my students wrote, "As we charged onto the field we looked like a team that was ready to win. We were INDOMITABLE (resolute and determined) and INDEFATIGABLE." These two sentences demonstrated a varied, accurate and apt vocabulary. My student received a 12 on her essay.

283. CIRCUMVENT

- *to cleverly go around or bypass a rule, to evade and thus avoid*

AP U.S. HISTORY

The Fifteenth Amendment (1870) prohibited states from denying black males the right to vote because of "race, color, or previous condition of servitude." During Reconstruction, however, the Southern states quickly found ways to CIRCUMVENT the amendment. Property qualifications, poll taxes, literacy tests, and the infamous grandfather clause, for example, all denied black males the vote without making skin color a determining factor. By the early 1900s, African Americans had effectively lost their political rights in the South.

284. ACQUIESCE

- *to accept passively; to give your assent to a plan or action without protest*

AP EUROPEAN HISTORY

The Treaty of Versailles demilitarized the Rhineland, a strategic strip of German land along the French border. In 1936 Adolf Hitler broke the treaty by sending German troops into the Rhineland. Although Hitler expected the French to retaliate, they instead ACQUIESCED to this blatant violation of the Versailles Treaty. Hitler later admitted, "The forty-eight hours after the march into the Rhineland were the most nerve-wracking in my life. If the French had then marched into the Rhineland, we would have had to withdraw." Emboldened by the French AQUIESCENCE, Hitler planned additional aggressive actions.

285. URBANE

- *characterized by elegant manners, DISCRIMINATING taste, and a BROAD education*

POP CULTURE

Have you seen "The Most Interesting Man in the World" commercial? The URBANE "Interesting Man" has elegant manners, discriminating taste, and is of course always surrounded by beautiful, admiring women. He is obviously a sophisticated person who is rich in stories and life experiences. However, his famous line "Stay thirsty, my friends" is very AMBIGUOUS (unclear). Does it mean to stay thirsty so you can acquire more knowledge and thus be even more URBANE? Or does it mean to stay thirsty so you can buy more Dos Equis beer? (I wonder what score the URBANE "Interesting Man" received on his SAT!).

286. SALUTARY

- *beneficial and thus tending to promote physical well-being*

IN YOUR LIFE

Taking the SAT, preparing for AP courses, applying to colleges, and participating in extracurricular activities can all be very stressful. Learning how to relax can have a SALUTARY effect on your mood and help restore balance into your hectic lifestyle. Popular relaxation techniques include meditating, breathing deeply, listening to soft music, watching a movie, and of course, reading this vocabulary book!

287. VOLATILE

- *subject to sudden and violent changes in temperament; unstable*

IN MY LIFE

Everyone in the high school where I taught knew that Greg had a VOLATILE personality. But we all underestimated just how VOLATILE his temper really was. Greg was dating a very pretty girl named Karen. Perhaps sensing that Greg was unstable, Karen decided to end their relationship right after lunch. As he returned to class, Greg's VOLATILE temper got the best of him as he violently punched a glass window. The blow caused severe lacerations and left a trail of blood in the hall. I'll never forget the horrified look on our students' faces as they saw Greg's bloody hand. Amazingly, Karen and Greg soon RECONCILED (reunited). Karen ignored Greg's VOLATILE temper and said the smashed window proved that he had strong feelings for her.

288. DILATORY

- *inclined to waste time and be habitually late; PRONE to tardiness*

IN YOUR LIFE

Like most SAT tutors, Christian and I repeat the following ADMONITION (earnest warning) at the end of every class: "Don't be DILATORY! Be sure to study a few of your Essential 600 words every day!" Needless to say, many of ours students still choose to be DILATORY, believing that they can learn all their vocabulary words a few days before the SAT. So at the risk of being REDUNDANT (repetitious), let us remind you that you are on a collision course with the SAT. So don't be DILATORY!

289. ARTIFICE

- *a deceptive maneuver; a crafty RUSE; a clever stratagem*

INSIDER INFO

ARTIFICE was the answer to a difficult sentence completion question on a recent PSAT. College Board test writers paired *ARTIFICE* with *RUSES* by saying that a person "ran out of RUSES when his ARTIFICES were exposed." George Washington's famous decision to cross the Delaware River and surprise the Hessians on Christmas Eve 1776 is perhaps the most famous ARTIFICE in American military history. The Trojan Horse that allowed the Greeks to conquer Troy in the historical epic the *Iliad* is the most famous ARTIFICE in literary history.

290. FORBEARANCE

- *to show great patience or tolerance*

INSIDER INFO

One way to remember *FOR<u>BEAR</u>ANCE* is to link the word *bear* with the popular expression, "Bear with me for a moment." When a coach, teacher, or parent asks you to bear with them, they are asking for your patience or FORBEARANCE.

PART 8

291. ENERVATE

- *to feel mentally and physically weakened; to lack strength and* energy

INSIDER INFO

Many students believe that *ENERVATE* means "energized." Although the two words do sound alike, they are actually antonyms. *ENERVATE* means "to lack energy or vigor." For example, many students understandably feel ENERVATED after a long day at school followed by band or athletic practice. But don't worry. You'll revive after reading the entertaining and DIDACTIC (instructive) examples in *The Essential Guide to SAT Critical Reading and Vocabulary*.

292. SQUALID

- *run-down and foul; very dirty and wretched*

AP U.S. HISTORY

In his book *How the Other Half Lives*, Jacob Riis documented the SQUALID conditions endured by late-19th-century immigrants living in New York City's Lower East Side. At that time, a single square mile in the Lower East Side contained 334,000 people, making it the most densely populated place in the world. Riis's photographs exposed the dirty, disease-ridden slums where families considered themselves lucky to live in a SQUALID one-room apartment lacking plumbing and proper ventilation.

293. JUXTAPOSITION

- *two or more contrasting people or things placed next to each other; a side-by-side comparison*

INSIDER INFO

The word *JUXTAPOSITION* drew a lot of attention on a recent SAT. A sentence completion described a modern sculptor who created a "sculpture wall" by JUXTAPOSING a number of contrasting objects. Many students incorrectly answered *SEMBLANCE*. *SEMBLANCE* refers to an outward appearance that is deliberately misleading. In contrast, *JUXTAPOSITION* refers to a side-by-side comparison.

294. UNEQUIVOCAL

- *admitting no doubt or misunderstanding; having only one meaning and interpretation*

POP CULTURE

In her song Stronger (What Doesn't Kill You), Kelly Clarkson's ex has left her alone. He thinks Kelly is "broken down" and will "come running back." But he was "dead wrong!" Kelly is a fighter who UNEQUIVOCALLY insists that "what doesn't kill you makes you stronger." Don't expect SAT authors to express opinions that are quite as emphatic as those expressed in Kelly's song. For example, in one recent passage Peter Schwartz expresses his UNEQUIVOCAL opposition to coal and other fossil fuels by writing that they are "driving climate change" and are "a luxury that a planet with six billion energy-hungry souls can't afford." Note that both Kelly Clarkson and Peter Schwartz can be characterized as UNEQUIVOCAL because of the strength of their convictions.

295. SCOURGE

- *something that causes misery, affliction, or destruction; a BANE*

IN YOUR LIFE

Have you ever read an Internet post written by a "troll"? If so, then you know that trolls are anonymous provokers who flood the Internet with inflammatory insults, threats, and profanity. Although trolls have existed since the beginning of the Internet, in recent years they have become a SCOURGE. Trolls often overwhelm website discussion boards with INVECTIVE-filled (verbally abusive) posts that are often profane and threatening.

296. IMPUNITY

- *freedom from punishment or pain*

IN THE NEWS

The Internet protects trolls (see Word 295) by allowing them to remain anonymous. In addition, the First Amendment protects the right of trolls to be as rude or offensive as they like. As a result of these protections, trolls can ASSAIL (attack) their victims with IMPUNITY. Fortunately, more and more websites are beginning to EXCISE (remove) objectionable posts from their comment boards.

297. IMPLACABLE

- *characterized by a relentless hatred that cannot be appeased; merciless and unforgiving*

POP CULTURE

What do the Evil Queen in the Snow White films and Raoul Silva in the James Bond film *Skyfall* have in common? Both share an IMPLACABLE hatred for their rivals. The Evil Queen is a villainous ruler who has an IMPLACABLE hatred for her beautiful stepdaughter Snow White. Raoul Silva is a ruthless cyberterrorist who has an IMPLACABLE hatred for M, the head of MI6, the British Secret Intelligence Service.

298. IMPUGN

- *to attack or ASSAIL with words; to verbally challenge something as false or wrong*

INSIDER INFO

The key to unlocking the meaning of *IMPUGN* is to know that the Latin root *pugnare* means "to fight." *IMPUGN* is used to describe situations in which someone uses words to attack another person verbally. For example, politicians often IMPUGN the credibility of their rivals, and lawyers often IMPUGN the testimony of witnesses.

299. POLEMIC

- *a controversial argument often published as an essay or pamphlet attacking a specific opinion or doctrine*

AP EUROPEAN HISTORY

In November 1894 a French court sentenced a Jewish artillery officer, Captain Alfred Dreyfus, to life imprisonment on Devil's Island in French Guiana. Although high-ranking members of the French General Staff were aware of Dreyfus' innocence, they FABRICATED (invented) a web of lies to convict Dreyfus. Emile Zola, a popular French novelist, published an open letter entitled "*J'Accuse*," attacking the irregularities in the Dreyfus trial. Zola concluded his POLEMIC by declaring, "The truth is on the march and nothing will stop it." Zola's famous POLEMIC forced the French courts to reopen the case and ultimately EXONERATE (free from guilt) Captain Dreyfus.

300. PERFIDIOUS

- *characterized by treacherous and deceitful behavior; traitorous*

POP CULTURE

In the movie *The Dark Knight Rises*, Miranda Tate pretends to be a wealthy socialite dedicated to using Wayne Enterprises' nuclear fusion technology to generate a clean source of energy. Tate soon becomes Bruce Wayne's trusted confidant and the new CEO of Wayne Enterprises. But in reality, Tate is a PERFIDIOUS villain who is actually Talia al Ghoul, the daughter of Batman's NEMESIS (a source of harm or ruin) Ra's al Ghoul. The PERFIDIOUS Talia's real goal is to crush Batman and fulfill her father's mission of destroying Gotham City.

PART 9

301. CURSORY

- *performed in a hasty and SUPERFICIAL manner without attention to details*

INSIDER INFO

Recent tests have included challenging questions that feature uses of the word *CURSORY*. For example, in one critical reading passage, the narrator is a young Korean girl who discovers a random page from a book. She then shows the page to her girlfriend Sunny. Far more interested in batting a shuttlecock, Sunny glances at the page and then tentatively identifies the print as *hangul*, a native Korean alphabet. Sunny's SUPERFICIAL glance is best described as CURSORY.

302. GALVANIZE

- *to energize and stir into action, to arouse*

AP U.S. HISTORY

On December 1, 1955, a white Montgomery City Lines bus driver BRUSQUELY (CURTLY, rudely) ordered Rosa Parks to give up her seat to a white passenger. Although she was tired from a long day at work, Rosa was even more tired of enduring the injustices of racial segregation. Rosa therefore refused the bus driver's order by saying just one fateful word—"No!" Rosa's historic refusal to give up her seat GALVANIZED Montgomery's black community and led to the successful Montgomery Bus Boycott. The boycott played a key role in GALVANIZING the Civil Rights Movement.

303. EXTEMPORIZE

- *to perform without preparation; IMPROVISE*

AP U.S. HISTORY

Political leaders now give speeches that are carefully written and delivered with the aid of a teleprompter. Students are therefore very surprised to learn that Dr. King EXTEMPORIZED most of his famous "I Have a Dream" speech. Dr. King's great speech left an INDELIBLE (can't be removed) impression on his listeners by successfully articulating the hopes and dreams of black and white Americans for a just society based upon racial equality.

304. TACITURN

- *RESERVED and not talkative; LACONIC*

POP CULTURE

In the *Men in Black* film series, Agent K (played by Tommy Lee Jones) is the MIB's top agent. Unlike his partner, the LOQUACIOUS (talkative) Agent J (played by Will Smith), Agent K is a TACITURN man who takes the MIB creed that "silence is your native tongue" very seriously. Agent K rarely jokes or smiles and typically responds to J's rambling thoughts with his trademark TACITURN expression, "All right, kid, here's the deal."

305. UNAMBIGUOUS

- *clear and precise; exhibiting no uncertainty; CATEGORICAL*

IN THE NEWS

Steve Jobs' innovative ideas changed the way technology is used in our society. For example, the iPod reinvented the way we listen to music and the iPhone reinvented the way we communicate with each other. These dramatic advances did not come easily. Jobs was an aggressive and demanding leader who insisted on maintaining high standards of excellence. "We have an environment where excellence is really appreciated," Jobs UNAMBIGUOUSLY asserted. That's my job – to make sure everything is great."

306. CONSTERNATION

- *a sudden, alarming feeling of amazement or dread that results in confusion, anxiety and dismay*

MEET LARRY'S STUDENTS: ARAVIND

The attack on the World Trade Towers on 9/11 left an INDELIBLE (can't be erased) memory on many of my students' families. For example, Aravind's dad was calmly reading a paper as his regular morning commuter train approached the tunnel to enter New York City. The train stopped suddenly, leaving Aravind's dad and his fellow passengers feeling confused. Their confusion turned to CONSTERNATION when the conductor grimly announced that terrorists had just attacked the World Trade Towers and that no trains, buses, or cars would be allowed to enter New York City. Fortunately, the train turned around, and Aravind's dad was able to finally return home.

307. PORTEND

- *to serve as an omen or warning; to foreshadow danger*

POP CULTURE

The movie *The Avengers* ends with the victory of the Avengers over Loki and the Chitauri invaders. However, after the first set of credits, viewers see a glimpse of the villain who sent Loki to Earth. He is Thanos, a sinister demi-god whose name is derived from Thanatos, the Greek god of death. Thanos is one of the most dangerous villains in the universe. His appearance PORTENDS future danger for Earth and for the Avengers. Many fans believe that Thanos and the Avengers will be on a collision course in *The Avengers 2*.

308. INSCRUTABLE

- *very hard to figure out; incomprehensible*

INSIDER INFO

SAT double-blank sentence completion questions often use unexpected examples and surprising cause and effect relationships. For example, on one recent question, fans of a new video game were CONFOUNDED (puzzled) by INSCRUTABLE new features. While I can imagine archaeologists being CONFOUNDED by INSCRUTABLE Mayan carvings, I find it unrealistic that modern gamers would be CONFOUNDED by INSCRUTABLE videogame features. But then, College Board test writers are often INSCRUTABLE.

309. CRYSTALLIZE

• *to take a definite form or shape*

IN YOUR LIFE

Your junior and senior years in high school can be a very stressful time. The SATs, college admission forms, and AP tests are all formidable hurdles that must be overcome. Although your plans have not CRYSTALLIZED, well-meaning parents, relatives, and teachers will all question you about a future that still seems NEBULOUS (not fully formed). But don't worry. You will achieve high test scores, college admission letters will arrive, and your plans will suddenly CRYSTALLIZE.

310. PUERILE

• *childish and immature; CALLOW*

POP CULTURE

What do Billy Madison, Happy Gilmore, and Lenny Feder have in common? All three are PUERILE characters portrayed by Adam Sandler in popular movies. Although critics have LAMBASTED (sharply criticized) these characters for their childish, immature, and often gross behavior, teenage audiences have enjoyed Sandler's slapstick humor and PUERILE antics. It is interesting to note that while your parents and teachers will not appreciate PUERILE behavior, Sandler's movies have grossed (no pun intended) over $2 billion dollars, and his personal fortune is estimated to be $300 million.

PART 10

311. PROFLIGATE

• *characterized by SQUANDERING (wasting) time and money*

POP CULTURE

When Justin Bieber's girlfriend Selena Gomez dropped a hint that she really wanted to see the movie *Titanic*, the Biebs decided to create a date she would never forget. JB surprised Selena by taking her to the Staples Center, the 20,000-seat home of the Los Angles Lakers. After a private dinner of steak and pasta at the Lexus Club, the evening became even more romantic when *Titanic* began playing on a huge screen in the empty arena. When my students heard about this amazing but extravagant date, most criticized JB for being a PROFLIGATE spender. After all, he could have rented *Titanic* for a lot less than the $100,000 it costs to rent the Staples Center for one night. But was Bieber really being PROFLIGATE? It turns out that Biebs was actually very FRUGAL (thrifty), because management allowed him to use the arena for free as a thank you for his string of three previous sold-out concerts.

312. FOREBODING

- *a strong inner feeling or premonition of future misfortune*

AP U.S. HISTORY

On December 7, 1941, the Japanese launched a surprise air attack on Pearl Harbor that sank or damaged eighteen American warships while losing just 29 planes. While his EXULTANT (triumphant) officers celebrated their victory, the Japanese commander Admiral Yamamoto spent the day sunk in apparent depression. Yamamoto had a FOREBODING that the war with America would end in disaster. "I fear all we have done," he warned, "is to awaken a sleeping giant and fill him with a terrible resolve." Yamamoto's feeling of FOREBODING proved to be correct. Resolved to crush Japan, an angry and now united America entered World War II.

313. IRASCIBLE

- *easily angered; PRONE to outbursts of temper*

INSIDER INFO

What do the words *IRATE* and *IRASCIBLE* have in common? Both words contain the Latin root *ira*, meaning "anger or rage." So if you are IRATE you are very angry, and if you are IRASCIBLE you are easily angered. *IRASCIBLE* is a negative trait that is often paired in double-blank sentence completion questions with other negative traits such as *BRUSQUE* (abrupt, CURT), *HEADSTRONG* (impulsive) and *CANTANKEROUS* (irritable, cranky).

314. INDULGENT

- *characterized by excessive generosity; overly lenient and tolerant*

POP CULTURE

According to celebrity magazines, Tom Cruise is determined to be an INDULGENT dad when he is with his young daughter Suri. For example, the newly single dad flew Suri on his private jet to Orlando, where she enjoyed a lavish four-day visit to Disney World. Her loving and INDULGENT father showered Suri with toys, treats, and an adorable *Little Mermaid* costume. Tom treated Suri like a princess as he arranged for her to chat with costumed characters and even spend a night in Disney's exclusive Cinderella Castle Suite.

315. PEDANTIC

- *characterized by being OSTENTATIOUS (showy) in displaying one's knowledge; bookish*

POP CULTURE

The character of Sheldon Lee Cooper on the TV program *The Big Bang Theory* is renowned for his PEDANTIC demonstrations of obscure information. Whether RUMINATING about Bose-Einstein condensates or describing the precise location of retroflectors on the moon's surface, Sheldon never misses an opportunity to show off what he knows.

316. OFFICIOUS

- *describes someone who acts more official than they actually are; annoyingly meddlesome*

POP CULTURE

OFFICIOUS is a tricky word that students often think refers to an office or an official. Instead, *OFFICIOUS* describes busybodies who act more official than they actually are. For example, in the *Harry Potter* series Percy Weasley is portrayed as having an unhealthy obsession with following rules. When the Ministry of Magic denies that Lord Voldemort has returned, the OFFICIOUS Percy insists that Harry and the members of the Order of the Phoenix accept the official but ERRONEOUS (wrong) viewpoint.

317. BOHEMIAN

- *describes a person who is known for UNCONVENTIONAL behavior; a nonconformist*

MEET LARRY'S STUDENTS:DHARA

I find that most of my students have never heard the word *BOHEMIAN*. My explanation that the 1950s beatniks and the late-1960s hippies both led BOHEMIAN lifestyles did not seem to RESONATE (evoke a shared feeling) with my 21st-century students. Fortunately, my student Dhara helped me by pointing out that the word *BOHEMIAN* reminded her of the Boho Chic style of clothing. Dhara's tip worked, and all of my students now remember that *BOHEMIAN* describes UNCONVENTIONAL behavior.

318. PROSCRIBE

- *to forbid or prohibit an activity*

IN MY LIFE

I recently attended my niece's wedding reception. I arrived early and went to the country club's now-empty bar to order a snack and a soft drink. The bartender stunned me by politely but firmly saying, "I'm sorry, but I can't serve you. Club rules PROSCRIBE serving gentlemen who are not wearing a jacket." I was impressed by the bartender's correct use of *PROSCRIBE* but furious at the club's INANE (absurd, silly) rule. The waiter made matters worse when he offered to let me wear a secondhand bright green sports jacket that was several sizes too large. Rather than look like a clown, I refused the offer and walked out.

319. FACETIOUS

- *cleverly amusing in tone; not meant to be taken seriously*

POP CULTURE

Richard Castle is one of the most FACETIOUS characters on television. His quick wit provides timely comedic relief on a program that focuses on solving gruesome murders. Castle's FACETIOUS sense of humor can be clearly seen in this exchange with his partner, Detective Beckett:

Beckett: "Crime scene. Dead body. Little respect here."

Castle: "I don't think he can hear me."

320. PUNCTILIOUS

- *strictly attentive to minute details of conduct; very precise and METICULOUS*

INSIDER INFO

Most of my students are BEFUDDLED (confused) by the word *PUNCTILIOUS*. They claim never to have seen it before and have no idea what it means. I then invite my students to take a close look at *PUNCTILIOUS*. It is really a combination of the word *PUNCTUAL*, meaning "prompt," and the suffix *-ous*, meaning "full of." So *PUNCTILIOUS* means "full of promptness," in the sense of paying careful attention to details. A PUNCTILIOUS person would not challenge traditions or take a CURSORY (hasty) glance at an important document.

PART 11

321. CRAVEN

- *characterized by being cowardly and fearful; faint-hearted*

POP CULTURE

In the *Harry Potter* saga, Peter Pettigrew is a CRAVEN character who more than lives up to his nickname, Wormtail. Pettigrew betrayed James and Lily Potter by revealing their secret home to Lord Voldemort. The CRAVEN Wormtail then faked his own death and framed Sirius Black for betraying the Potters. Pettigrew spent the next twelve years living undercover in his Animagus form as the Weasley family's CRAVEN pet rat, Scabbers. It is important to note that *CRAVEN* is typically used in SAT sentence completion questions to describe a person who wants to avoid conflict at all costs.

322. DEFUNCT

- *no longer living; dead or extinct*

INSIDER INFO

What do dinosaurs, Whigs, and Borders Bookstores have in common? All three are now DEFUNCT. The dinosaurs are thought to have vanished following a catastrophic meteor strike 65 million years ago. The Whigs were a political party that vanished following the political upheaval caused by the 1854 Kansas-Nebraska Act. And Borders Bookstores vanished following a series of management blunders and competitive pressure from Amazon. It is important to know the difference between DEFUNCT and MORIBUND. DEFUNCT is used to describe things that are dead while MORIBUND is used to describe things that are declining but not quite dead.

323. SCHISM

- *division of a group into opposing factions*

AP EUROPEAN HISTORY

Students are very surprised to learn that between 1378 and 1417 two rival popes each claimed to be the true and INFALLIBLE (unerring) leader of the Roman Catholic Church. Known in Church history as the Great Schism, the split left one pope in Rome and a second in Avignon, France. The rival popes promptly excommunicated each other and on one occasion the Roman pope proclaimed a "holy crusade" against the French pope. The Council of Constance finally ended the SCHISM in 1417. It is important to note that SCHISMS often occur within political parties and scientific communities.

324. PITHY

- *brief, precise and full of meaning*

AP U.S. HISTORY

The opening sentences of the Declaration of Independence and Lincoln's Gettysburg Address are both short but PITHY statements of America's founding principles. In one particularly PITHY sentence, Jefferson SUCCINCTLY (concisely) stated the key principles of human equality when he proudly proclaimed, "We hold these truths to be self-evident, that all men are created equal, that they are endowed by their Creator with certain unalienable rights, that among these are Life, Liberty, and the pursuit of Happiness." Lincoln REITERATED (repeated) Jefferson's PITHY principles when he firmly declared that "this government of the people, by the people, for the people, shall not perish from the earth."

325. PALLID

- *pale; lacking color*

POP CULTURE

Below-ground protective shelter will be one of the most important resources in a post-apocalyptic world. Although skyscrapers, malls, and other above-ground buildings will have been destroyed, many underground bunkers, subways, and basements will survive. People living in these underground structures will develop PALLID complexions from the lack of natural sunlight. Losing your summer tan and becoming a PALLID shelter-dweller may not be your idea of a great time, but hey—it's probably better than whatever will be lurking outside!

326. VIRULENT

- *extremely infectious; deadly*

AP EUROPEAN HISTORY

In the movie *World War Z*, a VIRULENT virus that suddenly spreads across the globe turns humans into zombies. Although the movie is of course fictitious, VIRULENT diseases have had a catastrophic impact upon real-world human populations. For example, an outbreak of bubonic plague called the Black Death claimed the lives of 25 million people—about one-third of Europe's population—in the five years between 1347 and 1352.

327. JADED

- *characterized by a CYNICAL fatigue caused by overindulgence*

POP CULTURE

In the *Hunger Games* saga, Panem's wealthiest and most powerful citizens live self-indulgent and JADED lives in the Capitol city. The JADED Capitol elite are dulled and satiated by their carefree lives. They enjoy imported luxuries from the outlying districts and spend an inordinate amount of time wearing FLAMBOYANT (dashing and colorful) fashions and, of course, watching the annual Hunger Games.

328. PROPITIATE

- *to please or PLACATE someone; to APPEASE in an attempt to conciliate*

POP CULTURE

In *Catching Fire*, Peeta realizes that the growing tension between Katniss and President Snow poses a threat to her safety. Hoping to PROPITIATE President Snow, Peeta publicly proposes to Katniss, thus proving that their actions at the end of the 74th Hunger Games were motivated by true love and not a spirit of rebellion. However, President Snow is not easily PROPITIATED. He OMINOUSLY (foreboding danger) warns that Katniss and the other Hunger Games victors "all pose a threat" and therefore "must be eradicated."

329. HABITUATE

- *to become accustomed to something*

IN YOUR LIFE

In a short time, you will probably move into a new dorm room. One very interesting thing about dorm life is how quickly you will HABITUATE to the room's relatively small size. Imagine walking in on the first day of freshman orientation and feeling like you were unfairly given the smallest room on the hallway. But don't despair. You will quickly HABITUATE to your new living quarters. You may even notice that less is more as you live more minimally and leave your room to meet new people. You could say you will HABITUATE to your cozy little-dorm room "habitat!"

330. VOLUBLE

- *very open and talkative*

POP CULTURE

Entertainment writers love to interview Bruno Mars. The pop superstar is both charming and VOLUBLE. Unlike many STILTED (unnatural and studied) media-trained celebrities, Mars is a natural who loves to express his views on almost any subject. Although College Board test writers probably don't read interviews with Bruno Mars, they do use *VOLUBLE* in challenging Level 5 sentence completion questions. It is important to remember that a VOLUBLE person is open and talkative, while a CRYPTIC person is deliberately vague and mysterious.

CHAPTER 11
THE TOP 110 LEVEL 4 WORDS

The SAT rates each question on a five-point scale of difficulty. Level 4 questions are the second most challenging questions on the test. At least 65 percent of all test-takers miss a Level 4 question. What makes these questions so difficult? In most cases, the questions call for a knowledge of little-known and often misunderstood vocabulary words. This chapter will define and illustrate 110 Level 4 vocabulary words. It is important to remember that the Level 4 questions are actually very easy if you know the words!

PART 1

331. AUSPICIOUS
- *favorable and promising; accompanied by good omens and therefore PROPITIOUS*

WORLD CULTURES

In Chinese culture certain numbers are believed to be either AUSPICIOUS or INAUSPICIOUS. For example, *two* is often considered an AUSPICIOUS number because "good things come in pairs." In contrast, *four* is often considered an INAUSPICIOUS number because its pronunciation is very similar to the word for death. As a result, many buildings in East Asia do not have a fourth floor. This is very similar to the Western practice of eliminating the thirteenth floor, since thirteen is believed to be an INAUSPICIOUS number.

332. EVOCATIVE

- *characterized by using the power of imagination to call forth a memory*

INSIDER INFO

On the SAT, *EVOCATIVE* describes an experience that has generated a number of answers for challenging sentence completion and critical reading questions. The questions typically deal with an EVOCATIVE portrayal of a person or an author's EVOCATIVE tone describing a place. For example, in one recent passage, an archaeologist's tone is EVOCATIVE because he imagines hearing "the echoes of the ancient city" and the voices of its residents "over pots of steaming coffee."

333. ENIGMA

- *a riddle shrouded in mystery and thus something that is puzzling and INSCRUTABLE*

POP CULTURE

In his song "6 Foot 7 Foot," Lil Wayne points out that being misunderstood is not necessarily bad when he asks, "What's a world without ENIGMA?" Lil Wayne is right. Life would be MUNDANE (commonplace) without ENIGMAS to discuss and solve. It is important to note that the adjective *ENIGMATIC* means "mysterious." For example, Da Vinci's *Mona Lisa* is world-famous for her ENIGMATIC smile.

334. SUPERFICIAL

- *shallow; lacking intellectual or emotional depth*

POP CULTURE

In the movie *Clueless*, Cher is an attractive, popular, and hip teenager at a fashion-obsessed Beverly Hills high school. However, these traits do not impress Josh, her socially conscious ex-stepbrother. Josh teases Cher for being selfish, vain, and most of all SUPERFICIAL. According to Josh, Cher's only direction in life is "toward the mall." Cher denies that she is SUPERFICIAL, pointing out that she is a serious person who donates her used clothes to charity. Cher may be "clueless," but at least she can define SUPERFICIAL!

335. PRECOCIOUS

- *characterized by the exceptionally early development or maturity of a talent*

IN MY LIFE

My niece Sierra is very PRECOCIOUS. Naturally, when I visit with Sierra I enjoy teaching her SAT vocabulary words. When she was just five years old, I told Sierra that she was PRECOCIOUS because she had a big vocabulary. Sierra then gleefully told everyone in the room that she was PRECOCIOUS!

336. STIGMATIZE

- *to brand or mark as inferior*

POP CULTURE

In his song "Thrift Shop," Macklemore boasts that he can "take some Pro Wings, make them cool." Pro Wings are an inexpensive brand of sneakers sold at Payless stores. SUPERCILIOUS (snobbish) middle-school kids often relentlessly tease classmates forced to wear these shoes. But Macklemore is so cool, he can take a STIGMATIZED brand of shoes and make them desirable to even the most arrogant sneaker head.

337. INFINITESIMAL
- *incalculably small; MINUSCULE*

AP BIOLOGY
Pfiesteria piscicida are microscopic one-celled microorganisms. The organism is INFINITESIMAL in size. Amazingly, thousands of them could fit on the exclamation point dot at the end of this sentence!

338. VITRIOLIC
- *characterized by a harsh and nasty tone; SCATHING*

AP U.S. HISTORY
In her groundbreaking book *Silent Spring*, Rachel Carson warned that the continued INDISCRIMINATE (not selective) use of DDT and other chemical pesticides posed a dire threat to wildlife and human health. The chemical industry promptly attacked both Carson and her book. VITRIOLIC critics denounced Carson as a "hysterical woman," "a fanatic," and "a Communist." Nevertheless, Carson demonstrated great courage and conviction by refusing to COMPROMISE her principles. Today, Rachel Carson is widely ACCLAIMED (praised) for her role in helping to ban DDT and GALVANIZE (energize) the global environmental movement.

339. PROLIFERATE
- *to grow rapidly; multiply quickly; to BURGEON*

DID YOU KNOW?
The song "Gangnam Style" has focused global attention on the lifestyle of the people who live in the Gangnam district of Seoul, South Korea. The "Gangnam style" includes a fascination with cosmetic plastic surgery. Visitors to Gangnam have noted the astonishing PROLIFERATION of plastic surgery clinics. There are now over 430 such clinics in the district, making it the plastic surgery center of South Korea. The PROLIFERATION of clinics has triggered a boom in cosmetic procedures. South Korea now has the highest per capita rate of cosmetic surgery in the world.

340. RESPLENDENT
- *characterized by great beauty, splendor, and dazzling jewel-like colors; not DRAB*

WORLD CULTURES
Traditional Indian weddings are often very elaborate affairs that can last for days. Brides and grooms are usually treated like royalty. Many brides wear sarees that are renowned for their RESPLENDENT jewel-like colors, gorgeous lace, and intricate embroidery.

PART 2

341. EXHORT

- *to spur on; to encourage*

IN MY LIFE

In *Harry Potter and the Order of the Phoenix*, Harry EXHORTED his classmates at Hogwarts to join "Dumbledore's Army" to learn how to fight the evil Lord Voldemort. On my InsiderTestPrep.com website, I EXHORT students to study my list of essential vocabulary words to fight evil questions on the SAT.

342. AMELIORATE

- *to improve; make better*

IN THE NEWS

America has a long list of notable reformers who have worked to AMELIORATE social problems. For example, in the early 20th century Jane Addams worked to AMELIORATE the condition of poor immigrants in Chicago. Today Brad Pitt's Make It Right Foundation is working to AMELIORATE a housing shortage in New Orleans' IMPOVERISHED (very poor) Ninth Ward.

343. COMPUNCTION

- *a feeling of deep regret caused by a sense of guilt;*
  great REMORSE and CONTRITION

POP CULTURE

In the movie *Snow White and the Huntsman*, the Evil Queen admits that she once felt COMPUNCTION for being the cause of bloody battles that claimed many innocent lives. "It once pained me," she confesses, "to know that I am the cause of such despair." But the Evil Queen's feelings have hardened, and she no longer feels any sense of COMPUNCTION for causing such great suffering. Instead, she defiantly proclaims, "their cries give me strength."

344. MENDACITY

- *the trait of being deliberately untruthful; DUPLICITOUS*

AP EUROPEAN HISTORY

Is lying ever justified? In his book *The Prince*, Machiavelli argued that for the good of the state, a prince should resort to MENDACITY to trick his enemies. His ideal ruler was the crafty Spanish king, Ferdinand of Aragon. When the king of France complained that Ferdinand had deceived him twice, the MENDACIOUS Ferdinand boasted, "He lies, the drunkard. I have deceived him more than ten times."

345. FORTUITOUS

- *an accidental but lucky chance; filled with good fortune*

IN THE NEWS

Tom Morris always bought three $1 Powerball tickets each week. On Saturday, August 13, 2011, Tom entered a SuperAmerica store to purchase his usual three tickets. He reached into his pocket and discovered that he only had a $5 bill. Tom briefly paused and then decided to buy five tickets and let the machine pick random numbers. Tom's spontaneous decision proved to be FORTUITOUS. The fourth set of numbers was the winner in a Powerball jackpot worth $228.9 million! The 61-year-old sales engineer celebrated his FORTUITOUS good luck by retiring from his job and promising his ECSTATIC (very happy) family, "We're going to have fun!"

346. DEBACLE

- *a complete disaster; a FIASCO*

AP U.S. HISTORY

On April 24, 1980, President Jimmy Carter ordered a daring mission to rescue 52 Americans held captive at the U.S. Embassy in Tehran, Iran. Code-named Operation Eagle Claw, the mission quickly turned into a DEBACLE when a sand cloud forced one helicopter to crash land and another to return to the aircraft carrier U.S.S. *Nimitz*. Carter then approved the ground commander's request to abort the mission. The DEBACLE became even worse when a helicopter crashed into a transport aircraft and caused the deaths of eight American servicemen. The humiliating DEBACLE damaged American prestige and played a key role in Carter's overwhelming defeat in the 1980 presidential election.

347. INADVERTENT

- *unintentional and accidental; unwitting*

MEET LARRY'S STUDENTS: MUKHI

Mukhi's full name is very long and very difficult to pronounce. Here it is—Saimukeshvarma Bhupatiraju. Needless to say, many people have trouble pronouncing this name. In fact, on the first day of school, teachers often address Mukhi as "the kid with the very long name." In the eighth grade, Mukhi earned an award for his high academic average. At the awards assembly the announcer INADVERTENTLY mispronounced Mukhi's name so badly that he did not know that he was being called to the stage. Thinking that Mukhi was absent, the announcer went on to the next person. Mukhi and his friends now remember the INADVERTENT slight as a humorous middle school incident. Mukhi wants everyone to know that he did receive his certificate a few days later.

348. PERFUNCTORY

- *characterized by casual INDIFFERENCE; performing in a routine manner*

IN MY LIFE

It is commonly assumed that students who achieve high SAT scores are smarter than students who achieve low scores. My experience suggests otherwise. Students who achieve high scores ASSIDUOUSLY (diligently) study vocabulary words, practice critical reading, and take several timed tests. In contrast, students who receive low scores typically make only a PERFUNCTORY effort. They postpone practice, make excuses, and conveniently forget to take practice tests.

349. AUSTERITY

- *great self-denial, especially when refraining from spending*

INSIDER INFO

Students who keep up with the news will recognize the word AUSTERITY. The economic crisis in Europe has forced governments in Greece, Italy, and Spain to enact AUSTERITY programs designed to cut government spending. Similarly, budget cuts have forced state and local governments in the United States to undertake AUSTERITY measures. Recent SAT sentence completions have also focused attention on the word AUSTERITY. Double-blank sentence completion questions often pair *AUSTERITY* with the word *CURTAIL*, meaning "to cut back, limit, or TRUNCATE (cut short)." For example, a town council would undertake AUSTERITY measures by CURTAILING the number of new public projects.

350. INDIGENOUS

- *a plant, animal, or person that is native or ENDEMIC to an area*

DID YOU KNOW?

The American Beauty rose is renowned for its exceptional beauty and fragrance. It is a particular favorite with home gardeners and is one of the MAINSTAYS (chief supports) of the cut-flower industry. Despite its name, the American Beauty rose is not INDIGENOUS to the United States. It is actually native to France and was first introduced in the United States in 1875 by the botanist George Valentine Nash. It is interesting to note that Nash had nothing to do with the use of roses on Valentine's Day.

PART 3

351. LITANY

- *a long and familiar list often recited by rote*

IN MY LIFE

My wife Susan once got a speeding ticket for driving 35 miles per hour in a 25-mph zone. She thought the ticket was unfair and prepared a good excuse. The traffic magistrate greeted a room filled with speeding offenders by warning everyone not to bother insulting his intelligence. He then recited a LITANY of tired excuses that included a broken speedometer (her excuse), rushing to a funeral, and worst of all claiming, "I had to go to the bathroom." After hearing the magistrate recite this LITANY of excuses, Susan decided to pay the $75 fine.

352. ESTRANGE

- *to alienate; drive apart*

INSIDER INFO
We often hear *ESTRANGE* used to describe the break-up of a celebrity marriage. This seems appropriate since *ESTRANGE* contains the word *strange*, suggesting that a couple has literally become strangers. Don't expect to see an SAT sentence completion question featuring a celebrity couple that has become ESTRANGED. While *ESTRANGE* is widely used to describe a personal relationship, it can also be used to describe a person's relationship to the environment. For example, massive and impersonal apartment complexes can ESTRANGE people from their surroundings.

353. GREGARIOUS

- *marked by a liking for companionship; sociable; AFFABLE*

AP BIOLOGY
Killer whales are very GREGARIOUS animals that live with their mothers in very stable family groups called *pods*. Since a female killer whale can live to be ninety years old, as many as four generations of whales can travel together. Their GREGARIOUS nature enables killer whales to develop sophisticated hunting techniques and vocal behaviors that marine biologists believe can be transmitted across generations.

354. IMPASSE

- *a deadlock or stalemate*

AP U.S. HISTORY
The election of 1860 marked a fateful moment in American history. Southern "fire-eaters" threatened to secede from the Union if the "sectional" Abraham Lincoln won the election. At the same time, northern abolitionists vowed to prevent the expansion of slavery into the western territories. The United States thus confronted a dangerous IMPASSE. Lincoln's election led to the secession of seven southern states. Senator Crittendon and other leaders worked tirelessly to craft a COMPROMISE that would break the IMPASSE and save the Union. But their efforts failed, and a civil war between the North and the South became inevitable.

355. ARDUOUS

- *describes a difficult task that requires a great deal of strenuous work*

MEET LARRY'S STUDENTS: ADITI
Aditi is committed to participating in Relay for Life activities designed to raise money for cancer research. For example, last year Aditi and her team wrote emails, sold cancer bracelets, and participated in a twelve-hour walk. Although these volunteer activities required long and ARDUOUS work, Aditi is proud that she raised $1,800 and that her team raised over $4,600. Way to go Aditi—we are all very proud of you!

356. ESCHEW

• *to avoid something deliberately*

WORLD CULTURES

Approximately 250,000 Amish live in North America. The Amish are known for ADHERING (strictly following) to a traditional lifestyle that ESCHEWS many modern conveniences. For example, Amish families ESCHEW using electricity, making telephone calls, and driving automobiles. In addition, the Amish ESCHEW modern clothing fashions, preferring to ADHERE (closely follow) to a strict dress code that rejects personal vanity.

357. PRECLUDE

• *to make impossible, especially beforehand; to prevent or to FORESTALL something from happening*

AP ART HISTORY

Vincent Van Gogh was not PRECLUDED from becoming famous by a lack of talent. One of history's most original artists, Van Gogh painted a variety of dazzling landscapes, vibrant still lifes, and revealing portraits that pioneered the Post-Impressionist style. Unrecognized and unappreciated in his own life, Van Gogh fought a desperate and ultimately losing struggle against poverty, hunger, alcoholism, and insanity. He fatally shot himself when he was 37, thus PRECLUDING the recognition and fame he deserved.

358. POSTHUMOUS

• *occurring or coming into existence after a person's death*

AP ART HISTORY

Vincent Van Gogh sold only one painting during his lifetime; however, his works enjoyed enormous POSTHUMOUS fame in the years following his death in 1890. Critics and the general public now recognize Van Gogh as one of history's greatest artists.

359. IMPETUS

• *the moving force behind something; a stimulus that moves something along*

AP EUROPEAN HISTORY

The spice trade provided the primary IMPETUS for the first Portuguese and Spanish voyages of exploration. Peppers that could be purchased in Calicut for three Venetian ducats could be sold in Europe for eighty ducats, a 2,700-percent markup. Profit thus provided the most compelling IMPETUS for the voyages of Vasco da Gama and Christopher Columbus.

360. PRISTINE

• *immaculately clean; unspoiled; free from contamination*

IN THE NEWS

In the early 1990s, Russian scientists discovered a PRISTINE lake two miles beneath the surface of Antarctica. Named Lake Vostok, the isolated body of water may be home to many unusual life forms. Researchers must now determine how to investigate the lake without contaminating its PRISTINE ecosystem.

PART 4

361. ERRONEOUS
* *incorrect; mistaken; wrong; filled with errors*

POP CULTURE
In the movie *The Social Network*, Lawrence Summers, the President of Harvard University, confidently predicted that Facebook would have limited public appeal and even less commercial value. Summers' prediction proved to be ERRONEOUS. Facebook now has over one billion active users, and its founder Mark Zuckerberg is one of the wealthiest people in the world.

362. ADMONISH
* *to counsel against, to warn EARNESTLY*

POP CULTURE
In 1995 J. K. Rowling, then an obscure single mom, began her search to find a publisher for a children's fantasy book she had just completed. One publishing executive ADMONISHED Rowling by warning her that young readers would not be able to identify with her characters and that there was little chance of making money by writing a children's book. Needless to say, his ADMONITION proved to be ERRONEOUS. Rowling's series of books about a boy wizard named Harry Potter have now sold over 450 million copies in 67 languages.

363. DEMARCATE
* *to clearly set or mark the boundaries of a group or geographic area*

AP U.S. HISTORY
Columbus's discoveries prompted the Spanish to ask Pope Alexander VI to DEMARCATE the boundaries between lands claimed by Spain and Portugal. The Pope obliged by issuing the Papal Line of DEMARCATION. As its name implies, the proclamation DEMARCATED or marked the boundaries of so-called "heathen lands" that would be controlled by Spain and by Portugal. Although the Line of DEMARCATION gave the lion's share of New World land to Spain, Portugal received title to lands that ultimately became Brazil.

364. FOSTER

- *to promote and encourage*

IN MY LIFE

I spent my second and third years of teaching at Jordan-Matthews High School in Siler City, North Carolina. The administration and staff at JM tried very hard to FOSTER a climate of racial harmony. But FOSTERING racial tolerance proved to be difficult. The community had to overcome a historic legacy in which the ancestors of some of our white students had owned the ancestors of some of our black students. Football played a key role in breaking down barriers and FOSTERING a greater sense of togetherness. As the Jordan-Matthews Jets won victory after victory, the school and community came together to support their team.

365. FLORID

- *excessively ornamental, as in a very flowery style of writing; neither plain nor STARK*

DID YOU KNOW?

The Italian city of Florence, the American state of Florida, and the SAT word *FLORID* all derive from the Old French word *flor*, meaning "flower." Florence is thus a flowery city, Florida is a flowery state, and *FLORID* is a flowery word. FLORID writers are known for using flowery descriptions. For example, Edward Bulwer-Lytton began his novel *Paul Clifford* with the following classic example of FLORID writing: "It was a dark and stormy night; the rain fell in torrents…rattling the housetop; and fiercely agitating the scanty flame of the lamps that struggled against the darkness."

366. CHURLISH

- *characterized by SURLY and rude behavior; sullen and devoid of CIVILITY*

IN THE NEWS

Serena Williams was once best known for her skill as a tennis player and flair as a fashion model. She is now increasingly known for her CHURLISH behavior during tennis matches. For example, in the 2011 U.S. Open, Williams called the official "a loser," "a hater," and "unattractive, on the inside." Williams continued to demonstrate CHURLISH behavior when she refused the customary post-match handshake with the umpire.

367. CIRCUMSCRIBE

- *to limit, restrict, or confine*

POP CULTURE

In her song "Fly," Nicki Minaj realizes that fame has a price. She protests that managers, producers, and even fans "try to box me in." Nicki doesn't want others to CIRCUMSCRIBE her life. She vows to soar and thrive. Don't expect College Board test writers to use lyrics from a Nicki Minaj song to test your knowledge of the word *CIRCUMSCRIBE*. Past SAT examples included social customs that CIRCUMSCRIBED the lives of Renaissance women and STRINGENT (very strict) rules that CIRCUMSCRIBED the range of paint colors available to a group of homeowners.

368. PROVISIONAL
- *temporary; not permanent*

INSIDER INFO
For most American teenagers the word *PROVISIONAL* calls to mind a PROVISIONAL driver's license. Don't expect to see this example on your SAT. Instead, test writers typically focus on PROVISIONAL theories of the universe that are not definitive and PROVISIONAL governments that are not permanent.

369. PASTORAL
- *an idealized portrayal of country life; RUSTIC; BUCOLIC*

AP ART HISTORY
John Constable is often described as England's greatest landscape artist. His PASTORAL paintings feature lush green meadows, picturesque villages, and lazy streams flowing under old stone bridges. To this day, his PASTORAL masterpieces draw large admiring crowds at London's National Gallery. The scenes he immortalized are preserved along a Painter's Trail in a portion of Suffolk now known as "Constable Country."

370. CONVIVIAL
- *characterized by being full of life and good company; JOVIAL and festive*

POP CULTURE
In the music video "Last Friday Night (TGIF)," Rebecca Black is the CONVIVIAL hostess of a "best ever" party that is "absolutely incredible." Rebecca generously welcomes her nerdy neighbor Kathy Beth Terry (Katy Perry) and quickly transforms her into a CONVIVIAL party girl. The festive guests enjoy a CONVIVIAL scene that includes Kenny G playing a sax solo on the roof and Hanson as the house band.

PART 5

371. BURGEON
- *to grow and multiply rapidly; to FLOURISH*

AP U.S. HISTORY
In the mid-19th century, as many as sixty to 100 million bison roamed the Great Plains. Less than three decades later the transcontinental railroads had enabled hunters to nearly exterminate these once-great herds. By 1912, a tiny herd of fewer than 100 bison remained in Yellowstone National Park; however, the determined work of dedicated conservationists has brought the bison back from the brink of extinction. The bison population is now BURGEONING, with an estimated 350,000 living on ranches and parks throughout the United States.

372. CONFOUND

- *to perplex and confuse; to leave baffled, BEWILDERED, and NONPLUSSED*

AP ART HISTORY

In 1950, Jackson Pollock stunned and CONFOUNDED the art world with an Abstract Expressionist painting entitled *Autumn Rhythm*. The painting did not contain images of Fall or any other recognizable objects. Instead, Pollock literally hurled paint onto a canvas and claimed that the resulting maze of lines and drips represented the process of painting. Needless to say, critics attacked Pollock's work and called him "Jack the Dripper." Even today, most museum visitors are still CONFOUNDED by Pollock's paintings and by his Abstract Expressionist message.

373. BEMOAN

- *to moan and groan; to express great regret; to LAMENT*

POP CULTURE

Laptop computers, advanced mobile devices, and social media such as Twitter are changing the way we communicate with each other. While many educators praise the positive effects of this communication boom, others BEMOAN the effect that shortcuts, alternative words, and other cyber-slang are beginning to have on students' writing skills. One veteran language arts teacher LAMENTED that "students are carrying over the writing habits they pick up through text messaging into school assignments."

374. QUIESCENT

- *marked by inactivity and quiet; a state of tranquility*

AP U.S. HISTORY

American college students have alternated between QUIESCENT periods of inactivity and restless periods of protest. For example, the Vietnam War and the Civil Rights Movement transformed the QUIESCENT 1950s into the turbulent 1960s.

375. REAFFIRM

- *to make a renewed commitment to something; to confirm*

IN THE NEWS

Malala Yousufzai is a teenage Pakistani human rights activist who has become a global symbol of defiance against Taliban oppression. In 2009, the Taliban issued a PEREMPTORY (arbitrary) order banning all girls from attending schools in the town in northwestern Pakistan where Malala lived. Malala refused to SUCCUMB (submit) to the Taliban and instead began a blog exposing the horrors they imposed on the girls in her hometown. The Taliban retaliated in October 2012 by attempting to assassinate Malala as she rode home on her school bus. Malala survived the attack and is now recognized as a courageous CHAMPION (supporter) of women's rights. UNDAUNTED (not discouraged) by continuing Taliban threats, Malala had REAFFIRMED her commitment to human rights vowing, "I shall raise my voice."

376. ACRIMONIOUS

• *marked by feelings of ill will and hostility; great resentment; RANCOROUS in tone*

AP U.S. HISTORY

The ACRIMONIOUS blood feud between the Hatfields and McCoys has fascinated Americans for over a century. The two rival families lived on opposite sides of the Big Sandy River in the mountains between Kentucky and West Virginia. The ACRIMONY began in 1878 when Randolph McCoy accused Floyd Hatfield of stealing one of his prized pigs. The incident sparked a lethal feud between the two families that lasted for decades. Over time the two clans finally RECONCILED and even appeared together in 1979 on the *Family Feud* game show. In 2012 a record television audience watched the History Channel's epic mini-series on the Hatfields and McCoys.

377. RANCID

• *having a rotten taste or smell; sour*

DID YOU KNOW?

Honey has special chemical properties that prevent it from spoiling or becoming RANCID. Archaeologists have found unspoiled honey stored in the tombs of ancient Egyptian pharaohs. Incredibly, the honey was still edible!

378. LARGESSE

• *generous giving; LIBERAL bestowing of gifts*

INSIDER INFO

LARGESSE is normally associated with generous acts of PHILANTHROPY and selfless giving. However, acts of LARGESSE can have ulterior motives. For example, the pharmaceutical industry in the United States is noted for its LARGESSE. The industry entertains lavishly and sponsors numerous medical conventions. But it also promotes its political interests by spending more on lobbyists than any other industrial group.

379. EPIPHANY

• *an unexpected moment of sudden inspiration*

IN MY LIFE

Back in the early 1990s, as I was driving home from an SAT class, I thought about how hard it is to teach students difficult SAT vocabulary words. I turned the radio channel to an oldies station just as the DJ began playing Bon Jovi's hit song "Livin' on a Prayer." I suddenly had an EPIPHANY. What if I used the stories in popular songs and movies to illustrate challenging SAT vocabulary words! For example, "Livin' on a Prayer" tells the story of a working class couple who are down on their luck. But Gina is RESOLUTE (determined) and refuses to SUCCUMB (give up). She EXHORTS (encourages) Tommy "to hold on to what we've got." This EPIPHANY marked the beginning of a revolutionary way to teach SAT vocabulary. The pop culture examples in this book all are inspired by my EPIPHANY as I listened to "Livin' on a Prayer."

380. VINDICATE

- *to justify or prove something's worth*

IN MY LIFE

I was very excited about my EPIPHANY (see Word 379) to use popular songs and scenes from movies to provide memorable examples of difficult SAT vocabulary words; SKEPTICS (doubters), however, questioned my new approach. They insisted that rote memorization and REPETITION were the best ways to learn SAT vocabulary words. I refused to let the critics dampen my enthusiasm. Within a short time my students reported dramatic increases in their critical reading scores. Being VINDICATED (proven right) felt good, and helping my students felt even better.

PART 6

381. AMBIGUOUS

- *open to more than one interpretation; unclear*

POP CULTURE

The movie *The Amazing Spider-Man* ends with an intentionally AMBIGUOUS mid-credits scene. Dr. Curt Conners (The Lizard) is incarcerated in a high-security cell for his diabolical plot to transform everyone in New York City into a reptile. A shadowy figure suddenly appears and asks Dr. Connors, "Did you tell the boy about his father?" Dr. Connors answers, "No," and the man in the shadows replies, "Well, that's very good, so we'll let him be for now." The boy is of course Peter Parker (Spider-Man); however, everything else is AMBIGUOUS. Who is the mysterious figure, and how did he get into the cell? Although there is much speculation, the scene is AMBIGUOUS, and the answers to these questions are all unknown. We'll have to wait for *The Amazing Spider-Man 2* to find out the truth.

382. ENTHRALL

- *fascinating and spellbinding; CAPTIVATING*

AP U.S. HISTORY

Frederick Douglass was a former slave who became America's foremost black abolitionist during the antebellum period. A gifted orator, Douglass ENTHRALLED audiences with his commanding personal presence and authentic stories about the horrors of slavery. For example, he told a spellbound audience in Massachusetts, "I appear before the immense assembly this evening as a thief and a robber. I stole this head, these limbs, this body from my master, and ran off with them."

383. VIVACIOUS

- *full of life and spirit; animated*

MEET LARRY'S STUDENTS: NICOLE

I am fortunate to have many VIVACIOUS students who enliven my classes with their spirit and energy. But few students can surpass Nicole's wit and VIVACITY. I can always count on Nicole for a funny story about the antics of celebrities such and Kim Kardashian, Snooki, and of course Kristen Stewart. In addition, Nicole has an uncanny ability to spontaneously use clever facial expressions and hand gestures to illustrate difficult vocabulary words.

384. IMPULSIVE

- *acting with a lack of forethought or deliberation; rash*

POP CULTURE

In her song "Call Me Maybe," Carly Rae Jepsen sees a hot guy and has a sudden innocent crush. Although Carly knows "this is crazy," she IMPULSIVELY gives the guy her number and says, "So call me, maybe?" If her IMPULSIVE action works out, it will be the perfect way to start a summer romance—or not!

385. AUDACIOUS

- *fearlessly and often recklessly bold and daring*

POP CULTURE

In the movie *The Hunger Games*, Katniss is forced to display her fighting skills during a private session with Seneca Crane and the other Gamesmakers. Normally a skilled archer, Katniss's first shot misses the target. Although Katniss's next shot is a bullseye, the bored Gamesmakers focus their attention on a roast pig placed on their banquet table. Furious that she has been ignored by the Gamesmakers and upstaged by a dead pig, Katniss AUDACIOUSLY targets an apple in the roast pig's mouth. Her arrow pierces the apple as the stunned Gamesmakers stare at her in disbelief. Impressed by her AUDACITY, the Gamesmakers award Katniss an eleven out of twelve for her skill and boldness.

386. BELLWETHER

- *a person, group, or statistic that serves as a leading indicator of future events*

AP ECONOMICS

Economists and Wall Street stock analysts use BELLWETHER statistics to help them predict changes in the economy. For example, economists use the consumer confidence index to predict future economic growth. Other fields also have BELLWETHERS. Paris and Milan are BELLWETHER cities for the high fashion industry. Copies of the clothes supermodels wear in these fashion centers will soon end up on store shelves in your nearby shopping mall.

387. FASTIDIOUS

- *marked by careful attention to details; METICULOUS*

MEET LARRY'S STUDENTS: SRUTI

What does your clothing closet look like? Are your clothes neatly arranged or are they placed in no particular order? I asked Sruti this question and she replied that her entire wardrobe is arranged by type and by color. Wow— Sruti is very FASTIDIOUS! However, not all of my students are so METICULOUS. Keyur admits that he puts his clothes in a big pile and then randomly picks out what to wear. He was not AFFRONTED (offended) when Sruti called him SLOVENLY (sloppy).

388. METEORIC

- *similar to a meteor in speed, brilliance, or BREVITY; characterized by a sudden, very rapid rise or fall*

POP CULTURE

Nicki Minaj's platinum single "Starships" is a good METAPHOR (comparison) for her METEORIC career rise. Just three years ago, Minaj was making dresses for herself in the basement of her home in Queens, New York. Now the rapper is a global superstar who headlines sold-out concerts and represents international companies such as Pepsi. Although Minaj is on top now, she should remember that in the music industry a METEORIC rise to fame is often followed by an equally METEORIC fall into obscurity.

389. CULL

- *to select from a large quantity or collection*

MEET LARRY'S STUDENTS: ALIN

Alin is the entertainment editor of *The Clarion*, the East Brunswick High School student newspaper. Alin admits that her job is not easy. Students often submit a number of reviews for popular movies, albums, and concerts. Alin must then CULL the best stories for publication. Because of space limitations, *The Clarion* must sometimes publish a TRUNCATED (abbreviated) version of the original article.

390. REVULSION

- *a strong feeling of REPUGNANCE or disgust*

AP U.S. HISTORY

In his muckraking novel *The Jungle* (1906), Upton Sinclair wrote the following graphic description of the filthy conditions in a Chicago meatpacking factory: "There would be meat stored in great piles in rooms; and the water from leaky roofs would drip over it; and thousands of rats would race about it." Sinclair's vivid and disturbing description produced a wave of public REVULSION. Congress responded to the public outcry by promptly passing the Meat Inspection Act and the Pure Food and Drug Act.

PART 7

391. INSIPID

- *lacking flavor or interest; flat and BLAND*

POP CULTURE

In the movie *Ratatouille*, Anton Ego is a sharp-tongued French food critic who is known as "the Grim Eater." Ego strikes fear into the hearts of proud French chefs by branding their dishes as INSIPID and unoriginal. It is important to remember that *INSIPID* can also be used to describe works of art and literature that lack flair or vitality.

392. SNIDE

- *expressing DISDAIN (contempt) in an insulting or contemptuous manner*

POP CULTURE

In the movie *Ratatouille*, Anton Ego (see Word 391 above) is a sharp-tongued French food critic who is known for his SNIDE remarks. For example, he gleefully tells the young and obviously nervous Linguini, "You're slow for someone in the fast lane." Note that on the SAT, an attitude of DISDAIN (contempt) is the key driving force behind a SNIDE remark.

393. SUCCUMB

- *to submit to an overpowering force or YIELD to an overwhelming desire; to give up or give in*

POP CULTURE

High school students are often urged to make good decisions and to avoid SUCCUMBING to the temptations of drugs, alcohol, and tobacco. If today's students would watch *Star Wars Episode III: Revenge of the Sith*, they would learn a valuable lesson about the danger of SUCCUMBING to temptation. As the movie begins, Anakin Skywalker is a justice-loving Jedi Knight who fights on behalf of the citizens of the Republic. But as the film progresses, Anakin's growing fears and insecurities combine with the MACHINATIONS (SINISTER schemes) of the evil Emperor Palpatine to tempt the young Jedi to go over to the Dark Side of the Force. Although his friend Obi-Wan Kenobi and his wife Padme try to prevent his downfall, Anakin finally SUCCUMBS to the Dark Side and becomes the Sith Lord, Darth Vader.

394. EXECRABLE

- *UNEQUIVOCALLY detestable, abominable, and repulsive*

INSIDER INFO

Do you think that *EXECRABLE* sounds like a "good" word or a "bad" word? When I asked my students this question, 100 percent confidently responded that *EXECRABLE* is a "bad" word. My students were right! Perhaps *EXECRABLE* sounds like a "bad" word because it is very similar to the word *excrement*. SAT test writers often use *EXECRABLE* to describe the extremely negative responses that critics and preview audiences have to abominable books and movies that contain detestable and repulsive content.

395. SHREWD

- *marked by mental alertness and clever calculation; ASTUTE*

POP CULTURE

What do Simon Cowell and Warren Buffett have in common? Both are SHREWD judges of talent. Cowell is best known as a judge of musical talent. He SHREWDLY formed One Direction to fill the need for a boy band. Buffett is best known as a judge of business talent. His SHREWD investments have made him the second richest person in the United States with a net worth of over $45 billion. Buffett is also known for his SHREWD common-sense advice. For example, he SHREWDLY warned investors that, "You can't make a good deal with a bad person."

396. ASSIDUOUS

- *characterized by being very diligent, industrious, and hardworking*

MEET LARRY'S STUDENTS: JOHN

John's musical career began in New Zealand when he was just ten years old. Hoping to learn how to play the drums, John visited a local music conservatory. The drum classes were full, however, and the only open classes were for the flute and clarinet. John rejected the flute as a "girly instrument" and chose the clarinet. His decision proved to be FORTUITOUS (fortunate). John worked ASSIDUOUSLY to develop his clarinet skills. His dedication paid off. Today, John is a distinguished musician who was selected to be part of America's All National Honor Ensemble.

397. AUTOCRATIC

- *having absolute power; dictatorial and DESPOTIC*

POP CULTURE

In the *Hunger Games* trilogy, Coriolanus Snow is the AUTOCRATIC ruler of the Capitol and all of Panem. Though seemingly laid-back, Snow's outward manner BELIES (misrepresents) the fact that he is in reality a cruel and manipulative ruler, determined to govern Panem with an iron hand.

398. POIGNANT

- *moving and heart-rending; deeply touching*

IN THE NEWS

Marina Keegan graduated from Yale on May 25, 2012. The future filled the 22-year-old aspiring writer with enthusiasm. In an essay written for the *Yale Daily News*, Marina confidently reminded her classmates, "What we have to remember is that we can still do anything. We can change our minds. We can start over… The notion that it's too late to do anything is comical. It's hilarious. We're graduating college. We're so young." Just a few days later Marina died in a car crash when her boyfriend lost control of his car. Marina's sudden and POIGNANT death stunned her family, friends, and classmates. Her devastated parents take SOLACE (comfort) from the knowledge that Marina's final, POIGNANT words are inspiring young people to live their lives to the fullest and to aspire always to make a difference.

399. TACTLESS

- *displaying a lack of consideration; thoughtless and INDISCREET*

MEET LARRY'S STUDENTS: RITIKA

Ritika and her family have a beloved pet dog named Leo. One day her sister shocked and upset her entire family by asking, "What will we do when Leo drops dead?" Although her sister's question raised an important point, it was very TACTLESS. Ritika scolded her sister and pointed out that it would have been far more TACTFUL (diplomatic) to ask, "What will we do when Leo is no longer with us?"

400. DEPRECATE

- *to show strong disapproval*

INSIDER INFO

The prefix *de-*, meaning "down," signals that *DEPRECATE* is a negative word that is used to express disapproval. For example, many Americans express their low approval of Congress by DEPRECATING politicians who seem unable to resolve pressing national issues. When people DEPRECATE themselves it is called SELF-DEPRECATION. For example, on the TV show *The X-Factor*, one very obese contestant SELF-DEPRECATINGLY asked the audience to "give a fat boy a chance." His inspirational performance thrilled the cheering audience.

PART 8

401. ANTHROPOMORPHIC
- *characterized by attributing human characteristics to animals or inanimate things*

POP CULTURE
What do Mickey Mouse, Donald Duck, and Goofy have in common? All three are world-famous ANTHROPOMORPHIC Disney characters. Mickey Mouse is a fun-loving, brave, and caring character who is the official host at Disney theme parks around the world. In contrast, Donald Duck is Micky's IRASCIBLE (easily angered), impatient, and often jealous rival. And finally, Goofy is an ANTHROPOMORPHIC dog who is lovable, loyal, and silly.

402. DISTRAUGHT
- *very upset; deeply agitated with emotional conflict or pain*

POP CULTURE
In the movie *The Life of Pi*, Pi is a sixteen-year-old boy who is stranded in the Pacific Ocean on a lifeboat with a 450-pound Royal Bengal tiger named Richard Parker. Pi and Richard Parker WARILY (cautiously) coexist as they overcome the threats posed by dehydration, predatory marine life, treacherous sea currents, and exposure to the elements. After 227 agonizing days at sea, the lifeboat finally washes ashore along the coast of Mexico. Richard Parker promptly and unceremoniously runs into the nearby jungle, disappearing forever. Richard Parker's failure even to look back once leaves Pi feeling DISTRAUGHT. Shaken by this "bungled goodbye," the DISTRAUGHT Pi weeps uncontrollably, saying that the pain "is like an axe that chops at my heart."

403. ALOOF
- *RESERVED and detached; distant*

INSIDER INFO
ALOOF is a high-frequency vocabulary word that is used in both sentence completion and passage questions. In double-blank sentence completions, ALOOF people are often contrasted with people who are outgoing and AFFABLE (friendly). *ALOOF* is typically used in passage questions to describe a character who is detached and RESERVED. For example, in one recent passage a landlady was ALOOF because she "always kept in the background."

404. EMULATE
- *characterized by imitation; striving to equal or match*

MEET LARRY'S STUDENTS: ROSHNI
Many of my students have younger brothers and sisters. One of my students wrote this example to illustrate how her younger brother EMULATED everything she did: "He ordered the same ice cream flavors as me, listened to the same music as me and played the same video games as me. He followed me around everywhere and even wanted

to go to the mall with me. EXASPERATED (annoyed) by this constant EMULATION, I complained to my dad. He patiently explained that my little brother was just looking up to me. His pattern of EMULATING my behavior was really a form of flattery."

405. COMPLICITY

- *association or involvement in a wrongful act*

POP CULTURE

In the *Harry Potter* saga, Peter Pettigrew betrayed James and Lily Potter's secret hiding place to Lord Voldemort. The Dark Lord then killed the couple but was THWARTED (blocked) in his attempt to kill Harry. Although he was COMPLICIT in this crime, Pettigrew successfully framed Sirius Black for the treacherous murders as well as the slaying of twelve innocent Muggles. The Ministry of Magic eventually EXONERATED (freed from blame) Black.

406. DISCREDIT

- *to cast doubt on the reputation of a person or the efficacy of an idea; to be held in low esteem*

IN THE NEWS

Tiger Woods was once known as a devoted husband and the world's greatest golfer. His smiling image graced billboard and televison advertisements across the world. Woods was DISCREDITED, however, following revelations that he repeatedly cheated on his wife. It is important to remember that ideas can also be DISCREDITED. For example, communism is now widely DISCREDITED as a failed economic philosophy.

407. OVERBEARING

- *having or showing an arrogant superiority to and DISDAIN for those one views as inferior or unworthy*

POP CULTURE

In the movie *Avatar*, Colonel Miles Quaritch is the OVERBEARING Chief of Security of Hell's Gate on Pandora. Quaritch has little respect for the Na'vi and other INDIGENOUS (native) life forms on Pandora. His OVERBEARING approach to diplomacy is clearly revealed when he informs new recruits that his strategy is, "Peace and prosperity to us all, through superior firepower."

408. REBUKE

- *to criticize sharply; to REPRIMAND*

AP EUROPEAN HISTORY

The Italian scientist Galileo Galilei is now REVERED (honored) for his key role in the rise of the Scientific Revolution. When he was alive, however, DOGMATIC (close-minded) church officials severely REBUKED Galileo for championing a heliocentric model of the solar system, in which the Earth orbits the sun. In a famous trial, Church authorities forced Galileo to RENOUNCE (take back) his views and spend the final years of his life under house arrest. The REBUKE of Galileo delayed, but did not reverse, the march of scientific progress.

409. VIRTUOSITY

- *great technical skill*

MEET LARRY'S STUDENTS: EMILY

Emily loves to draw. In fact, she began drawing her first pictures when she was just two or three years old. Emily admires the VIRTUOSITY of Old Masters who could depict delicate flowers, life-like animals, and even realistic tear drops rolling down a person's cheek. Even so, Emily admits that she finds the Old Masters a bit boring. So who is Emily's favorite artist? See Word 410 to find out!

410. VISCERAL

- *describes an instinctive and emotional approach to life and problem solving*

MEET LARRY'S STUDENTS: EMILY

Although Emily admires the VIRTUOSITY (great technical skill) of the Old Masters (Word 409), she is fascinated with the life and works of Vincent van Gogh. Unlike the CEREBRAL (intellectual) approach of the Old Masters, van Gogh's paintings emphasize a VISCERAL approach to his world. For example, Emily loves *The Starry Night* because van Gogh's stars seem to explode with life and energy.

PART 9

411. HAVOC

- *widespread disorder or destruction; mayhem*

POP CULTURE

In the movie *The Dark Knight Rises*, Bane more than lives up to his malevolent name by wreaking HAVOC on Gotham. After temporarily defeating Batman, Bane destroys Gotham's transportation links with the outside world. He then forcibly disbands the city's legal government, thus enabling his gang of mercenaries to loot the defenseless city. This HAVOC continues until Batman finally returns to Gotham to recapture the city and end Bane's reign of terror.

412. IMPERIL

- *to pose a threat to; to endanger*

AP BIOLOGY

More than half of the world's 633 types of primates are IMPERILED by RAMPANT (unrestrained) habitat destruction and illegal poaching. For example, 25 species of monkeys, lemurs, and gorillas are all on the brink of extinction and need global action to protect them.

413. CONFLATE

- *to combine; bring together; to MELD or blend together*

POP CULTURE

The assassination of President Kennedy remains one of the greatest unsolved mysteries in American history. The Oliver Stone movie *JFK* promotes the controversial theory that Lee Harvey Oswald did not act alone. The movie CONFLATES documentary footage and dramatizes re-enactments so skillfully that viewers sometimes do not know which scenes are real and which are not.

414. PAUCITY

- *a shortage or scarcity; a DEARTH of something*

MEET LARRY'S STUDENTS: DHARA

Dhara loves shoes. Her wardrobe currently includes fifteen pairs of shoes. Dhara complains that this is not enough, however, and that her wardrobe suffers from a PAUCITY of footwear. For example, she needs a pair of pumps, ballet shoes, combat boots, Sperries, Nike sneakers, and of course high heel platforms. While her friends all agree with Dhara, her parents think she has a PLETHORA (an abundance) of shoes.

415. SUPERFLUOUS

- *unnecessary and unneeded; nonessential*

INSIDER INFO

SUPERFLUOUS has recently become a frequent answer to challenging sentence completion and passage questions. It is important to remember that *SUPERFLUOUS* means "unnecessary and therefore nonessential." For example, a recent critical reading passage discussed how 8th-century B.C.E. Greek bards actually resisted the introduction of a written alphabet. It turns out that pre-alphabetic bards memorized and then chanted stories and legends. They therefore opposed the new alphabet because they had "little overt need for the new technology of reading and writing." The phrase "little overt need" tells us that ancient Greek bards thought that the alphabet was unnecessary and therefore SUPERFLUOUS.

416. UNTENABLE

- *incapable of being defended or justified; indefensible*

AP U.S. HISTORY

The Seneca Falls Convention in 1848 marked the beginning of a long and at times frustrating battle for women's suffrage. Opponents THWARTED (blocked) the women's suffrage movement by claiming that women were a "weaker sex" who should avoid public affairs and confine themselves to their domestic roles as wives and mothers. These arguments, however, finally proved to be UNTENABLE as a new generation of suffragists successfully argued that women's suffrage was consistent with America's commitment to equality. In 1920 the states ratified the Nineteenth Amendment, granting women the right to vote.

417. PRONE

- *having a tendency to do something*

MEET LARRY'S STUDENTS: KAVIN

Kavin is one of my go-to students when we need help solving a difficult Level 5 math problem. He is also a candidate master in chess who is currently ranked as one of America's top twenty players in his age group. Kavin is both a knowledgeable student of the game and a perceptive observer of his opponents. He reports that many players are PRONE to making rapid moves without carefully evaluating the consequences of their new positions. Kavin then ADROITLY (skillfully) exploits his opponent's vulnerable position.

418. RANCOR

- *having a feeling of deep or bitter anger and ill-will*

POP CULTURE

In the *Hunger Games* trilogy, the DESPOTIC (tyrannical) President Snow uses a combination of armed Peacekeepers, DRACONIAN (very severe) rules, and of course the Hunger Games to control Panem's oppressed citizens. Snow's harsh rule creates great RANCOR among the DESTITUTE (very poor) and powerless citizens of the twelve districts. Katniss ultimately turns this RANCOR into an outright rebellion against President Snow.

419. COVET

- *to desire and prize*

MEET LARRY'S STUDENTS: ALIN

Alin knew that she faced very low odds of winning one of Z-100's COVETED tickets to meet Justin Bieber. She would have to be the 100th person to call the popular New York City radio station immediately after they played a set of nine songs. Still, Alin felt that she had to try. So she placed her call and anxiously waited for an answer. To her shock and amazement the Z-100 DJ announced that Alin had won not one but two of the COVETED tickets. Needless to say, Alin was so EUPHORIC (very happy) that she jumped up and down screaming at the top of her lungs. She had an amazing time, and Justin Bieber is still her favorite recording artist.

420. RESTITUTION

- *the act of compensating a person or group for a loss, damage, or injury*

AP U.S. HISTORY

In the days and weeks following the attack on Pearl Harbor, frightened Americans displaced their rage against Japan onto the 110,000 people of Japanese birth and descent living on the West Coast. Although no specific charges were ever filed against these Japanese Americans, they were interned or confined in detention camps located on desolate lands owned by the federal government. In 1987, Congress approved a formal national apology and a tax-free RESTITUTION payment of $20,000 to more than 66,000 surviving Japanese Americans who were held in detention centers.

PART 10

421. STRINGENT

- *very strict; demanding close attention to details and procedures*

AP U.S. HISTORY

The Compromise of 1850 seemed to defuse the crisis between the North and the South. However, the hoped-for sectional peace proved to be FLEETING. The Compromise included the STRINGENT new Fugitive Slave Act, which imposed heavy fines and even jail sentences for those who helped runaway slaves escape. These STRINGENT regulations intensified antislavery sentiment because they required Northerners to enforce slavery.

422. BANE

- *anything that is a source of harm and ruin*

POP CULTURE

In *The Dark Knight Rises*, Bane is a villain who more than lives up to his name by being a BANE to Bruce Wayne and Gotham City. Bane's ruinous actions include bankrupting Wayne Industries, destroying Gotham's bridges, and threatening to devastate the isolated city with a nuclear bomb.

423. BOON

- *a timely benefit; a blessing*

POP CULTURE

At the beginning of *The Dark Knight Rises*, Bruce Wayne is a BROODING (preoccupied with depressing memories) man who has given up his role as Batman and now has nothing to live for. Bane then adds to Wayne's woes by viciously breaking his back and then locking him inside a foreign prison from which escape is virtually impossible. Ironically, these disasters actually prove to be a BOON. Bruce Wayne recovers from his injury, escapes from prison, and THWARTS (stops) Bane's plan to destroy Gotham.

424. OPAQUE

- *not transparent or clear, and thus dense and difficult*
  to understand; impenetrably dense

INSIDER INFO

OPAQUE is typically used to describe objects such as curtains that are not transparent and do not allow light to pass through them. However, *OPAQUE* can also be used to describe writing that is unclear and therefore difficult to understand. College Board test writers typically contrast *OPAQUE* with the antonym *LUCID*, meaning "clear." For example, newspaper editors would reject or rewrite a manuscript with OPAQUE writing, while they would accept a manuscript with LUCID writing.

425. LEVITY

- *lightness in manner or speech, especially an attempt to inject humor into an otherwise serious situation*

MEET LARRY'S STUDENTS: NICOLE, ROSHNI, & MEGHA

SAT classes typically require serious work. Fortunately, I have a number of students who can be counted on to add a touch of LEVITY to our classes. For example, Nicole delights in telling us PERTINENT (relevant) gossip about Kristen Stewart's ongoing relationship with Robert Pattinson. Roshni added some LEVITY to our vocabulary lesson when she pointed out that one way to remember AVARICE (greed) is to associate it with being greedy for rice. And not to be outdone, Megha pointed out that CAVALIER (arrogant) people are arrogant and HAUGHTY because they can afford to eat caviar.

426. REMUNERATION

- *the payment received for performing a job; compensation*

POP CULTURE

The REMUNERATION workers receive varies greatly from job to job. For example, the federal minimum wage in 2012 was $7.50 per hour. In contrast, Judge Judy earned an astounding $45 million a year for her small-claims court television show. Wow—now that is what I call REMUNERATION!

427. EGREGIOUS

- *CONSPICUOUSLY, outrageously, and flagrantly bad*

DID YOU KNOW?

The prefix e- means "out," and the root *greg* means "group." So *EGREGIOUS* literally means "out of the group." Originally *EGREGIOUS* meant "standing out from the group" in the sense of being really good. Today, however, *EGREGIOUS* means "standing out from the group" in the sense of being really bad. For example, common EGREGIOUS mistakes on the SAT include misbubbling an answer and stopping a section before the directions tell you to stop. Both of these EGREGIOUS errors can ruin your score.

428. LAUD

- *to praise, commend, EXTOL, ACCLAIM, and HAIL*

MEET LARRY'S STUDENTS: PALLAVI

The members of my East Brunswick SAT class helped Pallavi celebrate her Sweet Sixteen birthday party. The girls all enthusiastically LAUDED Pallavi for a fantastic evening. The party began with a chartered bus ride that took over twenty of Pallavi's friends to a special restaurant near Times Square in New York City. The girls enjoyed a SUMPTUOUS (splendid) buffet dinner at The View, a revolving roof-top restaurant. Everyone LAUDED the tasty desserts, EXTOLLED the spectacular PANORAMIC (sweeping) view of New York City, and of course ACCLAIMED Pallavi's amazing dress. All HAIL Pallavi!

429. DRAB

• *gloomy and depressing; dreary and cheerless*

POP CULTURE

In the movie *The Hunger Games*, District 12 is portrayed as Panem's most IMPOVERISHED (very poor) district. The people work in dangerous coal mines and live in DRAB homes that are covered by a layer of coal dust. Katniss describes her DRAB district as a place "where you can starve to death in safety."

430. DETER

• *to discourage or prevent someone from taking an action*

AP U.S. HISTORY

During the peak of the Cold War, the United States and the Soviet Union had enough nuclear weapons to destroy each other and most life on Earth. This "balance of terror" DETERRED leaders of the two superpowers from starting a catastrophic world war. Although the Cold War is over, the United States still maintains a powerful military to DETER hostile countries such as Iran and North Korea.

PART 11

431. MILIEU

• *the total environment or setting; surroundings*

IN YOUR LIFE

I know it is hard to believe right now, but the day will come when you receive college admission letters. You will then have to decide which college MILIEU offers the best fit for you. Although very important, academics are only part of a total campus MILIEU, which includes the school's social scene and physical environment.

432. FACSIMILE

• *an exact copy or reproduction of something*

IN MY LIFE

The word FACSIMILE caught both my students and me by surprise when it appeared as an answer to a recent SAT sentence completion question. Most of my students were surprised because they claimed to have never heard the word before. I was surprised because my students seemed confused when I said that a fax machine is actually short for a FACSIMILE machine. One PERPLEXED (puzzled) student declared: "Fax machines are really old. I thought everyone used scanners." So for the record, a fax machine is used to transmit a FACSIMILE or exact copy of a document. A FACSIMILE can also refer to an exact copy of a signature or a work of art.

433. TRANSGRESSION

- *the violation of a law, duty, or moral principle; the act of overstepping a boundary or limit*

POP CULTURE

At the conclusion of the 74th Hunger Games, Katniss and Peeta successfully defy the Capitol and outsmart the Gamesmakers by threatening to commit suicide, thus preventing the Games from ending with a single winner. Their desperate action works, and both Katniss and Peeta are allowed to win. However, President Snow views their actions as a TRANSGRESSION that breaches the rules and poses a threat to his power. What begins as an act of survival thus becomes a serious TRANSGRESSION against the Capitol that transforms Katniss into "a beacon of hope" that Snow vows to eliminate.

434. NOTORIOUS

- *well-known for a bad reason; infamous*

MEET CHRISTIAN

As soon I started to ride a motorcycle, I learned that in some people's minds I was now a public menace. Why? You already know the answer—"bikers" are NOTORIOUS for being anti-social, violent, dangerous criminals! Motorcycle clubs such as Hell's Angels or the fictional Sons of Anarchy have developed a NOTORIOUS reputation for a reason. I distinguish myself from these NOTORIOUS characters by referring to myself as a "motorcyclist," not a "biker." True, we may share a passion for a particular mode of transportation, but that hardly makes me a NOTORIOUS criminal!

435. MISCELLANY

- *a collection of different things*

IN YOUR LIFE

Setting up your first dorm room will be an exciting but formidable challenge. It won't take you long to realize that you are missing batteries, plastic wrap, q-tips and other household items you took for granted. But don't worry. You will soon accumulate a MISCELLANY of small items including headache medicine, sunscreen, bath towels, wall decorations, and packing tape. The word *MISCELLANY* is closely related to *miscellaneous*, which means "from many different types or kinds." Believe me, once you graduate and move into your first apartment, your MISCELLANY of random stuff will grow larger! Soon you'll need car parts, insurance documents, and a huge MISCELLANY of glasses, coffee mugs, pots, and pans. Your list of miscellaneous items will go on and on!

436. QUAGMIRE

- *an awkward, complex, or embarrassing situation that is difficult to get out of*

INSIDER INFO

In AP Human Geography a QUAGMIRE is a soft wet area that gives way under the feet. On the SAT, however, *QUAGMIRE* is typically used to describe awkward, complex, or embarrassing situations that are difficult to get out of. Note that in both definitions a QUAGMIRE is a place or situation in which you can become MIRED or stuck. For example, you could find yourself stuck in a social QUAGMIRE by accepting invitations to two parties on the same night or by supporting two sides of a controversial argument.

437. SKEW

- *to slant in one direction*

MEET MY STUDENTS: DHARA

Parallel parking is a BANE (source of distress) for many student drivers. Dhara admits that she was filled with TREPIDATION (fear) as she attempted to parallel park in downtown Princeton, where the drivers are NOTORIOUSLY impatient. Dhara was so afraid of hitting another car that she ended up parking at an angle toward the street. Her car looked very SKEWED compared to the other vehicles. It is important to note that *SKEW* can refer to anything that is slanted. For example, advertisers SKEW their commercials toward specific DEMOGRAPHIC (population) groups.

438. EMANATE

- *to flow out from a source or origin; to come forth*

POP CULTURE

Many students are fascinated by what life might be like in a post-apocalyptic world. They speculate that underground societies may cobble together a steam boiler that might burn trash and waste and then capture the heat that EMANATES from the fire. Don't expect College Board test writers to be fascinated by post-apocalyptic life. They are far more interested in scientific phenomena, such as the characteristics of Geminid meteor showers. It turns out that Geminid meteor showers are unique because they EMANATE from an asteroid and not a comet.

439. PROFUSION

- *an extraordinary abundance; an overflow*

POP CULTURE

Justin Bieber celebrated his sixteenth birthday by getting his first tattoo. Justin's growing PENCHANT (liking) for tattoos has sparked a PROFUSION of websites dedicated to revealing the inside story for each of his tattoos. For example, the angel image on his left arm is an exact replica of a Selena Gomez photograph from *Elle* magazine.

440. ONEROUS

- *burdensome; oppressive or troublesome; causing hardship*

POP CULTURE

In the movie *Man of Steel*, Clark Kent slowly realizes that he is an alien who possesses superhuman powers. This knowledge becomes an ONEROUS responsibility that forces Clark to consider what type of person he wants to be. At first, Clark views his powers as an ONEROUS problem he would like to ignore. But as the movie unfolds, Clark develops a sense of duty and morality that causes him to confront his destiny as the "Man of Steel."

CHAPTER 12
THE TOP 100 LEVEL 3 WORDS

The SAT rates each question on a five-point scale of difficulty. Level 3 questions are the third most challenging questions on the test. At least fifty percent of all test-takers miss a Level 3 question. What makes these questions so difficult? In most cases, the questions call for a knowledge of vocabulary words that seems familiar. There is a difference, however, between having heard a word and knowing its precise definition. This chapter will define and illustrate 100 commonly used Level 3 vocabulary words. It is important to remember that the Level 3 questions are actually very easy if you know the words!

PART 1

441. ADULATION
• *great public admiration and over-the-top praise*
IN THE NEWS
Lance Armstrong enjoyed widespread public ADULATION for much of his career. As a road-racing cyclist he won the prestigious Tour de France a record-shattering seven consecutive times between 1999 and 2005. In addition, he overcame cancer and founded the Lance Armstrong Foundation for cancer support. Public ADULATION translated into LUCRATIVE (very profitable) endorsements from a number of companies. But Armstrong's world changed forever when the U.S. Anti-Doping Agency issued a detailed report charging the cyclist with having used illicit performance-enhancing drugs. The overwhelming evidence in the report stunned Armstrong's fans and advertisers. The once-admired athlete is now REVILED (despised) as a cheat and a liar.

442. VACILLATE

- *to waver back and forth between conflicting actions; to OSCILLATE*

AP EUROPEAN HISTORY

In April 1521 Emperor Charles V summoned Martin Luther to appear before the Diet of Worms to either REAFFIRM or RENOUNCE his challenges to the Church's doctrines and practices. As the young emperor sternly watched, a papal legate demanded that Luther REPUDIATE (recant, take back) his writings and "the falsehoods they contain." Aware that he faced a MOMENTOUS (very important) decision, Luther did not VACILLATE. In an unwavering and clear voice Luther solemnly declared, "I cannot, I will not recant. Here I stand!"

443. ELUSIVE

- *hard to pin down; skillful at ELUDING capture; EVASIVE*

POP CULTURE

In the *Harry Potter* saga, the Golden Snitch is a very ELUSIVE object that can sprout wings and ELUDE (evade) even the most skillful Quidditch players. Each team has a designated Seeker, whose sole task is to capture the ELUSIVE snitch.

444. FUTILE

- *ineffectual; producing no result; vain*

DID YOU KNOW?

FUTILE actually comes from the Latin word *futilis*, meaning "leaky." So pouring water into a leaky bucket would of course be FUTILE. Don't expect College Board test writers to ask you the derivation of *FUTILE*. Instead, remember that a FUTILE project is doomed to failure.

445. CHAOTIC

- *disorganized and confused; lacking visible order or organization*

AP U.S. HISTORY

As the New York Stock Exchange opened on Thursday, October 29, 1929, the brokers hoped for a profitable day of rising prices. Instead they faced a CHAOTIC day of record selling and losses. By 1 PM the stock ticker had fallen 92 minutes behind the transactions on the floor. Frightened brokers could not get a true picture of what was happening. The CHAOTIC shouting of 1,000 brokers and their assistants created what one observer called a "weird roar." Now known as Black Thursday, the CHAOTIC market crash marked the beginning of the Great Depression.

446. OBSOLETE

- *no longer produced or used; ANTIQUATED; out-of-date; ARCHAIC*

IN YOUR LIFE

The electronic revolution is having a dramatic effect on how today's high school students learn and prepare for class. Once upon a time, high school students used slide rules to solve difficult math problems and multi-volume encyclopedias to find obscure information. Both slide rules and encyclopedias are now OBSOLETE. High school students now use sophisticated calculators to solve math problems and Wikipedia to look up information.

447. DISPARITY

- *the condition of being unequal; a noticeable difference in age, income, or treatment*

INSIDER INFO

Look closely at the word *DISPARITY*. The Latin root *par* means "equal." That's why when golfers are par for a course they are literally equal to the course. So *PARITY* means "equality." In contrast, the word *DISPARITY* signals an inequality. The DISPARITY can be in age, rank, income, or treatment. For example, legal experts criticize regional DISPARITIES in the sentencing of people convicted of comparable crimes.

448. ANTECEDENT

- *an event or occurrence that precedes something similar in time; a forerunner*

DID YOU KNOW?

Pizza is one of the most popular foods in the United States. Approximately three billion pizzas are sold in the United States each year, or about 46 slices per person. Yet few Americans realize that the ANTECEDENTS for pizza can be traced back to flatbreads prepared by ancient Roman bakers.

449. SOMBER

- *characterized by being dark, gloomy, and depressed*

AP U.S. HISTORY

On November 21, 1963, most Americans optimistically looked forward to a future of peace and prosperity led by their popular young president, John F. Kennedy. But history can be unpredictable. No one foresaw the terrible tragedy that occurred the next day in Dallas, Texas. As the news of President Kennedy's assassination flashed across the country, stunned Americans watched a SOMBER Vice President Lyndon B. Johnson take the oath of office inside the presidential plane as a grief-stricken Jacqueline Kennedy stood by his side.

450. AUGMENT

- *to make something greater; to increase*

IN YOUR LIFE

It is THEORETICALLY possible to AUGMENT almost anything. For example, surgeons can AUGMENT the size of a woman's breasts, and workers can take a second job to AUGMENT the size of their incomes. I often tell SAT students that one of my primary goals is to help them AUGMENT their LEXICON (dictionary) of SAT vocabulary words. Needless to say, this book is designed to help AUGMENT your SAT vocabulary so that you can achieve a higher critical reading score.

PART 2

451. STODGY

- *dull, uninspiring, and unimaginative*

IN MY LIFE

STODGY teachers can dampen the enthusiasm of even the most enthusiastic students. For example, one of my high school teachers dictated notes to us almost every day. Our test questions then required us to regurgitate our notes on a given topic. Although this STODGY teaching style lacked creativity, it did help me develop the outlining skills I would use to develop my first lessons and write my first books.

452. ABSTEMIOUS

- *characterized by moderation in eating and drinking*

AP WORLD HISTORY

Before gaining enlightenment, Buddha ate only a single grain of rice each day. His stomach became so empty that when he poked a finger into it he could touch his backbone. Buddha later RENOUNCED extreme deprivation. Instead, he urged his companions to follow an ABSTEMIOUS lifestyle based upon moderation in eating and drinking.

453. DIGRESS

- *to stray from a topic in writing, speaking, or thinking; to go off on a TANGENT*

IN YOUR LIFE

Have you ever heard a speaker DIGRESS or wander off his or her topic? Most audiences have little patience for a speaker who wastes time by DIGRESSING. The same principle applies to your SAT essay. College Board essay readers have little patience for student writers who DIGRESS from the assigned essay topic. So stay focused and don't go off on a TANGENT.

454. MISNOMER

- *an incorrect or inappropriate name*

DID YOU KNOW?

Dry cleaning, Chinese checkers, and the *funny bone* are all MISNOMERS. Dry cleaning actually uses chemicals, Chinese checkers originated in Germany, and the funny bone is actually a nerve.

455. LUCRATIVE

- *refers to an enterprise or investment that is profitable*

AP EUROPEAN HISTORY

The LUCRATIVE spice trade provided a compelling economic motive for the Portuguese and Spanish goal of reaching India. For example, da Gama and other Portuguese captains purchased 100 pounds of pepper in Calicut for just 3 Venetian ducats. They could then sell the pepper for 80 ducats in Venice for a 2,700 percent profit! Cinnamon, cloves, and nutmeg all commanded a similar LUCRATIVE markup.

456. SOLICITOUS

- *characterized by being overly attractive and caring; excessively concerned; INDULGENT*

POP CULTURE

It is all too easy for a boyfriend or girlfriend to be overly SOLICITOUS towards the person they care about. It is even possible to spoil a person by being too SOLICITOUS. For example, in his song *Grenade*, Bruno Mars admits that he would do anything for his girl. However, she is a taker who never gives back.

457. INTREPID

- *fearless and daring; bold; DAUNTLESS*

IN THE NEWS

Felix Baumgartner is an INTREPID and world-famous skydiver who is known as the "King of the Daredevils." Fearless Felix more than lived up to his reputation for undertaking extremely dangerous stunts when he jumped from a helium balloon floating at the edge of space, 24 miles above the Earth. As millions watched a streaming video on YouTube, the INTREPID Felix hurtled through the atmosphere at an estimated speed of up to 834 miles per hour. He thus became the first person to break the sound barrier without vehicular power.

458. AFFABLE

- *friendly and pleasant; gracious; GENIAL*

IN MY LIFE

Everyone in my high school liked Ann. She was captain of our cheerleading squad and our school's homecoming queen. Although Ann was very popular, she wasn't conceited or arrogant. Ann always greeted everyone with an AFFABLE smile and never complained. Sadly, cancer recently took Ann's life. At her funeral, her husband Harry noted that Ann never said a bad word about anyone. He challenged the mourners to remember Ann's AFFABLE hello and to try to go through each day without saying or thinking a negative thought.

459. FUNDAMENTAL

- *a belief, skill, or component that is essential and basic*

DID YOU KNOW?

FUNDAMENTAL has its roots in the Latin word *fundamentum*, meaning "foundation." So a FUNDAMENTAL idea is the foundation upon which a theory or plan is built. For example, the belief that government should be based upon the consent of the people is a FUNDAMENTAL cornerstone of democracy.

460. SCENARIO
- *a sequence of possible events that may occur*

IN YOUR LIFE

Worst-case SCENARIOS are often used in strategic planning to help people prepare for unexpected emergencies. For example, what would you do if your college roommate played loud music, never studied, and partied all night? Since this SCENARIO often happens to college freshmen, it would be wise to develop a mental set of "just in case" contingency plans.

PART 3

461. EMPATHY
- *great understanding of another person's feelings; great sympathy*

IN MY LIFE

Writing an SAT essay is not easy. I totally EMPATHIZE with students who feel a sense of nervous anticipation when the proctor finally says, "Open your test booklet to Section 1 and begin your essay." Like most of my students, I feel a sense of relief when I can think of two or three really good examples to illustrate my thesis.

462. PLAUSIBLE
- *believable; having a reasonable chance of something happening*

IN YOUR LIFE

Do you think the election of a female President of the United States in your lifetime is PLAUSIBLE? According to the Gallup Poll, that SCENARIO is not only PLAUSIBLE but likely. In 1955 just 52 percent of adults in the United States said that they would vote for a qualified woman for president. Today 92 percent of American adults say that they would vote for a qualified female presidential candidate.

463. HEYDAY
- *the peak of popularity and success of a movement, organization or person*

AP U.S. HISTORY

The late 1960s witnessed the HEYDAY of the hippie-led counterculture. Hippies believed that love was all America needed to end the Vietnam War and usher in a new era of peace and racial harmony. The Woodstock Festival in August 1969 marked the HEYDAY of the counterculture. Over 500,000 hippies watched 32 acts perform in a legendary outdoor concert promoted as "Three Days of Peace and Music."

464. INGENIOUS
- *a clever mix of creativity and inventiveness*

IN THE NEWS

In the fairy tale "Snow White and the Seven Dwarfs," the Wicked Queen uses a magic mirror to reveal who is "the fairest one of all." Now, thanks to the wizards at the New York Times Co. Research and Development Lab you too can own a "magic mirror." The Times' magic mirror is an INGENIOUS mix of sophisticated technology and basic human vanity. In addition to reflecting your image, the magic mirror can display a daily calendar, weather information, and news headlines. I wonder if it can also display an SAT vocabulary word-of-the-day. Now that would truly be INGENIOUS!

465. CONSPICUOUS

- *attracting attention by being unusual or very noticeable*

DID YOU KNOW?

Visitors who travel across the tropical savannas of Africa and Australia are surprised to see 25-foot-high sculpted hard earth mounds towering above the landscape. The mounds frequently resemble the towers of a castle and are often the region's most CONSPICUOUS natural feature. Believe it or not, the architects of these mounds are termites that are just 0.4 inches long. Relative to their small size, the termites construct the largest and by far the most CONSPICUOUS nests of any animal.

466. HIERARCHY

- *any system of persons, animals, or things that are ranked one above another*

DID YOU KNOW?

The mounds described in Word 465 house colonies that include millions of termites divided into a highly specialized HIERARCHY. Termite soldiers are armed with huge jaws and can emit a sticky toxic substance. The workers build the nest, produce food, cultivate fungi, and take care of the queen, eggs, and larvae. The queen is thirty times bigger than a worker. She lays eggs continuously, at a rate of about thirty per minute. The king is much smaller and mates with the queen for life.

467. EXASPERATE

- *to irritate; annoy; frustrate; VEX*

IN MY LIFE

No Jordan-Matthews High School student EXASPERATED my wife Susan more than Twig Wood. Twig employed an arsenal of excuses to explain his frequent absences from her class. Allegedly written by his mother, Twig's excuses ranged from "Twig, he have the toothache," to the classic "Twig, he have a little job to do." The notes were always signed, "Twig's mother, Lucille Wood." Although she was EXASPERATED at the time, Susan now fondly remembers Twig and his long list of grammatically incorrect but humorous excuses.

468. RESOLUTE

- *very determined and persistent; strong-minded*

MEET LARRY'S STUDENTS: MARC

Marc is an outstanding wrestler who refuses to quit. During one match he suffered a severe arm injury. Although he was forced to forfeit the match, Marc refused to become DISPIRITED (discouraged). Instead, he was RESOLUTE and vowed to return INVIGORATED (energized) and ready to go. Marc kept his promise and helped lead his team to a successful season.

469. MUNDANE

- *ordinary and commonplace*

IN THE NEWS

Amanda Knox was an American college student studying abroad who attracted world-wide attention when an Italian jury convicted her of murdering her roommate. But a second Italian jury overturned the verdict, allowing Amanda to return to her home in Seattle, Washington. After spending four years in a small concrete cell, Amanda yearned to enjoy the MUNDANE pleasures we take for granted. One of her first wishes, for example, was to sit on the green grass in her backyard.

470. SLOVENLY

- *characterized by being untidy in dress or appearance; messy and sloppy*

INSIDER INFO

Avoid confusing *SLOVENLY* with *CASUAL*. A SLOVENLY appearance would include wearing an unlaundered shirt and neglecting to shave for three days. For example, the cartoon character Homer Simpson is a SLOVENLY average guy who typically sits around in his underwear. In contrast, *CASUAL* would describe clothes you wear to an informal occasion like a backyard barbecue.

PART 4

471. DISPEL

- *to drive away or scatter; to remove*

IN YOUR LIFE

Many students believe that their college essay should focus on a lofty, "big" idea that will impress admissions officers. The College Board's authoritative guide book DISPELS this widespread but ERRONEOUS (wrong) idea. The College Board reminds students, "the greatest strength you bring to this essay is seventeen years or so of familiarity with the topic: YOU." Always remember that the key word in the Common Application essay prompt is "you"!

472. ADHERE

- *to follow closely; to stick with a policy or plan of action*

INSIDER INFO

The SAT word *ADHERE* is derived from a 15th-century French verb meaning "to stick." The same French verb also gives us the adjective *ADHESIVE* and the noun *ADHERENT*. All these words convey the quality of sticking with a plan or person. For example, if you ADHERE to a special diet, exercise program, or study plan, you stick with it. It is important to note that writers and artists can also ADHERE to a specific style. For example, the Harlem Renaissance author Zora Neale Hurston is known for her ADHERENCE to the use of authentic regional dialects to represent how her characters actually spoke.

473. TRIVIALIZE

- *to make TRIVIAL and thus insignificant; to minimize*

MEET LARRY'S STUDENTS: OLIVIA

Olivia loves to shop for clothes at Abercrombie & Fitch. However, when she recently returned a pair of jeans that had unexpectedly shrunk, the clerk questioned Olivia and seemed to minimize her complaint. Olivia stood her ground and displayed her formidable SAT vocabulary by telling the clerk, "You're TRIVIALIZING my complaint!" Although the clerk finally accepted the jeans, the incident left Olivia EXASPERATED (irritated) and angry. Vowing to take her business to Express, Olivia stormed out of the store.

474. NEGLIGENT

- *characterized by neglect and a careless lack of concern*

IN MY LIFE

Our first year of teaching at Jordan-Matthews High School presented my wife and me with a difficult problem. As graduation approached, the seniors at JM began to display the usual signs of senioritis by studying less and less. No senior was more NEGLIGENT in his work than Junior Hicks. He neglected to study for tests and failed to turn in required homework assignments. Junior's NEGLIGENT study habits brought him to the brink of failing both his required U.S. History and Senior English classes. If this happened, Junior would not graduate. See Word 475 to find out what happened!

475. ADEPT

- *demonstrating great skill in accomplishing a task or in achieving a goal; ADROIT*

IN MY LIFE

Junior panicked when my wife and I confronted him with his failing grades (see Word 474). After a long talk, he agreed to take make-up tests and turn in extra credit projects. Although Junior was not a good student, he was very ADEPT at charming his teachers. As a student in the Home Economics class, Junior had access to the school kitchen. Each day after school he delivered his extra credit projects and presented my wife and me with a special treat from the school kitchen. On one memorable occasion he presented my wife with a delicious vanilla ice cream sundae topped with whipped cream and a bright red cherry. Junior's ADEPT charm offensive worked. He pulled up his grades, barely passed his classes, and graduated with his classmates.

476. EMBELLISH

- *to enhance; to make more attractive with ornamentation*

INSIDER INFO

Note that the word *bell* is right in the middle of the word *EMBELLISH*. Bells are often used to decorate or EMBELLISH Christmas trees and other objects. So when you see the *bell* in *EMBELLISH*, think of ornaments used to enhance an object or even a story.

477. INSTILL

- *to gradually impart new values, attitudes, or skills*

IN YOUR LIFE

Religious leaders, parents, teachers, and coaches all attempt to INSTILL positive values and attitudes. For example, when coaches tell their players "No pain, no gain," they are attempting to INSTILL the importance of hard work and dedication.

478. EXACERBATE

- *to make worse; to aggravate a situation*

INSIDER INFO

EXACERBATE has appeared as a sentence completion answer on several recent tests. *EXACERBATE* is a negative word that always means "to make things worse." For example, the Boston Tea Party EXACERBATED tensions between the American colonists and the British.

479. IMPASSIONED

- *filled with passion and zeal; FERVENT*

AP U.S. HISTORY

On December 5, 1955, almost 7,000 African Americans crowded into the Holt Street Baptist Church to protest racial segregation on Montgomery city buses. They also came to listen to a speech by a young and untested minister named Dr. Martin Luther King, Jr. Dr. King urged the black community to continue its support for the bus boycott by saying, "There comes a time when people get tired of being trampled by the iron feet of oppression… We are determined here in Montgomery to work and fight until justice rushes down like water, and righteousness like a mighty stream." Dr. King's IMPASSIONED plea for justice GALVANIZED (electrified) the black community and marked his emergence as a national civil rights leader.

480. EUPHORIC

- *a feeling of great joy and overwhelming ELATION*

IN THE NEWS

Jack Andraka had a good reason to be proud and EUPHORIC. The Maryland teenager had just won the top award of $75,000 at the Intel Science and Engineering Fair for discovering an inexpensive and fast way to detect early-stage pancreatic cancer. When the Intel speaker announced his name, Jack reacted with unbridled joy as he ran to the stage to accept his award. Jack's EUPHORIC reaction quickly became a YouTube hit. You can see the video by searching for "Jack Andraka winning award." I promise that the video will leave you with an INDELIBLE (can't be erased) image of the meaning of EUPHORIC!

PART 5

481. MOCK

- *to make fun of or mimic someone with contempt, ridicule, or DERISION*

INSIDER INFO

In the movie *The Life of Pi*, Piscine Molitor Patel is regularly MOCKED by classmates who call him "Pissing Patel." Piscine escapes this MOCKING by shortening his first name to Pi. SAT examples of MOCKING will probably be more SUBTLE and challenging than the humorous but blatant example in *The Life of Pi*. For example, on one recent critical reading passage, Mo is a Chinese professor who is jealous of Duncan, an idealistic young American English teacher. The passage concludes by telling us that "Mo did not make a comment to Duncan that did not include the word *kind*. 'If you would be so kind,' he said. 'Just a kindly reminder. How very kind of you,'" Mo uses the word *kind* as an exaggerated form of flattery intended to MOCK Duncan.

482. CREDIBLE

- *apparently reasonable; believable*

IN YOUR LIFE

Have you ever been late to school or to work? If so, did you make up a fake excuse to explain why you were late? If you do use a fake excuse, try to make it CREDIBLE. Saying that you were in a long line at Starbucks may be true, but your vice principal or boss may not find it CREDIBLE. The most widely used and therefore most CREDIBLE excuse is saying that you were stuck in heavy traffic.

483. DIVISIVE

- *creating disunity and dissension; POLARIZING*

AP U.S. HISTORY

The Kansas-Nebraska Act (1854) was one of the most fateful and DIVISIVE pieces of legislation in American history. The furor over the act broke the uneasy truce between the North and the South. It incited a bitter public outcry that PRECIPITATED (hastened) the DEMISE (death) of the Whig Party and emergence of the Republican Party.

484. HERALD

- *to praise or enthusiastically greet the arrival of someone or something*

INSIDER INFO

At one time, a HERALD was an official who announced important news. That is why newspapers such as the *International Herald Tribune* have *HERALD* in their names. Although *HERALD* can still refer to a person, it typically appears on the SAT as a verb meaning "to praise" or "greet enthusiastically." For example, Aung Sang Suu Kyi has been HERALDED by freedom-loving peoples around the world for her courageous advocacy of democratic reforms in Burma.

485. DEVOUR

- *to eat VORACIOUSLY; consume greedily*

POP CULTURE

In the television program *The Simpsons*, Homer has a RAVENOUS (insatiable) appetite and DEVOURS almost any food in sight. He particularly delights in DEVOURING doughnuts covered with pink icing and rainbow sprinkles. Come to think of it, I would love to DEVOUR one of Homer's favorite doughnuts!

486. SHIRK

- *to avoid or neglect one's assigned duties or responsibilities*

AP U.S. HISTORY

John F. Kennedy became President on an inauguration day filled with high excitement and drama. The new President recognized that the Soviet Union was an IMPLACABLE (relentless, unappeasable) foe that had to be contained. JFK boldly refused to SHIRK his responsibility to defend freedom "in its hour of maximum danger." Kennedy welcomed America's duty to "pay any price, bear any burden…to assure the survival and the success of liberty" at home and around the world.

487. TENACIOUS

- *stubborn and unyielding; not easily letting go or giving up; RESOLUTE*

MEET LARRY'S STUDENTS: JASON

Many of my students hope to take the SAT just once and then be "one and done." The SAT is a formidable test, however, that requires hard work and TENACITY. For example, Jason needed a 2300 to qualify for a special program at an Ivy League college. The first two times he took the SAT, Jason scored a 2220 followed by a 2270. Although these were outstanding scores, Jason was TENACIOUS and refused to give up. He studied his vocabulary words, practiced writing essays, and focused on avoiding careless math mistakes. Jason's TENACITY paid off. He scored a 2320 and was accepted into the special program.

488. FEASIBLE

- *possible; capable of being achieved; VIABLE*

DID YOU KNOW?

Science fiction movies like *Back to the Future* regularly send characters backward and forward in time. But is time travel really FEASIBLE? According to Einstein, time travel is theoretically FEASIBLE if an object can travel faster than the speed of light. The problem, of course, is that nothing we know of can travel faster than light.

489. APPALL

- *to shock and outrage*

IN THE NEWS

On July 5, 2011, a Florida jury found Casey Anthony not guilty of murdering her two-year-old daughter. The verdict APPALLED many people who were convinced that the jury ignored evidence pointing to Anthony's guilt. Now REVILED (despised) as one of the most hated women in America, Anthony faces a PROBLEMATIC (unsettled) future as she lives in a secret location in Florida.

490. PERIPHERY

- *the outer boundary or fringe area of something;*
  MARGINAL and thus not part of the inner core

POP CULTURE

In the *Hunger Games* trilogy the Capitol is the political center of Panem. The city exercises absolute power over twelve surrounding districts. When the SAGA opens, Katniss Everdeen lives in District 12, an IMPOVERISHED (very poor) coal mining region located on the PERIPHERY of Panem. As the story unfolds, however, Katniss leads a rebellion that sparks a RESURGENCE (revival) of the once-PERIPHERAL twelve districts.

PART 6

491. **AUTONOMY**
- *independence; freedom from external control and restraints*

POP CULTURE

In her song "We Can't Stop," Miley Cyrus and her friends celebrate their AUTONOMY by proclaiming, "This is our house. This is our rules…We run this…It's our party we can do what we want." Although these lyrics may break her dad's achy-breaky heart, don't expect College Board test writers to pay attention to Miley's song. Instead, expect to evaluate sentence completion and passage-based questions that describe participants in academic studies and characters in novels who experience a condition of independence and thus AUTONOMY from external constraints.

492. **SAVOR**
- *to enjoy something to the fullest*

IN YOUR LIFE

In her June 2013 commencement speech at Randolph-Macon College in Virginia, Katie Couric urged the graduating seniors to SAVOR "the gifts that every day of your life will bring: your family, your friends, a beautiful sky at sunset…a baby's tiny hand." Katie is right. Life is a gift that we should all strive to SAVOR.

493. **SONOROUS**
- *characterized by a sound or speech that is full, rich and deep*

MEET CHRISTIAN

A great motorcycle is a treat for all the senses—a HEADY (intoxicating) mix of sight, touch, and smell. But nothing is as important to me as having a bike with a SONOROUS exhaust note. The deep, stuttering sound of my bike at start-up erupts into a mechanical symphony that fills my helmet with the rich sound of a high-performance racing engine at idle. A SONOROUS engine need not be loud. In fact, loudness alone is not enough to be considered SONOROUS. The easiest way to tell if an engine is SONOROUS is to simply apply the "goose-bump test." Does the motor's sound cause your hair to stand on end? If so, you have a full, rich, and deep sounding motor that qualifies as SONOROUS.

494. **DISPIRITED**
- *marked by a feeling of discouragement and dejection*

AP U.S. HISTORY

Nathaniel Hawthorne joined the Brook Farm utopian community in April 1841. Inspired by Brook Farm's IDEALISTIC vision of plain living and high thinking, Hawthorne looked forward to enjoying a "noble and unselfish life." However, long hours of hoeing potatoes, milking cows, and raking hay sapped Hawthorne's enthusiasm and left him feeling more and more DISPIRITED. After realizing that he was unsuited for a life "toiling in the sun," the DISPIRITED novelist returned to Boston.

495. TUMULT

- *a state of great commotion, confusion, and disruption*

POP CULTURE

When the movie *World War Z* opens, Gerry Lane and his family are trapped in Philadelphia traffic. They are suddenly confronted by an onslaught of zombies that triggers widespread TUMULT across the city. A VIRULENT (very infectious), fast-moving virus unleashes a tidal wave of living dead across the entire planet. As the zombie population grows, the ensuing TUMULT causes cities to fail and governments to collapse. Only Gerry Lane can find an antidote that will eradicate the virus and end the TUMULT.

496. SCRUTINIZE

- *to closely examine; to critically inspect*

POP CULTURE

What do President Obama and Kim Kardashian have in common? Both lead lives that are carefully SCRUTINIZED by the media and the public. For example, political PUNDITS (commentators) SCRUTINIZE the President's statements on every issue. At the same time, celebrity columnists SCRUTINIZE Kim Kardashian's clothes, hairstyles, romantic relationships, and family feuds.

497. MELANCHOLY

- *very sad and gloomy*

MEET CHRISTIAN

For me, the biggest downside of riding a motorcycle is how MELANCHOLY I become when Geraldine (my beloved motorcycle) requires repairs. Dejected and gloomy, I wonder about my poor Geraldine, and hope that her parts will be properly fixed. I think my MELANCHOLY mood comes partially from a feeling of guilt, the depressing sense that I am letting a stranger take care of a loved one. Since riding is my favorite way to forget about the stress of each day, frustrations can and do add up, making me feel more MELANCHOLY. But the day Geraldine returns home, my negative feelings evaporate and I EXUBERANTLY (joyously) leap into her saddle, ready to hit the road, together once again!

498. VERSATILE

- *having great diversity or variety*

MEET CHRISTIAN'S STUDENTS: SOPHIE

Sophie has a UNIQUE (one of a kind) idea for a business that utilizes her VERSATILE personal talents. Sophie is a talented poet who has a knack for math and calculating business figures. Sophie's skills are not limited to academic subjects. She also enjoys practical, hands-on skills like laying tile floors. Sophie says she will not be satisfied with a new career unless she finds a way to make use of all her VERSATILE talents. She recently had an EPIPHANY (sudden realization). Sophie hopes to form a tile-laying business and write PITHY (concise but full of meaning) verses of poetry on each individual floor tile. She plans to name her company—what else—"Verse-A-Tile!"

499. MINUTIAE
- *small or minor details*

POP CULTURE
Have you ever watched *Game of Thrones*? If so, do you know who Jon Snow's real mother is, or what Ned Stark's sister's name was? Can you draw the entire Targaryen family tree, from Aegon the Conqueror to Daenerys Stormborn? If so, congratulations! You are an expert on the MINUTIAE and trivia of this fascinating fantasy SAGA. You have mastered every "minute" (pronounced like "mine-yoot") detail of the television show. In fact, you could probably host a *Game of Thrones* game show with such detailed knowledge of its MINUTIAE!

500. GERMANE
- *relevant and appropriate*

MEET LARRY'S STUDENTS: MUKHI
Mukhi is a member of the Model UN club at Montgomery High School. One of the formalities of parliamentary procedure is for the Chair to determine if a new resolution is GERMANE. Before he knew the meaning of *GERMANE*, Mukhi went up to the chairperson and inquired why he repeatedly wanted to find out if a resolution was German. Mukhi naively asked if the Chair was seeking a resolution by Germany. Mukhi was MORTIFIED (very embarrassed) when the chairperson told him that *GERMANE* is a word that means "relevant to the topic."

PART 7

501. FLOP
- *to suddenly and abruptly fail; to collapse*

POP CULTURE
The stunning success of her starring role in the hit movie *Mean Girls* turned the 18-year-old Lindsay Lohan into a movie star with what seemed to be an unlimited future. Few predicted that within a few years Lohan's film career would FLOP. And yet, that is precisely what happened. A series of legal problems, probation violations, and repeated visits to rehabilitation facilities caused Lohan to lose several movie deals. Her once-promising Hollywood career hit a NADIR (bottom) in 2013 when her movie *InAPPropriate Comedy* made just $172,000 on its opening weekend, one of the worst U.S. box-office FLOPS in history.

502. PINPOINT
- *to precisely locate; to take aim at*

POP CULTURE
In his song "When I Was Your Man," Bruno Mars LAMENTS (regrets) that he has IRREVOCABLY (unalterably) lost his girl. Rather than blame her, Bruno PINPOINTS the problem on his own ego and "selfish ways." He sadly admits that he "should've given

you all my hours when I had the chance."

503. STATIC

- *stationary and unchanging; fixed; STAGNANT*

POP CULTURE

Kevin Feige, the president of Marvel Studios, believes that he cannot allow Iron Man to remain a STATIC superhero who does not grow and evolve. For example, as *Iron Man 3* opens, Tony Stark is not portrayed as a triumphant superhero who has just saved New York City from alien invaders. Instead, Stark is increasingly DISPIRITED as he admits that "nothing's been the same since New York." Fortunately, Stark rises to the occasion and ultimately defeats the SINISTER scientist Aldrich Killian. However, the desperate struggle with Killian leaves Stark a changed man. In a controversial ending, the no-longer STATIC superhero undergoes a successful surgery and then pitches his now-OBSOLETE chest arc reactor into the sea.

504. INTRICATE

- *very complex and elaborate*

MEET CHRISTIAN

Geraldine (that's my motorcycle) runs on one of the most fascinatingly INTRICATE small engines ever designed. Her so-called "Desmodromic" engine makes use of a complex and delicate mechanical system that is extremely rare compared with the simpler and more common styles of engine found in most motorcycles. Although Geraldine is "just" a machine, at times I feel that her INTRICATE engine is more complicated than some people I know!

505. PREEMINENT

- *exceeding all others; unchallenged superiority; EMINENT*

POP CULTURE

What do Michael Jordan and LeBron James have in common? Both illustrate the word *PREEMINENT*. Michael Jordan was universally recognized as the world's PREEMINENT basketball player during the 1990s. Fans, coaches, and opposing players all recognize that LeBron James is the PREEMINENT basketball player in the world today.

506. SURPASS

- *to outdo someone or something; to exceed*

POP CULTURE

LeBron James now owns two NBA championship rings, while Michael Jordan owns six. LeBron must win four more rings to tie MJ, and five more to SURPASS him.

507. MARGINALIZE

- *to relegate to an unimportant or powerless position on the fringe or margin of a group or society*

AP U.S. HISTORY

During the Jim Crow era, "separate but equal" laws and customs MARGINALIZED African Americans to the fringes of American life. For example, African Americans cooked and served food in restaurants where they could not dine. In Hollywood, studios MARGINALIZED African American actors by assigning them roles as maids, waiters, and common laborers.

508. CONDESCENSION

- *characterized by a PATRONIZING attitude and an air of superiority*

IN MY LIFE

I have a vivid memory of an experience that illustrates how it feels to be treated in a CONDESCENDING manner. As an inexperienced SAT teacher, I was filled with youthful EXUBERANCE (enthusiasm). I remember meeting with a veteran English teacher and enthusiastically saying, "I've discovered something important. I believe the College Board test writers select many of their vocabulary words from key synonym clusters like *ASSUAGE, MITIGATE, MOLLIFY,* and *ALLEVIATE.* The teacher rolled her eyes and said, "Everyone knows that." Her CONDESCENDING attitude stung but did not DETER my enthusiasm for finding ways to help my students.

509. EDICT

- *a formal or authoritative proclamation*

MEET CHRISTIAN'S STUDENTS: BRANDON

Sometimes an official EDICT can determine the course of a football game. Brandon plays defensive end for the Westwood High School Warriors. Everyone knows that in football, defensive players play defense, right? In a do-or-die championship game, Brandon alertly picked up what appeared to be a backwards lateral. He charged through opposing tacklers and sprinted to the end zone for a crucial touchdown. But was the play legal? The Lake Travis coaches VEHEMENTLY (loudly and emphatically) protested that their quarterback had in fact thrown an incomplete pass. The crowd waited in hushed suspense as the referees debated the legality of Brandon's touchdown. After what seemed like an eternity, the head referee announced their official EDICT—"Touchdown!" The crowd exploded with joy, and Brandon's teammates EXUBERANTLY (joyously) piled on top of him. In Texas, we take high school football very seriously!

510. CARTOGRAPHY

- *the science of making maps*

INSIDER INFO

I must admit that I was surprised to see *CARTOGRAPHY* used as a sentence completion answer. It is possible that the always crafty College Board test writers hoped careless students would confuse *CARTOGRAPHY* with the study of cars, carts, or even cards. Although the term *CARTOGRAPHY* was actually COINED (invented) in 1859, humans have drawn maps for thousands of years. Early CARTOGRAPHERS drew their maps on plaster walls and then parchment. Modern CARTOGRAPHERS use sophisticated computer software to create maps for Google and GPS devices.

PART 8

511. PREREQUISITE
- *a required prior condition; something that is required in advance*

POP CULTURE
In her song, "Just Give Me a Chance," Pink admits that she willingly opened her heart to Nate. Pink completely trusted Nate and let him "see the parts of me that weren't all that pretty." Pink let Nate steal her heart as an act of trust. She recognized that trust is a PREREQUISITE for a true love that will endure.

512. IMPEDIMENT
- *anything that slows, blocks, or THWARTS progress*

AP U.S. GOVERNMENT
What do the Electoral College and Senate filibusters have in common? Both are political IMPEDIMENTS that can THWART (block) majority rule. The Electoral College can enable a candidate to win the presidency without a majority of the popular votes. The Senate filibuster can enable senators to use long speeches to prevent action on a bill. Critics argue that the filibuster has become a serious IMPEDIMENT to needed reforms because it promotes gridlock in Congress.

513. INERTIA
- *resistance to change; a disposition to remain inactive or INERT*

IN MY LIFE
Today I teach highly motivated students who strive for top SAT and AP scores. But this was not always the case. During my first three years of teaching I taught fifteen straight classes of low-level students called Basics. I quickly learned that Sir Isaac Newton's theory of INERTIA could be applied to my students—a Basic at rest tends to stay at rest. This was particularly true on Monday mornings when my Basics pleaded, "We're tired, can we do nothing?" Needless to say, I tried to counter their Monday INERTIA by planning high-interest activities such as quiz bowls, bonus points, and the unveiling of posters with their pictures superimposed on the covers of *Time* and *Newsweek* magazines. Although I was not always successful, I often managed to overcome my students' INERTIA and jump-start a good week.

514. SCANT

- *characterized by a small amount of something; MEAGER*

IN YOUR LIFE

If and when you start your first business, you can expect to begin with SCANT resources. To put it bluntly, as a young and unproven entrepreneur, investors will not have a compelling reason to trust you with their money. You will thus have to start with your idea, your time, and your personal savings. But don't be DAUNTED (intimidated). Remember, where there is a will, there is a way. RESOLUTE (determined) entrepreneurs often enjoy the creative mindset required to work with SCANT starting materials, because of the feeling of accomplishment that comes from building something out of nothing. You too might begin with SCANT resources and build yourself a business empire!

515. DISILLUSION

- *to free from an illusion or false ideas*

MEET CHRISTIAN'S STUDENTS: JONAH

Jonah is a very intelligent student who did not have to work hard in school. Jonah ERRONEOUSLY (incorrectly) believed he could treat the SAT like any other school test. I tried to DISILLUSION him of this misconception by explaining that even very bright students must study hard if they expect to achieve high SAT scores. But my efforts were FUTILE (ineffective). Jonah remained OBDURATE (stubborn) until he received his first SAT scores. Needless to say, they did not live up to the scores in his imagination! At our next lesson, Jonah confessed that he was now DISILLUSIONED with his lazy schoolwork approach. He is now fully committed to a disciplined and focused study schedule that includes learning all the words in this book!

516. NOMADIC

- *migratory; moving from place to place*

MEET CHRISTIAN

I love taking long-distance motorcycle road trips. These solo adventures make me feel NOMADIC as I drift from town to town and explore offbeat sites, eat in special local diners, and see more of the American countryside. However, my carefree days as a NOMADIC traveler are all too short, since I always return home and resume preparing my students for the SAT.

517. CONSENSUS

- *a general agreement*

AP U.S. HISTORY

In the fall of 1941, Hitler's armies appeared to be invincible as they roared across Russia. At the same time, relations between the United States and Japan were rapidly deteriorating. Despite these OMINOUS (threatening) developments, there was still not a CONSENSUS in the United States about what foreign policy to follow. Some Americans still favored a policy of neutrality that would avoid entanglements in the wars in Europe and Asia. Others favored sending badly needed military supplies to Great

Britain and the Soviet Union. And finally, an increasingly vocal group argued that the United States had to enter World War II to stop Hitler and the Japanese warlords. The Japanese attack on Pearl Harbor ended all these doubts and forged an unbreakable CONSENSUS that America had to crush the Axis powers.

518. DRUDGERY
- *work that is hard, menial, and monotonous*

IN MY LIFE
At the end of my freshman year at UNC–Chapel Hill, I complained that I was tired of the DRUDGERY of writing papers and taking exams. So I got a job at a local factory. My job was to wrap metal strips around an iron pole to form parts for furniture and gates. It only took me a few hours to understand the true meaning of DRUDGERY. Bored from the monotonous work, I quit at the end of the day. I promptly enrolled in summer school and never complained again about preparing for my courses.

519. BLITHE
- *happy and carefree; LIGHTHEARTED*

MEET LARRY'S STUDENTS: NICOLE
Most students approach their junior year with feelings of dread, knowing that they will soon have to take numerous standardized high-stakes tests. However, Nicole was quite the opposite. Her BLITHE spirit, VIVACIOUS (lively) personality, and witty comments about famous personalities helped keep the mood in our SAT classes light and cheerful. For example, I could always count on Nicole for an up-to-date ANECDOTE (story) about the melodrama between K-Stew and R-Patz or Taylor Swift and her many boyfriends. Nicole's BLITHE spirit helped set a LIGHTHEARTED tone that relieved the stress and led to superb SAT scores for the entire class!

520. SYMBIOSIS
- *an interdependent relationship between two different organisms*

AP BIOLOGY
Many SAT tests include a sentence completion question devoted to an interesting fact about an unusual plant or animal. For example, lichens are actually composite organisms, consisting of a fungus and a photosynthetic partner living together in a SYMBIOTIC relationship. The SYMBIOSIS seems to work, since lichens can survive in extreme environments including arctic tundra, hot deserts, and even toxic slag heaps.

PART 9

521. **PROFOUND**
- *characterized by deep and insightful thinking*

AP U.S. GOVERNMENT

James Madison ranks as one of America's most PROFOUND political thinkers. In *Federalist 51* Madison admitted that, "If men were angels, no government would be necessary." As a PRAGMATIC (practical) politician, Madison recognized that men are not angels and that governments must "be administered by men over men." He therefore POSTULATED (asserted) this PROFOUND and enduring insight: "You must first enable the government to control the governed; and in the next place oblige it to control itself." Madison' PROFOUND political insight led to the system of checks and balances that is still in use today.

522. **DERIVATION**
- *the origin or root of something*

AP WORLD HISTORY

Vanilla and chocolate are the world's two most popular ice cream flavors. But few ice cream lovers realize that both words have interesting DERIVATIONS that can be traced back to the Aztecs. Like other Pre-Columbian Mesoamerican farmers, the Aztecs cultivated the vine of the vanilla orchid and the beans of the cacao tree. Led by the conquistador Hernan Cortes, the Spanish quickly developed a PENCHANT for both vanilla and chocolate. The word *vanilla* is DERIVED from the Spanish word *vaina*, or "little pod." The word *chocolate* is DERIVED from the Aztec word *xocolati*, meaning "bitter water."

523. **PROFICIENT**
- *having or showing knowledge, skill and aptitude*

MEET CHRISTIAN'S STUDENTS: KENDALL

Kendall is a PROFICIENT rower who is at such a high level of skill that she is considering an attempt to compete in the Olympics! She attends rowing camps to maximize her talent and has become PROFICIENT in both "sweep," in which each rower gets one oar, and "sculling," in which each rower gets two oars. I've learned from Kendall that being PROFICIENT as a rower requires strong back, leg, and arm muscles, plus an efficient and practiced stroke through the water. In fact, being a PROFICIENT rower is like being a "pro" at being "efficient!"

524. **OLFACTORY**
- *having to do with the sense of smell*

DID YOU KNOW?

Squirrels have a keen sense of smell. For example, eastern gray squirrels have a highly developed OLFACTORY system that enables them to locate where they have hidden nuts and also determine if the nuts have been infected by insects. Although squirrels look exactly alike, each one has a UNIQUE smell that enables it to identify other squirrels.

525. DISMISSIVE

- *showing INDIFFERENCE or disregard; rejective*

MEET LARRY'S STUDENTS: AVISHAI

It would be an UNDERSTATEMENT to say that Avishai disliked his math class. Bored by his teacher's SOPORIFIC (causing drowsiness) lessons, Avishai tried to entertain himself by folding pieces of paper into right triangles, squares, and other geometric shapes. Unfortunately, his teacher spotted the designs and sent Avishai to the principal's office. The principal was predictably unimpressed with Avishai's creative work. He DISMISSIVELY called them "paper airplanes" and dispatched Avishai to spend three hours in detention hall. Although SAT critical reading passages will not feature bored students and their DISMISSIVE principals, they often do feature critics who DISMISSIVELY reject plays, poems, and theories they disagree with.

526. CAPITULATE

- *to give in; to surrender without protest*

POP CULTURE

In 2008 Macklemore checked himself into rehab for drug addiction, alcoholism, and related obsessive behavior. The Seattle rapper celebrated two years of sobriety before relapsing in December 2011. Macklemore knew that he had betrayed his family, fans, and most of all himself. But Macklemore refused to CAPITULATE to his addictions. In his song "Start Over," he vowed to once again became "an example of getting sober."

527. SUPINE

- *lying on one's back*

AP ART HISTORY

How did prehistoric artists paint the walls of caves deep within the Earth? While we will never know for sure, art historians believe that since some of the paintings were drawn on a rough surface just two feet above the floor, the prehistoric artists must have worked in a SUPINE position. It is interesting to note that, contrary to popular belief, Michelangelo did not paint the Sistine Ceiling in a SUPINE position. He actually stood on a carefully constructed scaffold.

528. OBSEQUIOUS

- *behaving in an overly submissive manner; SERVILE and SUBSERVIENT*

POP CULTURE

In "The Simpsons," Waylon Smithers is an assistant who works for Mr. Burns, the owner of the Springfield nuclear power plant. Smithers is a devoted SYCOPHANT (servile yes-person) who always behaves in an OBSEQUIOUS manner. Here is an example of the always-OBSEQUIOUS Smithers catering to Mr. Burns's every passing whim:

Mr. Burns: Smithers, I've been thinking: Is it wrong to cheat to win a million-dollar bet?
Smithers: Yes, sir.
Mr. Burns: Let me rephrase that. Is it wrong if I cheat to win a million dollar bet?
Smithers: No, sir. Who would you like killed?

529. CRYPTIC

- *having a secret or hidden meaning; mysterious and mystifying; puzzling*

POP CULTURE

When *Harry Potter and the Chamber of Secrets* opens, Harry is in the midst of another dreadful summer with the Dursleys. Harry is eagerly looking forward to the end of the summer so he can return to Hogwarts and rejoin his friends. But then a house-elf named Dobby magically appears and delivers this CRYPTIC message: "Harry Potter must *not* go back to Hogwarts." Although Dobby's CRYPTIC message leaves Harry PERPLEXED (puzzled), he nonetheless returns to Hogwarts, only to find more CRYPTIC messages about a mysterious "Chamber of Secrets" and "Enemies of the Heir."

530. GUILE

- *clever and crafty behavior to attain a goal*

AP WORLD HISTORY

Philip of Macedon had a gift for leading men in battle. But he was also a SHREWD (cleverly calculating) judge of people who didn't hesitate to use GUILE instead of force. For example, Philip's discouraged commanders once reported that the impregnable walls of an enemy city would require a long and costly siege. "So impregnable," Philip asked, "even gold can't scale them?" Philip's willingness to use GUILE worked. He bribed a traitor who opened a hidden gate, allowing Philip's army to quickly conquer the city.

PART 10

531. SCAVENGE

- *to collect things that have been discarded by others*

POP CULTURE

The post-apocalyptic world will be a grim place, where humans and packs of vultures will SCAVENGE for scarce food in the wreckage of abandoned cities. Desperate survivors will surely value grocery stores as ideal locations to SCAVENGE for canned food. At the same time, the post-apocalyptic world will test human ingenuity as amateur inventors SCAVENGE for tools and used parts that can be reassembled into makeshift machines.

532. NOXIOUS

- *harmful to physical, mental, and political health; injurious*

INSIDER INFO

NOXIOUS is typically associated with foul smells EMANATING (coming out) from landfills and oil refineries. It is important to note that *NOXIOUS* can also be used to describe offensive political symbols, such as the Nazi swastika and the KKK emblem. College Board test writers have used *NOXIOUS* to describe propaganda plays performed in totalitarian countries.

533. RELINQUISH

- *to give up or let go of something; to RENOUNCE*

AP U.S. HISTORY

The American abolitionist William Lloyd Garrison published the first issue of *The Liberator* on January 1, 1831. Garrison boldly called upon Southern planters to voluntarily RELINQUISH control over all their slaves. Infuriated planters ADAMANTLY (stubbornly) rejected Garrison's demand, vowing to never RELINQUISH control over their valuable and supposedly contented labor force. Garrison, however, refused to give up, and the first issue of *The Liberator* marked a milestone in the American abolitionist movement.

534. ENGENDER

- *to produce, cause, or give rise to*

IN MY LIFE

When I was in high school it was not cool to be smart. I remember that bright students deliberately refrained from participating in class discussions, fearing that any perceptive comment would ENGENDER disapproving stares from jealous classmates. For example, I vividly remember asking our English literature teacher a perceptive question about a novel and receiving a prolonged icy stare from a pretty girl I hoped to date. Our class valedictorian was far more cautious than I was. Margaret rarely spoke in class and always claimed she was unprepared for tests. She understood that jealousy is a "green-eyed monster" that would undermine her popularity and ENGENDER muted hostility.

535. PLIANT

- *capable of being bent and shaped; easily influenced; MALLEABLE*

MEET CHRISTIAN'S STUDENTS: KYLIE

PLIANT is a challenging word to teach. I tried the traditional approach of explaining that *PLIANT* is derived from *plié*, a ballet term meaning "to bend one's knees into a graceful semi-crouch." But that attempt misfired and only elicited yawns. Then Kylie came to my rescue. She excitedly explained that while on a biology field trip, she discovered a soft willow stalk that was especially PLIANT. The bendable stalk gave Kylie an idea. If you drop the *I* in *PLIANT*, you are left with the word *PLANT*. Linking the word *PLIANT* with the bendable willow PLANT worked! Now all of my students remember that *PLIANT* means "bendable."

536. SPORADIC

- *occurring in irregular, unpredictable, or random instances*

MEET CHRISTIAN'S STUDENTS: TANNER

Tanner's family owns a ranch in central Texas. Unfortunately, SPORADIC assaults by wild hogs are a destructive force that wreak HAVOC (destruction) upon his family's land. There can be long intervals between pig attacks—sometimes just enough time for new crops and flower beds to gain a foothold in the rich earth—but then, unexpectedly, the hogs will strike again, uprooting vegetables and bluebonnets in a display of porcine passion for tasty snacks. Tanner and his family are not defenseless. Tanner often leads SPORADIC retaliations against the hogs by chasing them away with his all-terrain jeep and firing non-lethal weapons. But Tanner's "victories" are FLEETING (short-lived), as the hogs ultimately regroup and launch more SPORADIC attacks.

537. PROVOCATIVE

- *intending to deliberately provoke or stimulate a reaction*

POP CULTURE

Macklemore's songs are known for their signature mix of catchy rap verses, floor-thumping beats, and PROVOCATIVE lyrics. SKEPTICS (doubters) warned Macklemore that his PROVOCATIVE lyrics about his struggle with addiction and his tolerant views of same-sex marriage would never work. But Macklemore ignored the doubters and wrote about what was in his soul. For example, in "Same Love" he admits that at one time a "bunch of stereotypes" about gays filled his head. After much soul-searching, he PROVOCATIVELY concludes that "America the brave still fears what we don't know and 'God loves all his children' is somehow forgotten."

538. AFFECTATION

- *behavior that is deliberately PRETENTIOUS and unnatural; artificial*

INSIDER INFO

Don't confuse *AFFECTATION* with *AFFECTION*. *AFFECTION* is a positive word that that describes a warm emotional bond. In contrast, *AFFECTATION* is a negative word that describes behavior that is PRETENTIOUS, unnatural, and STILTED (artificial). For example, in his song "Thrift Shop," Macklemore DISDAINS (scorns) the deliberate AFFECTATION displayed by rappers who prize extravagant clothes and OSTENTATIOUS (showy) jewelry. Rather than buy expensive designer labels, Macklemore and his friends enjoy looking for bargains in a thrift shop.

539. FUROR

- *a sudden strong emotional reaction; an uproar*

POP CULTURE

Taylor Swift's video "You Belong with Me" won the 2009 MTV Music Award for Best Female Video. During Taylor's acceptance speech, rapper Kanye West suddenly appeared on stage, seized the microphone from Taylor's hand and told the stunned singer, "Yo, Taylor, I'm really happy for you and I'mma let you finish, but Beyonce had one of the best videos of all time." Kanye's action created a FUROR. Both fans and celebrities CASTIGATED (harshly criticized) Kanye for his BOORISH (rude and uncouth) behavior. As the FUROR slowly died down, the incident became an iconic moment that has often been PARODIED on YouTube.

540. TEPID

- *lukewarm and halfhearted support*

IN MY LIFE

After three years of teaching the Basics in North Carolina, I eagerly looked forward to my new job teaching social studies in Holmdel, New Jersey. The department head prided himself on being open to new ideas. I was therefore surprised by his TEPID support for including a unit on organized crime in my Problems in America course. Sensing his lukewarm enthusiasm, I agreed to drop the unit and focus more time on the environment and ethnic and racial relations. I later learned that there was a good reason for my department head's TEPID support for a unit on organized crime. In addition to being the home of Nobel Prize winners who worked at the Bell Lab, Holmdel was also the home of leading members of powerful organized crime families who worked in the metropolitan New York area.

CHAPTER 13
THE TOP FORTY WORDS WITH MULTIPLE MEANINGS

Many words in the English language have multiple meanings. For example, the word *BROAD* has fifteen different definitions! Most SATs contain one or two questions designed to test your knowledge of the less commonly known meanings of frequently used words. These questions are often the trickiest and most missed items on the test. this chapter discusses forty commonly tested words with multiple meanings. The definitions and examples all focus on how the word is typically tested on the SAT.

PART 1

541. ORNATE
- *elaborately decorated; marked by a flowery writing style*

INSIDER INFO
ORNATE is usually used to describe the decoration of a building. For example, the Taj Mahal, Versailles Palace, and St. Peter's Cathedral all feature ORNATE decorations. *ORNATE* can also be used to describe a style of writing that relies upon flowery descriptions and elaborate rhetorical devices. For example, Charles Dickens was famous for his ORNATE style of writing.

542. AUSTERE

- *unadorned and plain; bare and SPARE*

INSIDER INFO

AUSTERE is usually used to describe the absence of decoration. For example, a high-security prison cell and a monk's chamber would both have AUSTERE furnishings. AUSTERE can also be used to describe a style of writing based upon the use of a few unadorned words or what the College Board test writers call "an economy of expression." For example, Ernest Hemingway was famous for his AUSTERE prose in works such as *The Old Man and the Sea*. Modern tweets also provide good examples of AUSTERE writing that use just 140 unadorned characters.

543. SPARE

- *lacking EMBELLISHMENT or ornamentation; a plain style of writing or decoration*

INSIDER INFO

What first comes to your mind when you hear the word *SPARE*? When asked this question, my students unanimously replied "extra," as in a SPARE tire. It is important to remember that the word *SPARE* can also be used to describe both a plain and unadorned style of writing and a work of art that lacks ornamentation. For example, SAT test writers often use the phrase "economy of expression" to indicate that a writer has a SPARE prose style. When describing a work of art, *SPARE* is often used as a synonym for *AUSTERE* (plain) or as an antonym for *ORNATE* (lavish).

544. ECONOMICAL

- *thrifty and frugal with money and with words; not wasteful*

INSIDER INFO

ECONOMICAL is most commonly used to describe consumers who are thrifty and do not waste money. For example, an ECONOMICAL shopper would take advantage of bargain sales. However, ECONOMICAL can also be used to describe thrifty writers who are SUCCINCT (concise) and thus do not waste words. On one test, for example, College Board test writers used Lucille Clifton as an example of a poet who employed an ECONOMICAL writing style to discuss feminist themes and her African American heritage.

545. CAPTURE

- *to attract and hold*

INSIDER INFO

SAT test writers know that *CAPTURE* usually means "to seize someone or something by force." But *CAPTURE* can also mean "to attract and hold someone's attention." Steve Jobs and Apple CAPTURED the public's imagination with a series of INNOVATIVE iPhones and iPads. A writer can also CAPTURE a reader's attention. For example, Zora Neale Hurston was a Harlem Renaissance novelist who skillfully used colloquial idioms to create authentic characters that CAPTURED her reader's imaginations.

546. CHANNEL

• *a pathway through which information is transmitted*

INSIDER INFO

The *Free Online Dictionary* lists thirteen different definitions of the word *CHANNEL*. For example, *CHANNEL* can refer to a body of water like the English *CHANNEL* or to a frequency band for the transmission and reception of electromagnetic signals. College Board test writers typically use *CHANNEL* to refer to a pathway through which information is transmitted. For example, billions of people around the world now use the Internet as a *CHANNEL* for the almost instantaneous sharing of ideas and news.

547. PEDESTRIAN

• *commonplace and unimaginative; CONVENTIONAL; BANAL*

INSIDER INFO

PEDESTRIAN is a classic example of a word with multiple meanings. In everyday language, it is a noun that describes a person traveling on foot. On the SAT, however, *PEDESTRIAN* is often used as an adjective to describe a person or performance that is ordinary and *CONVENTIONAL*. Test writers typically use *PEDESTRIAN* as a negative word to describe plays with uninspired acting and books with *CONVENTIONAL* plots.

548. LIBERAL

• *generous and plentiful*

INSIDER INFO

AP Government students will immediately define the term *LIBERAL* as "a person or politician who is left of center on the political spectrum." Don't expect the SAT to test your knowledge of controversial political terms. Instead, be prepared to know that *LIBERAL* can also mean "generous and plentiful." For example, your mom will give you a *LIBERAL* helping of turkey on Thanksgiving, and a critic will hand out a *LIBERAL* dose of criticism to poets, playwrights, and architects.

549. ARREST

• *to check the expansion of something; to hold back*

INSIDER INFO

The word *ARREST* has a number of different meanings. Do not expect SAT test writers to be concerned with police *ARRESTING* criminals. Instead expect them to focus questions on *ARRESTING* the spread of a disease or *ARRESTING* the *DELETERIOUS* (harmful) effects of global warming.

550. BROAD

- *comprehensive; far-reaching*

IN YOUR LIFE

The *Free Online Dictionary* lists fifteen different definitions of *BROAD*, ranging from "wide" to "a slang word for a woman." Fortunately, SAT test writers will not expect you to know all of the different definitions of *BROAD*. Instead focus on the use of *BROAD* as a word meaning "comprehensive." For example, many college students take a BROAD range of courses.

PART 2

551. ODD

- *infrequent; irregular*

INSIDER INFO

What first comes to your mind when you hear the word *ODD*? Most high school math students probably think of integers that are not evenly divided by two, such as one, three, and five. Most everyday people probably think of *ODD* in the sense of being peculiar. As you have probably figured out, College Board test writers are not everyday people. They expect you to know that *ODD* also means "infrequent." For example, you might receive text messages from an old friend at ODD intervals.

552. SMART

- *elegant and stylish in manners or dress*

DID YOU KNOW?

Everyone knows that *SMART* is an easy Level 1 word meaning "intelligent." Yes, but very few SAT students also know that *SMART* means "elegant in manners or dress." For example, most high school girls would much rather wear a SMART dress to their prom than be seen in a DRAB and frumpy one.

553. LATITUDE

- *freedom from normal restraints and limitations*

INSIDER INFO

When most students hear the word *LATITUDE*, they first think of a geographic term referring to imaginary lines that are parallel to the equator. On the SAT, however, *LATITUDE* is typically used to describe freedom from normal restraints and limitations. For example, teachers can give their students wide LATITUDE in choosing topics for a term paper. In contrast, AUTOCRATIC (dictatorial) governments can severely restrict the LATITUDE given to their citizens.

554. DISCRIMINATING

- *characterized by selective judgment, especially in matters of taste*

INSIDER INFO

DISCRIMINATING is a very tricky word. Most students believe it is a negative word that describes the unfair treatment of a person or group on the basis of a prejudice. But DISCRIMINATION can also be a positive word that describes selective judgment, especially in matters of taste. SAT test writers typically use DISCRIMINATING as a synonym for *selective*. For example, sea otters are DISCRIMINATING eaters because they select only two or three types of prey from over thirty possible food sources. (Who says that you never learn new things on the SAT?)

555. COLD

- *lacking warmth or emotion; impersonal*

INSIDER INFO

What is the first thing you think of when you hear the word COLD? Most people probably think of either an annoying head COLD or a COLD snap in the weather. However, as you know, College Board test writers have a special PENCHANT (liking) for writing questions with uncommon uses of common words. Although it can be used to describe a viral infection or the weather, COLD can also be used to describe an impersonal lack of feeling. For example, Bharti Kirchner opens her novel *Darjeeling* by describing Manhattan's 52nd street as a "cold jumble of glass, concrete, chrome, and steel" that contrasted with the human warmth of the family-owned tea plantation in India where Aloka Gupta grew up. In this description, the word COLD means "impersonal," in the sense of showing no feeling.

556. DOCTOR

- *to falsify or alter; to tamper with*

POP CULTURE

The movie *Zero Dark Thirty* tells the story of the decade-long manhunt to find and eliminate terrorist leader Osama bin Laden. Although critics LAUDED (praised) the movie for its dramatic story, political and intelligence officials have criticized it for allegedly DOCTORING historic facts. For example, Senator John McCain complained that the film DOCTORS facts by suggesting that the use of torture played a crucial role in gathering intelligence that led to bin Laden's secret location in Pakistan.

557. ROUGH

- *approximate; not quite exact*

INSIDER INFO

ROUGH is a very versatile word with a number of commonly used meanings. For example, ROUGH can refer to a surface that is not smooth, a BOORISH (crude) manner of behaving, or a difficult experience. College Board test writers have recently used ROUGH to mean "approximate." For example, a ROUGH estimate of a statistic and a ROUGH sequence of events are not quite exact.

558. RESIGNATION
- *passive acceptance and submission*

INSIDER INFO
The word *RESIGNATION* has both an easy meaning, which most students know, and a very sophisticated meaning that most students don't know. *RESIGNATION* typically refers to the act of giving up or leaving a job. However, *RESIGNATION* can also refer to an attitude of passive acceptance. In a recent critical reading passage, the sentence "More silence, then a sigh" underscores a grandmother's sense of RESIGNATION about her inability to fully articulate her feelings. The word *sigh* conveys the grandmother's sense of RESIGNATION.

559. FURNISH
- *to provide something that is needed*

INSIDER INFO
The word *FURNISH* immediately calls to mind furniture. Thus we FURNISH a room by filling it with chairs and tables. But *FURNISH* is actually a versatile word that can be used to describe providing anything that is needed. For example, job applicants FURNISH answers to interview questions, and hosts FURNISH snacks for their guests. On a recent test, an employee was DISCONCERTED (unsettled) when his boss unexpectedly asked him to FURNISH a detailed report ahead of schedule.

560. FLAG
- *to experience a diminishing level of energy and attention; to become less intense*

INSIDER INFO
Everyone knows that a *FLAG* is a rectangular piece of cloth that contains a distinctive design used as a symbol, emblem, or signal. College Board test writers, however, often use *FLAG* as a verb to describe a person's diminishing level of energy. In one particularly tricky question, a student's attention never FLAGGED as she listened to a lengthy but fascinating lecture.

PART 3

561. EXHAUSTIVE
- *careful and thorough; comprehensive*

IN MY LIFE
After earning a master's degree in sociology at Wake Forest University, I applied for a teaching position at Holmdel High School in New Jersey. The school was in the final stages of an EXHAUSTIVE search for a new history teacher. More than 600 people had already applied, and now it was my turn. I answered questions in a series of EXHAUSTIVE interviews that lasted all day. I even had to teach a demonstration lesson on the Civil

War. Finally, at the end of a long and memorable day, the superintendent offered me a job. I was ECSTATIC, EXUBERANT, and ELATED (really happy)! My wife Susan and I left North Carolina and began a new life in New Jersey.

562. RETIRING

- *characterized by shy and modest behavior; SELF-EFFACING*

INSIDER INFO

RETIRING is a very tricky word. Everyone knows that when a person retires, he or she steps down from a job and doesn't intend to work anymore. But *RETIRING* can also be used to describe a person who is shy and modest. College Board test writers typically use *RETIRING* in sentence completion questions as a contrasting antonym with words such as *EXTROVERTED* (outgoing) and *controversial*.

563. TEMPER

- *to moderate or soften*

INSIDER INFO

TEMPER is typically associated with the emotion of anger. We try to control our TEMPER and usually regret it when we lose our TEMPER. Surprisingly, *TEMPER* can also mean "to moderate or soften" a feeling. On one sentence completion question, for example, a manager attempted to TEMPER, but not eliminate, the optimism of her overly ZEALOUS (very enthusiastic) sales force.

564. SHELVE

- *to put aside and postpone*

AP U.S. HISTORY

Lyndon B. Johnson began his presidency by promising to lead America on an IDEALISTIC quest to end racial segregation and wage war on poverty. The rising cost of the Vietnam War, however, forced LBJ to cut back and ultimately SHELVE many of his Great Society programs.

565. FASHION

- *to give something shape or form*

INSIDER INFO

Most people associate the word *FASHION* with trendy clothes and hip life styles. But clever College Board test writers know that *FASHION* can also mean "to give something shape or form." Over the years challenging sentence completion questions have asked students to realize that 18th-century artists FASHIONED a new artistic style and that contemporary Inuit sculptors are using traditional techniques to FASHION a modern cultural identity.

566. COMPROMISE

- *to expose to danger, suspicion, or disrepute*

POP CULTURE

American history students typically associate the word *COMPROMISE* with a middle ground where both sides make concessions. However, *COMPROMISE* can also mean "the act of exposing a person or organization to danger." In the movie *Skyfall*, for example, Patrice is a mercenary agent who has stolen a computer hard drive containing vital information about British agents placed undercover in terrorist organizations. If James Bond cannot recover it, the hard drive will COMPROMISE British intelligence activities around the world. Needless to say, no COMPROMISE is possible between Bond and Patrice's boss, the villainous cyberterrorist Silva.

567. COSMOPOLITAN

- *sophisticated and not limited by a narrow point of view; diverse and containing a variety of people*

INSIDER INFO

COSMOPOLITAN has two distinct definitions that are both tested in sentence completion questions. A COSMOPOLITAN person is sophisticated and not limited by a narrow, PROVINCIAL perspective. For example, the "Most Interesting Man in the World" commercials feature a COSMOPOLITAN man with a sophisticated knowledge of the world. In contrast, a COSMOPOLITAN place features a diverse and bustling population. New York City, Istanbul, and Hong Kong are all COSMOPOLITAN cities located at the crossroads of international trade.

568. PAROCHIAL

- *reflecting a narrow or limited point of view; PROVINCIAL*

INSIDER INFO

PAROCHIAL is derived from a Latin word meaning "of a parish." During the Middle Ages, a parish was a small section of a diocese that could support its own local church community. Today, *PAROCHIAL* is often used to refer to a church-supported school that provides both religious and CONVENTIONAL education. Do not expect to see this meaning of *PAROCHIAL* tested on your SAT. Instead, College Board test writers will focus on *PAROCHIAL* as a term used to describe a narrow or limited point of view. *PAROCHIAL* and its synonym *PROVINCIAL* are often used as antonyms of *COSMOPOLITAN* (Word 567).

569. TACKLE

- *to confront or take on a challenge*

IN THE NEWS

Jack Andraka is a Maryland teenager who won the top award at the 2012 Intel Science and Engineering Fair. (See Word 480 for Jack's EUPHORIC celebration.) Jack decided to TACKLE the problem of finding a way to detect pancreatic cancer after the disease claimed the life of his uncle. Jack contacted nearly 200 professors at Johns Hopkins University to ask for help with his project. He received almost 200 rejection letters.

UNDAUNTED (not discouraged), Jack refused to quit and continued to TACKLE the problem of devising a new test for pancreatic cancer. To find out what happened, see Word 570.

570. YIELD

- *to produce or provide; to generate*

IN THE NEWS

Jack finally received a positive response from Dr. Anirba Maitra, Professor of Pathology and Oncology at Johns Hopkins School of Medicine. Supported by Dr. Maitra, Jack's research began to YIELD impressive results. Jack's novel ideas have YIELDED a faster, cheaper, and more accurate technique for detecting pancreatic cancer than today's standard diagnostic techniques. Jack's breakthrough method can also be used to detect ovarian and lung cancer.

PART 4

571. STAPLE

- *a basic dietary item*

INSIDER INFO

When most students hear the word *STAPLE*, they probably think of the little pieces of wire used to fasten papers together. But *STAPLE* can also refer to a basic dietary item. For example, maize, beans, and squash formed a triad of key STAPLE crops grown by many pre-Columbian Native Americans.

572. HAUNT

- *to frequent a place*

INSIDER INFO

What is the first thing that comes to your mind when you think of the word *HAUNT*? Most people would probably say, "A HAUNTED house." As you have learned throughout this book, College Board test writers are not like most people. They expect you to know that *HAUNT* can also mean "to frequent or hang around a place." For example, during the 1870s Impressionist artists HAUNTED the Café Guerbois in Paris. Today, Dhara, Nicole, and many of my SAT students HAUNT the Starbucks in Hillsborough.

573. PORE

- *to focus one's attention on a specific task or problem*

INSIDER INFO
Most people would define a PORE as a tiny hole or opening that allows the passage of a liquid. When *PORE* is used as a verb, however, it means "to focus one's attention on a specific task or problem." For example, I spend hours PORING over released SATs. I carefully SCRUTINIZE (closely examine) the vocabulary on each test, looking for synonym clusters, key prefixes, and of course Level 5 words. The words in this book are all derived from this METICULOUS (very precise) process of PORING over long lists of SAT words.

574. SANCTION

- *to officially approve or disapprove of an action*

IN YOUR LIFE
SANCTION has the distinction of having two diametrically opposite definitions. It can mean "to approve something." For example, SAT test rules SANCTION the use of scientific or graphing calculators during the exam. It is important to note that *SANCTION* can also mean "to disapprove of something." For example, SAT test rules SANCTION calculators that have a keypad, use an electrical outlet, make noise, or have a paper tape.

575. TASTELESS

- *lacking AESTHETIC or social taste; inelegant and vulgar*

INSIDER INFO
We usually use the word *TASTELESS* to describe foods and drinks that lack flavor. However, *TASTELESS* can also be used to describe vulgar behavior and artistic styles. Although SAT critical reading passages rarely if ever describe vulgar behavior, they often quote critics who describe a movie, work of art, or architectural style as TASTELESS. For example, leading Post-Modern architects describe modernist buildings as TASTELESS glass and concrete boxes.

576. SPIRIT

- *a vital principle; the essence of a philosophy*

INSIDER INFO
Most people associate *SPIRIT* with a soul or ghost. Students might also associate *SPIRIT* with enthusiastic cheering for your school's athletic teams. It is important to know that *SPIRIT* can also be used to describe the essence of a philosophy. For example, "Man is the measure of all things" expresses the SPIRIT, or essence, of Greek artistic philosophy. Similarly, a belief in equal opportunity expresses the SPIRIT, or essence, of America's political philosophy.

577. SKEWER

- *to pierce with sharp criticism*

INSIDER INFO

A *skewer* is a long wooden or metal pin used to hold meat together while cooking. Keep in mind that *SKEWER* can also be used as a verb meaning "to pierce someone with sharp criticism." For example, FERVENT (very enthusiastic) sports fans lavish praise on victorious coaches. However, they promptly second-guess and SKEWER coaches who make questionable decisions that lead to a defeat. After being SKEWERED by critics for his role in the Bay of Pigs FIASCO (disaster, DEBACLE), President Kennedy MUSED (reflected) that "Victory has a thousand fathers, but defeat is an orphan."

578. ECLIPSE

- *to surpass; overshadow*

INSIDER INFO

The word *ECLIPSE* is commonly associated with a CELESTIAL (heavenly) event in which one body obscures another. For example, a solar ECLIPSE occurs when the moon briefly blocks our view of the sun. Don't expect to read about solar ECLIPSES on your SAT. Instead, College Board test writers typically use *ECLIPSE* to describe a situation in which one philosophy or type of technology ECLIPSES another. For example, traditional print media such as newspapers and magazines are being ECLIPSED by electronic media such as Internet blogs and Twitter tweets.

579. CULTIVATE

- *to carefully develop and ingratiate oneself*

INSIDER INFO

The word *CULTIVATE* is normally associated with farmers who CULTIVATE or raise a crop. It is important to note that *CULTIVATE* is not limited to agriculture. It can also be used to describe how people deliberately ingratiate themselves with others. For example, famous athletes use commercials to CULTIVATE their images; lobbyists use donations to CULTIVATE lawmakers; and DEMAGOGUES (political leaders who inflame popular passions) use scapegoats to distract and CULTIVATE their followers.

580. SOLID

- *substantial*

INSIDER INFO

SOLID is a perfect word for College Board test writers looking to test a student's ability to distinguish among the multiple meanings of a common word. The Free Online Dictionary lists fourteen different definitions of *SOLID*, including "firm," "reliable," and even "excellent." Given this range of options, it is impossible to predict which definition of *SOLID* the test writers will use. Nonetheless, it is important to note that recent tests have used *SOLID* as a synonym for "substantial." For example, scientists now believe that there is a SOLID body of evidence to support the Big Bang model of the early development of the universe.

CHAPTER 14

THE TOP TEN WORDS ABOUT KRISTEN STEWART & ROBERT PATTINSON

Kristen Stewart's cheating scandal generated intense media attention. Inquiring students want to know what happened. This chapter uses ten frequently used SAT vocabulary words to tell you all the news about K-Stew and R-Pattz.

581. CLANDESTINE &
582. SURREPTITIOUS

- *Both words describe FURTIVE activities and actions that are secret and hidden.*

POP CULTURE

The real-life romance between *Twilight* SAGA costars Kristen Stewart and Robert Pattinson captured the imagination of movie fans throughout the world. But fans were shocked when *Us Weekly* published pictures showing K-Stew having a CLANDESTINE romantic rendezvous with her *Snow White and the Huntsman* director, Rupert Sanders—a married father of two who is nineteen years older than Kristen. The pictures were taken by a photographer who SURREPTITIOUSLY followed Stewart and Sanders to a secluded place where they had what he called "a marathon make-out session."

583. REMORSEFUL &
584. CONTRITE

- *Both words describe feelings of regret and sorrow*

POP CULTURE

The pictures in *Us Weekly* forced Kristen to admit that she had indeed had a CLANDESTINE (secret) meeting with Rupert Sanders. Filled with REMORSE, K-Stew issued a public apology, declaring, "I'm deeply sorry for the hurt and embarrassment I've caused to those close to me and everyone that has been affected." The visibly CONTRITE actress then IMPLORED (begged) Pattinson to forgive her: "This momentary indiscretion has jeopardized the most important thing in my life, the person I love and respect the most, Rob. I love him. I love him. I'm so sorry."

585. SANCTUARY

- *a place where people go for peaceful tranquility and quiet introspection*

POP CULTURE

K-Stew's betrayal devastated R-Pattz. The *Twilight* star had believed that he and K-Stew were soulmates who would always be together. The MELANCHOLY (sad and depressed) star accepted Reese Witherspoon's invitation to stay at her secluded ranch in Ojai, northwest of Los Angeles. Reese's home served as a much-needed SANCTUARY where Rob reflected on what had happened.

586. IRE

- *an expression of strong anger*

POP CULTURE

While R-Pattz BROODED (dwelled anxiously) over what had happened to his seemingly perfect relationship, angry *Twilight* fans focused their IRE on Kristen. Angry fans branded her a "trampire" and refused to accept her public apology.

587. ANGUISH

- *a feeling of great distress, torment, and despair*

POP CULTURE

The apparent loss of R-Pattz and the IRE of her fans left K-Stew tortured by feelings of regret. Friends reported that the ANGUISHED star cried all night and was close to a total emotional meltdown.

588. ASSUAGE

- *to soothe, calm, and attempt to make less painful*

POP CULTURE

The guilt-ridden Kristen was determined to ASSUAGE Rob's pain and win back his trust. She bombarded Rob with phone calls and texts begging for forgiveness, swearing that her REMORSE was genuine, and promising that she would never betray his trust again. Kristen even openly wore a $40,000 locket Rob had previously given to her. It contained pictures of the couple and a Latin inscription that, when translated, reads, "Even if you can't see me, my love for you is always there."

589. RECONCILE

- *to restore a friendship or condition of harmony*

POP CULTURE

At first, RECONCILIATION between R-Pattz and K-Stew seemed impossible. Even though R-Pattz felt betrayed, he still loved Kristen and wanted to trust her. The two stars finally had a CLANDESTINE meeting, away from the prying cameras of intrusive paparazzi. Friends reported that "the frost between them is thawing." Within a short time the couple began appearing together in public, and their publicists confirmed that they had indeed RECONCILED.

590. PERSEVERE

- *to persist steadfastly, to hold on*

POP CULTURE

The RECONCILIATION (restoration of harmony) between Rob and Kristen proved to be FLEETING (short-lived). Unable to fully trust Kristen again, Rob called off their relationship. Although Kristen was devastated, she PERSEVERED. The painful experience taught Kristen that people sometimes change, and lovers sometimes rearrange. In life, there is nothing quite as sure as change.

CHAPTER 15
THE TOP TEN WORDS ABOUT PSY AND GANGNAM STYLE

Psy and his music video "Gangnam Style" have become global sensations. But who is Psy, and what are the hidden messages in the "Gangnam Style" video? This chapter uses ten frequently tested SAT vocabulary words to answer these and other "Gangnam Style" questions.

591. VERVE

- *an energetic style that is FLAMBOYANT and full of vitality*

POP CULTURE

The music video "Gangnam Style" has transformed a previously unknown South Korean rapper into a global superstar. Psy is full of VERVE as he raps catchy rhymes and performs energetic horse-riding dance moves. Psy's unique combination of VERVE, attitude, and wit have helped turn the "Gangnam Style" video into a YouTube sensation that has received almost two billion views. We agree (for now) with an EXUBERANT (very enthusiastic) liker who proclaimed, "Psy is boss!"

592. FRIVOLOUS VERSUS
593. TRENCHANT

- *FRIVOLOUS describes behavior that is silly and not serious. In contrast, TRENCHANT describes observations that are penetrating, incisive, and sharply perceptive.*

POP CULTURE

At first glance, "Gangnam Style" is a LIGHTHEARTED (carefree) and FRIVOLOUS (silly) video that displays Psy as he dances his way through a HODGEPODGE (jumble) of seemingly disconnected misadventures. Beneath the surface, however, "Gangnam Style" is a TRENCHANT social commentary on life in the Gangnam district of Seoul, South Korea. Gangnam is the wealthiest and most COVETED (desired) place to live in Seoul. It is the home of fashionable boutiques, trendy clubs, and prestigious prep schools. Psy's TRENCHANT video exposes the love-hate relationship South Koreans have with the PRETENTIOUS (self-important) people who live, work, and play in Gangnam.

594. DILAPIDATED

- *run-down, decaying, and shabby*

POP CULTURE

Gangnam is now known for its trendy stores and wealthy residents. Surprisingly, less than thirty years ago Gangnam was an IMPOVERISHED (very poor) and NONDESCRIPT (lacking interesting features) area, best known for its DILAPIDATED apartment buildings and streets lined with MALODOROUS (foul-smelling) drainage ditches.

595. APPREHENSIVE

- *describes an uneasy feeling of anxiety and worry*

POP CULTURE

Gangnam's wealthy residents inspire feelings of both envy and APPREHENSION. Many traditional South Koreans are APPREHENSIVE that the district's obsession with materialism will erode their country's traditional values of hard work and sacrifice. Their uneasy feeling contributes to a national sense of AMBIVALENCE (mixed feelings) that Psy skillfully captures in his "Gangnam Style" video.

596. OSTENTATIOUS

- *marked by showy and often tasteless displays of wealth*

POP CULTURE

Gangnam is the wealthiest district in South Korea. This AFFLUENCE has created an OSTENTATIOUS look known as the "Gangnam style." The self-important people who live in Gangnam prize OSTENTATIOUS clothes and expensive jewelry purchased at posh boutiques. In his official making of the "Gangnam Style" video, Psy expresses his disgust for this OSTENTATIOUS display of material possessions when he disdainfully notes, "Human society is so hollow."

597. DERIDE

- *to ridicule and make fun of; treat with scorn; DEPRECATE*

POP CULTURE

In his song "Gangnam Style," Psy DERIDES vain people who mindlessly pursue symbols of material wealth. For example, the song's lyrics DERIDE the Gangnam obsession with expensive coffee shops. In Gangnam trendy women and men often scrimp on food so they can splurge on drinks at boutique coffee shops. In his song, Psy's character proudly boasts that he is a guy who is so rich that he can "one-shot his coffee before it even cools down." Naturally, Psy wants to meet "a classy girl who knows how to enjoy the freedom of a cup of coffee."

598. QUIRKY

- *characterized by ECCENTRIC habits and odd mannerisms; peculiar*

POP CULTURE

Psy is a stage name derived from the first three letters of the word *psycho*. Psy has always viewed himself as a QUIRKY outsider. Unlike most K-pop (Korean pop) performers, he is not handsome, tall, or muscular. Instead, the QUIRKY Psy describes himself as "a guy who has bulging ideas rather than muscles." Psy is a thoughtful recording artist who writes his own songs and choreographs his own videos. At the same time, however, the QUIRKY Psy boasts that he is "a guy who goes completely crazy when the right time comes."

599. SALIENT

- *standing out in an obvious way; noticeable and prominent*

POP CULTURE

In an interview on NBC's *Today Show*, Psy acknowledged that he is neither handsome nor muscular. He then paused and correctly noted the most SALIENT point about his current status: "But I'm sitting here." Psy is right. He has succeeded where the other K-pop superstars have failed. The 35-year-old rapper has become the first K-pop artist to successfully crack the LUCRATIVE (very profitable) American music market.

600. VANGUARD

- *the leading position in a trend or movement*

MEET LARRY'S STUDENTS: CHRISTIN

Christin is proud of her Korean heritage. She taught me how to pronounce Gangnam and also pointed out some of the hidden cultural points in the "Gangnam Style" video. The man in the bright yellow suit, for example, is actually a very popular South Korean comedian and TV personality. The beautiful redhead Psy meets on the subway is the leader of a very famous K-pop girl group named 4Minute. Christin predicts that Psy is in the VANGUARD of a wave of K-pop recording artists who are poised to invade the COVETED (desired) but ELUSIVE (hard to reach) American music market.

PART II
THE ESSENTIAL GUIDE TO SENTENCE COMPLETIONS

CHAPTER 16
INTRODUCING SENTENCE COMPLETIONS

Chapters 1–15 provide you with definitions and illustrations of 600 key words frequently tested on the SAT. These words will help you become a more articulate writer and speaker. They will also help you achieve a higher Critical Reading score.

Each SAT contains three sections devoted to Critical Reading. These sections include a total of nineteen sentence completion questions and 48 passage-based questions. Vocabulary plays a particularly important role in the challenging Level 4 and Level 5 questions. In many ways, the Critical Reading section can be viewed as a sophisticated vocabulary test.

Part II of *The Essential Guide to SAT Critical Reading and Vocabulary* is designed to provide you with a comprehensive overview of sentence completion questions. Chapters 17–20 explain and illustrate four basic types of sentence completion questions. Chapter 21 contains 170 practice sentence completion questions that will give you an opportunity to practice most of the 600 words in Chapters 1–15. And finally, Chapter 22 contains a practice set of 19 sentence completions. This set is arranged in groups of eight, six, and five questions, just as they appear on actual SATs.

BASIC INFORMATION

Each SAT contains nineteen sentence completion questions. These sentences contain one or two blanks. Your task is to fill in the blanks with a word or set of words which best fits the meaning of the sentence as a whole. According to the College Board, sentence completion questions are designed to test your vocabulary and "your ability to understand how the different parts of a sentence fit logically together."

ORDER OF DIFFICULTY

Each critical reading section will begin with a set of either eight, six, or five sentence completion questions. The sentence completions are arranged in order of difficulty. The first question will be relatively easy, and the next questions will become increasingly difficult. Here's what to expect:

- In the set of eight sentence completions, numbers 1–3 are usually easy, numbers 4–5 are of medium difficulty, and numbers 6–8 are hard.
- In the set of six sentence completions, numbers 1–2 are usually easy, numbers 3–4 are usually of medium difficulty, and numbers 5–6 are usually hard.
- In the set of five sentence completions, number 1 is usually easy, numbers 2–3 are usually of medium difficulty, and numbers 4–5 are usually hard.

THE GOLDEN RULE

College Board test writers can't just use any sentence and arbitrarily leave out a word. They must provide enough information to make the correct choice indisputably right and the incorrect choices indisputably wrong. This information takes the form of key words, phrases, and examples. The Golden Rule for answering sentence completions is: ALWAYS FIND THE KEY WORD, PHRASE, OR EXAMPLE. IT WILL LEAD YOU TO THE CORRECT ANSWER.

A SAMPLE QUESTION

Take a look at the sample sentence completion below, and select the missing word:

The textbook on African history provides a _____ treatment of a diverse subject.
  (A) compassionate
  (B) deceptive
  (C) chaotic
  (D) fascinating
  (E) chronological

Which answer did you choose? Why? Are the other answers clearly incorrect?

In this example, all five of the answer choices could be correct. The textbook treatment of African history could be compassionate, deceptive, chaotic, fascinating, or chronological. The sentence doesn't provide us with enough information to determine the best answer.

Now take a look at this version of our sample sentence completion question:

> The textbook on African history provides a _____ treatment of a diverse subject; it carefully describes the sequential development of a complex series of events.
>   (A) compassionate
>   (B) deceptive
>   (C) chaotic
>   (D) fascinating
>   (E) chronological

Which answer did you choose this time? Why? The key phrase "the sequential development" tells you that the textbook's treatment of African history must be CHRONOLOGICAL. No other answer choice will fit this defining phrase.

Every sentence completion on the SAT will have a key word, phrase, or illustrative example that will lead you to the correct answer. Your prime directive is to identify the key word or phrase and then match it with the appropriate answer choice. The chapters in Part II will examine and illustrate different types of key words that will help you answer sentence completion questions correctly.

THE IMPORTANCE OF SENTENCE COMPLETION QUESTIONS

The nineteen sentence completion questions comprise 28 percent of the 67 Critical Reading questions on your SAT. Although this is a significant percentage, the importance of sentence completion questions transcends their number.

It is important to remember that each set of sentence completion questions ends with two to three challenging Level 4 and 5 questions. As a result, the nineteen sentence completions typically generate seven to nine Level 4 and 5 questions. As a general rule, each SAT contains between fifteen and twenty Level 4 and 5 questions. Challenging sentence completion questions thus comprise between forty and fifty percent of the tough Level 4 and 5 questions on a given SAT.

Level 4 and 5 sentence completion questions can have a particularly significant impact on the Critical Reading scores of students aspiring to score above a 700. The May 2013 SAT, for example, contained eight Level 4 and 5 sentence completion questions. These questions all tested challenging vocabulary words that are in this book. A student who missed these eight questions and correctly answered all the remaining 59 critical reading questions would have received a score of 690. These eight Level 4 and 5 questions were thus worth a total of 110 points!

CHAPTER 17
DEFINITIONAL SENTENCE COMPLETIONS

In the previous chapter you learned to analyze each sentence completion by first looking for key words, phrases, and examples. Now examine the following three sentence completion examples:

1. **Discussions at the town hall meetings were usually _____, focusing on solving practical community problems.**
   (A) subversive
   (B) acrimonious
   (C) soporific
   (D) pragmatic
   (E) eclectic

2. **Some of the guests were _____, speaking rudely to their host and generally displaying deplorable manners.**
   (A) uncouth
   (B) despondent
   (C) euphoric
   (D) earnest
   (E) candid

3. **President Coolidge presents a challenge to would-be biographers because he was both _____ and _____: he said very little and accomplished even less.**
   (A) overbearing .. prescient
   (B) taciturn .. ineffective
   (C) aloof .. productive
   (D) audacious .. incompetent
   (E) indefatigable .. energetic

What type of pattern do you think the key words and phrases in these three questions have in common? In each sentence, the key group of words is a definition. In Sentence 1, the key phrase "focusing on solving practical community problems" tells you that the answer is (D) PRAGMATIC (Word 4). In Sentence 2, the key phrases "speaking rudely" and "displaying deplorable manners" tell you that the answer is (A) UNCOUTH (Word 121). In Sentence 3, the key phrase "said very little" tells you that the answer to the first blank is (B) TACITURN (Word 304). The key phrase "accomplished even less" tells you that the answer to the second blank is (B) ineffective.

In all three of these definitional sentences, the key words and phrases are definitions. The answer is therefore a word that is defined or explained in the sentence.

PRACTICE EXAMPLES

The following ten examples will give you an opportunity to practice the skill of identifying key definitional words, phrases, and examples. They will also give you an opportunity to use vocabulary words from Part I.

1. Mayor Jenkins is one of the most _____ politicians in the state; he is never candid, frequently insincere, and always calculating.
   (A) bombastic
   (B) disingenuous
   (C) vacillating
   (D) dilatory
   (E) paradoxical

2. Nishant laughed exuberantly and embraced his teammates, so _____ was he about leading his team to victory in the fencing tournament.
   (A) forlorn
   (B) indifferent
   (C) disdainful
   (D) euphoric
   (E) wistful

3. Richard Serra, an influential modern sculptor, is best known for his _____ and _____ style that combined eccentric themes with controversial images that sparked heated public debates.
   (A) idiosyncratic .. contentious
   (B) naïve .. nuanced
   (C) bizarre .. conciliatory
   (D) insipid .. inscrutable
   (E) audacious .. prodigious

4. Popular in 18th-century Paris, Rococo art was both _____ and _____: it emphasized elaborate decorations along with frivolous scenes of aristocrats at play.
   (A) pastoral .. somber
   (B) ornate .. superficial
   (C) stark .. cerebral
   (D) unadorned .. fickle
   (E) convoluted .. profound

5. Cortez, Pizarro, and other Spanish conquistadores coveted gold and silver, and with this _____ came a ruthless willingness to conquer the Aztec and Inca empires.
   (A) lethargy
   (B) altruism
   (C) avarice
   (D) prescience
   (E) prudence

6. Viruses are _____; they are found in almost every ecosystem on Earth and are the most abundant type of biological entity.
   (A) auspicious
   (B) audacious
   (C) ubiquitous
   (D) ravenous
   (E) meticulous

7. The committee's report was completely _____; it was filled with inaccurate facts, unfounded innuendoes, and biased sources.
   (A) verifiable
   (B) corroborated
   (C) infallible
   (D) erudite
   (E) erroneous

8. Many beneficial scientific breakthroughs began by chance with the _____ discovery of _____ finding that deviated from accepted patterns and thus could not be explained by existing theoretical models.

    (A) premeditated .. an atypical

    (B) inadvertent .. a conventional

    (C) fortuitous .. an anomalous

    (D) predictable .. a revolutionary

    (E) calculated .. a trivial

9. Critics denounced the company's president for his _____ policies that lacked foresight and failed to address important trends in consumer tastes.

    (A) histrionic

    (B) prolific

    (C) trenchant

    (D) sagacious

    (E) myopic

10. During his negotiations with the Senate over the League of Nations, Woodrow Wilson was both _____ and _____: he refused to compromise and displayed a disdainful attitude toward senators whom he viewed as inferior and unworthy.

    (A) obstinate .. affable

    (B) flexible .. cavalier

    (C) fastidious .. altruistic

    (D) intransigent .. overbearing

    (E) frank .. surreptitious

ANSWERS

1. B: The key definitional phrase "never candid, frequently insincere, and always calculating" leads you to a person who is dishonest and deceitful. The correct answer is therefore DISINGENUOUS (Word 252).

2. D: The key definitional phrase "laughed exuberantly and embraced his teammates" leads you to a person who is very happy. The correct answer is therefore EUPHORIC (Word 480).

3. A: The key definitional word "eccentric" leads you to IDIOSYNCRATIC for the first blank. The key definitional word "controversial" leads you to CONTENTIOUS for the second blank. The correct answer is therefore IDIOSYNCRATIC (Word 233) .. CONTENTIOUS (Word 278).

4. B: The key definitional phrase "elaborate decorations" leads you to ORNATE for the first blank. The key definitional phrase "frivolous scenes" leads you to SUPERFICIAL for the second blank. The correct answer is therefore ORNATE (Word 541) .. SUPERFICIAL (Word 334).

5. C: The key definitional phrase "coveted gold and silver" leads to a word that means "great greed." The correct answer is therefore AVARICE (see Word 260).

6. C: The key definitional phrase "found in almost every ecosystem on Earth" indicates that you are looking for an answer that means "found everywhere." The correct answer is therefore UBIQUITOUS (Word 237).

7. E: The key phrase "inaccurate facts, unfounded innuendoes, and biased sources" tells you that the report was inaccurate. The correct answer is therefore ERRONEOUS (Word 361).

8. C: The key definitional phrase "began by chance" leads you to either (B) INADVERTENT or (C) FORTUITOUS. Since the finding "deviated from accepted patterns" and therefore "could not be explained by existing theoretical models," it would be atypical and thus ANOMALOUS. The correct answer is therefore FORTUITOUS (Word 345) .. ANOMALOUS (Word 19).

9. E: The key definitional phrase "lacked foresight" leads to a word that means "shortsighted." The correct answer is therefore MYOPIC (Word 244).

10. D: The key definitional phrase "refused to compromise" leads you to either (A) OBSTINATE or (D) INTRANSIGENT. Since Wilson also "displayed a disdainful attitude," he was OVERBEARING. The correct answer is therefore INTRANSIGENT (Word 166) .. OVERBEARING (Word 407).

CHAPTER 18
CONTRAST SENTENCE COMPLETIONS

In the previous chapter you learned that the key word or group of words in many sentence completion questions is a definition or explanation. Now read the following three sentence completions:

1. **The diplomat was not at all _____; on the contrary, he was a duplicitous person who could not be trusted.**
    (A) vivacious
    (B) unscrupulous
    (C) disingenuous
    (D) frank
    (E) slovenly

2. **The compromise proposal avoids _____; its appeal is instead to a new spirit of harmony.**
    (A) acrimony
    (B) novelty
    (C) austerity
    (D) amiability
    (E) credibility

3. **The participants in the study considered themselves _____, but in yielding to the wishes of the group they were assuming _____ values.**
    (A) cooperative .. communal
    (B) traditional .. orthodox
    (C) innovative .. conventional
    (D) egalitarian .. elitist
    (E) diligent .. industrious

What type of pattern do the key words and groups of words in these three sentences have in common? Each sentence contains a word or group of words that signals a change in direction. In Sentence 1, the phrase "on the contrary" signals that you are looking for an answer that is the reverse of "duplicitous." In Sentence 2, the phrase "is instead" signals that you are looking for an answer that is the reverse of "harmony." In Sentence 3, the word "but" signals that you are looking for a pair of opposites.

"On the contrary," "is instead," and "but" are all reversal words that alert you to expect a contrast or change of direction in the sentence. The list below includes the most common reversal words used in SAT contrast sentence completion questions:
- BUT
- IN CONTRAST TO
- ON THE CONTRARY
- INSTEAD OF
- ALTHOUGH
- HOWEVER
- NEVER
- NEVERTHELESS
- YET
- NOT KNOWN FOR
- PARADOXICALLY

Sentences containing reversal words are called *contrast sentences*. In this type of sentence completion, the answer will be a word that contrasts with the key word or group of words. For example, in the three sentences above FRANK (Word 7) contrasts with duplicitous, ACRIMONY (Word 376) contrasts with harmony, and INNOVATIVE (Word 88) and CONVENTIONAL (Word 2) make up a contrasting pair of antonyms. Note that CONVENTIONAL is supported by the definitional phrase "yielding to the wishes of the group."

PRACTICE EXAMPLES

The following ten practice examples will give you an opportunity to practice the skill of identifying key contrast words and phrases. They will also give you an opportunity to use vocabulary words from Part I.

1. Akhil was not _____ and instead preferred to participate in team sports and join a variety of social clubs.
   - (A) shrewd
   - (B) ebullient
   - (C) impulsive
   - (D) aloof
   - (E) venal

2. Ernest Hemingway's distinctive writing style was characterized by a simplicity of expression, a _____ sentence structure that contrasted with the elaborate and often _____ prose of 19th-century British writers.
   - (A) subservient .. docile
   - (B) verbose .. succinct
   - (C) varied .. eclectic
   - (D) spare .. ornate
   - (E) mundane .. mediocre

3. As a civilization, the ancient Greeks were full of contradictions: _____ and yet prizing utility, egalitarian and yet sometimes prone to _____ philosophies.
   - (A) pragmatic .. communal
   - (B) expedient .. autocratic
   - (C) sensible .. reciprocal
   - (D) aesthetic .. elitist
   - (E) empathetic .. democratic

4. Madison's surprisingly _____ explanation contrasted with her usual _____ manner of speaking.
   - (A) succinct .. loquacious
   - (B) garrulous .. verbose
   - (C) brusque .. curt
   - (D) candid .. forthright
   - (E) disingenuous .. deceptive

5. Although the speaker was in fact quite perturbed by the rowdy crowd, she managed to remain outwardly _____.
   - (A) unflappable
   - (B) agitated
   - (C) irascible
   - (D) disconcerted
   - (E) apprehensive

6. Kurt's dispassionate and objective explanation sharply contrasted with his usual _____ point of view.
   - (A) soporific
   - (B) biased
   - (C) provisional
   - (D) disinterested
   - (E) pristine

7. Nothing in Anchal's speech was _____: instead she recited carefully documented facts and recounted carefully rehearsed anecdotes.
   - (A) succinct
   - (B) coherent
   - (C) objective
   - (D) corroborated
   - (E) extemporized

8. Never _____, Rebecca instead treated everyone she knew with respect and and as an equal.
   - (A) indomitable
   - (B) cavalier
   - (C) quixotic
   - (D) laconic
   - (E) conspicuous

9. Some people alternate between contrasting temperaments; either they are _____ or they are _____.
   (A) haughty .. imperious
   (B) eccentric .. idiosyncratic
   (C) compliant .. submissive
   (D) overwrought .. histrionic
   (E) somber .. lighthearted

10. Never _____, Zack was instead a _____ person whose effervescent personality enlivened school parties.
   (A) capricious .. mercurial
   (B) despondent .. morose
   (C) altruistic .. magnanimous
   (D) obstinate .. recalcitrant
   (E) reticent .. gregarious

ANSWERS

1. D: The reversal phrase "and instead" signals that you are looking for an answer that contrasts with participating in team sports and and joining a variety of social clubs. Akhil would not be ALOOF, because an ALOOF person prefers to be detached from groups. The correct answer is therefore ALOOF (Word 403).

2. D: The reversal phrase "contrasted with" signals that you will be looking for a pair of antonyms. The phrase "a simplicity of expression" will lead you to "a SPARE sentence structure." This would contrast with the "elaborate" and therefore "ORNATE prose of 19th-century British writers." The correct answer is therefore SPARE (Word 543) .. ORNATE (Word 541).

3. D: The key phrase "full of contradictions" alerts you to look for a pair of antonyms. The first blank must be filled with a word that is the opposite of "prizing utility." The second blank must be filled with a word that is the opposite of "egalitarian." The correct answer is therefore AESTHETIC (Word 1) .. ELITIST (Word 213).

4. A: The reversal phrase "contrasted with" alerts you to look for a pair of opposites. Only answer choice A meets this test. The correct answer is therefore SUCCINCT (Word 16) .. LOQUACIOUS (Word 169).

5. A: The reversal word "although" alerts you to look for an answer that contrasts with the key word "perturbed." The correct answer is therefore UNFLAPPABLE (Word 192).

6. B: The reversal phrase "sharply contrasted with" alerts you to look for an answer that contrasts with a "dispassionate and objective explanation." The correct answer is therefore BIASED (Word 48).

7. E: The reversal word "instead" alerts you to find an answer that contrasts with reciting "carefully documented facts" and recounting "carefully rehearsed anecdotes." The correct answer is therefore EXTEMPORIZED (Word 303).

8. B: The reversal word "instead" alerts you to find an answer that contrasts with treating people "with respect as an equal." The correct answer is therefore CAVALIER (Word 151).

9. E: The reversal phrase "alternate between contrasting temperaments" alerts you to look for a pair of opposites. The correct answer is therefore SOMBER (Word 449) .. LIGHTHEARTED (Word 59).

10. E: The reversal word "instead" alerts you to find an answer for the first blank that contrasts with the answer for the second blank. A person who has an "effervescent personality" that enlivens school parties would be GREGARIOUS. In contrast, a person who is RETICENT would not have this characteristic. The correct answer is therefore RETICENT (Word 10) .. GREGARIOUS (Word 353).

CHAPTER 19
USING POSITIVE AND NEGATIVE WORDS TO SOLVE SENTENCE COMPLETION QUESTIONS

SAT sentence completion questions frequently use challenging vocabulary words and complex sentence structures. As a result, even the best students are not always sure of the answer to each question.

If you are having trouble answering a sentence completion question, don't give up. There are effective strategies you can use to eliminate distracters and focus in on the correct answer.

A STRATEGY FOR USING POSITIVE AND NEGATIVE WORDS

Suppose a friend said to you, "I don't recommend the video game, it is too complicated and _____." What word would you put in the missing blank? Words like "violent" and "boring" quickly come to mind. Why is that? Why don't words like "interesting" and "entertaining" come to mind?

The answer of course, is that your friend specifically said, "I don't recommend the video game." As a result, you expect to hear negative words to complete the statement. If your friend had said, "I strongly recommend the video game," you would expect to hear positive words to explain this statement.

Like your everyday conversations, SAT sentence completion questions often use positive and negative words. Knowing this can help you master some of the test's toughest sentence completion questions. Here is a three-step strategy for using positive and negative words:

First, use contextual clues to determine if the missing word (or words) is most likely a positive word or a negative word. A positive word is one with good connotations, while a negative word is one with bad connotations. As you determine the meaning of the sentence, write a positive sign (+) in the blank if it requires a positive word or a negative sign (–) if it requires a negative word.

Second, write a positive or negative sign next to each of the answer choices.

Third, match the symbols you placed in the sentence blanks with the symbols you placed beside the choices.

CASE EXAMPLES

Let's apply this three-step procedure to the following two case examples:

1. **Climatologists have long warned that global warming will have _____ effect, raising sea levels, flooding coastal areas, and endangering arctic wildlife.**
   (A) an auspicious
   (B) an exhilarating
   (C) an uplifting
   (D) a deleterious
   (E) a lucrative

STEP 1:

Use contextual clues to determine if the missing word is positive or negative. This sentence clearly calls for a negative word, since climatologists are warning that global warming will lead to a series of negative consequences. Therefore place a (–) sign in the blank.

STEP 2:

Write a positive or negative symbol beside each of the answer choices:

(A) AUSPICIOUS means "favorable" and is thus a positive word.
(B) EXHILARATING means "refreshing and exciting" and is thus a positive word.
(C) UPLIFTING means "elevating to a higher social or moral level" and is thus a positive word.
(D) DELETERIOUS means "very harmful" and is thus a negative word.
(E) LUCRATIVE means "profitable" and is thus a positive word.

STEP 3:

Find answer choices that match your sentence symbols. Since you are looking for a negative answer, you can eliminate answer choices (A), (B), (C), and (E). The correct answer is (D) DELETERIOUS (Word 111).

2. During the late 1940s, the theories published by William Foote Whyte on the social structure of an Italian street gang were dismissed or even _____, but now they are _____ and unanimously praised by sociologists.

    (A) derided .. lauded
    (B) celebrated .. circumvented
    (C) refuted .. bemoaned
    (D) revered .. truncated
    (E) scorned .. neglected

STEP 1:

Use contextual clues to determine if the missing words are positive or negative. This sentence clearly calls for a strong negative first word, since Whyte's theories were originally "dismissed." The second blank, however, clearly calls for a positive word, since Whyte's theories are now "unanimously praised by sociologists." Therefore, place a (–) sign in the first blank and a (+) sign in the second blank.

STEP 2:

Write positive and negative symbols beside each answer choice:

(A) DERIDE means "to treat with scorn" and is thus a negative word. LAUD means "to praise" and is thus a positive word.
(B) CELEBRATE means "to rejoice" and is thus a positive word. CIRCUMVENT means "to go around or bypass something" and thus can be either a positive or a negative word.
(C) REFUTE means "to prove that something is false" and thus can be either a positive or a negative word. BEMOAN means "to express disapproval or regret" and is thus a negative word.
(D) REVERE means "to show great respect" and is thus a positive word. TRUNCATE means "to cut short" and thus can be either a positive or a negative word.
(E) SCORN means "to express open dislike" and is thus a negative word. NEGLECT means "to pay little or no attention to" and is thus a negative word.

STEP 3:

Find answer choices that match your sentence symbols. Since you are looking for a negative–positive combination, you can eliminate choices (B), (C), (D), and (E). The correct answer is (A) DERIDED (Word 597) .. LAUDED (Word 428).

PRACTICE EXAMPLES

The following ten examples will give you an opportunity to practice the skill of using positive and negative words to answer sentence completion questions. They will also give you an opportunity to practice using vocabulary words from Part I.

1. Although it had been promoted as the plane of the future, the new airliner proved to be a _____: it cost too much, leaked oil, and had faulty lithium ion batteries.
   (A) a landmark
   (B) a fiasco
   (C) a triumph
   (D) a colossus
   (E) an anachronism

2. Investigators uncovered the politician's _____ when a hidden surveillance camera recorded him accepting bribes from a local businessman seeking special favors.
   (A) probity
   (B) charisma
   (C) venality
   (D) forbearance
   (E) idiosyncrasies

3. Chadni's _____ behavior had its usual _____ effect on her colleagues, who put aside their differences and reached a reasonable compromise.
   (A) conciliatory .. salutary
   (B) quirky .. soporific
   (C) earnest .. adverse
   (D) lighthearted .. autocratic
   (E) belligerent .. elusive

4. Critics called the new play bland, because its plot was _____ and its poorly executed dialogue relied upon repetitious and mindless _____.
   (A) hackneyed .. platitudes
   (B) innovative .. redundancies
   (C) discerning .. anecdotes
   (D) scintillating .. allusions
   (E) trite .. subtleties

5. Although President Harding was personally honest, the Teapot Dome scandal tarnished his reputation and ultimately _____ his presidency.
   (A) bolstered
   (B) dignified
   (C) redeemed
   (D) discredited
   (E) rejuvenated

6. Recent promising advances have led proponents of renewable energy sources to predict confidently that solar panel technology will soon enter a new and more _____ phase of development.
   (A) ominous
   (B) perplexing
   (C) contentious
   (D) auspicious
   (E) inscrutable

7. Tyler's _____ was the inverse of his sister's _____: he was tolerant and generous while she was vengeful and unforgiving.
   (A) munificence .. benevolence
   (B) vivacity .. lethargy
   (C) diffidence .. prudence
   (D) ineptitude .. dexterity
   (E) magnanimity .. vindictiveness

8. The unruly students were not merely scolded, they were _____ during a lengthy _____ by their irate vice-principal.
  (A) extolled .. eulogy
  (B) excoriated .. rebuke
  (C) extrapolated .. manifesto
  (D) exonerated .. pronouncement
  (E) expunged .. tribute

9. The skillful store manager was able to _____ the irate customer by offering her a sincere apology and a valuable gift certificate.
  (A) exasperate
  (B) mollify
  (C) stigmatize
  (D) admonish
  (E) confound

10. Although the new high-speed rail line met with _____ from passengers, it also had its _____ who protested that it was very expensive to build and operate.
  (A) acclaim .. critics
  (B) derision .. detractors
  (C) approbation .. proponents
  (D) accolades .. benefactors
  (E) enmity .. zealots

ANSWERS

1. B: The sentence calls for a strong negative answer, since it lists three negative characteristics of the new airliner. Answers (A) and (C) can be eliminated because they are positive words. Answer (D) can be eliminated because a colossus is a huge object. Answer (E) can be eliminated because an anachronism (Word 232) is a person, event, or object that is chronologically out of place. The correct answer is therefore (B), since a FIASCO is a disaster (see Word 346).

2. C: The sentence calls for a negative word, since the hidden camera recorded the politician accepting bribes. Answers (A), (B), and (D) can all be eliminated since they are positive words. Answer (E) can be eliminated since an idiosyncrasy (Word 213) is an eccentric behavior. The correct answer is therefore (C), because VENALITY describes behavior that is corrupt and dishonest (Word 230).

3. A: The sentence calls for two positive words, since Chadni's behavior caused her colleagues to "put aside their differences" and reach "a reasonable compromise." Answers (B), (C), (D), and (E) can all be eliminated because they contain at least one negative word. The correct answer is therefore (A), since CONCILIATORY (Word 273) means "willing to make concessions" and SALUTARY (Word 286) means "beneficial."

4. A: The sentence calls for two negative words, because the critics called the play "bland" and criticized the dialogue for being "repetitious and mindless." Answers (B), (C), (D), and (E) can all be eliminated since they contain at least one positive word. The correct answer is therefore (A), since HACKNEYED (Word 188) means "trite" and PLATITUDE (Word 187) means "commonplace, unoriginal, and mindless."

5. D: The sentence calls for a negative word that contrasts with the positive word "honest." Answers (A), (B), (C), and (E) can all be eliminated because they are positive words. The correct answer is therefore (D), since DISCREDIT (Word 406) means "to cast doubt on the reputation of a person."

6. D: The sentence calls for a positive word, since "promising advances" have led proponents of renewable sources of energy to confidently predict that panel technology will soon enter a new phrase of development. Answers (A), (B), (C), and (E) can all be eliminated, because they are negative words. The correct answer is therefore (D), since AUSPICIOUS means "favorable" (Word 331).

7. E: The sentence calls for a pair of antonyms, featuring a positive first word that is compatible with "tolerant and generous" and a negative second word that is compatible with "vengeful and unforgiving." Answers (C) and (D) can be eliminated, since diffidence is a negative trait that means "lacking self-confidence," and ineptitude is a negative trait that means "lacking skill." Answer (A) can be eliminated since both munificence and benevolence are positive words meaning "generous" and "kind" respectively. Answer (B) can be eliminated because vivacity means "full of life" and lethargy means "lazy." Although vivacious is a positive trait and lethargy is a negative trait, these words are not supported by the definitional phrases in the sentence. The correct answer is therefore (E) since MAGNANIMITY (Word 201) means "generous" and VINDICTIVENESS (Word 202) means "vengeful and unforgiving."

8. B: The sentence calls for a pair of negative words, since the irate (angry) vice-principal strongly scolded the "unruly students." Answers (A), (D), and (E) can all be eliminated because they contain positive words. Answer (C) can be eliminated, because extrapolate means "to project," and a manifesto is a public declaration of beliefs. The correct answer is therefore (B), because EXCORIATE (Word 174) means "to harshly denounce" and REBUKE (Word 408) means "to reprimand."

9. B: The sentence calls for a positive word that is consistent with using a "sincere apology and a valuable gift certificate" to placate the irate customer. Answers (A), (B), (D), and (E) can all be eliminated, because they are negative words. The correct answer is therefore MOLLIFY (see Word 3), meaning "to calm or lessen."

10. A: The sentence calls for a positive first word and a negative second word that describes a person who protests that the high-speed rail line is too expensive. Answers (B) and (E) can be deleted, since derision (ridicule) and enmity (animosity) are both negative first words. Answers (C) and (D) can be deleted, since proponents and benefactors are both positive second words. The correct answer is therefore (A), because ACCLAIM (Word 428) means "to praise," and a CRITIC is someone who expresses dissatisfaction.

CHAPTER 20
ANSWERING THE MOST CHALLENGING SENTENCE COMPLETION QUESTIONS

The most challenging sentence completion questions are easy to find. They always appear at the end of each of the three sets of sentence completion questions. You can expect to have seven to nine challenging sentence completion questions, worth over 110 points of your critical reading score.

CHARACTERISTICS OF CHALLENGING SENTENCE COMPLETION QUESTIONS

Challenging Level 4 and 5 sentence completions are easier to find than to answer. What characteristic features make these questions so difficult? Their degree of difficulty is based upon two key factors:

1. CHALLENGING VOCABULARY

Level 4 and 5 sentence completion questions contain a number of difficult vocabulary words. These challenging words are used in both the answer choices and in the sentence. In order to successfully answer these tough questions, you must have a strong vocabulary. Chapter 10 defines and illustrates 110 Level 5 words. Chapter 11 defines and illustrates 110 Level 4 words.

2. COMPLEX SENTENCE STRUCTURE

The most challenging sentence completion questions employ a combination of definitions, contrast words, and positive and negative vocabulary. In addition, recent tests have included questions asking you to determine the logical connection between the answer choices. For example, you may be asked to find a cause-and-effect relationship between key words in the sentence and the answer choices.

CASE EXAMPLE 1: CHALLENGING VOCABULARY

EAGER TO AVOID APPEARING FRENETIC AND PROVINCIAL, PRANAY CULTIVATED A PUBLIC PERSONA THAT MADE HIM APPEAR TO BE BOTH _____ AND _____.

    (A) imperturbable .. cosmopolitan
    (B) imperious .. tenacious
    (C) brusque .. ostentatious
    (D) unflappable .. parochial
    (E) overwrought .. urbane

Pranay wants to avoid appearing frenetic (wildly excited) and provincial (limited and narrow). You must therefore find a pair of positive answers that contrast with these two negative traits. Answer choice (D) is a possibility, since *unflappable* (calm and poised) is a positive antonym of *frenetic*. You must eliminate (D), however, since *parochial* is a negative synonym of *provincial*. Answer choices (B), (C), and (E) can all be eliminated because they contain negative first words that are not antonyms of *frenetic*. The correct answer is therefore (A), since IMPERTURBABLE (Word 191) is a positive word that contrasts with *frenetic*, and COSMOPOLITAN (Word 567) is a positive word that contrasts with *provincial* (Word 568).

CASE EXAMPLE 2: COMPLEX SENTENCE STRUCTURE

THE TEACHER WARNED HER STUDENTS THAT THE AP PREP BOOK WAS TOO _____ TO HELP THEM PREPARE FOR THE EXAM, GIVEN ITS _____ TREATMENT OF A COMPLEX SUBJECT.

    (A) coherent .. disjointed
    (B) superficial .. cursory
    (C) encyclopedic .. narrow
    (D) methodical .. haphazard
    (E) unsophisticated .. shrewd

This sentence asks you to find a pair of words that are logically connected. For example, you can eliminate (A) because a prep book that is too coherent or organized would not offer a disjointed or unconnected treatment of a complex subject. Choices (C), (D), and (E) can all be eliminated for the same reason. *Encyclopedic* does not imply narrow, *methodical* does not imply haphazard, and *unsophisticated* does not imply shrewd. Only (B) provides a pair of logically related words. A teacher would warn her students to avoid a SUPERFICIAL (Word 334) prep book, because it would provide a CURSORY (Word 301) treatment of a complex subject.

PRACTICE EXAMPLES

The following ten examples will give you an opportunity to practice the skill of answering challenging sentence completion questions. They will also give you an opportunity to practice using vocabulary words from Part I.

1. A long week of demanding homework assignments, challenging tests, and grueling soccer practices drained Lindsay's energy: she felt to _____ to do anything but sleep.
   (A) resilient
   (B) galvanized
   (C) enervated
   (D) unfettered
   (E) unnerved

2. Recent advances in solar technology indicate that energy independence is feasible, but environmentalists are quite _____ in their public statements, mindful of prior claims that proved _____.
   (A) impulsive .. ephemeral
   (B) audacious .. illusory
   (C) equivocal .. prescient
   (D) jovial .. irrevocable
   (E) prudent .. erroneous

3. Professor Duncan has a well-deserved reputation as _____: he disdains tradition and regularly attacks cherished beliefs.
   (A) a dilettante
   (B) a zealot
   (C) a demagogue
   (D) an iconoclast
   (E) a progenitor

4. Although Navajo sand paintings have been created for centuries, their artistic merits remain _____, because they have always been _____ works of art that medicine men promptly destroy.
   (A) enigmatic .. indelible
   (B) authenticated .. elusive
   (C) conclusive .. therapeutic
   (D) beguiling .. futile
   (E) uncorroborated .. ephemeral

5. The comedian is _____ by nature: he has a penchant for displaying a disrespectful attitude in situations that call for a serious response.
   (A) flippant
   (B) wistful
   (C) prudent
   (D) jovial
   (E) didactic

6. The new sales manager was not at all _____; on the contrary, she was cooperative, open-minded, and always willing to listen.
   (A) peremptory
   (B) pragmatic
   (C) docile
   (D) conciliatory
   (E) shrewd

7. Fortunately, the committee's confidence in its appointee's abilities was _____: an investigation uncovered her participation in several _____ business ventures.
   (A) justified .. unsavory
   (B) vindicated .. lucrative
   (C) warranted .. unscrupulous
   (D) reciprocated .. licentious
   (D) premature .. exemplary

8. The shy and _____
behavior of the platypus accounts for
the _____ of confirmed
observations about its life cycle in the
wild.
   (A) gregarious .. dearth
   (B) reticent .. confluence
   (C) retiring .. paucity
   (D) mercurial .. plethora
   (E) contentious .. coherence

9. The Internet embodies
_____ inquiry, since the
system encourages free and open access
to a vast trove of facts, opinions, and
images.
   (A) specialized
   (B) impeded
   (C) unfettered
   (D) frenzied
   (E) coerced

10. The fable of Arachne centers on a human's
_____, the overweening
pride that makes a mortal believe she can
defeat a goddess.
   (A) hubris
   (B) diffidence
   (C) histrionics
   (D) duplicity
   (E) versatility

ANSWERS

1. C: The key word "drained" leads you to a word that means "to feel mentally and physically weakened." The correct answer is therefore ENERVATED (Word 291).

2. E: The sentence asks you to find a pair of words that are logically connected. Logically, the environmentalists would be very careful or PRUDENT (Word 76), because they are mindful that prior claims proved to be wrong or ERRONEOUS (Word 361).

3. D: The key definitional phrase "disdains tradition and regularly attacks cherished beliefs" leads you to describe Professor Duncan as an ICONOCLAST (Word 85).

4. E: This sentence asks you to find a pair of words that are logically connected. Logically, the artistic merits of Navajo sand paintings must remain unproven or UNCORROBORATED (Word 123) and therefore EPHEMERAL (Word 250) since the medicine men promptly destroy them.

5. A: The key definitional phrase, "a penchant for displaying a disrespectful attitude in situations that call for a serious response," leads you to describe the comedian as someone who has a FLIPPANT (Word 63) nature.

6. A: The key reversal phrase "on the contrary" tells you to look for an answer that is the opposite of the key definitional phrase "cooperative, open-minded, and always willing to listen." The correct answer is therefore PEREMPTORY (Word 20).

7. B: This sentence asks you to find a pair of words that are logically connected. The key word "fortunately" signals that both answers will be positive words. The correct answer is therefore VINDICATED (Word 380) .. LUCRATIVE (Word 455).

8. C: This sentence asks you to find a pair of words that are logically connected. The key word "shy" will lead you to either "reticent" or "retiring" for the first blank. Shy and retiring behavior will logically lead you to a paucity or shortage of confirmed observations. The correct answer is therefore RETIRING (Word 562) .. PAUCITY (Word 414).

9. C: The key definitional phrase "free and open access" leads you to describe the Internet as a system that embodies UNFETTERED (Word 122) inquiry.

10. A: The key definitional phrase "overweening pride" leads you to conclude that the fable of Arachne centers on a human's HUBRIS (Word 150).

CHAPTER 21
SENTENCE COMPLETION PRACTICE EXERCISES— SETS I–XV

The Essential Guide to SAT Critical Reading and Vocabulary provides you with definitions and illustrations of 600 key words frequently tested on the SAT. These words will help you become a more articulate writer and speaker. *Essential* is more than just a vocabulary book. In order to achieve a high score on the SAT, it is not enough to simply learn vocabulary words. You must also know how to apply them to sentence completion questions.

This chapter gives you an opportunity to apply the vocabulary learned in this book to 170 practice sentence completion questions. The questions are arranged in practice sets of 10–15 questions that correspond with the vocabulary chapters. Each practice set is followed by a list of answers and explanations.

PRACTICE SET I: CHAPTER 1, THE TOP TWENTY WORDS

1. As she became increasingly reluctant to approach new people, Janet became ever more _____ to share her thoughts and feelings with others.
   (A) nostalgic
   (B) frank
   (C) impatient
   (D) resolved
   (E) reticent

2. Because Wari craftsmen created complex ceramic patterns that were very different from those produced by other Pre-Columbian Andean cultures, art historians have described the anonymous designers as _____ artists.
   (A) pragmatic
   (B) beguiling
   (C) ominous
   (D) anomalous
   (E) altruistic

3. There was a certain _____ quality to Anthony's actions that belied his forced attempt to be assertive.
   (A) succinct
   (B) diffident
   (C) peremptory
   (D) nostalgic
   (E) altruistic

4. The candidate's statements during the debate were so _____ that even her most critical opponents admitted that she demonstrated keen insight and good judgment on pressing national issues.
   (A) discerning
   (B) peremptory
   (C) ominous
   (D) conventional
   (E) aesthetic

5. The candidate's statements during the debate were so _____ that even her most ardent supporters criticized her for being overly cautious and willing to conform with established ideas.
   (A) conventional
   (B) prescient
   (C) discerning
   (D) subtle
   (E) frank

6. At the class reunion Avi was surprised to find his former friend serious and somber, the _____ of her formerly lighthearted and carefree self.
   (A) anomaly
   (B) artifact
   (C) reminiscence
   (D) bulwark
   (E) antithesis

7. The proposed redesign of the museum's famous Old Master galleries was lauded as both _____ and _____: it was tasteful and refined and yet functional and efficient.
   (A) altruistic .. pragmatic
   (B) aesthetic .. utilitarian
   (C) economical .. redundant
   (D) dubious .. innovative
   (E) discerning .. beguiling

8. The party leaders see themselves as realistic and _____, but their detractors describe them as _____ and unwilling to support compromise proposals.
   (A) patronizing .. condescending
   (B) peripheral .. marginal
   (C) peculiar .. idiosyncratic
   (D) contentious .. argumentative
   (E) pragmatic .. intransigent

9. Although in most of Rhea's blogs her allusions to controversial political issues are _____, in one of her recent postings, Rhea's criticism of venal officials is blunt and even scathing.

   (A) blatant
   (B) altruistic
   (C) subtle
   (D) undiscerning
   (E) indiscreet

10. The policies of the company's new board of directors were _____: they demonstrated great foresight by making provisions for new product development.

   (A) antithetical
   (B) aesthetic
   (C) prescient
   (D) convenitional
   (E) nastalogic

ANSWERS FOR PRACTICE SET I

1. E: The key definitional word "reluctant" leads you to describe Janet as being RETICENT (Word 10).

2. D: The key definitional phrase "very different" leads you to describe the Wari craftsmen as ANOMALOUS (Word 19).

3. B: The key word "belied" signals that you are looking for a word that contrasts with "assertive." The correct answer is therefore DIFFIDENT (Word 6).

4. A: The key definitional phrase "keen insight" leads you to describe the candidate as being DISCERNING (Word 17).

5. A: The key definitional phrase "overly cautious and willing to conform with established ideas" leads you to describe the candidate as being CONVENTIONAL (Word 2).

6. E: The key word "surprised" alerts you to look for a word that describes the sharp contrast between a friend who was formerly "lighthearted and carefree" and is now "serious and somber." The correct answer is therefore ANTITHESIS (Word 11).

7. B: The first blank must be filled with an answer that means "tasteful and refined," and the second blank must be filled with an answer that means "functional and efficient." The correct answer is therefore AESTHETIC (Word 1) .. UTILITARIAN.

8. E: The first blank must be filled with an answer that is consistent with "realistic." The second blank must be filled with an answer that is consistent with "unwilling to compromise." The correct answer is therefore PRAGMATIC (Word 4) .. INTRANSIGENT (Word 166).

9. C: The reversal word "although" signals that you are looking for an answer that contrasts with the key word "blatant." The correct answer is therefore SUBTLE (Word 9).

10. C: The key definitional phrase "demonstrated great foresight" leads you to realize that the board of directors were PRESCIENT (Word 12).

PRACTICE SET II: CHAPTERS 2–3, THE TOP TWENTY RHETORICAL DEVICE WORDS AND THE TOP TEN WORDS USED TO EVALUATE ARGUMENTS

1. Michael publicly advocates caution and self-control, but _____ enough, seems to admire most those people who achieve great success through bold risk-taking.
   (A) coherently
   (B) peremptorily
   (C) succinctly
   (D) ominously
   (E) ironically

2. Prehistoric cave paintings present contemporary art historians with _____: how is it that works of art hidden from view for over 12,000 years now fit naturally in the Western cultural tradition?
   (A) a euphemism
   (B) a eulogy
   (C) a paradox
   (D) an analogy
   (E) an allusion

3. Although Zoee was willing to _____ a small point about the issue, she was completely unwilling to acknowledge the overall logic of her opponent's argument.
   (A) lampoon
   (B) eulogize
   (C) conjecture
   (D) concede
   (E) postulate

4. The young child delighted his parents with a memorable _____ when he innocently exaggerated the value of his new toys by proudly announcing that they would give him "wealth, power, and great fame."
   (A) analogy
   (B) qualification
   (C) euphemism
   (D) hyperbole
   (E) refutation

5. Jenny's farewell speech was little more than a long _____, an attempt to disprove accusations she considered slanderous.
   (A) refutation
   (B) paradox
   (C) metaphor
   (D) eulogy
   (E) anecdote

6. For the late 17th-century English philosopher John Locke, the natural right of each person to life, liberty, and property was _____, an essential presupposition upon which he based his social contract theory of government.
   (A) an incongruity
   (B) a postulate
   (C) a rebuttal
   (D) an irony
   (E) an allusion

7. Although evidence is incomplete, modern art historians _____ that the low ceilings of many caves may have forced prehistoric artists to work in a supine position.
   (A) reciprocate
   (B) stipulate
   (C) amalgamate
   (D) connive
   (E) conjecture

8. Greek comic playwrights often
_____ philosophers;
in the play The Clouds, Aristophanes
_____ Socrates as the
owner of a "Think Shop."
   (A) lampooned .. satirized
   (B) glorified .. ridiculed
   (C) neglected .. eulogized
   (D) exonerated .. vilified
   (E) provoked .. appeased

9. An American in China by Shawn Roundy is
actually a series of _____;
these sketches recount the author's
experiences as he travelled across China
and Taiwan.
   (A) sagas
   (B) vignettes
   (C) euphemisms
   (D) understatements
   (E) allusions

10. Teachers commended Sahib for writing
_____ essay that
defended his thesis with a clear and
balanced progression of facts and logical
relationships.
   (A) a biased
   (B) a coherent
   (C) a euphemistic
   (D) a hyperbolic
   (E) an anomalous

ANSWERS FOR PRACTICE SET II

1. E: There is an IRONIC contradiction between what Michael advocates and what he actually admires. The correct answer is IRONY (Word 28).

2. C: Prehistoric cave paintings present contemporary art historians with a PARADOX, because the paintings are very old but seem very recent. The correct answer is PARADOX (Word 26).

3. D: It is important to note that Zoee is "willing" to accept a "small point" but "unwilling to acknowledge" her opponent's overall argument. This contrast indicates that Zoee is willing to CONCEDE a point. The correct answer is CONCEDE (Word 42).

4. D: The key definitional word "exaggerate" leads you to the correct answer, HYPERBOLE (Word 32).

5. A: The key definitional phrase "an attempt to disprove accusations" leads you to the correct answer, REFUTATION (Word 44).

6. B: The key definitional phrase "essential presupposition" leads you to the correct answer, POSTULATE (Word 41).

7. E: Since modern art historians are making a hypothesis from incomplete evidence, the correct answer is CONJECTURE (Word 50).

8. A: The question asks you to find a pair of words that are logically connected within the context of the passage. Only LAMPOON (Word 38) .. SATIRIZED (Word 35) meets this test.

9. B: The key definitional word "sketches" leads you to describe Roundy's book as a series of VIGNETTES (Word 22).

10. B: The key definitional phrase, "a clear and balanced progression of facts and logical relationships," leads you to describe Sahib's essay as COHERENT (Word 47).

PRACTICE SET III: CHAPTER 4, THE TOP THIRTY ATTITUDE, MOOD, AND TONE WORDS

Directions: Mark the answer for each of the following five sentence completion questions. Try to complete the entire set in 3.5 minutes. When you have finished, use the space provided to record how long you took to complete the set and how many questions you answered correctly.

1. Because the editors refused to take a position on controversial issues, their magazine acquired a reputation for being impartial and _____.
   (A) controversial
   (B) objective
   (C) whimsical
   (D) vehement
   (E) sardonic

2. Although the novel portrays suburban characters who share occasional _____ moments of carefree fun, the book's overall tone is one of disdain and at times _____ toward the oppressive conformity and excessive materialism that dominated American life in the 1950s.
   (A) lighthearted .. indignation
   (B) somber .. ambivalence
   (C) jovial .. wistfulness
   (D) earnest .. indifference
   (E) subtle .. pragmatism

3. Professor Singh's essays on pivotal presidential decisions are considered _____ and _____ because they are carefully researched, thoughtful, and impartial.
   (A) pompous .. objective
   (B) earnest .. biased
   (C) diffident .. peremptory
   (D) scholarly .. evenhanded
   (E) conversational .. hyperbolic

4. Ms. D'Costa cautions her children to be _____ watching horror movies; she believes that viewing them will give her young daughters nightmares.
   (A) wary of
   (B) exhilarated by
   (C) enthralled by
   (D) ambivalent about
   (E) nonchalant about

5. Always _____, Neeraj was deliberately cautious, but once he reached a conclusion he was a forceful and _____ spokesperson.
   (A) circumspect .. wavering
   (B) impetuous .. vehement
   (C) prudent .. emphatic
   (D) biased .. evenhanded
   (E) scholarly .. capricious

6. Labor leaders confidently predicted a short strike, but dubious reporters were _____ because management still refused to compromise on a key negotiating issue.
   (A) conversational
   (B) exuberant
   (C) nonchalant
   (D) skeptical
   (E) flippant

7. Although very entertaining, the YouTube training video was also very _____ because it provided an informative guide that clearly illustrated how to install a new scanner.
   (A) exorbitant
   (B) didactic
   (C) superficial
   (D) flippant
   (E) pompous

8. Prior to the Japanese attack on Pearl Harbor, Charles Lindbergh was an outspoken and at times even _____ supporter of a foreign policy based upon isolationism.
   (A) tepid
   (B) ambivalent
   (C) indifferent
   (D) evenhanded
   (E) vehement

9. The journalism teacher admonished her students to avoid writing _____ reviews that have a disrespectful and sharply critical tone.

(A) ambivalent
(B) caustic
(C) cryptic
(D) somber
(E) evasive

10. Although the movie critic's overall tone fell short of being truly _____, he did write a negative review that playfully mocked the director for using unrealistic special effects.

(A) ambivalent
(B) cryptic
(C) clandestine
(D) sanguine
(E) sardonic

ANSWERS FOR PRACTICE SET III

1. B: The key definitional word "impartial" and the key phrase "refused to take a position on controversial issues" lead you to describe the editors as being OBJECTIVE (Word 79).

2. A: The key definitional phrase "moments of carefree fun" will lead you to look for a positive first word. Both LIGHTHEARTED and JOVIAL meet this test. The key reversal word "although" and the key definitional word "disdain" signal that the second word will be negative. Only LIGHTHEARTED (Word 59) .. INDIGNATION (Word 61) meets these tests.

3. D: The key definitional phrase "carefully researched, thoughtful" supports SCHOLARLY and the key word "impartial" supports EVENHANDED. The correct answer is therefore SCHOLARLY (Word 58) .. EVENHANDED (Word 75).

4. A: The key definitional word "cautious" will lead you to WARY OF (Word 69) as the correct answer.

5. C: The key definitional phrase "deliberately cautious" will support either CIRCUMSPECT or PRUDENT for the first blank. The key reversal word "but" and the key definitional word "forceful" tell you to look for a second answer that is an antonym of your first answer. Only EMPHATIC meets this test. The correct answer is therefore PRUDENT (Word 76) .. EMPHATIC (Word 54).

6. D: The key definitional word "dubious" will lead you to describe the reporters as being SKEPTICAL (Word 64).

7. B: The key words "training" and "informative" will lead you to DIDACTIC (Word 53) to best describe the YouTube video.

8. E: The key word "outspoken" will lead you to describe Charles Lindbergh as a VEHEMENT (Word 67) supporter of isolationism.

9. B: The key definitional phrase "disrespectful and sharply critical" leads you to CAUSTIC (Word 68) as the correct answer.

10. E: The key phrase "a negative review that playfully mocked" leads you to SARDONIC (Word 62) as the correct answer.

PRACTICE SET IV: CHAPTER 5, THE TOP THIRTY PEOPLE

1. Jodi was not really _____ ; it was just that she enjoys complaining from time to time about people who aggravate her.
   (A) an interloper
   (B) an underdog
   (C) a misanthrope
   (D) a hedonist
   (E) a zealot

2. The novel Brave New World portrays a future society in which psychological manipulation and operant conditioning have been used to transform citizens into mere _____, preprogrammed humans who act in a robotic fashion.
   (A) automatons
   (B) demagogues
   (C) pundits
   (D) renegades
   (E) heretics

3. Because MC Sir Mix-a-Lot paved the way for later Pacific Northwest rappers such as Macklemore, he is considered _____ of that musical style.
   (A) a progenitor
   (B) a renegade
   (C) a neophyte
   (D) an underdog
   (E) an automaton

4. Although Nikita's blog has not received widespread recognition, her political essays have been recognized by knowledgeable _____, commentators who strive to offer their readers diverse opinions on controversial issues.
   (A) interlopers
   (B) hedonists
   (C) philanthropists
   (D) pundits
   (E) demagogues

5. Although he considered himself a valuable helper, Sal was actually an annoying _____ known for his inept work and botched jobs.
   (A) purist
   (B) bungler
   (C) polymath
   (D) heretic
   (E) sage

6. _____ believe that they have a duty to question and sometimes even attack cherished ideas and traditions.
   (A) benefactors
   (B) hedonists
   (C) demagogues
   (D) iconoclasts
   (E) progenitors

7. As he aged, Uncle Steven gained a well-deserved reputation for being an ill-tempered _____ who constantly grumbled about everything.
   (A) bungler
   (B) zealot
   (C) curmudgeon
   (D) progenitor
   (E) demagogue

8. Russell was keenly aware of how easily jealousy could transform the appreciation due to a generous _____ into an attitude of dislike and even outright _____.
   (A) philanthropist .. amity
   (B) benefactor .. enmity
   (C) mentor .. congeniality
   (D) misanthropist .. malevolence
   (E) nemesis .. antipathy

9. Kavin gained a reputation for being a _____ because he excelled in fields as diverse as mathematics, physics, chess, and history.
   (A) polymath
   (B) renegade
   (C) purist
   (D) bungler
   (E) curmudgeon

10. Like a true _____,
Claressa's seemingly frank and open demeanor was actually a disingenuous strategy to secure her partner's confidence.

 (A) heretic
 (B) misanthrope
 (C) neophyte
 (D) dilettante
 (E) charlatan

ANSWERS FOR PRACTICE SET IV

1. C: The key definitional phrase "complaining from time to time about people" signals that you should begin by looking for a negative person. Although Jodi is not a true MISANTHROPE, she does complain about people. The correct answer is therefore MINANTHROPE (Word 92).

2. A: The key definitional phrase "preprogrammed humans who act in a robotic fashion" leads you to AUTOMATONS (Word 107) as the correct answer.

3. A: The key definitional phrase "paved the way" leads you to describe Sir Mix-a-Lot as a PROGENITOR (Word 99).

4. D: The key definitional phrase "commentators who strive to offer their readers diverse opinions" leads you to PUNDITS (Word 97) as the correct answer.

5. B: The key definitional phrase "known for his inept work and botched jobs" leads you to BUNGLER (Word 110) as the correct answer.

6. D: The key definitional phrase "attack cherished ideas and traditions" leads you to ICONOCLASTS (Word 85) as the correct answer.

7. C: The key definitional words "ill-tempered" and "constantly grumbled" lead you to CURMUDGEON (Word 102) as the correct answer.

8. B: The key words "appreciation" and "generous" lead you to look for a positive first person. PHILANTHROPIST, BENEFACTOR, and MENTOR all meet this test. The key definitional phrase "attitude of dislike" leads you to look for a negative second word. Only BENEFACTOR (Word 87) .. ENMITY (Word 143) meets this test.

9. A: The key definitional phrase "excelled in fields as diverse as" leads you to describe Kavin as a POLYMATH (Word 103).

10. E: The key definitional phrase "seemingly frank and open demeanor" and the key word "disingenuous" lead you to CHARLATAN (Word 109) as the correct answer.

PRACTICE SET V: CHAPTER 6, THE TOP THIRTY WORDS WITH PREFIXES

1. The shoppers were visibly stunned by what they considered the _____ prices; everyone agreed that the new handbags and shoes were unreasonably expensive.
   (A) malicious
   (B) debased
   (C) unerring
   (D) unpretentious
   (E) exorbitant

2. Critics initially feared that the urban renewal project would have a _____ effect, replacing long-established tightly knit neighborhoods with impersonal high-rise apartments.
   (A) didactic
   (B) nostalgic
   (C) deleterious
   (D) indiscernible
   (E) subtle

3. Zack's controversial life-style attracted _____ criticism from pundits who failed to fully understand his motives for living in a remote commune that forbade cell phones and other communication devices.
   (A) objective
   (B) unwarranted
   (C) discerning
   (D) anomalous
   (E) indiscernable

4. The company's once _____ managers had to reevaluate their pessimistic forecasts when a sudden surge in sales prompted a more _____ outlook.
   (A) gloomy .. pessimistic
   (B) despondent .. sanguine
   (C) exuberant .. wistful
   (D) wary .. skeptical
   (E) pompous .. condescending

5. The entrepreneur had a well-deserved reputation for _____, having overcome a series of adversities that included a personal bankruptcy and a deep national recession.
   (A) despondency
   (B) reciprocation
   (C) resilience
   (D) succinctness
   (E) reticence

6. During the early 1800s a new wave of religious _____, called the Second Great Awakening, _____ church membership across the United States.
   (A) indifference .. rejuvenated
   (B) ambivalent .. exhilarated
   (C) subtlety .. unfettered
   (D) fervor .. revitalized
   (E) reverence .. repelled

7. The chief executive officer's _____ business tactics _____ board members who insisted that company policies and practices be a model of professional integrity.
   (A) unscrupulous .. troubled
   (B) unerring .. exasperated
   (C) unwarranted .. mollified
   (D) prescient .. unnerved
   (E) pragmatic .. incensed

8. Modest and unassuming, Chris is the model of an _____ person who carefully avoided the limelight.
   (A) unscrupulous
   (B) unsavory
   (C) undaunted
   (D) unpretentious
   (E) uncouth

9. Many contemporary theologians argue that people today are overwhelmed by a profound spiritual unease, _____ that is engendered by the social anxieties and uncertainties of modern life.

    (A) an exuberance
    (B) a lightheartedness
    (C) a whimsicality
    (D) a malaise
    (E) a redundancy

10. A model of _____ behavior, Carolyn ate and drank to excess.

    (A) intemperate
    (B) indifferent
    (C) indiscernible
    (D) insurmountable
    (E) infinite

ANSWERS FOR PRACTICE SET V

1. **E:** The key definitional phrase "unreasonably expensive" leads you to EXORBITANT (Word 116) as the correct answer.

2. **C:** The key phrase, "replacing long-established tightly knit neighborhoods with impersonal high-rise apartments," tells you to look for a negative answer that means "harmful." Only DELETERIOUS (Word 111) meets this test.

3. **B:** The key phrase "failed to fully understand his motives" leads you to conclude that the pundits' criticism was uncalled for and thus UNWARRANTED (Word 133).

4. **B:** The key phrase "pessimistic forecasts" tells you to look for a negative first word. GLOOMY, DESPONDENT, and WARY all meet this test. The key phrase "a sudden surge in sales" is good news that tells you to look for a positive second word. Only SANGUINE meets this test. The correct answer is therefore DESPONDENT (Word 113) .. SANGUINE (Word 51).

5. **C:** The key definitional phrase "having overcome adversities" leads you to RESILENCE (Word 118).

6. **D:** This question asks you to look for a pair of words that are logically related. For example, you can reject answer (A) since a wave of religious INDIFFERENCE would not REJUVENATE church membership. The correct answer is (D), since a wave of religious FERVOR (Word 56) would REVITALIZE (Word 120) church membership.

7. **A:** This question asks you to find a pair of answers that are logically connected. Also note that the answers must be negative words that would upset board members who "insist that company policies be a model of professional integrity." Only answer choice (A) meets these tests, since UNSCRUPULOUS (Word 129) business tactics would violate standards of professional integrity and thus TROUBLE the board members.

8. **D:** The key definitional phrase "modest and unassuming" leads you to UNPRETENTIOUS (Word 130) as the correct answer.

9. **D:** The key definitional phrase "profound spiritual unease" leads you to MALAISE (Word 139) as the correct answer.

10. **A:** The key definitional phrase "ate and drank to excess" leads you to describe Carolyn as INTEMPERATE (Word 138) as the correct answer.

PRACTICE SET VI: CHAPTER 7, THE TOP TWENTY WORDS WITH A HISTORY

1. Elizabeth Blackwell's career demonstrates her _____, her steadfast refusal to allow male doctors to deter her goal of becoming the first woman in the United States to earn a medical degree.
    (A) versatility
    (B) pomposity
    (C) inscrutability
    (D) indomitability
    (E) reciprocity

2. Although frequently used in the 1920s to describe fashionable men and women, the terms "sheik" and "sheba" are now considered _____ because they are out-of-date and no longer used.
    (A) derogatory
    (B) discerning
    (C) revealing
    (D) artful
    (E) antediluvian

3. Chloe's behavior was so _____ that it is was offensive to many: few people liked her because she was excessively _____.
    (A) narcissistic .. self-effacing
    (B) moribund .. exuberant
    (C) maudlin .. emotional
    (D) cavalier .. unpretentious
    (E) quixotic .. pragmatic

4. Because their previous supervisor had been especially _____ and understanding, the staff members were resentful of the _____ rules imposed by the new director.
    (A) dictatorial .. unwarranted
    (B) lenient .. draconian
    (C) rigid .. cavalier
    (D) jovial .. didactic
    (E) irritable .. trivial

5. Prone to being excessively self-absorbed, Marvin displayed the chief characteristics of a _____ personality.
    (A) narcissistic
    (B) moribund
    (C) quixotic
    (D) laconic
    (E) mercurial

6. As a college professor at Princeton, Woodrow Wilson gained a well-deserved reputation for _____: his carefully researched lectures demonstrated unrivalled knowledge and scholarship.
    (A) erudition
    (B) narcissism
    (C) sophistry
    (D) hubris
    (E) unscrupulousness

7. A model of _____ conversation, President Coolidge was renowned for his _____ statements.
    (A) voluble .. terse
    (B) duplicitous .. forthright
    (C) prescient .. myopic
    (D) jovial .. somber
    (E) laconic .. succinct

8. Tana's behavior was so _____ that it offended many of her colleagues: few people liked her because she was extremely haughty and overbearing.
    (A) erudite
    (B) urbane
    (C) exuberant
    (D) cavalier
    (E) earnest

9. The popular historian Will Durant once said that a large number of factors led him to write his acclaimed Story of Civilization; that is, the causes were _____.
    (A) exorbitant
    (B) didactic
    (C) myriad
    (D) anecdotal
    (E) redundant

10. Once a very lucrative business, the candy shop was now _____ and on the verge of bankruptcy as more and more of its customers switched to healthy food choices.

    (A) protean
    (B) prolific
    (C) voluptuous
    (D) nefarious
    (E) moribund

ANSWERS FOR PRACTICE SET VI

1. D: The key definitional phrase "steadfast refusal to allow doctors to deter" leads you to choose INDOMITABILITY (Word 153) as the best word to describe Blackwell's career.

2. E: The key phrase "out-of-date and no longer used" leads you to ANTEDILUVIAN (Word 152) as the correct answer.

3. C: The key phrase "offensive to many" signals that you should look for a pair of related negative words that describe an "excessive" behavior. Only choice (C) MAUDLIN (Word 159) .. EMOTIONAL meets this test.

4. B: The key word "understanding" indicates that you should look for a related positive first word. Both LENIENT and JOVIAL meet this test. The key words "resentful" and "rules imposed" indicate that you should look for a negative second word that contrasts with your first word. Only LENIENT .. DRACONIAN (Word 155) meets these criteria.

5. A: The key definitional phrase "excessively self-absorbed" leads you to NARCISSISTIC (Word 142) as the correct answer.

6. A: The key definitional phrases "carefully researched lectures" and "unrivalled knowledge and scholarship" lead you to ERUDITION (Word 160).

7. E: This sentence asks you to find two words that form a logical definition. Only LACONIC (Word 147) .. SUCCINCT (Word 16) meets this test.

8. D: The key definitional phrase "extremely haughty and overbearing" leads you to describe Tana as CAVALIER (Word 151).

9. C: The key definitional phrase "a large number of factors" leads you to MYRIAD (Word 141).

10. E: The key phrases "once a very lucrative business" and "on the verge of bankruptcy" tell you that the candy shop is rapidly approaching its demise. The candy shop is therefore MORIBUND (Word 143).

PRACTICE SET VII: CHAPTERS 8–9, THE TOP TWENTY SYNONYM PAIRS AND THE TOP TEN ANTONYM PAIRS

1. The divisive bill ignited a _____ national debate that inflamed _____ passions on all sides of the issue.
   (A) measured .. fervent
   (B) subdued .. histrionic
   (C) tendentious .. partisan
   (D) contentious .. innocuous
   (E) indifferent .. indignant

2. Paradoxically, this successful and popular politician is publicly egalitarian and privately surprisingly _____.
   (A) compassionate
   (B) savvy
   (C) elitist
   (D) theoretical
   (E) droll

3. The Slovak Republic was formed by negotiation and compromise, not by conquest and _____.
   (A) coercion
   (B) conciliation
   (C) irreverent
   (D) histrionics
   (E) platitudes

4. Although segregationists repeatedly tried to _____ his progress, Jackie Robinson overcame their racially imposed obstacles and in 1947 succeeded in becoming the first African American to break Major League Baseball's color barrier.
   (A) exhort
   (B) foster
   (C) underscore
   (D) revitalize
   (E) thwart

5. The child is given to emotional excesses: she can be disturbingly agitated one moment and completely _____ the next.
   (A) adamant
   (B) irreverent
   (C) histrionic
   (D) unflappable
   (E) theoretical

6. Picasso's _____ drawing manifest itself at an early age: when he was just two years old, Picasso preferred drawing to writing and even talking.
   (A) aversion to
   (B) predilection for
   (C) listlessness for
   (D) indifference toward
   (E) ineptitude at

7. Richard's _____ attitude, demonstrated in his constant refusal to follow instructions, made him a source of _____ for his coaches.
   (A) intransigent .. inspiration
   (B) pliant .. irritation
   (C) reflective .. rumination
   (D) jovial .. annoyance
   (E) recalcitrant .. exasperation

8. Brandon was _____ and even merciless person; he had none of his sister's _____.
   (A) a vindictive .. spite
   (B) a ruthless .. compassion
   (C) a cavalier .. haughtiness
   (D) an urbane .. sophistication
   (E) an imperturbable .. equanimity

9. Despite their attempt to maintain the appearance of _____, Ethan and Olivia could barely suppress the underlying _____ that divided them.
   (A) affability .. esteem
   (B) reconciliation .. forgiveness
   (C) collegiality .. enmity
   (D) melancholy .. conviviality
   (E) discretion .. civility

10. A model of _____ behavior, Rohan generously forgave former opponents who had insulted him.
   (A) irreverent
   (B) overwrought
   (C) magnanimous
   (D) esoteric
   (E) intransigent

ANSWERS FOR PRACTICE SET VII

1. C: The key word "divisive" tells you that the first word will either be TENDENTIOUS or CONTENTIOUS. Since the debate "inflamed passions," there must be a cause-and-effect relationship between the correct answers. You can eliminate (D) since a CONTENTIOUS debate would not lead to INNOCUOUS or harmless passions. Only (C) TENDENTIOUS (Word 171) .. PARTISAN (Word 172) establishes a logical cause-and-effect relationship.

2. C: The reversal word PARADOXICALLY signals that you should look for an answer that is the opposite of the key word EGALITARIAN. The correct answer is therefore ELITIST (Word 213).

3. A: The key reversal word "not" signals that you should look for an answer that is the opposite of the key words "negotiation" and "compromise." The correct answer is therefore COERCION (Word 210).

4. E: The key phrase "racially imposed obstacles" signals that THWART (Word 199) is the correct answer.

5. D: The key phrase "emotional excesses" signals that you should look for an answer that is the opposite of "disturbingly agitated." The correct answer is therefore UNFLAPPABLE (Word 192).

6. B: The key word "preferred" leads you to the correct answer PREDILECTION (Word 196).

7. E: The key definitional phrase "constant refusal to follow instructions" leads you to either INTRANSIGENT or RECALCITRANT for the first blank. The second blank must be filled by a word that is a logical consequence of being either INTRANSIGENT or RECALCITRANT. The correct answer is therefore RECALCITRANT (Word 166) .. EXASPERATION (Word 467).

8. B: The key definitional phrase "merciless person" leads to VINDICTIVE, RUTHLESS, or even CAVALIER for the first blank. The reversal phrase "he had none of his sister's" indicates that that the second blank requires a word that is the opposite trait of the first blank. The correct answer is therefore RUTHLESS (Word 207) .. COMPASSION.

9. C: The key phrase "despite their attempt" signals that you should look for a pair of antonyms. The key definitional phrase "that divided them" signals that the second word must be negative. Only answer choice (C) COLLEGIALITY .. ENMITY (Word 163) meets these tests.

10. C: The key definitional phrase "generously forgave" leads you to MAGNANIMOUS (Word 201) as the correct answer.

PRACTICE SET VIII: CHAPTER 10, THE TOP 110 LEVEL 5 WORDS (#221–270)

1. The Kenroku-en Garden in Japan leaves an _____ impression on visitors, so that once seen it is impossible to forget.
   (A) ambivalent
   (B) indelible
   (C) innocuous
   (D) insipid
   (E) ephemeral

2. Certain people alternate between opposing moods; either they are _____ or they are _____.
   (A) magnanimous .. munificent
   (B) diffident .. self-effacing
   (C) petulant .. capricious
   (D) taciturn .. aloof
   (E) frank .. disingenuous

3. Advertisements for the popular candidate for governor have become _____, so prevalent are they on billboards and posters throughout the state.
   (A) enigmatic
   (B) anomalous
   (C) metaphorical
   (D) ubiquitous
   (E) pernicious

4. Juhee criticized the recently announced government edict as _____, just another failure of politicians to use foresight to identify future trends.
   (A) cryptic
   (B) redundant
   (C) discerning
   (D) acerbic
   (E) myopic

5. At the science museum we observed a group of tourists who were being led by a _____ tour guide who made little effort to _____ the visitors.
   (A) charismatic .. enlighten
   (B) draconian .. control
   (C) belligerent .. antagonize
   (D) soporific .. edify
   (E) loquacious .. engage

6. The defense lawyer was admired for her _____; she always conducted herself with great personal and professional integrity.
   (A) verbosity
   (B) diffidence
   (C) symbolism
   (D) rectitude
   (E) profligacy

7. Paleontologists believe that a huge meteor struck the Yucatan Peninsula 65 million years ago, producing a _____ cloud of dust and ash that lowered global temperatures and triggered the mass extinction of dinosaurs and other animals.
   (A) redundant
   (B) infinitesimal
   (C) tenuous
   (D) ravenous
   (E) prodigious

8. Misplacing a high school student's prom dress mortified Wendi, and then forgetting to remove a conspicuous stain only increased her _____.
   (A) exultation
   (B) chagrin
   (C) credibility
   (D) ubiquity
   (E) aplomb

9. Moving west to start a new life is _____ part of the American experience that remains solidly established, even though parts of California and other western states have become overcrowded.
   (A) a vacillating
   (B) a fleeting
   (C) a pernicious
   (D) an inconsequential
   (E) an entrenched

10. The writer is a sarcastic and often _____ writer who makes telling points by gleefully _____ human follies.
   (A) subtle .. personifying
   (B) acerbic .. satirizing
   (C) altruistic .. eulogizing
   (D) officious .. underscoring
   (E) lugubrious .. elucidating

11. Pope Leo X grew increasingly _____ during the debates about Martin Luther's criticism of the Church; the papal advisors had never seen the pontiff so irate.
   (A) apopleptic
   (B) soporific
   (C) ethereal
   (D) disingenuous
   (E) licentious

12. Because Jefferson's opening lines in the Declaration of Independence are not narrowly focused on _____ political disputes, they seem as influential and _____ today as they did over two hundred years ago.
   (A) ephemeral .. enduring
   (B) universal .. momentary
   (C) ubiquitous .. venal
   (D) entrenched .. irrelevant
   (E) anachronistic .. transient

13. Because Napoleon was such a powerful and _____ ruler, his defeat at the Battle of Waterloo was _____, marking a momentous change of course from an age of democratic revolutions to a period of conservative restoration.
   (A) marginal .. an amalgam
   (B) charismatic .. a triviality
   (C) crucial .. an anomaly
   (D) pivotal .. a watershed
   (E) lugubrious .. an anachronism

14. Postmodern architect Michael Graves successfully _____ traditional and modernist elements thereby combining features from a variety of styles.
   (A) aggrandizes
   (B) habituates
   (C) amalgamates
   (D) disassociates
   (E) marginalizes

15. Paradoxically, the personnel manager was both _____ and _____: she uncritically accepted each job applicant's personal anecdotes but often expressed doubts about a candidate's ability to perform key tasks.
   (A) credulous .. skeptical
   (B) discerning .. perspicacious
   (C) reverent .. irreverent
   (D) theoretical .. empirical
   (E) merciless .. ruthless

ANSWERS FOR PRACTICE SET VIII

1. B: The key definitional phrase "impossible to forget" leads you to INDELIBLE (Word 253) as the correct answer.

2. E: The key phrase "alternate between opposing moods" signals that the answer will be a pair of antonyms. Only FRANK (Word 7) .. DISINGENUOUS (Word 252) meets this test.

3. D: The key definitional word "prevalent" leads you to UBIQUITOUS (Word 237) as the correct answer.

4. E: The key definitional phrase "failure of politicians to use foresight" leads you to MYOPIC (Word 244) as the correct answer.

5. D: The question asks you to find two words that are logically connected. The key phrase "little effort" tells you that the second word will have a negative relationship with the first word. Only choice (D) SOPORIFIC (Word 241) .. EDIFY (Word 246) meets these tests, since a SOPORIFIC tour guide would not EDIFY the visitors.

6. D: The key definitional phrase "great personal and professional integrity" leads you to RECTITUDE (Word 239) as the correct answer.

7. E: Since the cloud of dust and ash "lowered global temperatures and triggered the mass extinction of dinosaurs and other animals," it must have been very large. This facts leads you to PRODIGIOUS (Word 242) as the correct answer.

8. B: The key definitional word "mortified" leads you to CHAGRIN (Word 269) as the correct answer.

9. E: The key definitional phrase "remains solidly established" leads you to ENTRENCHED (Word 259) as the correct answer.

10. B: The first word should be consistent with the key word "sarcastic." The second work should be consistent with "gleefully" portraying "human follies." Only ACERBIC (Word 247) .. SATIRIZING (Word 38) meets these two tests.

11. A: The key definitional phrase "so irate" leads you to describe Pope Leo X as APOPLECTIC (Word 245).

12. A: Since Thomas Jefferson's opening lines are "not narrowly focused" and still seem "influential," you should look for a pair of logically related antonyms. Both answer choices (A) and (B) meet this test. However, you can eliminate (B) since UNIVERSAL does not mean "narrowly focused." The correct answer is therefore EPHEMERAL (Word 250) .. ENDURING.

13. D: The first word must be consistent with the key word "powerful," and the second word must be consistent with the key definitional phrase "a momentous change of course." Only choice (D) PIVOTAL .. WATERSHED (Word 236) meets these tests.

14. C: The key definitional phrase "combining features" leads you to AMALGAMATES (Word 258).

15. A: The key reversal word "PARADOXICALLY" signals that you should look for a pair of antonyms. The key definitional phrases "uncritically accepted" and "expressed doubt" lead you to CREDULOUS (Word 224) .. SKEPTICAL (Word 64).

PRACTICE SET IX: CHAPTER 10, THE TOP 110 LEVEL 5 WORDS (#271–330)

1. Confused readers originally found James Joyce's novel *Ulysses* _____ because it included seemingly incomprehensible stream-of-conscious narratives and an array of obscure literary allusions.
   - (A) foreboding
   - (B) inscrutable
   - (C) implacable
   - (D) truncated
   - (E) unambiguous

2. In sharp contrast to the original insights revealed in his _____ essay on the rise and fall of empires, Nelson's second book repeated _____ that could be found in any introductory history textbook.
   - (A) craven .. conundrums
   - (B) officious .. analogies
   - (C) seminal .. platitudes
   - (D) inscrutable .. banalities
   - (E) conventional .. juxtapositions

3. The climatologist's report is truly _____: it predicts that a confluence of factors, including rising global temperatures and melting polar ice caps, _____ an alarming rise in sea levels that will threaten many coastal cities.
   - (A) fortuitous .. stymies
   - (B) discerning .. thwarts
   - (C) flippant .. heralds
   - (D) ominous .. portends
   - (E) lighthearted .. underscores

4. Like a true _____, Kevin was _____ enemy whose hatred could not be appeased.
   - (A) scourge .. a conciliatory
   - (B) charlatan .. a volatile
   - (C) nemesis .. an implacable
   - (D) renegade .. an officious
   - (E) mentor .. an urbane

5. Zubyn was a woman of surprising contrasts: she was reserved and even _____ at work and talkative and even _____ at home.
   - (A) refractory .. unruly
   - (B) taciturn .. voluble
   - (C) phlegmatic .. lethargic
   - (D) puerile .. callow
   - (E) enervated .. indefatigable

6. Henry Kissinger's detailed analysis of the negotiations that ended the Vietnam War is not _____ reading, but a student who carefully studies the book will be rewarded with many valuable insights.
   - (A) scholarly
   - (B) cursory
   - (C) profound
   - (D) painstaking
   - (E) edifying

7. Although critics attempted to _____ the mayor's credibility by assailing him with false accusations, he emerged from the ordeal with his reputation intact.
   - (A) juxtapose
   - (B) ruminate
   - (C) crystallize
   - (D) propitiate
   - (E) impugn

8. Although we understood that Henry was still young, immature, and impressionable, we were nevertheless surprised and dismayed by his continued _____ behavior.
   - (A) puerile
   - (B) insatiable
   - (C) indefatigable
   - (D) effusive
   - (E) urbane

9. Derek was considered
_____ because he loved
to show off his command of obscure
knowledge and _____
because he loved to provoke heated
arguments.
   (A) taciturn .. acerbic
   (B) pedantic .. contentious
   (C) scholarly .. affable
   (D) officious .. facetious
   (E) didactic .. punctilious

10. A full day of classes, fencing practice, and
homework assignments drained Vikram's
vitality: he felt too _____
to do anything but go to sleep.
   (A) crystallized
   (B) enervated
   (C) galvanized
   (D) truncated
   (E) extemporized

11. The accountant habitually engaged in
_____ filing practices by
not sending out her clients' tax reports
until the last possible day.
   (A) indefatigable
   (B) perfidious
   (C) dilatory
   (D) belligerent
   (E) bohemian

12. Professor Shah pointed out that the
Federalists, Whigs, and Populists are all
_____ political parties that
lost popular support and vanished during
the 19th century.
   (A) moribund
   (B) redundant
   (C) pedantic
   (D) defunct
   (E) punctilious

13. String theory has created a deep
_____ within the scientific
community by dividing theoretical
physicists into proponents who hail the
controversial theory's potential and
_____ who believe it is an
abject failure.
   (A) dialogue .. detractors
   (B) setback .. dilettantes
   (C) impasse .. enthusiasts
   (D) schism .. detractors
   (E) reconciliation .. partisans

14. The diplomatic envoys for the
Hapsburg dynasty were known for
being _____; they were
treacherous and deceitful even during
routine negotiations.
   (A) perfidious
   (B) candid
   (C) perfunctory
   (D) affable
   (E) phlegmatic

15. The report was _____
about the future of the faltering economy,
concluding pessimistically that conditions
would _____ within weeks.
   (A) disingenuous .. revive
   (B) reassuring .. rebound
   (C) unambiguous .. rally
   (D) sanguine .. decline
   (E) foreboding .. deteriorate

ANSWERS FOR PRACTICE SET IX

1. B: The key words "incomprehensible" and "obscure" lead you to INSCRUTABLE (Word 308) as the correct answer.

2. C: The reversal phrase "in sharp contrast" alerts you to look for a pair of contrasting words. The key definitional phrase "original insights" leads you to SEMINAL (Word 277) as the answer for the first blank. The key phrase "found in any introductory history textbook" leads you to PLATITUDES (Word 187) for the second blank.

3. D: The key words "alarming" and "threaten" signal that the report will be very negative and that it will issue a warning. Only answer (D) OMINOUS (Word 15) .. PORTENDS (Word 307) satisfies these conditions.

4. C: The key definitional phrase "enemy whose hatred could not be appeased" leads you to describe Kevin as a NEMESIS (Word 104). Since an IMPLACABLE (Word 297) hatred is a characteristic of a NEMESIS, the correct answer is (C) NEMESIS .. IMPLACABLE.

5. B: The key reversal phrase "surprising contrasts" tells you to look for a pair of opposites. The key definitional word "reserved" leads you to TACITURN of the first blank. The key definitional word "talkative" leads you to VOLUBLE for the second blank. The correct answer is therefore TACITURN (Word 304) .. VOLUBLE (Word 330).

6. B: The combination of the key reversal word "not" and the key definitional phrase "carefully studies" signals that you should look for an answer that does NOT describe a careful reader. The correct answer is therefore CURSORY (Word 301). Note that answer choices (A), (C), (D), and (E) can be eliminated, since Kissinger's analysis is SCHOLARLY, PROFOUND, PAINSTAKING, and EDIFYING.

7. E: The key definitional phrase "assailing him with false accusations" leads you to IMPUGN (Word 298).

8. A: The key definitional phrase "young, immature, and impressionable" lead you to PUERILE (Word 310).

9. B: The key definitional phrase "loved to show off his command of obscure knowledge" will lead you to PEDANTIC, SCHOLARLY, or even DIDACTIC. The key definitional phrase "loved to provoke heated arguments" leads you to CONTENTIOUS. The correct answer is therefore PEDANTIC (Word 315) .. CONTENTIOUS (Word 278).

10. B: The key definitional phrase "drained Vikram's vitality" leads you to ENERVATED (Word 291).

11. C: The accountant's habit of waiting to file tax reports "until the last possible day" leads you to describe her as DILATORY (Word 288).

12. D: The key definitional word "vanished" tells you that all three political parties are dead or DEFUNCT (Word 322). Although MORIBUND (Word 143) is a tempting choice, it is incorrect. It is important to remember that MORIBUND means "approaching death."

13. D: The key word "dividing" signals that the first word will describe a split or disagreement. Possible answers include SETBACK, IMPASSE, and SCHISM. The second word will be an antonym of "proponents," since this group believes that string theory has been "an abject failure." Only answer (D) SCHISM (Word 323) .. DETRACTORS meets this test.

14. A: The key definitional words "treacherous and deceitful" lead you to describe the Hapsburg envoys as PERFIDIOUS (Word 300).

15. E: The word "pessimistically" leads you to look for a pair of negative words to describe both the report and its conclusion. Only choice (E) FOREBODING (Word 312) .. DETERIORATE meets this test.

PRACTICE SET X: CHAPTER 11, THE TOP 110 LEVEL 4 WORDS (#331–380)

1. During the last few years many ambitious entrepreneurs have _____ working for established companies, preferring instead to create their own start-up businesses.
(A) embraced
(B) reaffirmed
(C) eschewed
(D) festered
(E) vindicated

2. Some mistook Matthew's _____ for arrogance because he was exceptionally talented; they assumed he was _____.
(A) precocity .. cavalier
(B) reticence .. aloof
(C) churlishness .. vindictive
(D) conviviality .. frivolous
(E) mendacity .. flippant

3. The tutor's comments on Morgan's practice essay were both _____ and _____: they lacked depth and were purely routine.
(A) evocative .. fortuitious
(B) superficial .. perfunctory
(C) earnest .. prescient
(D) profound .. cursory
(E) desultory .. meticulous

4. Baz Luhrmann's film The Great Gatsby is a powerful _____: it calls forth the extravagant sights and sounds that made the Roaring Twenties such a memorable decade.
(A) demarcation
(B) exhortation
(C) compunction
(D) evocation
(E) vindication

5. Saying that all the leading economic indicators were favorable, Varun announced that it was _____ time to launch his new Internet company.
(A) an enigmatic
(B) a perfunctory
(C) a quiescent
(D) an auspicious
(E) an arduous

6. After a long _____ day of intensive studying for a series of difficult exams, Vivian felt completely _____ and just wanted to get some well-deserved rest.
(A) acrimonious .. indefatigable
(B) benign .. indomitable
(C) futile .. exhilarated
(D) arduous .. enervated
(E) effortless .. galvanized

7. Historians praise the settlement house movement for successfully using English and vocational classes to _____ the condition of the urban poor in late 19th-century America.
(A) ameliorate
(B) bemoan
(C) stigmatize
(D) reaffirm
(E) evoke

8. Alexander Fleming's discovery of penicillin was _____; he was actually investigating the properties of staphylococci at the time.
(A) clandestine
(B) premeditated
(C) tenuous
(D) inadvertent
(E) lighthearted

9. Negotiations between the two nations soon became so _____ that reaching any agreement was inconceivable: they had reached _____.
(A) fortuitous .. a conundrum
(B) rampant .. an edict
(C) rancorous .. a resolution
(D) amicable .. a conjecture
(E) acrimonious .. an impasse

10. The renowned science fiction writer had a well-deserved reputation for creating _____ characters whose puzzling actions were shrouded in mystery.

(A) execrable
(B) condescending
(C) enigmatic
(D) blithe
(E) caustic

11. Both _____ and _____, the tour guide's descriptions of the royal family and their historic place were long, boring, and surprisingly shallow.

(A) tedious .. superficial
(B) realistic .. reassuring
(C) provocative .. profound
(D) indispensible .. suerfluous
(E) monotonous .. euphemistic

12. Gertrude Stein helped _____ the development of early 20th-century avant-garde artists by promoting, displaying, and purchasing their works.

(A) stigmatize
(B) eschew
(C) foster
(D) circumscribe
(E) confound

13. Although cats are as _____ as many other animals, some people think of them as solitary creatures.

(A) reclusive
(B) multifarious
(C) sedentary
(D) malevolent
(E) gregarious

14. Novelist David Fan is well known for creating profoundly moving characters who experience _____, unexpected moments of sudden inspiration, that help them overcome tragic situations.

(A) demarcations
(B) epiphanies
(C) reaffirmations
(D) litanies
(E) debacles

15. Cedric was bewildered by the unexpected turn of events, so _____ that he did not know what to think, say, or do.

(A) consoled
(B) habituated
(C) confounded
(D) mollified
(E) exhilarated

ANSWERS FOR PRACTICE SET X

1. C: The key phrase "preferring instead" leads you to ESCHEW (Word 356), because ambitious entrepreneurs prefer to avoid or forgo established companies.

2. A: The key definitional phrase "exceptionally talented" leads you to PRECOCITY, and the key definitional word "arrogance" leads you to CAVALIER. The correct answer is therefore PRECOCITY (Word 335) .. CAVALIER (Word 151).

3. B: The key definitional phrase "they lacked depth and were purely routine" leads you to SUPERFICAL (Word 334) .. PERFUNCTORY (Word 348) as the correct answer.

4. D: The key definitional phrase "calls forth the extravagant sights and sounds" leads you to EVOCATION (Word 332) as the correct answer.

5. D: The key definitional word "favorable" leads you to AUSPICIOUS (Word 331) as the correct answer.

6. D: This sentence asks you to find a logical cause-and-effect relationship between the two correct answers. For example, a FUTILE day would not lead Vivian to feel EXHILARATED. The correct answer is ARDUOUS (Word 355) .. ENERVATE (Word 291) because a long ARDUOUS day would lead Vivian to feel ENERVATED and ready for some "well-deserved rest."

7. A: The key word "praise" signals that you should look for a positive word to describe the impact of the settlement house movement on the urban poor. Only AMELIORATE (Word 342) meets this test.

8. D: Alexander Fleming's discovery is best described as INADVERTENT (Word 347) because he was actually investigating the properties of something else when he accidentally discovered penicillin.

9. E: The key phrase "reaching any agreement was inconceivable" tells you to look for a negative first word. Both (C) RANCOROUS and (E) ACRIMONIOUS meet this test. The key phrase "agreement was inconceivable" eliminates RESOLUTION in choice (C) and leads you to choice (E) AN IMPASSE. The correct answer is therefore ACRIMONIOUS (Word 376) .. IMPASSE (Word 354).

10. C: The key definitional phrase "puzzling actions were shrouded in mystery" leads you to ENIGMATIC (Word 333) as the correct answer.

11. A: The key definitional phrase "long, boring, and surprisingly shallow" leads you to TEDIOUS (Word 32) .. SUPERFICIAL (Word 334) as the correct answer.

12. C: The key definitional phrase "promoting, displaying, and purchasing" indicates that Gertrude Stein's actions were very positive. This leads you to FOSTER (Word 364) as the correct answer.

13. E: The key reversal word "although" signals that you should look for an answer that is the opposite of the key word "solitary." The correct answer is therefore GREGARIOUS (Word 353).

14. B: The key definitional phrase "unexpected moments of sudden inspiration" leads you to EPIPHANIES (Word 379) as the correct answer.

15. C: The key definitional word "bewildered" and the key phrase "did not know what to think, say, or do" lead you to CONFOUNDED (Word 372) as the correct answer.

PRACTICE SET XI: CHAPTER 11, THE TOP 110 LEVEL 4 WORDS (#381–440)

1. Dismayed coaches reprimanded Jonah for _____ decisions that _____ his leadership by casting doubts on his ability to act with careful forethought.
   - (A) egregious .. enhanced
   - (B) impulsive .. discredited
   - (C) audacious .. underscored
   - (D) prudent .. undermined
   - (E) capricious .. vindicated

2. The new personnel officer vowed to eliminate the insensitive, outrageous, and at times _____ violations of basic rules of courtesy that plagued his predecessor's administration.
   - (A) vivacious
   - (B) fastidious
   - (C) onerous
   - (D) egregious
   - (E) anthropomorphic

3. The autocratic government enforced repressive policies that became so repulsive that dissidents demanded that the detestable officials be promptly removed for their _____ actions.
   - (A) execrable
   - (B) shrewd
   - (C) impulsive
   - (D) insipid
   - (E) assiduous

4. The College Board insists that its procedures for grading AP essays are very _____; readers must follow detailed procedures that are very strict.
   - (A) rancorous
   - (B) skewed
   - (C) enthralling
   - (D) untenable
   - (E) stringent

5. Never_____, Ankit treated everyone he knew with respect and consideration.
   - (A) tactless
   - (B) onerous
   - (C) visceral
   - (D) discreet
   - (E) drab

6. Charita's tweets are _____ to _____, because they have a tendency to be unclear and open to more than one interpretation.
   - (A) disposed .. frankness
   - (B) disinclined .. altruism
   - (C) prone .. ambiguity
   - (D) susceptible .. rancor
   - (E) opposed .. notoriety

7. The controversial positions taken by the third-party candidate were both _____ and _____: they were unnecessary and indefensible.
   - (A) superfluous .. untenable
   - (B) indispensable .. unorthodox
   - (C) redundant .. sustainable
   - (D) egregious .. execrable
   - (E) vital .. discredited

8. Emily was a remarkably _____ commodities trader: she impressed her clients with her quick thinking, clever calculations, and astute judgment.
   - (A) impulsive
   - (B) snide
   - (C) tactless
   - (D) distraught
   - (E) shrewd

9. Junko Tabei, the world's first woman to reach the summit of Mount Everest, was considered _____ because she boldly chose a risky, little-used path to the summit.
   - (A) opaque
   - (B) overbearing
   - (C) perfunctory
   - (D) audacious
   - (E) dilatory

10. Opened in 1872, Yellowstone National Park established a model of park design that other impressed nations rushed to _____.

    (A) discredit
    (B) eschew
    (C) emulate
    (D) undermine
    (E) admonish

11. Paradoxically, the governor was both _____ and _____: she was publicly full of charm and personal magnetism and privately uninteresting and bland.

    (A) pedestrian .. banal
    (B) elitist .. supercilious
    (C) charismatic .. insipid
    (D) enchanting .. enthralling
    (E) snide .. sardonic

12. Although alarmed ornithologists reported a _____ of bald eagles in the contiguous United States in the 1950s, they now optimistically report that populations are beginning to _____, due to the banning of DDT and other strict protective measures.

    (A) dearth .. proliferate
    (B) paucity .. shrink
    (C) profusion .. expand
    (D) plethora .. migrate
    (E) scarcity .. regress

13. In the years following Richard Nixon's resignation, public response to his presidency has oscillated between _____ for his bold role in promoting better relations with China and _____ for his covert role in trying to cover up the Watergate scandal.

    (A) indifference .. apathy
    (B) condemnation .. abhorrence
    (C) plaudits .. acclamation
    (D) acclaim .. disdain
    (E) indignation .. antipathy

14. The YouTube video was both _____ and _____: although instructional, it was surprisingly touching.

    (A) exorbitant .. frugal
    (B) superficial .. lugubrious
    (C) didactic .. poignant
    (D) empirical .. pragmatic
    (E) erudite .. inane

15. Because Myra had always been shy and even _____, her _____ attitude during the college admissions interview came as a complete and unpleasant surprise.

    (A) audacious .. timid
    (B) fastidious .. exacting
    (C) aloof .. detached
    (D) diffident .. overbearing
    (E) vivacious .. lighthearted

ANSWERS FOR PRACTICE SET XI

1. B: The key words "dismayed" and "reprimanded" tell you to look for a negative word to describe Jonah's decisions. EGREGIOUS, IMPULSIVE, CAPRICIOUS, and even AUDACIOUS are all possible answers. Jonah's poor decisions had a negative effect on his leadership. Only answer choice (B) provides you with two negative answers that fit the sentence. The correct answer is therefore IMPULSIVE (Word 384) .. DISCREDITED (Word 406).

2. D: The key words "insensitive" and "outrageous" lead you to describe the previous administrator's behavior as EGREGIOUS, because it violated "basic rules of courtesy". The correct answer is therefore EGREGIOUS (Word 427).

3. A: The key words "repulsive" and "detestable" lead you to describe the actions of the autocratic officials as EXECRABLE (Word 394).

4. E: The key phrase "detailed procedures that are very strict" leads you to STRINGENT (Word 421) as the correct answer.

5. A: The key reversal word "never" signals that you should look for an answer that has the opposite meaning of treating everyone "with respect and consideration." The correct answer is therefore TACTLESS (Word 399).

6. C: The best strategy for this question is to begin with the second blank. The key definitional phrase "unclear and open to more than one interpretation" leads you to AMBIGUITY. The correct answer is therefore PRONE (Word 417) .. AMBIGUITY (Word 381).

7. A: The key definitional word "unnecessary" leads you to either SUPERFLUOUS or REDUNDANT. The key definitional word "indefensible" leads you to UNTENABLE. The correct answer is therefore SUPERFLUOUS (Word 415) .. UNTENABLE (Word 416).

8. E: The key definitional phrase "quick thinking, clever calculations, and astute judgment" leads you to SHREWD (Word 395) as the correct answer.

9. D: The key definitional phrase "boldly chose a risky, little-used path" leads you to AUDACIOUS (Word 385) as the correct word to describe Junko Tabei.

10. C: The key phrase "model of park design that other impressed nations" signals that you should look for a positive answer that means "imitate." EMULATE (Word 404) is therefore the correct answer.

11. C: The word PARADOXICALLY signals that you should look for a pair of answers that have opposite meanings. The key definitional phrase "full of charm and personal magnetism" leads you to either CHARISMATIC or ENCHANTING. The key definitional phrase "uninteresting and bland" leads you to INSIPID. The correct answer is therefore CHARISMATIC (Word 262) .. INSPID (Word 391).

12. A: The key word "alarmed" leads you to look for a negative first word. A DEARTH, PAUCITY, or SCARCITY of bald eagles would all alarm ornithologists. The key word "optimistically" and the strict new "protective measures" all lead you to look for a positive second word. The correct answer is therefore DEARTH (Word 414) .. PROLIFERATE (Word 339).

13. D: The key word "oscillate" signals that you should look for a pair of antonyms to describe public responses to Richard Nixon's presidency. The key phrase "bold role" leads you to either PLAUDITS or ACCLAIM for the first word. The key phrase "covert role" leads you to look for a negative second word. Only answer choice (D) meets these tests. The correct answer is therefore ACCLAIM (Word 428) .. DISDAIN (Word 66).

14. C: The key definitional word "instructional" leads you to DIDACTIC, EMPIRICAL or possibly ERUDITE. The key phrase "surprisingly touching" leads you to POIGNANT. The correct answer is therefore DIDACTIC (Word 53) .. POIGNANT (Word 398).

15. D: The key word "shy" leads you to either ALOOF or DIFFIDENT for the first blank. The second blank must be filled with a word that would come as a "complete and unpleasant surprise" to a college admissions officer. Since OVERBEARING means "arrogant and disdainful," it would be incongruous with Myra's normally DIFFIDENT manner. The correct answer is therefore DIFFIDENT (Word 6) .. OVERBEARING (Word 407).

PRACTICE SET XII: CHAPTER 12, THE TOP 110 LEVEL 3 WORDS (#441–490)

1. "Bedlam," a popular name for the first English insane asylum, has come to signify any _____ scene of turmoil and confusion.
   - (A) subtle
   - (B) paradoxical
   - (C) chaotic
   - (D) coherent
   - (E) ingenious

2. The term "funny bone" is actually _____, since this part of the body is actually a nerve.
   - (A) an allusion
   - (B) an understatement
   - (C) a misnomer
   - (D) a paradox
   - (E) a personification

3. Despite high expectations, the popular novelist's new blog was surprisingly _____: every entry was ordinary and commonplace.
   - (A) divisive
   - (B) mundane
   - (C) poignant
   - (D) egregious
   - (E) lucrative

4. Guneet cannot tolerate a situation that is _____, where there is no hope of effective action.
   - (A) euphoric
   - (B) futile
   - (C) slovenly
   - (D) feasible
   - (E) somber

5. The guidance counselor demonstrated great understanding of the student's feelings, thereby enhancing her reputation for being _____.
   - (A) divisive
   - (B) exasperating
   - (C) obsolete
   - (D) empathetic
   - (E) euphoric

6. Justin was _____ and _____, a man of great courage and conviction.
   - (A) craven .. credible
   - (B) punctilious .. taciturn
   - (C) adept .. tenacious
   - (D) impassioned .. affable
   - (E) intrepid .. resolute

7. Carson was a gloomy and _____ person; he had none of his brother's _____.
   - (A) stodgy .. credibility
   - (B) fastidious .. rancor
   - (C) somber .. vivacity
   - (D) slovenly .. empathy
   - (E) abstemious .. vacillation

8. Conrad Anker is a world-famous mountain climber who is renowned for his _____ and _____: he is very inventive and never gives up on a challenge.
   - (A) ingenuity .. tenacity
   - (B) ineptitude .. indomitability
   - (C) adeptness .. inertia
   - (D) negligence .. futility
   - (E) elusiveness .. aloofness

9. Because of its out-of-date features, reviewers have roundly criticized the printer for its use of _____ technology.
   - (A) trivial
   - (B) obsolete
   - (C) plausible
   - (D) mundane
   - (E) credible

10. Because she has a great need for praise and admiration, Rihanna enjoys the public _____ that comes with being a famous recording artist.

    (A) adulation
    (B) empathy
    (C) disparity
    (D) mockery
    (E) levity

ANSWERS FOR PRACTICE SET XII

1. C: The key definitional phrase "scene of turmoil and confusion" leads you to CHAOTIC (Word 445) as the correct answer.

2. C: Since the "funny bone" is actually a nerve, its name is incorrect and therefore a MISNOMER (Word 454).

3. B: The key definitional phrase "ordinary and commonplace" leads you to MUNDANE (Word 469) as the correct answer.

4. B: The key definitional phrase "no hope of effective action" leads you to FUTILE (Word 444) as the correct answer.

5. D: The key definitional phrase "great understanding of the student's feelings" leads you to EMPATHETIC (Word 461) as the correct answer.

6. E: The key definitional phrase "great courage" supports INTREPID, and the key definitional word "conviction" supports RESOLUTE. The correct answer is therefore INTREPID (Word 457) .. RESOLUTE (Word 468).

7. C: The sentence calls for a first word that is synonymous with "gloomy" and a second word that offers a sharp contrast. The correct answer is therefore SOMBER (Word 449) .. VIVACITY (Word 383).

8. A: The key definitional phrase "is very inventive and never gives up on a challenge" leads you to describe Conrad Anker as a person known for his INGENUITY (Word 464) .. TENACITY (Word 487).

9. B: The key definitional phrase "out-of-date features" leads you to OBSOLETE (Word 446) as the correct answer.

10. A: The key definitional phrase "praise and admiration" leads you to ADULATION (Word 441) as the correct answer.

PRACTICE SET XIII: CHAPTER 12, THE TOP 110 LEVEL 3 WORDS (#491–540)

1. Addison's use of clever strategies and crafty behavior to overcome seemingly insurmountable obstacles suggested a talent for _____ that impressed her colleagues.
   (A) loquacity
   (B) autonomy
   (C) empathy
   (D) guile
   (E) condescension

2. The message was frustratingly _____: it contained hidden meanings that we were unable to fully understand.
   (A) obsequious
   (B) cryptic
   (C) sporadic
   (D) versatile
   (E) blithe

3. The studio delayed the movie's release when lukewarm reviews by critics and preview audiences indicated that the film would have _____ support at the box office.
   (A) effusive
   (B) raucous
   (C) prodigious
   (D) chaotic
   (E) tepid

4. The defense lawyer insisted that the Instagram pictures were _____ evidence that provided relevant insight into her client's motives and subsequent behavior.
   (A) illusory
   (B) superfluous
   (C) germane
   (D) incidental
   (E) innocuous

5. Critics _____ Jodi Hooper's latest play for its convoluted plot, banal dialogue, and _____ characters who were overly sad and gloomy.
   (A) excoriated .. melancholy
   (B) acclaimed .. contemptible
   (C) extolled .. taciturn
   (D) castigated .. candid
   (E) marginalized .. provocative

6. Ancient Mayan civilization consisted of _____ city-states that were unrestrained by a unifying central authority.
   (A) innocuous
   (B) autonomous
   (C) magnanimous
   (D) dilapidated
   (E) hierarchical

7. Scientists have discovered that our sense of smell is surprisingly acute; our _____ system is capable of distinguishing thousands of chemical odors.
   (A) demographic
   (B) topography
   (C) olfactory
   (D) auditory
   (E) cartographical

8. Noah has an indisputably _____ manner: he is a _____ who fawns on anyone whom he perceives to be his superior.
   (A) straightforward .. charlatan
   (B) meticulous .. bungler
   (C) affable .. curmudgeon
   (D) obsequious .. sycophant
   (E) conventional .. heretic

9. The theological discussions were often _____, raising deep and challenging insights into the nature of good and evil.
   (A) profound
   (B) supine
   (C) static
   (D) sonorous
   (E) dismissive

10. Because the drudgery of continuous work left her exhausted, Halley preferred to work only _____ at any tedious project or activity.

    (A) incessantly
    (B) cryptically
    (C) sybiotically
    (D) tenaciously
    (E) sporadically

ANSWERS FOR PRACTICE SET XIII

1. D: The key definitional phrase "clever strategies and crafty behavior" leads you to GUILE (Word 530) as the best word to describe Addison.

2. B: The key definitional phrase "hidden meanings that we were unable to fully understand" leads you to CRYPTIC (Word 529) as the correct answer.

3. E: The key definitional word "lukewarm" leads you to TEPID (Word 540) as the correct answer.

4. C: The key definitional word "relevant" leads you to GERMANE (Word 500) as the correct answer.

5. A: The key words "convoluted plot" and "banal dialogue" signal that the critics were harshly critical of Jodi Hooper's play. EXCORIATE and CASTIGATE are both possible choices for the first blank. The key definitional phrase "overly sad and gloomy" leads you to MELANCHOLY for the second blank. The correct answer is therefore EXCORIATE (Word 174) .. MELANCHOLY (Word 497).

6. B: The key definitional phrase "unrestrained by a unifying central authority" leads you to AUTONOMOUS (Word 491) as the correct answer.

7. C: The key definitional phrase "sense of smell" leads you to OLFACTORY (Word 524) as the correct answer.

8. D: This question asks you to match a person with his defining characteristic. The key definitional phrase "fawns on anyone whom he perceives to be his superior" leads you to OBSEQUIOUS (Word 528) .. SYCOPHANT (Word 528) as the correct answer.

9. A: The key definitional phrase "deep and challenging insights" leads you to PROFOUND (Word 521) as the correct answer.

10. E: Because "the drudgery of continuous work left her exhausted," we can conclude that Halley preferred work that was not continuous. The correct answer is therefore SPORADICALLY (Word 536).

PRACTICE SET XIV: CHAPTER 13, THE TOP FORTY WORDS WITH MULTIPLE MEANINGS (#541–580)

1. Although the professor occasionally allowed her students the _____ to select their own research projects, she typically imposed strict guidelines, which severely limited their freedom of choice.
   (A) latitude
   (B) channel
   (C) stipulation
   (D) antecedent
   (E) resignation

2. Professor Tuttle's new world history text is both _____ and _____: although his prose is unimaginative, the book is very comprehensive.
   (A) intriguing .. didactic
   (B) banal .. parochial
   (C) compelling .. versatile
   (D) pedestrian .. exhaustive
   (E) tasteless .. spare

3. In surprising contrast to the austere homes build in this neighborhood, the homes built in the adjacent town are surprisingly _____.
   (A) tasteless
   (B) economical
   (C) capricious
   (D) ornate
   (E) symmetrical

4. Eager to appear sophisticated and genial, Eric cultivated a public image that was both _____ and _____.
   (A) parochial .. gregarious
   (B) urbane .. enigmatic
   (C) cosmopolitan .. affable
   (D) aesthetic .. laconic
   (E) temperate .. craven

5. Although the mayor tried to _____ the soaring optimism engendered by the large private grant, her pleas for moderation were largely ignored.
   (A) arrest
   (B) doctor
   (C) eclipse
   (D) shelve
   (E) temper

6. The new director of the charitable trust announced that his primary focus would be on broad global problems rather than on _____ issues with limited consequences.
   (A) provincial
   (B) nostalgic
   (C) disputatious
   (D) universal
   (E) autonomous

7. The restaurant chef was noted for her _____ taste; she carefully selected only organic vegetables and grass-fed beef for her menu.
   (A) retiring
   (B) discriminating
   (C) austere
   (D) odd
   (E) provincial

8. Rather than _____ the building project, the college president called upon alumni to launch an immediate and aggressive fundraising drive.
   (A) shelving
   (B) tackling
   (C) commencing
   (D) galvanizing
   (E) cultivating

9. Hoping that her exhaustive analysis would yield insights that had eluded previous scholars, the archaeologist _____ the ancient artifacts.
   (A) neglected
   (B) shelved
   (C) doctored
   (D) obscured
   (E) pored over

10. Although usually _____
and reluctant to draw attention to herself,
Neve publicly announced a bold plan to
_____ her community's
pressing need for a new park.

    (A) retiring .. tackle
    (B) gregarious .. confront
    (C) diffident .. forego
    (D) provocative .. embrace
    (E) cavalier .. address

ANSWERS FOR PRACTICE SET XIV

1. A: The reversal word "although" signals that you want an answer that contrasts with the key phrase "typically imposed strict guidelines, which severely limited their freedom of choice." The correct answer is therefore LATITUDE (Word 553).

2. D: The key word "unimaginative" will lead you to either BANAL or PEDESTRIAN. The second key word "comprehensive" will lead you to EXHAUSTIVE. The correct answer is therefore PEDESTRIAN (Word 547) .. EXHAUSTIVE (Word 561).

3. D: The reversal phrase "in striking contrast" tells you to look for an answer that is the opposite of AUSTERE. The correct answer is therefore ORNATE (Word 541).

4. C: The key definitional word "sophisticated" will lead you to either URBANE or COSMOPOLITAN. The key definitional word "genial" will lead you to either GREGARIOUS or AFFABLE. The correct answer is therefore COSMOPOLITAN (Word 567) .. AFFABLE (Word 458).

5. E: The mayor tried to limit or soften the "soaring optimism." Her pleas for "moderation" therefore represent an attempt to TEMPER "the soaring optimism." The correct answer is therefore TEMPER (Word 563).

6. A: The reversal phrase "rather than" signals that you want an answer that is the opposite of "broad global problems" and is consistent with "limited consequences." The correct answer is therefore PROVINCIAL (Word 568).

7. B: The key definitional phrase "carefully selected" leads you to DISCRIMINATING (Word 554) as the best answer.

8. A: The reversal phrase "rather than" tells you to look for an answer that has the opposite meaning of "immediate and aggressive." The correct answer is therefore SHELVING (Word 564).

9. E: This sentence asks you to find a logical relationship between the archaeologist's "exhaustive analysis" that would "yield insights" and the ancient artifacts. The archaeologist can only achieve her goal by PORING OVER (Word 573) the ancient artifacts.

10. A: The key phrase "reluctant to draw attention to herself" will lead you to either RETIRING or DIFFIDENT for the first blank. The key phrase "bold plan" tells you that Neve will TACKLE her community's "pressing need for a new park." The correct answer is therefore RETIRING (Word 562) .. TACKLE (Word 569).

PRACTICE SET XV: CHAPTERS 14 & 15, THE TOP TWENTY WORDS ABOUT K–STEW & R–PATTZ AND PSY & GANGNAM STYLE (#581–600)

1. Because so many important artistic movements originated there, Paris was said to be in the _____ of 19th-century art.
   (A) vanguard
   (B) sanctuary
   (C) scenario
   (D) juxtaposition
   (E) forbearance

2. The treaty, instead of promoting _____ and unity, actually _____ tensions between the two nations.
   (A) discord .. inflamed
   (B) diplomacy .. alleviated
   (C) collegiality .. ameliorated
   (D) reconciliation .. exacerbated
   (E) amity .. rectified

3. In contrast to the _____ maneuvers of his fellow diplomats, Ambassador Chavan's negotiations were always open and aboveboard.
   (A) superficial
   (B) surreptitious
   (C) chaotic
   (D) rancorous
   (E) pious

4. Controlled explosions are often used to destroy _____ buildings that are run-down and can no longer be saved.
   (A) redundant
   (B) chaotic
   (C) dilapidated
   (D) rancorous
   (E) nostalgic

5. Although Rajvi's podcasts have occasional anecdotes that seem _____ and silly, her overall message is _____ desire to help his listeners deal with their personal problems.
   (A) trenchant .. a solemn
   (B) frivolous .. an earnest
   (C) capricious .. a trifling
   (D) apprehensive .. an impassioned
   (E) elusive .. a flippant

6. Because the subject of the painting was _____ and often eccentric local personality, the artist's choice of a _____ setting seemed inappropriate.
   (A) an ostentatious .. pedestrian
   (B) an idiosyncratic .. harmonious
   (C) a clandestine .. congruous
   (D) a quirky .. conventional
   (E) a retiring .. anguished

7. Because they distrust people, _____ habitually enjoy _____ human projects and activities.
   (A) innovators .. creating
   (B) misanthropists .. deriding
   (C) narcissists .. admiring
   (D) pundits .. describing
   (E) hedonists .. enjoying

8. Although Lucas was usually unapologetic, he pleased his friends and fans by issuing a _____ apology for his embarrassing antics.
   (A) clandestine
   (B) divisive
   (C) superficial
   (D) contrite
   (E) tasteless

9. After completing his PowerPoint presentation on the origins of the Cold War, Professor Binderman emailed his students a carefully prepared list of _____ points he wanted them to remember.

    (A) trivial
    (B) rough
    (C) inadvertent
    (D) salient
    (E) archaic

10. Himali's _____ is astonishing; she is always exuberant and full of vitality.

    (A) lethargy
    (B) apprehension
    (C) ire
    (D) anguish
    (E) verve

ANSWERS FOR PRACTICE SET XV

1. A: The key phrase "originated there" tells you that Paris was in the VANGUARD (Word 600) of 19th-century art.

2. D: The key word "instead" tells you to look for a pair of answers with contrasting meanings. The key word "unity" leads you to DIPLOMACY, COLLEGIALITY, RECONCILIATION, or AMITY for the first blank. Knowing that the second blank must be filled with a negative word that contrasts with your first word leads you to EXACERBATE. The correct answer is therefore RECONCILIATION (Word 589) .. EXACERBATE (Word 478).

3. B: The key reversal phrase "in contrast to" tells you to look for an answer that has the opposite meaning of "always open and aboveboard." The correct answer is therefore SURREPTITIOUS (Word 582).

4. C: The key definitional phrase "run-down and can no longer be saved" leads you to DILAPIDATED (Word 594) as the correct answer.

5. B: The key word "silly" leads you to either FRIVOLOUS or CAPRICIOUS for the first blank. The key reversal word "although" signals that you should look for a contrasting second word. Only FRIVOLOUS (Word 592) .. EARNEST (Word 55) passes these tests.

6. D: The key definitional word ECCENTRIC leads you to either IDIOSYNCRATIC or QUIRKY for the first blank. Given these choices, a CONVENTIONAL setting would seem inappropriate. The correct answer is therefore QUIRKY (Word 598) .. CONVENTIONAL (Word 2).

7. B: This question asks you to match a defining characteristic with a specific type of person. Only choice (B) MISANTHROPISTS (Word 92) .. DERIDING (Word 597) matches this test.

8. D: The key reversal word "although" tells you to look for a word that is opposite in meaning to the phrase "usually unapologetic." The correct answer is therefore CONTRITE (Word 584).

9. D: The key phrase "carefully prepared list of" tells you to look for an answer that means "important and prominent." The correct answer is therefore SALIENT (Word 599).

10. E: The key definitional phrase "always exuberant and full of vitality" leads you to VERVE (Word 591) as the best word to describe Himali.

CHAPTER 22
SENTENCE COMPLETIONS— PRACTICE SET

Try to recall a situation in which you were performing under the pressure of a ticking clock. Athletes, entertainers, and writers often have to "beat the clock," "keep a schedule," and "make a deadline." The pressure builds whenever you feel like you don't have enough time to do what you are capable of doing. Learning how to handle time pressure requires practice, patience, and confidence.

The SAT will require you to perform well while working at a brisk pace. Students aspiring for top scores should strive to answer all or almost all the sentence completion questions. The vocabulary chapters, strategies, and practice exercises you have completed so far are designed to enable you to master even the most challenging sentence completion questions.

Each of the three SAT critical reading sections will begin with a set of either eight, six, or five sentence completion questions. You should spend an average of about forty seconds on each sentence completion question. This means devoting about five minutes to the set of eight questions, four minutes to the set of six questions, and about 3.5 minutes to the set of five questions. This pace is designed to leave you with ample time to complete the critical reading passages.

PRACTICE SET 1: GROUP OF EIGHT

Directions: Mark the answer for each of the following eight sentence completion questions. Try to complete the entire set in five minutes. When you have finished, use the space provided to record how long you took to complete the set and how many questions you answered correctly.

1. Jean Piaget has _____ the study of cognitive development by fundamentally altering the way people think about how infants and children understand the world.
   (A) readjusted
   (B) revolutionized
   (C) discredited
   (D) coveted
   (E) hindered

2. Each painting for the Picasso exhibit was carefully selected and then _____ according to a carefully designed chronological and thematic pattern.
   (A) muddled
   (B) abandoned
   (C) renounced
   (D) ignored
   (E) positioned

3. Attending support groups can have _____ effect: they help people heal personal troubles and restore psychological health.
   (A) a deleterious
   (B) a therapeutic
   (C) a counterproductive
   (D) a perplexing
   (E) an unusual

4. Many club members report feeling _____ after participating in strenuous exercise workouts with physical trainer Marc Vindas, but he, in contrast, is _____.
   (A) fatigued .. indefatigable
   (B) diminished .. shriveled
   (C) resplendent .. radiant
   (D) uncommunicative .. taciturn
   (E) replenished .. rejuvenated

5. West African folklore consists of _____ mix that includes a wide range of songs, legends, and oral histories.
   (A) an eclectic
   (B) an inscrutable
   (C) an egregious
   (D) a bland
   (E) a homogeneous

6. Although he was very modest about his achievements, Kavin was not a _____; he was in fact an accomplished chess player.
   (A) misanthrope
   (B) pundit
   (C) heretic
   (D) connoisseur
   (E) neophyte

7. The governor's term in office was marked by _____ as he became entangled in a series of _____ and disgraceful scandals.
   (A) approbation .. seminal
   (B) idealism .. divisive
   (C) rectitude .. appalling
   (D) ignominy .. esteemed
   (E) chicanery .. venal

8. Karl's behavior was so _____ that it offended many club members: few people liked him because he was _____ and arrogant.
   (A) deplorable .. affable
   (B) exemplary .. amiable
   (C) cavalier .. overbearing
   (D) conciliatory .. despotic
   (E) execrable .. egalitarian

TIME: _____

NUMBER CORRECT: _____

PRACTICE SET 1: GROUP OF SIX

Directions: Mark the answer for each of the following six sentence completion questions. Try to complete the entire set in four minutes. When you have finished, use the space provided to record how long you took to complete the set and how many questions you answered correctly.

1. In contrast to Abhin's _____ response, Helen delayed completing the questionnaire and thus did not receive an interview.
   (A) hesitant
   (B) monotonous
   (C) irrelevant
   (D) prompt
   (E) argumentative

2. Art and literature _____ during the European Dark Ages: modern historians have noted _____ of creative endeavors.
   (A) retreated .. an abundance
   (B) unfolded .. an absence
   (C) languished .. a rebirth
   (D) stagnated .. a dearth
   (E) flourished .. paucity

3. The purpose of the arbiter's mission was to mediate the dispute by helping labor and management _____ their differences.
   (A) reconcile
   (B) exacerbate
   (C) prolong
   (D) ignore
   (E) deprecate

4. Francis Parkman's monumental seven-volume history of the European colonization of North America featured _____ narrative style that included elaborate descriptions of people, places, and events.
   (A) an unadorned
   (B) an ornate
   (C) an evenhanded
   (D) an oversimplified
   (E) an incoherent

5. Fatigued from the start, the athlete became even more _____ as the strenuous game continued.
   (A) inscrutable
   (B) enervated
   (C) taciturn
   (D) indulgent
   (E) officious

6. Outraged Church officials accused the heretic of being _____ because he was a morally unprincipled person who would never reform his _____ lifestyle.
   (A) an iconoclast .. virtuous
   (B) a hedonist .. righteous
   (C) a toady .. laudable
   (D) a raconteur .. unorthodox
   (E) a reprobate .. depraved

TIME: _____

NUMBER CORRECT: _____

PRACTICE SET 1: GROUP OF FIVE

Directions: Mark the answer for each of the following five sentence completion questions. Try to complete the entire set in 3.5 minutes. When you have finished, use the space provided to record how long you took to complete the set and how many questions you answered correctly.

1. The presidency of James Monroe is often called "the Era of Good Feelings" because it was a _____ period that was relatively free of controversy.
   (A) heterogeneous
   (B) skeptical
   (C) chaotic
   (D) tranquil
   (E) contentious

2. While everyone agrees that the President and Congress should work together, this _____ vanishes once the politicians confront contentious political issues.
   (A) consensus
   (B) analogy
   (C) speculation
   (D) metaphor
   (E) allusion

3. The landlord complained that the negligent tenant abandoned his apartment and left it in _____ condition: the paint was peeling off the walls and the pipes were encrusted with rust.
   (A) pristine
   (B) tolerable
   (C) dilapidated
   (D) enhanced
   (E) punctilious

4. The group responded to Srishti's _____ story with tearful support that verged on becoming _____.
   (A) poignant .. maudlin
   (B) ominous .. lighthearted
   (C) wistful .. callous
   (D) uplifting .. disdainful
   (E) beguiling .. indifferent

5. Bismarck unified Germany by intimidation and _____, not by encouragement and _____.
   (A) persuasion .. coaxing
   (B) compromise .. conciliation
   (C) conjecture .. fidelity
   (D) rumination .. nostalgia
   (E) coercion .. cajolery

TIME: _____

NUMBER CORRECT: _____

PRACTICE SET 1: ANSWERS
GROUP OF EIGHT

1. B: The key definitional phrase "fundamentally altering" leads you to a word that describes a significant change. The correct answer is therefore REVOLUTIONIZED.

2. E: The key phrases "carefully selected" and "carefully designed" lead you to a word that means "placed." The correct answer is therefore POSITIONED.

3. B: The key definitional phrase "help people heal" indicates that you want a positive word that means "to heal" or "to help." The correct answer is therefore THERAPEUTIC.

4. A: The key reversal phrase "in contrast" indicates that you want a pair of antonyms. Only choice (A) meets this criterion. The correct answer is therefore FATIGUED .. INDEFATIGABLE (Word 282).

5. A: The key definitional phrase "mix that includes a wide range" leads you to a word that means "varied." The correct answer is therefore ECLECTIC (Word 222).

6. E: The reversal word "not" indicates that you are looking for a word that means the opposite of "an accomplished chess player." The correct answer is therefore NEOPHYTE (Word 94).

7. E: This sentence asks you to find a pair of words that are logically connected. The key phrase "disgraceful scandals" tells you to look for a pair of related negative words. Only answer (E) meets these criteria. The correct answer is therefore CHICANERY (Word 231) .. VENAL (Word 230).

8. C: The sentence asks you to find a pair of words that are logically connected. They key words "offended" and "arrogant" tell you to look for negative answers that mean "arrogant." The correct answer is therefore CAVALIER (Word 151) .. OVERBEARING (Word 407).

GROUP OF SIX

1. D: The key reversal phrase "in contrast to" tells you to look for an answer that means the opposite of "delayed." The correct answer is therefore (D) PROMPT.

2. D: This sentence asks for you to find a pair of words that are logically connected. The correct answer is therefore STAGNATED .. a DEARTH (Word 414).

3. A: The key definitional word "mediate" tells you that the arbiter is trying to help labor and management find a solution to their dispute. The correct answer is therefore the positive word RECONCILE (WORD 589).

4. B: The key definitional word "elaborate" tells you to look for an answer that means "embellished." The correct answer is therefore ORNATE (Word 541).

5. B: The key word "fatigued" and the key phrase "even more" tells you to look for an answer that means "very tired." The correct answer is therefore ENERVATED (Word 291).

6. E: The key definitional phrase "morally unprincipled person" tells you to look for a very negative word for the first blank. The second word must then be a logical characteristic of this "morally unprincipled person." The correct answer is therefore REPROBATE (Word 82) .. DEPRAVED.

GROUP OF FIVE

1. D: The key definitional phrase "relatively free of controversy" tells you to look for an answer that means "calm." The correct answer is therefore TRANQUIL.

2. A: The key definitional phrase "everyone agrees" tells you to look for an answer that means "general agreement." The correct answer is therefore CONSENSUS.

3. C: The key word "negligent" and the deteriorating condition of the paint and pipes tell you to look for a negative answer that means "run-down." The correct answer is therefore DILAPIDATED (Word 594).

4. A: The sentence asks you to find a pair of words that are logically connected. The first word must describe a story that would bring the group to tears. The second word must describe a state of excess emotion. The correct answer is therefore POIGNANT (Word 398) .. MAUDLIN (Word 159).

5. E: The sentence asks you to find a first word that is consistent with "intimidation" and a second contrasting word that is consistent with "encouragement." The correct answer is therefore COERCION (Word 210) .. CAJOLERY (Word 209).

PART III

THE ESSENTIAL GUIDE TO CRITICAL READING

CHAPTER 23
INTRODUCING CRITICAL READING PASSAGES AND QUESTIONS

Part I provided you with definitions and illustrations for 600 key words frequently tested on the SAT. These words will help you become a more articulate writer and speaker. They will also help you achieve a higher Critical Reading score.

Each SAT contains three sections devoted to Critical Reading. These sections include a total of 19 sentence completion questions and 48 passage-based questions. Vocabulary plays a particularly important role in the challenging Level 4 and Level 5 questions. In many ways, the Critical Reading section can be viewed as a sophisticated vocabulary test.

The Critical Reading passages and questions on the SAT are designed to measure your abilities as a critical reader. It is important to remember that good readers, like good scientists, writers, and athletes, got that way through practice and hard work.

The "best" approach to reading any material depends on the purpose for which you are reading it. When you take the SAT, you are reading strictly for the purpose of answering 48 passage-based questions. This special purpose requires a variety of unique strategies.

Part III of *The Essential Guide to SAT Critical Reading and Vocabulary* is designed to provide you with a comprehensive overview of the passage-based questions. Chapter 23 will begin our presentation by discussing key points about Critical Reading passages and passage-based questions. Chapters 24–25 will describe the characteristics of right and wrong answers. Chapter 26 will describe and illustrate a focused and efficient Critical Reading strategy that takes advantage of the micro questions that numerically dominate the test. Chapter 27 will show you how to identify and answer main idea questions. Chapters 28–30 will focus on questions that test rhetorical devices, attitude, tone and mood, and vocabulary-in-context questions. Chapters 31–32 will examine and illustrate both the short and the long dual or paired passages.

THREE TYPES OF PASSAGES

Each SAT contains seven Critical Reading passages that can be assigned to one of the following three categories:

1. SHORT PASSAGES

Each test contains two short paragraph-length passages. Each of these passages contains ten to fifteen lines and is followed by two questions.

2. LONG PASSAGES

Each test contains three long passages that range from fifty to ninety lines in length. The passages are typically followed by six, nine, or thirteen questions.

3. PAIRED OR DUAL PASSAGES

Each SAT contains two paired or dual passages. The paired passages focus on a related topic. The authors of these passages support, oppose, and sometimes complement each other. The short paired passages are just two paragraphs long and are followed by 4 to 5 questions. The long paired passages contain 80 to 90 lines and are followed by 12 or 13 questions.

THREE TYPES OF QUESTIONS

Most SAT passage-based questions can be assigned to one of the following three categories:

1. GENERAL QUESTIONS

General questions test your overall understanding of a passage. They usually ask you to
• identify the main idea, theme, or purpose of a passage
• distinguish the author's attitude, tone, or mood

2. VOCABULARY–IN–CONTEXT QUESTIONS

These questions ask you to infer the meaning of a word or short phrase from its context.

3. SPECIFIC QUESTIONS

These questions ask you about a specific paragraph, sentence, or phrase. Specific questions comprise over two-thirds of all passage-based questions. There are two basic types of specific questions:
• Literal comprehension questions ask you about facts or points directly stated in the passage. The correct answer is usually a restatement or paraphrasing of words found in the text of the passage.
• Extended reasoning questions ask you to draw inferences or conclusions from information stated in the passage. Typical extended reasoning questions ask you to understand the implications of what is stated, follow the logic of an argument, and evaluate the author's assumptions.

ORDER OF DIFFICULTY

As you have seen, sentence completion questions are presented in order of difficulty. In contrast, passage-based questions are NOT presented in order of difficulty. As a result, you may find that the first two questions are very difficult. Don't despair! Every passage is followed by easy, medium, and hard questions.

Passages, like the questions, will also vary in difficulty. As a general rule, two of the seven passages will be relatively easy, three will be of medium difficulty, and two will be challenging. However, the degree of difficulty of a passage is subjective and will vary from reader to reader. For example, students who enjoy science may find a difficult science passage easy and an easy social science passage quite challenging.

TIME ALLOCATION

The Critical Reading passages require time and concentration. As a general rule you should allow about seventy seconds for each passage-based question. One way to quickly compute how much time you need for a passage is to add the number 2 to the total number of questions following a passage. For example, you should allocate fifteen minutes to a paired passage that contains thirteen questions.

WHY IS CR SO HARD?

Many students complain that no matter how hard they try, they just can't seem to raise their CR scores. Indeed, most SAT tutors agree that CR scores are the most difficult part of the SAT to improve.

The Critical Reading score is difficult to improve for three interrelated reasons:

1. THE PASSAGES ARE CHALLENGING

Have you ever become bored and found your attention wandering as you read a CR passage? If so, you are not alone. Many students complain that the passages are a hodgepodge of long, tedious, and confusing paragraphs. As a result, many test-takers often become bored and "lost" in a passage.

2. THE QUESTIONS ARE CHALLENGING

Have you ever had the experience of feeling that you understood the passage and the question, only to find that none of the answers seem to be correct? Once again, you are not alone. SAT answers are carefully crafted to sound plausible and thus lure you into choosing a wrong answer. As a result, finding the right answer can be frustratingly difficult.

3. THE VOCABULARY IS CHALLENGING

Have you ever been frustrated by difficult vocabulary words that seem to deliberately obscure the meaning of an answer? As always, you are not alone. Both the passages and the questions contain challenging vocabulary words. The presence of these words is one of the hallmarks of Level 4 or Level 5 questions. In order to correctly answer these challenging questions you must have a strong vocabulary. Of course, that is why this book begins with 600 words you absolutely, positively should know.

A NEW ANALYTICAL APPROACH

The CR section is conquerable; however, you will need to learn a new analytical approach to reading the passages and answering the questions. Most students approach an SAT passage as if it were a short story in their literature class. They focus on the passage's characters, plot, and themes. Their approach is typically subjective and interpretive.

This subjective approach is perfectly valid in your literature class, but it has limited value in helping you correctly answer SAT passage-based questions. SAT passages are not intended to entertain you. They are instead designed to test your ability to be an analytical reader who can summarize different points of view, dissect logical arguments, and understand how different rhetorical devices contribute to an author's argument.

CHRISTIAN SAYS:

Don't blow past this incredibly important info! Students commonly make the mistake of personally reacting to the SAT reading passages. That's often what you focus on in English class. In contrast, the SAT requires a more objective, fact-based and analytical mindset. You're an observer, not a participant, in a carefully choreographed discussion between questions, passages, and answers. It would be impossible to design a reading test that allowed two million students per year to offer their own perspectives. So instead of "This answer is the answer because I like it," adopt Larry's viewpoint: "An answer is an answer because it has support in the passage."

DON'T GIVE UP!

The Critical Reading passages and questions will be the ultimate test of your indomitable will. Learning how to become a skilled analytical reader takes time and sustained practice. The following chapters are designed to teach you a carefully sequenced set of skills that will ultimately combine to produce a significant increase in your CR score!

CHAPTER 24
THE CHARACTERISTICS OF RIGHT ANSWERS

Finding right answers is the only way to earn Critical Reading points. So what are the characteristics of a right answer? Let's begin your quest for right answers and CR points with the following short passage. Read the paragraph and then answer the following question:

It is April 2009, and I'm seated on a bus that just passed through the main gate at Parris Island. Like the other Marine recruits on the bus, I am filled with nervous anticipation. The decision we have all taken is now irreversible. For the next thirteen weeks we will all be completely cut off from the civilian world.

The author's description of the recruits on the bus suggests that
- (A) they will not receive a warm welcome
- (B) they will only be able to communicate with their parents
- (C) they are about to begin a detailed but flexible itinerary
- (D) they are all handling a difficult situation with aplomb
- (E) they have made a decision that is irreversible

Did you have any trouble finding the right answer? Probably not. Choice (E) provides the correct answer by giving you a direct quote from the passage. Now reread the passage and answer the following question:

The author's description of the recruits on the bus suggests that
- (A) they will not receive a warm welcome
- (B) they will only be able to communicate with their parents
- (C) they are about to begin a detailed but flexible itinerary
- (D) they are all handling a difficult situation with aplomb
- (E) they are taking a step that is irrevocable

What is the difference between this test item and the previous version? As you can see, the two questions are identical, with the exception of Choice (E). Although the two choice (E) answers do not have a single word in common, both are correct. The phrase "they are taking a step that is irrevocable" is a restatement, or paraphrase, of the author's statement that the "decision we have all taken is irreversible."

THE GOLDEN RULE

This simple example illustrates an extremely important point. Every SAT Critical Reading question has one objective answer that restates relevant ideas or information from the passage. When answering passage-based questions, always remember this Golden Rule: AN ANSWER IS AN ANSWER BECAUSE IT HAS SUPPORT IN THE PASSAGE. This support will take the form of key words, phrases, and examples. Never go outside the passage to find support for your answers.

A SOPHISTICATED GAME OF MATCHING

Since correct answers are restatements of information from the passage, your job is to match key ideas from the text with accurate restatements in each question. The College Board is asking you to play a sophisticated game of verbal matching. The following activity is designed to help you begin the process of recognizing the types of paraphrases you will encounter in the CR sections of your SAT. Match the original passage material in the left column with the restatements in the right column.

1. _____ overpowering and threatening	A. pervasive attention
2. _____ a disorderly traffic flow	B. an ominous threat
3. _____ a menacing presence	C. overwhelming and intimidating
4. _____ vast and infinite	D. a chaotic jumble
5. _____ unable to agree	E. an immense expanse
6. _____ widespread appeal	F. a rustic view
7. _____ we have not cared at all	G. a lack of consensus
8. _____ a pastoral scene	H. complete indifference

The correct answers are 1–C; 2–D; 3–B; 4–E; 5–G; 6–A; 7–H; 8–F.

READ CR PASSAGES AS IF YOU ARE A LAWYER

Passage-based questions are not designed to reward creative thinking and original interpretations. This all-important but often overlooked fact comes as a surprise to many students. After all, English teachers encourage their students to come up with imaginative interpretations. Don't fall into this trap. Instead, pretend that you are a lawyer and the passage is a legal document. Your job is to spot key words that support arguments, points of view, and attitudes. You will then look for objective answers that restate this information without changing its meaning.

GUIDED PRACTICE

Knowing how to identify a restatement is an essential skill for answering passage-based questions. Always match your answers with key material contained in the passage. Answer each of the following questions by looking for words found in the text. Then compare your answers with the detailed explanations that follow each question.

1. **The sheer novelty of the first talking pictures mesmerized audiences, but their vapid content and banal dialogue dismayed critics.**

Which of the following best describes how audiences responded to the first talking pictures?
 (A) outrage
 (B) disappointment
 (C) indifference
 (D) ambivalence
 (E) fascination

The question asks you how audiences responded to the first talking movies. According to the passage, the audiences were "mesmerized" by the new invention. The key word "mesmerized" will lead you to the positive answer choice (E) FASCINATION. Note that if the question had asked you how the critics responded to the talking pictures, the word "dismayed" would have led you to the negative answer choice (B) DISAPPOINTMENT.

2. **A good investigative reporter must ask probing and even embarrassing questions. Like the great muckrakers in the early 1900s, a journalist must dispute accepted facts and argue with officials who attempt to conceal the truth.**

The "officials" (line 5) would most likely describe the narrator as
 (A) genial
 (B) profound
 (C) contentious
 (D) charismatic
 (E) misunderstood

The question asks you how the "officials" would most likely describe the narrator. According to the passage, the narrator would "dispute" facts and "argue" with officials. These key words will lead you to choice (C) CONTENTIOUS (Word 278). Note that this is a Level 5 question because it contains difficult vocabulary. However, if you have mastered the *Essential 600* words in Chapters 1–15, then this question should have been easy. This underscores an important paradox—on the SAT, the hard questions are easy if you know the vocabulary!

3. I don't know why I thought your Mama Day would be a big, tall woman. From the stories you told about your clashes with her, she had loomed that way in my mind. Hard. Strong. Yes, it definitely showed in the set of her shoulders. But she was barely five feet and could have been snapped in the middle with one good-sized hand… "I'm Mama Day to some, Miss Miranda to others. You decide what I'll be to you." That type of straightforward honesty would cheapen anyone returning less than the same.
(from *Mama Day* by Gloria Naylor)

Lines 1–13 characterize Mama Day as being
(A) decrepit and even senile
(B) vigorous but also duplicitous
(C) diminutive and supercilious
(D) forceful and forthright
(E) brusque and aloof

Questions 1 and 2 asked you to match key words from a passage with a single-word answer choice. In contrast, Question 3 asks you to match key words from a passage with two-word answer choices. It is very important to understand that both words must be supported by the passage. A favorite test writer trick is to provide you with an answer choice in which one of the words is supported by the passage while the second word is unsupported. For example, in choice (C) Mama Day is diminutive or small but she is not supercilious or arrogant. Mama Day is best described as FORCEFUL because she is "Hard" and "Strong," and FORTHRIGHT because of her "straightforward honesty."

INDEPENDENT PRACTICE

The following ten examples are designed to give you an opportunity to practice the skill of identifying answers that paraphrase words found directly in the text. Circle the correct answer.

1. Today, standing at the base of the Great Pyramid at Giza, millions of awed tourists have asked themselves: "How could this mountain of stone have been built by people who had not even begun to use the wheel?" Each perfectly cut stone block weighs at least 2.5 tons. Some weigh 15 tons. More than 2 million of these blocks are stacked with precision to a height of 481 feet. The entire structure covers more than 13 acres.

The author's description emphasizes the Great Pyramid's
(A) aesthetic beauty
(B) impressive size
(C) diverse functions
(D) economic importance
(E) isolated location

2. Coach McClamrock's rules were as fixed as the laws of physics. And they were clearly spelled out.

Coach McClamrock's rules are described as
(A) immutable and punitive
(B) elusive and unpredictable
(C) biased and scholarly
(D) unvarying and definitive
(E) superfluous and universal

3. Ninety-five percent of Greenland is covered by ice. Towns and villages cling to the coastline; at their backs loom glaciers a thousand meters thick: gleaming, white, blue, clear, transparent ice.
(from *Frozen Earth* by Doug Macdougall)

Which of the following words best describe the towns and villages?
  (A) wretched and forlorn
  (B) defiant and truculent
  (C) imperturbable and incomprehensible
  (D) volatile and frivolous
  (E) exposed and vulnerable

4. As the first female Hispanic judge in a small Georgia town, Ms. Hernandez made certain that she rendered her decisions in a calm, unvarying voice, since opinions tentatively offered were usually questioned. If she chose to talk to the press at all, she made sure that she was both clear and succinct. She didn't want to be either misquoted or interrupted.

As described in lines 1–9, Ms. Hernandez's manner of speaking is best characterized as
  (A) oddly melancholy
  (B) intentionally incoherent
  (C) carefully calculated
  (D) overtly hostile
  (E) noticeably irreverent

5. Although Mr. Myers rarely smiled, he was both compassionate and considerate of others. However, his lofty bearing and reserved temperament left many with the erroneous impression that he was cold and detached.

Mr. Myers' manner is best described as
  (A) sympathetic but aloof
  (B) imperious but jovial
  (C) surreptitious and beguiling
  (D) sarcastic and flippant
  (E) prudent and impulsive

6. Art historian Marilyn Stokestad argues that in all of known history only three major artists appeared on the scene by themselves: 14th-century Renaissance artist Giotto, 17th-century Baroque artist Caravaggio, and 20th-century Cubist artist Picasso. Every other artist was part of a movement or a specific style.

The passage indicates that Giotto, Caravaggio, and Picasso are best viewed as
  (A) artistic anomalies
  (B) inspired dilettantes
  (C) rival contemporaries
  (D) precocious novices
  (E) benevolent mentors

7. I realized from the beginning that Mr. Williams was a natural teacher. But he was not a great educator in any conventional sense. Of course he had a deep understanding of all the seminal works of American literature. But he also had an intuitive grasp of his teenage students. He repeatedly demonstrated an uncanny ability to link our lives to great works of literature. And most of all, he was a talented raconteur who enthralled us with his personal anecdotes.

As explained by the narrator, Mr. Williams is best described as
  (A) genial but soporific
  (B) redundant but taciturn
  (C) visceral but reticent
  (D) erudite but superficial
  (E) gifted but unorthodox

8. The ancient Sumerians worshipped over 3,000 different gods. Archaeologists speculate that the Sumerians created clay dolls of their gods to help their children learn how to identify their various deities. The dolls thus functioned as learning tools and not as venerated sacred objects.

According to the passage, archaeologists speculate that the Sumerians used clay dolls of their gods as
   (A) didactic tools
   (B) revered idols
   (C) frivolous toys
   (D) nostalgic relics
   (E) popular heroes

9. I grew up on what seemed at the time like the edge of the world—in a remote corner of northeastern Tennessee. Our humble home had few books or magazines, and no television. Apart from a few people who occasionally visited Johnson City, virtually nobody we knew travelled outside our county. We lived in a closed society that thought of itself as self-sufficient.

The author characterizes the environment in which he grew up as
   (A) bohemian and quirky
   (B) provincial and autonomous
   (C) peripheral but scintillating
   (D) pastoral but chaotic
   (E) drab but unique

10. When *Luncheon on the Grass* by Edouard Manet was first exhibited at the 1863 Salon des Refuses in Paris, it created a sensation. The painting was both embraced and reviled. Outraged critics accused Manet of deliberately provoking a scandal. But his small group of avant-garde defenders lauded the work as a groundbreaking challenge to the rigid conventions of academic art. Today, *Luncheon on the Grass* is widely acclaimed as the first modern painting, and Manet is recognized as the first modern artist.

The passage indicates that in 1863 *Luncheon on the Grass* was met with
   (A) universal praise
   (B) unquestioning derision
   (C) perfunctory queries
   (D) measured assessments
   (E) antithetical judgments

The painting *Luncheon on the Grass* is best described as
   (A) an egregious error in judgment
   (B) a watershed event in Western art
   (C) a provocative but fleeting work of art
   (D) a pioneering work that appealed to traditionalists
   (E) a diversion from the historic events taking place in Paris in 1863

ANSWERS

1. B: The author emphasizes the Great Pyramid's vast weight and size by telling us that the structure is 481 feet high and covers 13 acres. These details support (B) IMPRESSIVE SIZE.

2. D: The passage tells us that Coach McClamrock's rules were "fixed" and "clearly spelled out." These key words support (D) UNVARYING and DEFINITIVE. It is interesting to note that the passage does support immutable or unchanging in choice (A). However, the passage does not support describing the rules as punitive or punishing.

3. E: According to the passage, the "towns and villages cling to the coastline" while enormous glaciers "loom" above them. The key words "cling" and "loom" indicate that the towns and villages occupy an unprotected and thus (E) EXPOSED and VULNERABLE position along the coastline. The passage does not support wretched (pitiful) and forlorn (despondent); defiant (rebellious) and truculent (belligerent); imperturbable (calm) and incomprehensible (bewildering); or volatile (very changeable) and frivolous (silly).

4. C: The passage provides a great deal of information to support describing Ms. Hernandez's manner of speaking as (C) CAREFULLY CALCULATED. For example, her decisions are not "tentative." In addition, Judge Hernandez always makes sure that her interaction with the press is "both clear and succinct" and therefore not careless or impromptu. As a person who carefully calculates her words, Judge Hernandez does not want to be "either misquoted or interrupted."

5. A: The key words "compassionate," "considerate," and "reserved" all support choice (A) SYMPATHETIC but ALOOF (Word 403). Although imperious in choice (B) is supported by Mr. Myers' "lofty bearing," there is no evidence to support describing him as jovial or humorous.

6. A: This passage tells us that Giotto, Caravaggio, and Picasso are all atypical because they each "appeared on the scene by themselves." They are therefore artistic ANOMALIES (Word 19), since "every other artist was part of a movement or a specific style."

7. E: The key phrases "natural teacher," "deep understanding," and "talented raconteur" all support GIFTED in choice (E). The key phrase "not a great educator in any conventional sense" supports the second word UNORTHODOX in choice (E). Mr. Williams is therefore best described as GIFTED but UNORTHODOX (Word 183).

8. A: The key phrase "learning tools" supports describing the clay dolls as DIDACTIC (Word 53) tools. You can eliminate choice (B), because the dolls were not used as venerated or revered objects.

9. B: The key phrases "remote corner" and "closed society" both support PROVINCIAL (see Word 568). This is further supported by the fact that the author's home had "few books or magazines, and no television." In addition, very few people travelled outside the author's home county. The author concludes by saying that the people believed they were "self-sufficient." This clearly supports the second word in choice (B), AUTONOMOUS (Word 491) or self-reliant.

10. E: The passage tells us that *Luncheon on the Grass* was both "embraced and reviled." It is important to note that "embraced" is a positive word. In contrast, "reviled" is a very negative word that means "to scorn or denounce." This pair of antonyms clearly supports choice (E), ANTITHETICAL (Word 11) judgments.
    B: The passage underscores the importance of *Luncheon on the Grass* by concluding that it is "the first modern painting." This clearly supports calling the work "a WATERSHED (Word 236) event in Western art." Note that the first part of choice (D), "a pioneering work," is correct. However, the second part of this answer, "that appealed to traditionalists," is incorrect. Be alert for answers that are half true and half false. Test writers often use this trick to lure students into choosing a wrong answer.

CHAPTER 25

THE CHARACTERISTICS OF WRONG ANSWERS

In the previous chapter, you learned that correct passage-based answers must be fully supported by specific evidence in the passage. Correct answers, however, can sometimes elude even the best students. When this happens, don't panic and make a wild guess. Instead, calmly and methodically use the process of elimination to identify and cross out the wrong answers.

Fortunately, College Board test writers use a number of predictable types of wrong answers. So once again, strive to think like an objective, fact-driven lawyer, determined to disprove answers as a way to find the correct answer. This chapter will examine six of the most common types of wrong answers:

CHRISTIAN SAYS:

Skillful, practiced elimination of wrong answers is my personal favorite way to deal with hard Critical Reading questions. When the going gets tough, I stop looking for the right answer and start identifying wrong answers in an effort to whittle my choices down to a "last man or woman standing" correct answer. Larry's six characteristics of wrong answers are by far the most frequent styles of deception used by the authors of the SAT; learn them well so you will never be fooled again.

I. PARTIALLY TRUE = TOTALLY WRONG

This type of wrong answer features correct information that accurately restates key information in the passage. However, the answer is undermined by the presence of an inaccurate phrase or even a single erroneous word. This type of wrong answer is particularly common in Level 3–5 questions. The following three examples are designed to Illustrate the characteristic features of answers that are Partially True:

1. **I had not realized that Shakespeare's plays could be so exciting. His treatment of topics as diverse as war, comedy, and romance struck me, as it still does, as a miracle of language and construction.**

   To the author, Shakespeare's plays were
   (A) intellectually stimulating but emotionally exhausting
   Note that the phrase "intellectually stimulating" is supported by the passage. However, there is no support for the phrase "emotionally exhausting." So this Partially True answer is totally wrong!
   (B) wondrous and well-crafted
   This answer is an accurate paraphrase of the author's statement that Shakespeare's plays are a "miracle of language and construction."

2. **The Martin Luther King Jr. National Memorial in Washington, D.C., opened on August 22, 2011. Since then, millions of tourists have visited the memorial to pay tribute to Dr. King and to honor his vision of a just society. After admiring the thirty-foot statue of Dr. King, many people stand in front of the Inscription Wall and reverently read the inscribed excerpts from his most inspiring sermons and public addresses.**

   Lines 1–5 ("The Martin...addresses.") primarily serve to
   (A) show the strong appreciation people have for Civil Rights workers
   Note that the phrase "show the strong appreciation people have for" is supported by the passage. However, the passage does not discuss "Civil Rights workers." So this Partially True answer is totally wrong!
   (B) indicate the esteem people feel for Dr. King and his message
   This answer is an accurate paraphrase of the author's statement that "many people stand in front of the Inscription Wall and reverently read the inscribed excerpts."

3. **Mr. Gamble was a quiet fixture at our afternoon football practices. He stood in the same spot, partially concealed by the bleachers. Mr. Gamble was determined to avoid being confused with parents who sporadically dropped by to watch their sons. As a former captain of the Greyhound varsity team, he was a quietly passionate supporter who was a distant observer of everything we did.**

   The description of Mr. Gamble suggests that the narrator views him as
   (A) brooding and detached
   Note that the passage does support describing Mr. Gamble as being "detached." However, there is no support for describing Mr. Gamble as a "brooding" person. So this Partially True answer is totally wrong!
   (B) focused and aloof
   This answer is an accurate paraphrase of the author's description of Mr. Gamble as "a distant observer of everything we did."

II. TOTALLY IRRELEVANT = TOTALLY WRONG

This type of wrong answer features information that is not found in the the passage and is thus Totally Irrelevant. It typically attracts confused test-takers who don't understand the passage. Totally Irrelevant wrong answers can be found in most passage-based questions. The following two examples are designed to illustrate the characteristic features of answers that are Totally Irrelevant:

1. "Archana, I'm really apprehensive about leaving home and going to a college in the South. The people are so different in that part of the country. I'll never fit in. And I'll miss the Rocky Mountains. They are always in the background towering above the Plains. I should stay here in Boulder."

Archana did not appreciate my litany of complaints. "You're a spoiled brat!" she scornfully upbraided. Archana sounded irate, and she was. "Madison, you've led a sheltered life here in the Boulder bubble. It's time for you to go out and experience a new place and meet new people."

Archana would most likely characterize Madison as

(A) an underachiever who lacks motivation
Note that this answer is Totally Irrelevant, since the passage does not say anything about Madison's lack of achievement or motivation. So this Totally Irrelevant answer is totally wrong!
(B) a naïve person who needs to overcome her provincial outlook
This answer accurately paraphrases the author's statement that Archana has "led a sheltered life here in the Boulder bubble" and that it is time for her to "go out and experience a new place and meet new people."

2. Dr. Kreskey dominated the Bell Laboratory during a period of exhilarating scientific discoveries and demoralizing budget cuts. Everyone had an opinion about "the boss." To his admirers, Dr. K was a leader of unquestioned integrity, sincere dedication, and lofty standards of excellence. To his critics, Dr. K was a humorless and imperious tyrant who stubbornly insisted that his vision was best for the organization. In spite of his faults, Dr. Kreskey nevertheless had a knack for instilling an invincible sense of professional pride into each research scientist. For example, whenever he evaluated a new project, Dr. K would convince himself, and us, that it was "the greatest idea since Einstein."

The author's overall evaluation of Dr. Kreskey's leadership is best described as

(A) an exposé of Dr. Kreskey's questionable conduct before he came to the Bell Laboratory
Note that this answer is Totally Irrelevant, because the passage does not discuss Dr. Kreskey's career before the Bell Laboratory. So this Totally Irrelevant answer is totally wrong!
(B) an evenhanded appraisal of Dr. Kreskey's strengths and weaknesses
This answer accurately summarizes the author's balanced portrayal of Dr. Kreskey's strengths and weaknesses.

III. DIRECT ANTITHESIS = TOTALLY WRONG

This type of wrong answer features information that directly contradicts something in the passage. On first glance, this would appear to be an easy answer to delete. However, many test-takers often misunderstand the passage. As a result, they are surprisingly susceptible to this type of wrong answer. The following two examples are designed to illustrate the characteristic features of answers that are the Direct Antithesis of information in the passage.

1. **With its red roofs and Renaissance architecture, Florence is incredibly beautiful from every angle. Standing high atop the Duomo affords awed visitors a panoramic view of the entire city. It feels like turning the pages of an illustrated art history book.**

   Lines 1–7 ("With its...book.") suggest which of the following about the author's reaction to Florence?
   (A) She is bored by the city's mundane sights.
   Note that this directly contradicts the author's excited response to Florence. So this Direct Antithesis of the passage is totally wrong!
   (B) She sees a romanticized version of the city.
   This answer accurately summarizes the author's idealized view of Florence.

2. **Some baseball fans think that instant replay should be restricted to boundary home run calls, while others prefer that it be extended to include base-running calls. Still others prefer to eliminate instant replay and let the umpires call the game.**

   Which generalization about the use of "instant replay" (line 1-2) is most directly supported by the passage?
   (A) There is a strong accord on how to use instant replay.
   Note that this directly contradicts the fact that there are a number of different views on how to use instant replay. So this Direct Antithesis of the passage is totally wrong!
   (B) There is currently no consensus on how to use instant replay.
   This answer accurately summarizes the fact that there are a number of different views on how to use instant replay.

IV. A STEP TOO FAR = TOTALLY WRONG

This type of wrong answer features an unsupported extension of information in the passage. It has great appeal to test-takers who believe that making conjectures is a way to demonstrate their creativity and originality. Avoid this trap! Always remember that your primary objective is to find answers that are supported by the passage. The following two examples are designed to illustrate the characteristic features of answers that go A Step Too Far:

1. **After Gary's father retired, he began to actively use Twitter. Each day he sent Gary a concise, impersonal statement of the things he was doing: "Planted a new row of hostas." Occasionally there was a sentence about a current event or a neighbor. But there was never a sense of his father's presence in these terse messages. It was a one-sided correspondence. His tweets never asked questions, never asked for a reply and never asked for a personal connection.**

The primary function of the passage is to
(A) forecast a probable confrontation between Gary and his father
Note that this answer goes A Step Too Far by speculating on how the relationship between Gary and his father might deteriorate. While it is possible that there will be a confrontation between Gary and his father, this outcome is not certain and it is not specifically supported by the passage. It therefore goes A Step Too Far and is totally wrong!
(B) describe a predictable pattern of behavior between Gary and his father
This answer is an accurate summary of the routine correspondence between Gary and his father.

2. **I grew up on a small town dominated by a large furniture factory. Each morning at exactly 7:45 AM, a long row of cars passed by our house carrying workers to the plant. My friends and I knew it was just after 4:00 PM when we spotted the first cars leaving the factory. The routine seemed an eternal part of our local universe. So it came as a great surprise when the factory closed and the workers and their cars disappeared.**

The passage supports which of the following statements about the workers?
(A) Their jobs were unfulfilling.
Note that this answer goes A Step Too Far by speculating on how the workers viewed their jobs. While it is possible that the workers did think that there jobs were unfulfilling, this inference is not specifically supported by information in the passage. It therefore goes A Step Too Far and is totally wrong!
(B) Their schedule was unvarying.
This answer is an accurate summary of the daily routine described in the passage.

V. TRUE STATEMENT FROM THE WRONG LOCATION = TOTALLY WRONG

This type of wrong answer features a true statement that is supported by information taken from a part of the passage that is not specified by the question. It is designed to trap test-takers who do not carefully read the question. Most questions now direct you to specific line reference. Beware of answers that are taken from earlier or later portions of the passage. The following two examples are designed to illustrate the characteristic features of answers that are True Statements From The Wrong Location:

1. **David was proud of his father's large library and academic accomplishments. But he was also dismayed that his father often became overly absorbed in his work. When David arrived at his father's office, the greeting was always the same. His father would look up, startled, genuinely surprised but glad to see his son. He would then check his watch. "Am I late?" he would say, knowing he was, but enjoying the daily routine.**

   Lines 7–10 ("His father...late?'") indicate that the father views David's arrival as
   (A) an enjoyable ritual
   Note that on first glance this answer appears to be supported by specific phrases in the passage. For example, lines 6–7 say that "the greeting was always the same," and line 11 specifically states that the father enjoyed "the daily routine." So why is this answer incorrect? Note that the question specifically directs you to look for an answer between the words "His father" and "late." Answers based upon information before or after this specific information are wrong. Although this answer is supported by the passage, it is a True Statement From The Wrong Location and is therefore totally wrong!

(B) an unanticipated pleasure
This answer is fully supported by information taken directly from the lines specified in the question. The key word "startled" supports "unanticipated," and the key word "glad" supports "pleasure."

2. **Margaret Miller always liked to pretend that she would do poorly on our calculus tests. She insisted that she didn't understand the material and was certain to fail the next big test. Of course, when no one was looking, Margaret was hard at work studying. In addition to our textbook, she purchased several prep books and even hired a tutor from the local community college. When the test day finally arrived, Margaret was fully prepared. I glanced at her during the test and what do you know—her fingers effortlessly hit the buttons on her expensive calculator, and the correct answer miraculously flashed on her screen. Needless to say, Margaret modestly attributed her high score to good luck.**

   Lines 1–18 ("Margaret Miller...luck") primarily depict Margaret Miller as a
   (A) shrewd student who will be accepted at an elite college
   Note that on first glance this answer is unsupported by the passage and is therefore obviously wrong. It is important to point out that the actual passage was longer than the paragraph reprinted here. In the full passage, an elite college accepted Margaret in the last paragraph. The answer is thus a True Statement From The Wrong Location and is thus totally wrong!
   (B) resourceful but disingenuous student
   This answer is fully supported by information from the passage. Margaret is "resourceful" because she "purchased several prep books and even hired a tutor." She is "disingenuous" because she "liked to pretend she would do poorly."

VI. REPEATED WORD = PROBABLY WRONG

This type of wrong answer features words and even phrases that are picked up from the passage and then repeated in an answer. It can have great allure for many test-takers. After all, tutors and prep books (including this one) stress that it is important to match key words from the passage with a paraphrased answer. So what is wrong with an answer that repeats a key word from the passage? Technically, there is nothing wrong with this type of answer. Experience indicates, however, that most of the time a repeated word is a strong signal that the answer is indeed wrong. So if you do spot a repeated word, be careful and do not immediately assume that the answer is either right or wrong. The following two examples are designed to illustrate the characteristic features of wrong answers that use Repeated Words:

1. **The Russian artist Wassily Kandinsky was the first to paint works that completely abandoned any reference to recognizable reality. Kandinsky's revolutionary discovery that he could convey emotion irrespective of content was influenced by earlier artists. For example, Kandinsky admired Turner's swirling masses of radiant color and Van Gogh's deliberate use of color to express raw emotions.**

The author mentions Turner and Van Gogh to make the point that

(A) Kandinsky was part of a group of artists who admired and supported each other
Note that this answer is very tempting because it repeats the word "admire." The answer is wrong, however, because there is no evidence to support the statement that Kandinsky, Turner, and Van Gogh were part of a "group of artists who admired and supported each other." In this example, "admire" is a Repeated Word designed to lead you to a wrong answer.

(B) Kandinsky drew upon the work of artistic forerunners
This answer is fully supported by the passage. Turner and Van Gogh were artistic forerunners who influenced Kandinsky.

2. **The cheetah may be a gorgeous, sleek sports car among mammals, able to sprint at speeds approaching seventy miles an hour, yet it has not been able to run away from its many miseries. Once the cat ranged throughout the African continent, the Near East, and into southern India; now it is extinct almost everywhere but in scattered patches of sub-Saharan Africa…To make the magnificent cat's story more poignant still, many scientists have concluded that the species is severely inbred, the result of a disastrous population crash thousands of years ago from which the poor animals have hardly had a chance to recover.**
(from Cheetahs by Linda C. Wood)

The author primarily portrays the cheetah as a

(A) poignant but miserable creature
Note that this answer is very tempting, because it repeats the words "poignant" and alludes to "miseries." However, the answer is wrong because the passage does not primarily portray the cheetah as a "poignant but miserable" creature. In this example, "poignant" is a Repeated Word designed to lead you to a wrong answer.

(B) magnificent creature that faces formidable problems
This answer is fully supported by the passage. The cheetah is "magnificent" because it is "a gorgeous, sleek sports car among mammals." It "faces formidable problems" because it is "severely inbred."

WHAT ABOUT EXTREME WORDS?

Many prep books include a tip encouraging students to identify and then eliminate wrong answers that contain extreme words. The prep books then provide examples that do seem egregiously extreme. This "tip" has two problems. First, College Board answers are usually subtle and typically do not include extreme language. Second, on recent tests strong words such as VEHEMENT (Word 67), EMPHATIC (Word 54), INDIGNANT (Word 61), SARDONIC (Word 62), and IRREVERENT (Word 216) have been used frequently as correct answers. Many students may incorrectly assume that these words are "extreme" and then cross them out. Given these problems, I believe that it is prudent to use this "tip" with great caution.

CHAPTER 26
HOW TO READ SHORT AND LONG NARRATIVE PASSAGES

The following questions and answers always occur at the beginning of my first Critical Reading lesson:

ME: Today's lesson will be devoted to Critical Reading passages.

STUDENT 1: Mr. Krieger, what do you think is the best strategy for Critical Reading?
ME: What have your heard is the best strategy?

STUDENT 1: I've heard that it's best to read the whole passage and then answer the questions.

ME: Well that is a traditional approach that is used by many test-takers. Does anyone have any other ideas?

STUDENT 2: I've heard that the best strategy is to read the questions first and then read the passage.

ME: Actually, I used to do that back in the old days, when the passages were shorter and there were fewer questions.

STUDENT 3: What do you do now?

ME: Good question! In today's lesson, I will teach you how to use a revolutionary Critical Reading strategy that is focused and efficient. It has helped my students achieve a significant improvement in their Critical Reading scores. Let's get started!

MICRO AND MACRO QUESTIONS

The debate over whether to read the passage first or read the questions first has dominated discussions on SAT Critical Reading passages for years. Both approaches have strengths and weaknesses; however, both approaches ignore the fundamental reality of the types of questions used on both the short and the long narrative passages. (Chapters 31 and 32 will discuss strategies for reading the short and long dual passages).

Let me begin by distinguishing between "micro" questions and "macro" questions. Micro questions contain line references that direct your attention to specific words, phrases, and sentences. Micro questions are almost always focused on parts of a specific paragraph. In contrast, macro questions are general and typically ask you about the main idea of a passage.

Older versions of the SAT contained a significant number of macro questions. As a result, prep books recommended a macro strategy, based upon first reading the entire passage to gain a sense of the author's main idea and feeling tone. However, this strategy became much less effective when the balance between micro and macro questions dramatically changed with the debut of the new SAT in March 2005.

The SAT you will take features a variety of short and long narrative passages, dominated by micro questions. A content analysis of five released tests from January 2012 to May 2013 reveals that the short and long narrative passages on each test generate between 31 and 32 passage-based questions. These five tests had a combined total of 157 passage-based questions, of which 133, or 85 percent, were micro questions. The 24 remaining questions were divided among 18 main idea questions, three "if true then" questions, two overall tone questions, and one "all of the following EXCEPT" question.

MICRO QUESTIONS RECOMMEND A MICRO STRATEGY

The statistical dominance of micro questions strongly recommends that you adopt a Micro Critical Reading Strategy. Here is a step-by-step guide to the Micro Strategy I teach to my students:

STEP 1: READ THE BLURB
Always begin by reading the italicized blurb. It will provide you with a sense of what the passage will be about. In addition, it usually identifies the characters in fictional passages.

STEP 2: LOOK AT THE FIRST FEW QUESTIONS
Avoid the temptation to go directly to the passage. Instead, look at the questions and identify those that apply to the first paragraph. Now use the line references to underline the words and bracket the sentences identified in each of the paragraph 1 questions.

STEP 3: WHAT IF THE FIRST QUESTION IS A MACRO MAIN IDEA QUESTION?

About a third of the short and long narrative passages begin with a main idea question. This does not mean that you should read the entire passage. Instead, simply skip that question and return to it when you have answered all of the micro questions.

STEP 4: READ THE FIRST PARAGRAPH

Now read the first paragraph and answer each of the micro questions that refer to it. Focus on the key words and line references that you have underlined and bracketed. Always remember that correct answers must have specific support from the passage (See Chapter 24). Don't despair if a question is difficult. Use the process of elimination described in Chapter 25 to cross out wrong answers.

STEP 5: WHAT IF THERE ARE NO FIRST PARAGRAPH QUESTIONS?

Most first paragraphs do generate at least one micro question. If the paragraph does not have a micro question, you should read it anyway. The first paragraph is important because it establishes the setting and tone for the rest of the passage. Would you skip the first ten minutes of a movie? Probably not. So don't be lazy. Always read the first paragraph of an SAT Critical Reading passage.

STEP 6: WHAT IF THE FIRST PARAGRAPH IS VERY LONG?

Hard passages often begin with long first paragraphs. If this happens, break the paragraph into discrete chunks based upon the sequence of micro questions. This approach will help you focus on the key words that will lead you to the correct answers.

STEP 7: NOW GO BACK AND FORTH FROM QUESTIONS TO PARAGRAPHS

Once you have finished the first paragraph, repeat a back-and-forth procedure by looking at the questions, underlining key words, and bracketing referenced sentences.

STEP 8: WHAT IF THERE IS AN INTERIOR MACRO QUESTION?

College Board test-writers sometimes include an interior macro question that applies to a long paragraph. For example, a passage on the October 2010 SAT included the following question: "The final paragraph (lines 48 – 81) is primarily concerned with..." Note that this question asks test-takers to read 33 lines. As always, don't panic. Instead, simply skip this question and proceed to the next set of micro questions. It is interesting to note that the paragraph from lines 48 to 81 generated six micro questions. After you have answered the micro questions go back and answer the macro questions.

STEP 9: NOW ANSWER THE MACRO QUESTIONS

Most (but not all) passages do have one or two macro questions. Once you have answered all the micro questions, you will have read the entire passage. Now go back and answer the macro questions. You will find that the macro questions are usually very straightforward. Of the 24 macro questions asked on the tests from January 2012 to May 2013, six were Level 2, thirteen were Level 3, four were Level 4, and just one (an EXCEPT) question was a Level 5.

STEP 10: NOW BUBBLE IN YOUR ANSWERS

I recommend that you bubble in all the answers to each passage at the same time. This will prevent you from skipping a macro question and then accidentally bubbling it with a micro question. It is important to stress that this is an optional procedure. If you feel more comfortable bubbling in each question as you answer it, then by all means do so. Always be certain that you correctly match each question and answer.

CHRISTIAN SAYS

Before you go on, make sure that you understand exactly how micro and macro questions can be identified, which type you should answer first, and why. Larry's research into the statistics of he Critical Reading breakdown is unique. His special advice offers you a real chance to make a big breakthrough in your Critical Reading score in a short time! (Of course, augmenting your SAT lexicon is also a great way to raise your CR score)!

GUIDED PRACTICE

The following passage and questions are designed to give you an opportunity to apply our Micro Critical Reading Strategy to a practice example. The questions are followed by an annotated set of answers.

Questions 1–9 are based on the following passage.

The following passage was adapted from a memoir published in 1920.

Line

When I first met Harrold at university, he had already dedicated himself to a life as a poet, a "voice," as he liked to say, "for our age." In anyone else, of course, this would have been the rankest pretension, but Harrold's sincere goodwill disarmed all criticism. Besides, with his handsome inheritance, the specific choice of career did
5 not much matter. Poet he would be, and though he was an artist more by predilection than by gift, Harrold made up for what he wanted in native talent with an admirable and affecting diligence.

Then there was his fiancée, Jenny. We all wondered at Harrold's incredible fortune in finding such a girl. It was not that her personal address stunned. On closer
10 acquaintance, one was struck by an ineffable warmth and rightness: Jenny was a magnet that drew us all. Her voice was emblematic of her nature. Though surprisingly low, it was at the same time so liquid and soothing that I remember thinking a wood

Line

thrush would have to speak so if a wood thrush could speak. For all her admiration of Harrold, she was not timid with him in the least and would chaff him over this or
15 that manifestation of male obtuseness with such graceful irreverence that I could have wished myself the daily object of whatever mock scorn she should choose to heap upon me.

Our paths parted. After their wedding, Harrold and Jenny took up residence in a Tuscan villa where the climate was conducive to a "creative harvest," as he called it.
20 I saw them only once after, at the wedding of a mutual friend. Harrold seemed to glow with an inner fire and talked of their life in Italy as though he had gained access to some terrestrial paradise. I had not been particularly impressed by the slender volumes of his verse that appeared at yearly intervals, but I would have gladly let myself be stripped of all talent if I might live in such a state of bliss as my old friend.

25 The bliss was not to last. Back in Tuscany, Jenny contracted malaria and succumbed. Without her, the villa was no longer a paradise, and Harrold returned to London. I made a valiant effort to console him, and he made as valiant an effort to be consoled, but the task was too great, and we both knew it. The burden of shared memory was unbearable, and I think it was with almost a sense of gratitude that Harrold
30 accepted my near-complete withdrawal from his life. I would always write a few lines congratulating him heartily on the publication of every new volume as it appeared, but I only feigned enthusiasm out of compassion: it was clear that Harrold was losing his way as a poet. What before had been mediocrity had since degenerated into mere sterility. Harrold's poems had become all thought, no feeling. One read them,
35 to be sure, but one would never think of reading them aloud or hearing them read. They had no voice.

Then I received his note. I must come at once. The prospect was not encouraging: a dreary hour our two spent so carefully avoiding the one topic that might unite us that we could only end more disunited and dissatisfied than we began.

40 But of course I did go. Harrold met me at the door, and I saw immediately that he was changed. No longer the stoic mask he had worn so gracelessly, his face now enjoyed a mobility that brought out wrinkles yet somehow also made him look younger. "I have something I want you to see," he announced holding a sheaf of papers, then, changing his mind, invited me to sit while he read aloud.

45 It was an elegy, an ode, and a hymn all in one. There was no line but had Jenny as its theme. In the poem, so unlike any other he had written, Harrold stretched the bounds of expression to bursting. I was so overwhelmed by the poem's profusion of emotion that I did not mark the poet's. He stopped halfway through a verse, unable to continue. His eyes were full, but he did not weep. Smiling, rather, he handed
50 me the papers and told me they were mine. At a complete loss what to say or do, I thanked him and left.

Once outside, I made a direct path for Hyde Park* and the nearest bench. I felt I must finish the poem. By the time I read its last line, my sense of connection with the

Line

world around me had become indistinct as the fog rolling up from the Serpentine.*
55 But I was certain I could hear a voice, low, liquid, and clear; that I had been hearing it, in fact, for some time now. Was it only the sound of water splashing distantly in the lake? Or could it be that Harrold the poet had succeeded at last and beyond my wildest imaginings?

*Hyde Park is a large park in west-central London; the Serpentine is a lake in the park.

1. The author indicates in lines 4–7 ("Besides...diligence.") that Harrold chose his particular career primarily because he
   (A) had a pronounced natural ability
   (B) wanted to transcend his personal limitations
   (C) was drawn by a strong personal preference
   (D) needed to find a lucrative career
   (E) felt satisfaction in hard, disciplined work

2. The second paragraph characterizes Jenny as being
   (A) indelible but sarcastic
   (B) lighthearted but supercilious
   (C) timorous but ungainly
   (D) enchanting and self-assured
   (E) impudent and altruistic

3. The author found Jenny's "scorn" (line 16)
   (A) captivating
   (B) ominous
   (C) repugnant
   (D) prescient
   (E) wistful

4. Lines 21–23 ("I had...friend.") suggest that at the time when they were written, the author
   (A) was not a prolific writer
   (B) overrated his own abilities
   (C) was envious of Harold's literary success
   (D) was not completely satisfied with his own life
   (E) underestimated the quality of Harrold's life

5. Lines 31–34 ("it was...voice.") indicate that Harrold's poetry had become
   (A) painfully sentimental
   (B) overly cerebral
   (C) surprisingly fertile
   (D) spontaneously didactic
   (E) carelessly exuberant

6. At the time, the author assumed his visit to Harrold would be "dreary" (line 36) because
   (A) Harrold would still be jealous of the author
   (B) Harrold would be defensive about his poetry
   (C) they would argue endlessly about Harrold's decision to live in Tuscany
   (D) they would spend hours reminiscing about the good times they shared at the university
   (E) it would be difficult to skirt an uncomfortable topic

7. The description of Harrold in lines 38–40 ("Harrold...younger.") reveals
  (A) an alarming juxtaposition
  (B) an expected transformation
  (C) a forlorn condition
  (D) a disingenuous façade
  (E) a surprising contrastl

8. Listening to Harrold read his poem left the author feeling
  (A) nonplussed because he was speechless
  (B) distraught because he was upset
  (C) exasperated because he was irritated
  (D) somber because he was disconsolate
  (E) wary because he was cautious

9. The passage is best described as a
  (A) technical analysis of the qualities of good poetry
  (B) meditation of the values of forgiveness and humility
  (C) recollection of a difficult time in the author's life
  (D) diatribe against privilege and pretension
  (E) reflection on the evocative power of love and loss

STRATEGIC OVERVIEW

Questions 1–8 are micro questions, while Question 9 is the only macro question. This is a typical pattern of questions that is found on many SAT passages. Although Question 8 does not have a line reference, it is a micro question that can be answered from lines 45–46. It is important to remember that the questions are arranged in consecutive order in all short and long narrative passages.

ANSWERS

1. C: The key phrase "more by predilection than by gift" leads you to choice (C) as the correct answer.

2. D: Jenny is best described as "enchanting," because she "was a magnet that drew us all," and "self-assured," because she was "not timid with him."

3. A: The author found Jenny's "mock scorn" a positive characteristic that he wished he could experience each day. This leads us to the positive answer "captivating." Note that "captivating" reinforces the description of Jenny as "enchanting" in Question 2.

4. D: We can conclude that the author "was not completely satisfied with his own life," because he admits that he "would gladly let myself be stripped of all talent" if he could be with Jenny.

5. B: The key sentence, "Harrold's poems became all thought, no feeling," leads you to "cerebral" as the correct answer.

6. E: Choice (E) is a restatement of the key phrase "carefully avoiding the one topic that might unite us."

7. E: The key phrase "I saw immediately that he had changed" leads you to choice (E).

8. A: The key definitional phrase "at a complete loss what to say or do" leads you to "nonplussed because he was speechless" as the correct answer.

9. E: Answer choice (E) succinctly summarizes the twin emotions that dominate the passage.

INDEPENDENT PRACTICE

The Official SAT Study Guide (also known as the "Blue Book") opens with three real SATs that were given in October 2006, January 2007, and May 2007. These three tests contain an excellent selection of short and long narrative passages that will enable you to practice the Micro Critical Reading Strategy.

CHAPTER 27
ANSWERING MAIN IDEA QUESTIONS

Have you ever had the experience of reading a poorly organized blog or magazine article? After impatiently reading paragraph after paragraph, did you wish you could ask the author, "What's your point?"

Reading an unfocused argument is frustrating. Fortunately, you will not have this experience on the SAT. The authors of SAT Critical Reading passages will always present a well-organized argument that is clearly focused and logically presented. The passages may sometimes be boring, but they will never be disjointed or incoherent.

IDENTIFYING MAIN IDEA QUESTIONS

As we discussed in the previous chapter, the short and long narrative passages typically generate three to four main idea questions per test. These questions are designed to test your ability to identify and summarize an author's overall purpose, concern, or argument. Main idea questions are almost always either the first or the last question listed after a passage. As a general rule, they are moderately easy Level 2 and 3 questions.

Main idea questions are very easy to spot. Here are examples of the formats used on recent tests:

- The primary purpose of the passage is to
- The author's primary purpose in the passage is to
- The passage is best described as
- The primary focus on the passage is on
- The passage is primarily concerned with

A CASE EXAMPLE

Read the following passage, and then answer the main idea question. Remember, the answer will accurately summarize the author's purpose and content.

> In 1900, an English archaeologist, Arthur Evans, announced a startling discovery on the island of Crete. He had uncovered ruins that resembled a vast palace similar to the one described in ancient myths. Evans promptly named the people who built the palace the Minoans after their mythological leader King Minos. Excavations soon uncovered a fascinating and extraordinary lost civilization. Wall paintings found in the palace depict a lively people with a zest for athletic contests, festivals, and stylish dress. Clad in ruffled gowns, women of the court wore delicate gold jewelry and styled their hair into long, graceful coils. They took part in activities ranging from dancing to strenuous sports. Unlike Ancient Egypt and Mesopotamia, the Minoans have left no paintings or statues depicting belligerent gods or warrior chieftains leading troops into battle. Is it possible that the Minoans were history's first pacifists?

> The primary purpose of the passage is to
> (A) compare Minoan and Ancient Egyptian cultures
> (B) highlight the role of women in Minoan culture
> (C) speculate on reasons why the Minoans were history's first pacifists
> (D) criticize the methods Arthur Evans used to discover the Minoan palace
> (E) introduce absorbing and distinctive features of Minoan culture

The correct answer is (E). It succinctly and accurately paraphrases the author's main point that excavations "uncovered a fascinating and extraordinary lost civilization."

IDENTIFYING WRONG MAIN IDEA ANSWERS

Suppose that you were asked to write a main idea question for an SAT passage. Writing the question is easy. All you have to do is choose one of the five main idea question formats listed above. Writing the correct answer is also fairly simple. All you have to do is clearly and accurately summarize the author's key argument. But your job is still not finished. The hard part is to write four other answer choices that are attractive but still indisputably wrong.

At first glance, writing the incorrect choices would appear to be a very arduous task. As you might have already guessed, appearances are once again deceiving. In fact, College Board test writers follow a recognizable pattern when they design the incorrect choices for main idea questions. Knowing this pattern will help you eliminate the distractors and use the process of elimination to find the correct answer.

1. ONE OR MORE ANSWERS ARE TOO BROAD

A broad answer goes well beyond the facts provided in the passage. In the Minoan question above, choice (A) is too broad because it goes well beyond what is covered in the passage.

2. ONE OR MORE ANSWERS ARE TOO NARROW

A narrow answer only covers a small portion of the passage. Narrow responses may be true, but they only apply to a paragraph or to a sentence. In the Minoan question above, choices (B) and (C) are too narrow.

3. ONE OR MORE ANSWERS WILL BE INACCURATE

Inaccurate answers are often tempting, because they frequently use actual words from the passage. However, the statement contradicts or is not supported by information in the passage. In the Minoan question above, choice (D) is inaccurate.

Identifying broad, narrow, and inaccurate answer choices will help you eliminate wrong answers and zero in on the correct answer. It is important to point out that College Board test-writers do not have to include a broad, narrow, and inaccurate choice in every main idea question. For example, a question could include one broad choice and three narrow ones. The most important point is to always remember that the correct answer will summarize the main idea and embrace the passage as a whole.

PRACTICE EXAMPLES

The following five examples provide you with an opportunity to practice the skill of answering main idea questions. Answer each question, and then check your response with the explanations in the next section.

1. The cockroach is roughly 250 million years old, which makes it one of the planet's oldest living insects. As it happens, the cockroach is a particularly popular test subject for laboratory research. It adapts well to captivity, lives relatively long, reproduces quickly, and will subsist in full vigor on Purina Dog Chow. The largest American species, up to two inches in length and known as *Periplaneta Americana*, is even big enough for easy dissection. One eminent physiologist has written fondly: "The laboratory investigator who keeps up a battle to rid his rat colony of cockroaches may well consider giving up the rats and working with the cockroaches instead. From many points of view the roach is practically made to order as a laboratory subject. Here is an animal of frugal habits, tenacious of life, eager to live in the laboratory and very modest in its space requirements."
(from *Natural Acts* by David Quammen)

   The primary purpose of the passage is to
   (A) suggest a plan for exterminating cockroaches
   (B) explain why the cockroach received the name *Periplaneta Americana*
   (C) deliver a pointed critique of the ethics of using animals as test subjects in laboratory experiments
   (D) explain why the cockroach is widely used in laboratory experiments
   (E) reveal why cockroaches have survived for over 250 million years

2. To the modern reader, the complex rules of etiquette that precisely regulated Louis XIV's life at the Versailles Palace appear to be a ridiculous and comical waste of time. But Louis knew better. The King explained, "The people over whom we reign, being unable to apprehend the basic reality of things, usually derive their opinion from what they can see with their eyes." Louis was insightful. In France, "the basic reality of things" was that Louis XIV ruled as an absolute monarch by divine right. Unlike the King of England, Louis exercised an undisputed monopoly over all the power of the French government. Viewed from this perspective, the daily rituals at Versailles were an accurate visual display of the power and grandeur of the French monarchy.

The author's primary purpose in the passage is to
(A) scold modern readers for being overly superficial
(B) explain the symbolic function of Louis XIV's daily routine
(C) compare the power of monarchs in France and England
(D) enumerate the rules that regulated daily life at the Versailles Palace during the reign of Louis XIV
(E) trace the development of court etiquette

3. Albrecht Dürer's engraving *The Fall of Man (Adam and Eve)* is the first successful fusion of Northern Renaissance and Italian Renaissance artistic traditions. As a native German, Dürer was heir to an artistic tradition renowned for precise naturalistic details and hidden symbols. Dürer's engraving includes a forest with meticulously drawn foliage and several symbolic animals. But at the same time, Dürer was the first northern artist to visit Italy and absorb the lessons of the Italian Renaissance masters. Thus his graceful figures of Adam and Eve stand in idealized poses, reminiscent of classical statues. Dürer's innovative art brought him unprecedented recognition and financial independence.

The primary purpose of the passage is to
(A) trace the history of Italian Renaissance art
(B) call attention to famous classical statues
(C) describe Dürer's trip to Italy
(D) defend the superiority of Northern Renaissance art
(E) describe how Dürer successfully joined two artistic traditions

4. The recent apparently successful prediction by mathematical models of an appearance of El Niño—the warm ocean current that periodically develops along the Pacific coast of South America—has excited researchers and even the general public. Jacob Bjerknes pointed out over thirty years ago how winds might create either abnormally warm or abnormally cold water in the eastern equatorial Pacific. Nonetheless, until the development of the models, no one could explain why conditions should regularly shift from one to the other, as happens in the periodic oscillations between appearances of the warm El Niño and the so-called anti-El Niño. The answer, at least if the current model that links the behavior of the ocean to that of the atmosphere is correct, is to be found in the ocean.

The author's primary purpose in the passage is to
(A) describe and explain a phenomenon
(B) reject a popular hypothesis
(C) critique a new model
(D) point out the fallacies of using mathematical models
(E) champion a discredited theory

5. Growing up in the Lower East Side, I experienced a vibrant juxtaposition of cultures. At school I learned about my new American homeland and its democratic government. But when the final bell rang, the densely packed streets became my new classroom. The streets had their own rhythm and rules. I knew the names of each gang and the alleys they ruled. I also knew which shopkeepers would give a young boy an extra piece of candy. I'm thankful for both worlds. I know the Gettysburg Address by heart, and I also know how to read and understand the silent language of the street.

   The passage is primarily concerned with the author's
   (A) longing to return to his homeland
   (B) acceptance by street gangs
   (C) desire to learn more about American government
   (D) failure to adjust to the dual cultures he experienced
   (E) ability to learn lessons both in and out of school

ANSWERS

1. D: The second sentence states, "the cockroach is a particularly popular subject for laboratory results." The rest of the passage is devoted to explaining this central point. Choice (D) correctly restates this main idea. Choices (A) and (C) are incorrect because they are inaccurate. Choice (B) is incorrect because it is too narrow, while choice (E) is incorrect because it is too broad.

2. B: The author believes that the complex rules of etiquette followed by Louis XIV were not a waste of time. He explains that they were "an accurate visual display of the power and grandeur of the French monarchy." Choice (B) correctly restates this main idea. Choice (A) is incorrect because it is inaccurate. Choices (C), (D), and (E) are all incorrect because they are too broad.

3. E: The author states that "Dürer's engraving *The Fall of Man (Adam and Eve)* is the first successful fusion of Northern Renaissance and Italian Renaissance artistic traditions." He then devotes the rest of the passage to explaining how Dürer merged these two artistic styles. Choice (E) correctly restates this main idea. Choice (D) is incorrect because it is inaccurate. Choices (B) and (C) are incorrect because they are too narrow, while answer (A) is incorrect because it is too broad.

4. A: The passage is devoted to explaining that El Niño causes weather conditions to "regularly shift." Answer (A) is correct, because it restates this central idea. Choices (B), (C), (D), and (E) are all incorrect because they are inaccurate.

5. E: The author proudly states that he "experienced a vibrant juxtaposition of cultures" growing up on the Lower East Side. He then explains that he is "thankful" for the lessons he learned in the classroom and on the street. Choice (E) is correct because it restates this primary focus of the passage. Choices (A), (B), and (D) are incorrect because they are inaccurate. Choice (C) is incorrect because it is too narrow.

CHAPTER 28
ANSWERING RHETORICAL DEVICE QUESTIONS

What do the terms SIMILE, PARADOX, and PARALLEL STRUCTURE have in common? All three are rhetorical devices that you have probably studied in your language arts and literature classes. All three are frequently tested in SAT passage-based questions. And finally, all three are discussed and illustrated in Chapter 2 of this book.

In recent years, College Board test-writers have begun to ask more and more rhetorical device questions. These questions are not difficult if you have a full command of the key rhetorical devices discussed and illustrated in Chapter 2. This chapter is designed to give you an opportunity to apply these terms to passage-based questions.

CASE EXAMPLES

Knowing how to identify rhetorical devices is an important skill for achieving a high Critical Reading score. The following three examples are designed to introduce you to how rhetorical devices are used in SAT passages and questions.

1. **The apple-green Cadillac with the white vinyl roof and Florida plates turned into Brewster like a greased cobra.**
(from *The Women of Brewster Place* by Gloria Naylor)

    Lines 1–3 make use of which of the following rhetorical devices?
    (A) simile
    (B) understatement
    (C) satire
    (D) irony
    (E) paradox

    Lines 1–3 contain a very vivid SIMILE (Word 23) that compares a Cadillac to a "greased cobra." SIMILES are one of the most frequently tested rhetorical devices. Always remember that a SIMILE is often introduced by the words "like" or "as."

2. **Uncle Amos stood out splendidly above all my uncles because he did not stand out at all. That was his distinction. He was the averagest man I ever knew.**
(from *My Average Uncle Amos* by Robert P. T. Coffin)

    The statement in lines 1–3 ("Uncle Amos… all.") is an example of
    (A) a metaphor
    (B) a euphemism
    (C) a paradox
    (D) an understatement
    (E) an irony

    The statement in lines 1–3 is an excellent example of a PARADOX (Word 26). The author uses a contradictory statement to illustrate a truth about his uncle. Always remember that a PARADOX is based upon a contradiction.

3. **I have the right to education. I have the right to play. I have the right to sing. I have the right to talk. I have the right to go to market. I have the right to speak up.**
(from a 2011 interview with Malala Yousufzai)

    Lines 1–4 ("I have…up.") are notable chiefly for their use of
    (A) hyperbole
    (B) understatement
    (C) paraphrase
    (D) vignette
    (E) parallel structure

    Malala's eloquent statement uses PARALLEL STRUCTURE (Word 30) to underscore her passion and commitment to the cause of women's rights in Pakistan. Malala's repetition of the phrase "I have the right to" provides a particularly powerful example of PARALLEL STRUCTURE. It is important to point out that College Board test-writers sometimes use REPETITION as an answer choice instead of PARALLEL STRUCTURE. Don't let this confuse you. The two terms are equivalent.

PRACTICE EXAMPLES

The following ten examples are designed to give you an opportunity to practice the skill of identifying rhetorical devices. Circle the correct answer.

1. New York City is an ever-changing kaleidoscope of revealing human interactions. For example, I once stood in a long line at a popular Central Park vending stand. A well-known celebrity saw the line and walked around to the back of the cart where I heard him ask if he could avoid the line. When the vendor refused, the pompous celebrity indignantly asked, "Don't you know who I am?" Like a true Jacksonian democrat, the egalitarian vendor replied, "Of course! But you still gotta wait in line!"

This passage makes use of which of the following rhetorical devices?
I.   metaphor
II. allusion
III. anecdote

(A) I only
(B) II only
(C) I and II only
(D) II and III only
(E) I, II, and III

2. Nobody else could see much of anything through this telescope, nor did I have a great deal of initial success, lacking experience as I did—and having been a bit unnerved when, on one of my first attempts to use the thing, I looked through its four-power finder scope and was confronted by the grotesquely magnified image of a flying cockroach who had just landed on the tube and was scurrying away.
(from *Seeing in the Dark* by Timothy Ferris)

This paragraph makes use of which rhetorical device?
(A) a witty lampoon
(B) a hypothetical conjecture
(C) an obscure allusion
(D) a humorous anecdote
(E) a dramatic hyperbole

3. Countless suspicious eyes followed Dorothea Lange as she entered a sprawling cardboard slum that its Depression-era residents called a "Hooverville." As she approached a homeless woman the famed photographer asked, "How are you today?" The destitute but proud woman looked Lange directly in the eye and said, "Let me give you a tour of my cardboard palace."

The homeless woman's use of the word "palace" (line 10) is best characterized as
(A) anecdotal
(B) belligerent
(C) ironic
(D) conditional
(E) neighborly

4. Uhmma's hands are as old as sand. They have always been old, even when they were young. In the mornings, they would scratch across our sleeping faces as she smoothed our foreheads, our cheeks, and tell us quietly, Wake up. Time for school.
(from *A Step From Heaven* by An Na)

The paragraph makes use of which of the following rhetorical devices?
I.   simile
II. understatement
III. paradox

(A) I only
(B) II only
(C) I and II only
(D) I and III only
(E) II and III only

5. The question "Why have there been no great women artists?" is simply the top tenth of an iceberg of misinterpretation and misconception; beneath lies a vast dark bulk of shaky ideas about the nature of art and its situational concomitants, about the nature of human abilities in general and of human excellence in particular, and the role that the social order plays in all this.
(from *Why Have There Been No Great Women Artists* by Linda Nochlin)

The iceberg (line 3) functions as
   (A) a satirical commentary
   (B) an apt metaphor
   (C) a subtle understatement
   (D) a personal anecdote
   (E) an extended allegory

6. Menhaden have always been an integral, if unheralded, part of America's history. This was the fish that Native Americans taught the Pilgrims to plant with their corn. This was the fish that made larger-scale agriculture viable in the eighteenth and early nineteenth centuries for those farming the rocky soils of New England and Long Island. As the industrial revolution transformed the nation, this was the fish whose oil literally greased the wheels of manufacture, supplanting whale oil as a principal industrial lubricant and additive by the 1870s.
(from *The Most Important Fish in the Sea: The Menhaden and America* by H. Bruce Franklin)

Lines 3–11 ("This was..the") are notable for their use of
   (A) repetition
   (B) outrageous hyperbole
   (C) symbolic motifs
   (D) play on words
   (E) parenthetical expression

7. Marine biologist Sara Gottlieb, author of a groundbreaking study on menhaden's filtering capability, compares their role with the human liver's: "Just as your body needs its liver to filter out toxins, ecosystems also need those natural filters." Overfishing menhaden, she says, "is just like removing your liver."
(from *The Most Important Fish in the Sea: The Menhaden and America* by H. Bruce Franklin)

Sara Gottlieb makes use of which of the following rhetorical devices?
   (A) analogy
   (B) allusion
   (C) personification
   (D) euphemism
   (E) hyperbole

8. I remember the walk we took one morning… About halfway down the beach there was a tall wooden platform shaped like a castle turret. During the summer months lifeguards stood up there and kept an eye on the swimmers…I simply couldn't believe that I was about to move to a place where there was no ocean… Because the ocean had always been there, in good times as well as the bad times of my life…the tide rising and falling just as it always did, no matter what and it seemed to me that even if you weren't actively letting your emotions ride its surface, the ocean still went on giving you something, teaching you some sort of lesson.
(from *Goodbye Tsugumi* by Banana Yoshimoto)

The author makes use of which of the following rhetorical devices?
   I. analogy
   II. figurative language
   III. personification

   (A) I only
   (B) II only
   (C) I and II only
   (D) I and III only
   (E) II and III only

9. It's April 1979, and I'm standing in a crowded living room on the Upper Westside, sipping wine and surveying the surroundings. The room, modest except for the walls lined with magisterial bookshelves—this is mostly a literary, or at least a writing crowd—is buzzing with the noise of animated group-talk... In the group next to me, the subject of discussion is X, a well-known writer and literary critic whose opinions, in the opinion of this group, are terribly wrong. "The man has a regrettable penchant for Saul Bellow. It's his Achilles heel," a short, pudgy man pronounced with languid deliberation.
(from *Lost in Translation* by Eva Hoffman)

The passage makes use of which of the following rhetorical devices?
   (A) literary allusion
   (B) hyperbole
   (C) qualification
   (D) rebuttal
   (E) paradox

10. The sightseer (at the Grand Canyon) may be aware that something is wrong. He may simply be bored; or he may be conscious of the difficulty: that the great natural wonder yawning at his feet somehow eludes him. The harder he looks at it the less he can see. It eludes everybody.
(from *The Message in the Bottle* by Walker Percy)

The passage includes an example of which rhetorical device?
   (A) extended anecdote
   (B) dramatic foil
   (C) humorous caricature
   (D) paradox
   (E) euphemism

ANSWERS

1. **E:** In order for METAPHOR to be the correct answer, the author must compare two unrelated objects. The opening sentence meets this test by comparing New York City to "an ever-changing kaleidoscope." In order for ALLUSION to be the correct answer, there must be a reference to a historical or literary person or place. The passage meets this test when the author calls the vendor "a true Jacksonian democrat." This is an ALLUSION to the value President Andrew Jackson placed on the importance of common man. In order for ANECDOTE to be the correct answer, there must be a short story intended to illustrate a key point. The story about the street vendor meets this test by illustrating the egalitarian nature of contemporary American social norms. The correct answer is (E), since the passage includes a METAPHOR (Word 24), ALLUSION (Word 33), and ANECDOTE (Word 21).

2. **D:** In order for ANECDOTE to be the correct answer, there must be a short, personal story that illustrates a key point. The description in this passage meets both of these tests. The story is short, personal, and it illustrates the author's lack of initial success. The correct answer is therefore ANECDOTE (Word 21). Note that by College Board standards this is a humorous story!

3. **C:** In order for IRONY to be the correct answer, the author must say one thing while implying something else. The homeless woman's use of the word "palace" meets this test. A palace is a large opulent building. In contrast, the woman actually lives in a cardboard shack. The correct answer is therefore IRONIC (Word 28).

4. **D:** In order for SIMILE to be the correct answer, the author must use "like" or "as" to compare two unlike things. The description in line 1 meets this test, since Uhmma's hands are compared to sand. In addition, the passage contains a PARADOX, since the author describes Uhmma's hands as being "old, even when they were young." This contradictory statement expresses a truth about Uhmma. The correct answer is therefore SIMILE (Word 23) and PARADOX (Word 26).

5. B: In order for METAPHOR to be the correct answer, the author must compare two unrelated objects without using "like" or "as." The author uses the iceberg as a METAPHOR for a huge mass of "misinterpretation and misconception." The correct answer is therefore AN APT METAPHOR (Word 24).

6. A: In order for REPETITION to be the correct answer, the author must repeat words and phrases that are similar in meaning and structure. The author's repetition of the phrase, "This was the fish," meets this test. The correct answer is therefore REPETITION. Note that PARALLEL STRUCTURE (Word 30) would also have been a correct answer.

7. A: In order for ANALOGY to be the correct answer, an author must compare an unfamiliar idea or object with a familiar one. Sara Gottlieb's quote meets this test by comparing the menhaden's filtering function with the human liver's filtering function. The correct answer is therefore ANALOGY (Word 36).

8. E: In order for FIGURATIVE LANGUAGE to be the correct answer, an author must use either a SIMILE or a METAPHOR or both. The author meets this test by comparing the "tall wooden platform" to a "castle turret." In addition, the author uses PERSONIFICATION by giving the ocean the human ability to teach a lesson. The correct answer is therefore FIGURATIVE LANGUAGE (see Words 23 and 24) and PERSONIFICATION (Word 25).

9. A: In order for LITERARY ALLUSION to be the correct answer, the passage must include a direct reference to an author, work of literature, or literary figure. The passage meets this test by referring to both the well-known 20th-century author Saul Bellow and the legendary Greek hero Achilles. The correct answer is therefore LITERARY ALLUSION (Word 33).

10. D: In order for PARADOX to be the correct answer, the passage must include a contradictory statement that expresses a truth. The sentence, "The harder he looks at it the less he can see," meets this test. The correct answer is therefore PARADOX (Word 26).

CHAPTER 29
ANSWERING ATTITUDE, TONE, AND MOOD QUESTIONS

Take a close look at the following list of words. What do they all have in common?
- HAPPINESS
- SADNESS
- FEAR
- ANGER
- SURPRISE
- DISGUST

Each of these words describes a different mood. A MOOD is a predominant emotion. If you are with a friend, how can you determine if he or she is angry or happy? In our everyday conversations, we pay close attention to a person's tone of voice and body language. For example, a person who is angry will often raise his or her voice and frown.

Interpreting a person's mood requires good human relation skills. Interpreting a writer's mood requires a good vocabulary and good critical reading skills. Each author has an ATTITUDE, or state of mind, toward the subject he or she is writing about. While authors cannot literally frown or smile at the reader, they can reveal their attitudes by the descriptive phrases and examples they use.

ATTITUDE, MOOD, AND TONE QUESTIONS
SAT test-writers often ask you to determine an author's attitude, mood, or tone. These questions are easy to spot. Here are examples of the formats used on typical tests:
- The author's attitude toward X is best described as
- The author's tone in the passage is best described as
- The tone of lines xx–yy is best described as
- The author uses the word _____ to express
- The author's attitude toward X changed from _____ to _____
- Compared to the tone of Passage 1, the tone of Passage 2 is more _____

THE IMPORTANCE OF USING POSITIVE AND NEGATIVE WORDS

In Chapter 19, you learned how to use positive and negative words to help you answer sentence completion questions. The same skill can help you master attitude, tone, and mood questions. Since most of these questions direct you to a sentence or paragraph, always carefully examine these lines for positive and negative words and phrases. Positive words and phrases indicate that the author approves of a person, place, or idea. Negative words and phrases indicate that the author disapproves of a person, place, or idea. Once you have gained a sense of whether the author is positive or negative about a subject, delete the choices that do not reflect this view. Chapter 4 defines and illustrates thirty key attitude, tone, and mood words.

CASE EXAMPLES

Knowing how to identify an author's attitude, tone, and mood is an important skill for achieving a high Critical Reading score. The following two examples are designed to illustrate how key words can completely change an author's attitude toward a subject.

1. **For as long as I can remember, in our town people idolized Coach J. D. Harris and spoke about him with awe and respect. Both his former and current players praise Coach Harris' dedication, work ethic, and ability to inspire his teams to perform at a championship level.**

   According to the narrator, the town's attitude toward Coach Harris is best characterized as
   (A) indifferent
   (B) disdainful
   (C) adulatory
   (D) amused
   (E) ambivalent

   The narrator uses a number of positive words to describe how the town views Coach Harris. For example, he is an "idolized figure" who is spoken of with "awe and respect." In addition, his players all consistently praise Coach Harris. These positive descriptive words all support ADULATORY (Word 441) as the correct answer to this question.

2. **For as long as anyone can remember, Coach J.D. Harris has been a controversial figure in our town, where he is spoken about with both awe and jealousy. Both his former and current players praise Coach Harris' determination, work ethic, and ability to inspire his teams to perform at a championship level. However, former assistant coaches describe Coach Harris as vain, autocratic, and willing to do anything to win.**

   According to the narrator, the town's attitude toward Coach Harris is best characterized as
   (A) indifferent
   (B) disdainful
   (C) adulatory
   (D) amused
   (E) ambivalent

   Note that the narrator now tempers his portrayal of how the town views Coach Harris. For example, he is now described as a "controversial figure" who is spoken of with both "awe and jealousy." While Coach Harris' players continue to praise his performance, his assistant coaches have a negative view. They describe Coach Harris as "vain" and "autocratic." Taken together, these mixed views support AMBIVALENT (Word 71) as the correct answer to this question.

PRACTICE EXAMPLES

The following ten examples are designed to give you an opportunity to practice the skill of identifying an author's attitude, tone, and mood. Circle the correct answers.

1. On October 4, 1957, the Soviet Union stunned the world by launching Sputnik, the first human-made satellite to orbit the Earth. The American public worried about what this ominous event meant and impatiently waited to see how President Eisenhower would respond.

   The American public's attitude toward the launch of Sputnik can best be described as
   (A) energized
   (B) belligerent
   (C) skeptical
   (D) apprehensive
   (E) despondent

2. The director's meticulous attention to plot, dialogue, and costume are among the highlights of a brilliant film that clearly establishes Sanjana Mehta as a rising star in the film industry.

   The tone of the sentence is best described as
   (A) scathing
   (B) effusive
   (C) cryptic
   (D) maudlin
   (E) exasperated

3. Jazz is filled with eccentrics—idiosyncratic people with odd habits and prickly personalities. Jelly Roll Morton, however, is at the head of the pack. A boaster, con man, liar, gambler, he nonetheless possessed a winning charm and a high musical intelligence. He claimed to have invented jazz and, like the boxer Muhammad Ali, insisted that he was its greatest practitioner, but in his music he was both honest and deadly serious. (from *The Great Jazz Artists* by James Lincoln Collier)

   The author's attitude toward Jelly Roll Morton is best described as
   (A) open disdain
   (B) undisguised envy
   (C) evenhanded respect
   (D) nostalgic regret
   (E) amused skepticism

4. There is only one way to shield the United States from the deleterious effects produced by our national addiction to fossil fuels. We must launch a sustained program to develop such green alternatives as wind and solar power. Such a farsighted policy will yield numerous benefits. It will end our dangerous dependence upon importing oil from nations that are often hostile to our national interest. It will also spur economic growth by creating new industries and new jobs.

The tone of lines 1–13 ("There is…jobs.") is best described as
   (A) unequivocal
   (B) impartial
   (C) resigned
   (D) triumphant
   (E) whimsical

5. The Anasazi, or Ancient Ones, lived in the valleys and canyons of the American Southwest. Like other people in pre-Columbian America, the Anasazi did not have horses, mules, or the wheel. Instead, they relied on human labor to quarry sandstone from the canyon walls and move it to the site. Skilled builders then used a mud-like mortar to construct walls up to five stories high.

The author's overall tone in lines 1–10 ("The Anasazi…high.") is best described as
   (A) disdainful and judgmental
   (B) brooding and distant
   (C) bewildered and incredulous
   (D) concerned and inquisitive
   (E) objective and scholarly

6. Almost 200,000 Jews managed to survive the horrors of the Nazi death camps. Many clung to life so that they could bear witness to what had happened. The survivors' efforts were not in vain. When a Nazi commander named Adolf Eichman was asked about his hideous deeds, he replied, "I will obey, obey, obey." The Holocaust demonstrated that evil orders must never be obeyed and that the values of tolerance and respect for others must be preserved.
(from *World History Perspectives on the Past* by Larry Krieger)

The author's tone in the final sentence ("The Holocaust…preserved.") is best characterized as
   (A) condescending
   (B) sardonic
   (C) dismissive
   (D) intrigued
   (E) didactic

7. Growing up in the Lower East Side of New York City, I experienced a jarring juxtaposition of cultures. At school I learned about my new American homeland and its democratic government. But when the final bell rang, the densely packed streets and impersonal playgrounds became my new classrooms. I quickly learned to avoid the suspicious eyes of vigilant shopkeepers watching for young shoplifters. I was wary of both worlds. I knew the Gettysburg Address by heart and I also knew how to read and understand the silent language of the street. I soon became someone else. It wasn't hard to imagine that great dangers lay ahead.

The author's overall attitude toward the Lower East Side is best described as
   (A) unalloyed fear
   (B) weary cynicism
   (C) cautious unease
   (D) cheerful optimism
   (E) studied neutrality

8. The belief that teenagers will inevitably succumb to peer pressure is both widespread and erroneous.

   The tone of this statement is best described as
   (A) caustic
   (B) dismayed
   (C) emphatic
   (D) ambivalent
   (E) apologetic

9. I thought about my late husband as I sat beneath our favorite tree. I am sure I had a soft, distant smile on my face as I remembered our shared dreams. We always imagined a happy retirement blessed with good health. But then cancer took away our future, and I am left with a slow and painful dance with grief.

   The narrator's mood in lines 1–6 ("I thought... health.") is best characterized as
   (A) wistful
   (B) lighthearted
   (C) exasperated
   (D) morose
   (E) nonchalant

10. Margaret Miller always liked to pretend that she would do poorly on our calculus tests. She insisted that she didn't understand the material and was sure to fail the next big test. Of course, when no one was looking, Margaret was hard at work studying. In addition to our textbook, she studied several prep books and even hired a tutor from the local community college. When the test day finally arrived, Margaret was fully prepared. I glanced at her during the test and what do you know—her fingers effortlessly hit the buttons on her expensive calculator, and the correct answer miraculously flashed on her screen. Needless to say, Margaret modestly attributed her high score to good luck.

    In context, which best describes the author's tone in the final two sentences ("I glanced... luck.")?
    (A) empathetic
    (B) measured
    (C) confounded
    (D) sardonic
    (E) laudatory

ANSWERS

1. D: The American public's attitude toward the launch of Sputnik is defined by the key words "worried" and "impatiently." These words will lead you to select an answer that conveys a feeling of unease and misgiving. The correct answer is therefore APPREHENSIVE.

2. B: The tone of this sentence is conveyed in the series of positive words that the author uses to describe Sanjana's work. The key words "meticulous" "brilliant," and "a rising star" all convey a feeling of lavish and unrestrained praise. The correct answer is therefore EFFUSIVE (Word 229).

3. C: The author's attitude toward Jelly Roll Morton is complex. On the one hand, he lists a series of negatives that include describing Morton as "a boaster, con man, liar, gambler." However, these negative traits are balanced by the author's list of positive characteristics that include "a winning charm," and "high musical intelligence." The author thus provides an EVENHANDED (Word 75) description of Jelly Roll Morton. The author's concluding statement that "in his music he was both honest and deadly serious" conveys the author's concluding attitude of respect. The correct answer is therefore EVENHANDED RESPECT.

4. A: The author's tone is clearly established in the first five words, when he confidently asserts, "There is only one way." This sense of strong conviction establishes a tone that is UNEQUIVOCAL (Word 294).

5. E: The author uses a straightforward presentation of facts to establish an overall tone that is impartial, academic, and learned. The correct answer is therefore OBJECTIVE AND SCHOLARLY (Word 58).

6. E: The author's final sentence is intended to convey an important message about refusing to obey evil orders while also defending the values of "tolerance and respect for others." The correct answer is therefore DIDACTIC (Word 53).

7. C: The author succinctly summarizes his attitude toward the Lower East Side's "jarring juxtaposition of cultures" when he declares, "I'm wary of both worlds." The key word "wary" tells us that the author is cautious. His final acknowledgement that "great dangers lay ahead" expresses his sense of unease. The correct answer is therefore CAUTIOUS UNEASE.

8. C: The author unambiguously declares that the widespread belief that teenagers "will inevitably succumb to peer pressure" is "erroneous." The author's forceful statement conveys a feeling of great conviction. The correct answer is therefore EMPHATIC (Word 54).

9. A: The narrator's overall mood is complex and nuanced. Although she is clearly very sad, the narrator is not MOROSE or deeply depressed. As she reflects on the passing of her husband, the narrator is neither lighthearted (Word 59) nor exasperated (Word 467). The key phrase, "I had a soft, distant smile on my face," supports the view that her overall mood is sadly thoughtful. The correct answer is therefore WISTFUL (Word 73).

10. D: The author prepares us for his final two sentences by stating that Margaret "liked to pretend that she would do poorly in calculus." However, while no one was looking, Margaret SURREPTITIOUSLY (Word 582) studied prep books and even hired a personal tutor. These CLANDESTINE (Word 581) activities helped prepare Margaret to achieve a high score on her calculus test. Given this context, it comes as no surprise that the author mocks Margaret's "effortless" performance and false modesty. SARDONIC (Word 62) best captures the author's very sarcastic tone.

CHAPTER 30

ANSWERING VOCABULARY–IN–CONTEXT QUESTIONS

Many words in the English language have multiple meanings. For example, the *Free Online Dictionary* lists seven different definitions or uses of the word *common*. Possible definitions of *common* include: "shared" (common interests), "widespread" (a common saying), "ordinary" (a common person), "coarse" (common manners), "familiar" (a common sight), "plain" (a common face), and "frequent" (a common occurrence).

When a word has many different meanings, how do you know which one the author is using? The intended meaning clearly depends upon the context in which the word is being used. For example, what does the word *common* mean within the context of this sentence: "She didn't see herself as a hero but simply as a common citizen." Since the author tells us that the woman did not see herself as a hero, we are looking for a definition of *common* that means the opposite of "hero." Within the context of this sentence, *common* means "ordinary."

VOCABULARY–IN–CONTEXT QUESTIONS
College Board test-writers are well aware of the large number of common words that have uncommon definitions. Recent tests have included more and more questions designed to test your knowledge of these words. Chapter 13 defines and illustrates forty key multiple meaning words.

Vocabulary-in-context questions are specifically designed to test your ability to use contextual clues to determine the meaning of a word or phrase with multiple meanings. Your SAT will include three to five vocabulary-in-context questions. Fortunately, these questions are very easy to spot. Here are the two most frequently used question stems:
- In line 15, the word "common" most nearly means
- In context, the phrase "XYZ" is best understood to mean

A CASE EXAMPLE

Read the following paragraph, and then answer the accompanying vocabulary-in-context question:

> In 1492, two complex but totally different cultures collided. Europeans believed that land could be bought, sold, and divided. In contrast, Native Americans viewed land as a common resource that, like water and air, could be used by everyone.

> In line 3, "common" most nearly means
> (A) coarse
> (B) plain
> (C) frequent
> (D) familiar
> (E) shared

All vocabulary-in-context questions provide a line reference. Your first step is to use this reference to go back to the passage and locate the appropriate sentence. It is wise to read both the sentence you are referred to and the ones that precede and follow it. This will provide you with a more complete context.

Vocabulary-in-context questions are very similar to sentence completion questions. As you have learned, each sentence completion question contains a key word or phrase that will lead you to the correct answer. The same principle applies to vocabulary-in-context questions. In the example above, Native Americans are described as viewing land as a "common resource that...could be used by everyone." In contrast, Europeans "believed that land could be bought, sold, and divided." Native Americans viewed land as a resource that should be shared by everyone. Although choices (A), (B), (C), and (D) are all possible meanings of *common*, none of them is supported by contextual clues in the passage. Choice (E) is therefore the correct answer.

In this example, all of the answer choices are different definitions of the word *common*. It is important to remember that vocabulary-in-context answer choices can also include unrelated words. Don't let unrelated words fool you. They are distractors and should be deleted.

PRACTICE EXAMPLES

Read each of the following ten paragraphs. Then use the contextual clues to determine the best answer for each question. Circle the correct answer.

1. There is only one way to shield the United States from the deleterious effects produced by our national addiction to fossil fuels. We must launch a sustained program to develop such green alternatives as wind and solar power. Such a farsighted policy will yield numerous benefits. It will end our dangerous dependence upon importing oil from nations that are often hostile to our national interests. It will also spur economic growth by creating new industries and new jobs.

In line 8, "yield" most nearly means
   (A) surrender
   (B) concede
   (C) produce
   (D) collapse
   (E) retain

2. In 1883, Paul Gauguin left his family and a comfortable job to pursue a career as an artist. Gauguin promptly abandoned traditional paintings for what he called his "savage instinct." Seeking pure sensation untainted by decadent French civilization, Gauguin spent the final ten years of his life in Tahiti. He lived in a native hut and painted vividly colored, symbolic works that drew their inspiration from Tahitian carvings and customs.

In line 10, "drew" most nearly means
   (A) sketched
   (B) lured
   (C) derived
   (D) pumped out
   (E) repelled

3. In Stanley Milgram's famous series of experiments on obedience, his naïve subjects were innocent of the experiment's true purpose. Milgram cleverly told them that he was testing the effects of punishment on learning and memory. In reality, Milgram was testing factors that promote obedience to a person who is perceived as a legitimate authority figure.

In line 3, "innocent" most nearly means
   (A) blameless
   (B) unaware
   (C) trusting
   (D) unsullied
   (E) harmless

4. Sonia Sotomayor is the first Hispanic and the third woman appointed to the United States Supreme Court. In her book *My Beloved World* Sotomayor recounts her life, from growing up in a crime-ridden Bronx housing project to attending Yale Law School and serving on the nation's highest court. Although her family lacked many material comforts, Sotomayor's home was always rich in love and understanding.

In line 10, "rich" most nearly means
   (A) wealthy
   (B) splendid
   (C) filling
   (D) deep
   (E) abundant

5. Creating a world history textbook proved to be a difficult and often arduous undertaking. My first step was to write down a preliminary list of topics and then quickly group them into a rough chronological sequence. My editor promptly ordered me to reduce the list to 36 chapters, one for each week of the school year.

In line 5, "rough" most nearly means
   (A) rugged
   (B) harsh
   (C) untamed
   (D) boorish
   (E) approximate

6. A massive wave of "new" immigrants from southern and eastern Europe began to pour into American cities during the 1890s. They soon received a cold reception from unsympathetic Americans who kept their distance from the alien newcomers and their strange customs. One Italian saying expressed the sense of disillusionment felt by many immigrants: "I came to America because I heard the streets were paved with gold. When I got here, I found out three things: First, the streets weren't paved with gold; second, they weren't paved at all; and third, I was expected to pave them."

In line 4, "cold" most nearly means
(A) impersonal
(B) freezing
(C) stale
(D) unconscious
(E) animated

7. Lyndon Johnson was one of the most influential Senate majority leaders in American history. Standing six foot three, the tall Texan dominated any room he entered. Johnson demonstrated great skill in the give-and-take needed to reach an agreement. People called his legendary ability to persuade senators to support his bills "the Johnson treatment." The Johnson treatment included a liberal use of flattery, supplemented with generous special favors.

In line 10, "liberal" most nearly means
(A) freethinking
(B) tolerant
(C) broad
(D) plentiful
(E) progressive

8. The kidnapping of Charles Lindbergh, Jr., the son of the world famous aviator Charles Lindbergh, was one of the most highly publicized crimes in the 20th century. The twenty-month-old child was abducted from his family home near Hopewell, New Jersey, on the evening of March 1, 1932. After an exhaustive investigation that took over two years, authorities arrested Bruno Hauptmann. A solid body of circumstantial evidence linked Hauptmann to the crime, convincing jurors to find him guilty. But Hauptmann never confessed, and he proclaimed his innocence until his execution on April 3, 1936.

In line 11, "solid" most nearly means
(A) substantial
(B) unbroken
(C) rugged
(D) uniform
(E) unanimous

9. Mr. Hosokawa chose *Rusalka* as a measure of his respect for Miss Coss. It was the centerpiece of her repertoire and would require no extra preparation on her behalf, a piece that surely would have been in her program had he not requested it…He simply wanted to hear her sing *Rusalka* while standing close to her in a room. (from *Bel Canto* by Ann Patchett)

In line 1, "measure" most nearly means
(A) dimensions
(B) quantity
(C) plan
(D) indicator
(E) procedure

10. In his book *Cyber War*, government security expert Richard A. Clarke defines cyberwarfare as "actions by a nation-state to penetrate another nation's computers or networks for the purposes of causing damage or disruption." Clarke warns that China, Russia, and North Korea are devoting significant resources to preparing for cyber attacks against vulnerable American transportation, financial, and utility networks. At a major security conference he called upon the President and Congress to develop a broad plan to protect these vital U.S. facilities from hostile cyber attacks.

In line 14, "broad" most nearly means
(A) focused
(B) comprehensive
(C) open
(D) deep
(E) roomy

ANSWERS

1. C: The passage tells you that an energy policy based on green alternatives "will yield numerous benefits." The next two sentences then describe some of these benefits. Given this context, you can conclude that YIELD (Word 570) has a meaning that is similar to "create." The correct answer is therefore PRODUCE.

2. C: The passage tells you that Gauguin "abandoned traditional paintings." Instead he spent his final year in Tahiti, where he drew his inspiration from local carvings and customs. Given this context, you can conclude that DREW has a meaning that is the opposite of "abandoned" and is consistent with "obtained." The correct answer is therefore DERIVED.

3. B: The passage tells you that Milgram's "naïve subjects were innocent" of the real purpose of his experiments. Instead of revealing the truth, Milgram told his subjects that the experiment was about "the effects of punishment on learning and memory." Given this context, you can conclude that INNOCENT has a meaning that is consistent with being naïve or not properly informed. The correct answer is therefore UNAWARE.

4. E: The passage tells you that although Sotomayor's family "lacked many material comforts," it "was always rich in love and understanding." The key reversal word "although" tells you to look for a meaning of RICH that contrasts with "lacked." Given this context, you can conclude that RICH has a meaning that is the opposite of "lacked" and is consistent with "full." The correct answer is therefore ABUNDANT.

5. E: The passage tells you that after writing "a preliminary list of topics," the narrator quickly grouped them in "a rough chronological sequence." The key phrase "quickly grouped" tells you to look for a meaning of ROUGH (Word 557) that is similar in meaning to "nearly accurate." Given this context, the correct answer is therefore APPROXIMATE.

6. A: The passage tells you that the new

immigrants "received a cold reception from unsympathetic Americans who kept their distance from the alien newcomers and their strange customs." The key phrases "unsympathetic Americans" and "kept their distance" tell you that the immigrants did not receive a warm welcome. Given this context, you can conclude that COLD (Word 555) has a meaning similar to "detached and distant." The correct answer is therefore IMPERSONAL.

7. D: The passage tells you that the "Johnson treatment included a liberal use of flattery, supplemented with generous special favors." The key word "generous" tells you that Lyndon Johnson made great use of flattery. Given this context, you can conclude that LIBERAL (Word 548) has a meaning similar to "extensive." The correct answer is therefore PLENTIFUL.

8. A: The passage tells you that a "solid body of circumstantial evidence linked Hauptmann to the crime." The key word "circumstantial" tells you that the evidence involved at least some conjectures. In addition, Hauptmann always maintained his innocence. Given this context, you can conclude that SOLID (Word 580) has a meaning that is similar to "considerable." The correct answer is therefore SUBSTANTIAL.

9. D: The passage tells you that "Mr. Hosokawa chose *Rusalka* as a measure of his respect for Miss Coss." The passage concludes by telling you that Mr. Hosokawa "wanted to hear her sing *Rusalka* while standing close to her in a room." The key phrase "standing close to her in a room" demonstrates Mr. Hosokawa's great respect for Miss Coss. Given this context, you can conclude that MEASURE has a meaning that is similar to "point to or show." The correct answer is therefore INDICATOR.

10. B: The passage tells you that security expert Richard A. Clarke warns that hostile cyber attacks could threaten vulnerable American "industrial, financial, and governmental targets." Clarke has therefore called upon the President and Congress to develop "a broad plan to protect vital facilities." Given this context, you can conclude that BROAD (Word 550) has a meaning that is similar to "extensive." The correct answer is therefore COMPREHENSIVE.

CHAPTER 31
INTRODUCING PAIRED PASSAGES

Have you ever asked your friends what they thought of a new movie? Did everyone have the same opinion? Probably not. Some of your friends may have liked the special effects, while others may have thought that the plot was pedestrian. People often have different opinions about the same movie, television program, YouTube video or national issue, because they look at these things from different points of view.

A person's point of view is the way he or she interprets topics or events. Learning how to identify and compare different points of view is an important critical thinking skill. As citizens of a democracy, you are often asked to evaluate different viewpoints on an issue. Because of the importance of this skill, each SAT includes both a short and a long pair of passages, written by two authors who have contrasting viewpoints on a topic.

SHORT PAIRED PASSAGES

1. FORMAT
Short paired passages consist of two 10–13 line paragraphs written by two different authors. The passages are brief but focused statements on the same topic. The two authors will typically present contrasting viewpoints on the same issue. For example, in one recent short paired passage, the author of Passage 1 discussed the advantages of a flexible work schedule. The second author then presented a possible negative consequence of this policy.

2. LOCATION
Short paired passages can appear in either of the two 25-minute Critical Reading sections. They are often located in the 25-minute section that includes five sentence completions and two narrative passages. Short dual passages will never appear in the 20-minute Critical Reading section.

3. NUMBER OF QUESTIONS

Each short paired passage will be followed by four or five questions. An analysis of eight released SATs from January 2011 to May 2013 revealed that six tests had short passages that were followed by four questions, while two were followed by five questions.

4. TYPE OF QUESTIONS

Short paired passages include two types of questions. The overwhelming majority will be dual questions, which ask you to compare and contrast the two passages. In six of the eight released tests from January 2011 to May 2013, all of the questions involved dual-passage comparisons. A few short paired passages do include one or at most two micro questions that focus on a word or sentence in one of the passages.

5. A BASIC READING STRATEGY

The statistical dominance of dual-passage comparison and contrast questions forces you to adopt the following three-step approach to reading short paired passages:

- First, read Passage 1. Make sure that you can identify the topic and the author's attitude toward that topic. For example, is the author's tone positive or negative? Then look for a Passage 1 micro question. If there is not a Passage 1 micro question, proceed to Passage 2.
- Second, read Passage 2. Make sure that you can identify the topic and the author's attitude toward that topic. For example, is the author's tone positive or negative? Then look for a Passage 2 micro question. If there is one, answer it now. If there are no Passage 2 micro questions, proceed to the next step.
- Third, now answer each of the dual comparison and contrast questions. Chapter 32 will provide a detailed discussion of the different types of dual-passage comparison and contrast questions.

LONG PAIRED PASSAGES

1. FORMAT

Long paired passages consist of two 40–45 line passages, written by two different authors. The two authors typically present contrasting viewpoints on the same topic. For example, one recent long paired passage dealt with the causes of the Cold War. The author of Passage 1 summarized the traditionalist view that Soviet expansion into Eastern Europe triggered the Cold War. The second author presented the revisionist view that American economic expansion caused the Cold War.

2. LOCATION

Long paired passages can appear in any of the three Critical Reading sections. An analysis of eight released SATs from January 2011 to May 2013 revealed that four long paired passages appeared in the 25-minute sections, while four appeared in the 20-minute section.

3. NUMBER OF QUESTIONS
Each long paired passage will be followed by seven, twelve, or thirteen questions. Our analysis of eight SATs released from January 2011 to May 2013 revealed that one dual passage (January 2011) had seven questions, while four had twelve questions, and three had thirteen questions.

4. TYPE OF QUESTIONS
Long paired passages include both micro and dual-passage comparison and contrast questions. Many prep books assert that micro questions from either Passage 1 or Passage 2 comprise about two-thirds of the total questions, while the both passage questions comprise the remaining one-third of the total. Our analysis of eight released tests from January 2011 to May 2013 reveals that, in fact, the dual-passage comparison and contrast questions now comprise slightly more than one-half of the total long paired passage questions.

5. A BASIC READING STRATEGY: DIVIDE AND CONQUER
On first glance, a paired passage might look twice as hard as a single narrative passage. Fortunately, appearances can be deceiving. There is no reason for you to be worried. The best way to approach a long paired passage is to cut it down to size by using the following five-step "divide and conquer" strategy:
- First, read the italicized blurb. It will identify the topic and provide useful background information.
- Second, read Passage 1. As always, identify the topic and the author's attitude toward that topic.
- Third, now answer all of the Passage 1 micro questions. Don't worry about finding the questions. Long paired passage questions contain specific line and passage references that will enable you to determine which passages they relate to. Focusing on the Passage 1 questions will enable you to avoid trap answers that contain information from Passage 2. It is very important to note that long paired passages now almost always begin with one to three both-passage questions. Do not let this deter you from using our divide-and-conquer strategy. For now, skip these questions.
- Fourth, now read Passage 2. As always, identify the topic and the author's attitude toward that topic. Then answer all of the Passage 2 micro questions.
- Fifth, now go back and answer all of the dual-passage comparison questions. Since you skipped them before, be very careful to bubble your answers into the proper circles. Chapter 32 will provide a discussion of the different types of dual-passage comparison and contrast questions.

CHRISTIAN SAYS:
Be super-careful to bubble the correct bubbles! Larry's strategy is brilliant, but it is your responsibility to avoid any careless mistakes while moving from question to question.

CHAPTER 32
ANSWERING COMPARISON AND CONTRAST QUESTIONS

Have you ever asked your friends what they thought of a new movie? Did everyone have the same opinion? Probably not. Some of your friends may have liked the special effects, while others may have thought that the plot was pedestrian. People often have different opinions about the same movie, television program, YouTube video or national issue, because they look at these things from different points of view.

College Board test-writers recognize the importance of comparing and contrasting different points of view. That's why each SAT includes a short paired passage and a long paired passage. Chapter 31 provided you with basic information about the passages and questions used in this type of Critical Reading passage. As you learned, some of the short paired passages and all of the long paired passages include micro questions that are identical to the micro questions found in the narrative passages. However, the short paired passages and the long paired passages include a total of nine to eleven "comparison and contrast questions." These questions ask you to recognize similarities and differences between the two passages. This chapter will focus on the skills you need to answer comparison and contrast questions. Correctly answering these questions is essential for students striving for top Critical Reading scores.

FIVE TYPES OF COMPARISON AND CONTRAST QUESTIONS

Making comparisons and contrasts is an important part of our everyday lives. For example, as high school students you compare teachers, colleges, cars, cell phones, singers, ideas, and many other things. But what does it mean to make comparisons and contrasts? Making a comparison involves examining two or more ideas, objects, people, or events to discover ways in which they are alike. Making a comparison involves examining two or more ideas, objects, people, or events to discover ways in which they are different.

Paired passages can be compared and contrasted in a number of different ways. College Board test-writers have primarily focused on the following five types of comparison and contrast questions:

1. COMPARING AND CONTRASTING MAIN IDEAS

In Chapter 27 you learned that each SAT passage contains a main idea and supporting details. As you read each passage, it is very important to identify the author's primary purpose. Questions that ask you to compare and contrast main ideas are easy to spot. Here are examples of the formats used on recent tests:
• Both authors make the point that
• Both passages are chiefly concerned with
• The two authors differ in their approach to
• Unlike the author of Passage 1, the author of Passage 2

2. COMPARING AND CONTRASTING TONE

In Chapter 29 you learned that each author has a tone or attitude toward the subject he or she is writing about. Many paired passages include a question asking you to evaluate the differences in tone between two passages. Here are examples of the formats used in recent tests:
• The tone of each passage is best described as
• The tone of the opening sentence of each passage is best described as

3. COMPARING AND CONTRASTING ASSUMPTIONS

An assumption is a belief that underlies a statement or action. Although assumptions may be stated, they are often unstated. For example, Alexander Hamilton's statement that the government should be entrusted to the "rich, well-born, and able" was based upon the assumption that the mass of people were incapable of self-government. Many paired passage questions ask you to evaluate the assumptions upon which the authors base their arguments. Here are examples of the formats used in recent tests:
• Which of the following is an assumption made in Passage 1 about the trend toward electric cars that is contradicted in Passage 2?
• The passages imply that the Founding Framers shared which assumption about human nature?

CHRISTIAN SAYS:

Assumption questions give many of my students the most difficulty. If stuck, try referring to the relevant part of the passage and then say to yourself: "If that was what I truly believed, what else might I believe?" Following this line of imaginative reasoning can sometimes dislodge the right answer from its hiding place.

4. DETERMINING A POINT OF AGREEMENT

The authors of the two paired passages often disagree on key issues and ideas. However, this does not mean that they disagree on everything. Point-of-agreement questions are very easy to spot. Here are examples of the formats used on recent tests:

- Which of the following statements would the authors of Passage 1 and Passage 2 agree with?
- Both Passage 1 and Passage 2 emphasize the need to
- Both passages conclude with

5. DETERMINING HOW ONE AUTHOR WOULD REACT TO THE OTHER AUTHOR

These challenging questions ask you to use your knowledge of one author's viewpoint to determine how he or she would react to a point made by the other author. It is very important to note that many passages include multiple points of view. For example, an author may quote someone that he or she disagrees with. Test-writers are very quick to spot and ask questions about multiple viewpoints. Here are examples of the formats used on recent tests:

- The author of Passage 2 would most likely consider that the "perspective" mentioned in line 10, Passage 1 is
- The author of Passage 2 would most likely characterize the "scholars" (line 23) as
- The progressives described in Passage 1 would have responded to Morris's view of Theodore Roosevelt by asserting that
- The author of Passage 2 would most likely offer which response to the question posed in lines 17–18 in Passage 1?

PRACTICE: SHORT PAIRED PASSAGES

The following three short paired passages are designed to give you an opportunity to practice the skill of answering comparison and contrast questions. Read each passage and circle the best answer for each question. Answers and explanations follow each passage.

Questions 1–4 are based on the following passages.

PASSAGE 1

Line

Many Americans cherish Emanuel Leutze's painting *Washington Crossing the Delaware* as an image of heroic patriotism at a critical moment in the Revolutionary War. But iconoclasts such as Ina Jaffe have enthusiastically debunked the painting. Jaffe points out that the Leutze image contains a number of egregious flaws. For
5   example, the flag the men are carrying was not adopted until 1777, one year after the crossing. "What's more," Jaffre added, "the boats used by the Continental army were different, the time of the day is wrong, and the jagged chunks of ice floating near the boat would have been smoothed over by the flow of the river." To Jaffe's skeptical eye, the painting was both inaccurate and absurd. "There's no way,"
10   Jaffe declared, "Washington could have stood up for the journey without losing his footing and being tossed into the freezing water."

PASSAGE 2

Line

Historian David Fischer agrees that debunkers such as Ira Jaffe are right about some of the details in Leutze's painting. However, he also argues that the critics rarely ask about the accuracy of the painting's major themes: "To do so is to discover that the larger ideas in Emanuel Leutze's art are true to the history that inspired it. The artist
5   was right in creating an atmosphere of high drama around the event, and a feeling of desperation among the soldiers in the boats." Indeed, to read the writings of the men and women who were there is to find that they believed the American cause was very near collapse on Christmas night in 1776. The small army that crossed the Delaware River was near the end of its resources. They believed that another defeat
10   could destroy the Cause, as they called it. Leutze accurately captured their sense of urgency, in what was truly a watershed moment for American history.

1. The authors of both passages would most likely agree that
 (A) Jaffe is an inept art critic
 (B) Jaffe grasped the essence of what Leutze was attempting to portray
 (C) Leutze's painting is a revered icon that should not be criticized
 (D) Leutze's painting depicts a pivotal event
 (E) accurate details are more important than broad themes

2. How would the author of Passage 2 respond to Jaffe's point in lines 9–10 ("There's no...water.")?
 (A) He would concede Jaffe's point but focus on the bigger picture.
 (B) He would dismiss Jaffe's point as inaccurate and irrelevant.
 (C) He would supplement Jaffe's point with additional supporting evidence.
 (D) He would refute Jaffe's point and attempt to undermine her credibility.
 (E) He would ignore Jaffe's point and focus on other flaws in the painting.

3. Passage 2 suggests that the attitude of "the men and women" (line 16) toward Jaffe's criticism would be
 (A) emphatic support
 (B) reluctant acceptance
 (C) scholarly respect
 (D) pensive detachment
 (E) outspoken disagreement

4. Which of the following statements best characterizes the relationship between the two passages?
 (A) Passage 1 presents claims that are systematically debunked in Passage 2.
 (B) Passage 1 provides a historical perspective on an event that is largely ignored in Passage2.
 (C) Passage 2 furnishes a larger context for the specific errors described in Passage 1.
 (D) Passage 2 uses primary source accounts to corroborate the errors enumerated in Passage 1.
 (E) Passage 2 uses material presented in Passage 1 to correct popular misconceptions.

ANSWERS

1. D: Passage 1 describes the image of Washington crossing the Delaware as "a critical moment in the Revolutionary War." Passage 2 calls it "truly a watershed moment for American history." Both passages would therefore agree that "Leutze's painting depicts a pivotal event." The correct answer is therefore (D).

2. A: The author of Passage 2 concedes that Leutze's painting contains inaccurate details. However, he also stresses that Leutze correctly portrays the major themes or big picture. The correct answer is therefore (A).

3. E: The author stresses that "the men and women" wrote that "the American cause was very near collapse" as Washington prepared to cross the Delaware. These men and women understood the gravity of the situation. They would therefore have a negative view of Jaffe's focus on the painting's inaccurate but inconsequential details. The correct answer is therefore (E).

4. C: Passage 1 points out several specific errors, including the incorrect flag and the historically wrong boats. In contrast, Passage 2 is concerned with the larger setting or big picture. The correct answer is therefore (C).

Questions 5–8 are based on the following passages.

PASSAGE 1

Line

The entertainment industry in America has become increasingly formulaic. For example, reality programs are now the staple of network television schedules. The blueprint is irresistibly simple. Select a mix of everyday people and place them in a competitive situation with a clearly defined prize. Because they don't require highly-
5   paid writers and actors, reality shows are relatively inexpensive to produce and thus very profitable. The popularity of reality programs should come as no surprise to those who already believe that Newton Minow was right when in 1961 he called television "a vast wasteland." Little has changed.

PASSAGE 2

Line

The hallmark of the Hollywood superhero movie is a comic book hero who possesses
10   a distinctive power. A spate of recent superhero movies included a Norse god who wields a cosmic hammer, a man in a pulsating lime-green bodysuit who sculpts objects made from his mind entirely of light, and a bionically enhanced paramilitary stoic who protects himself with an impenetrable shield. The backstories that power superhero movies are becoming increasingly redundant and banal. We seem to be
15   watching the same stories over and over again. Of course, given Hollywood's long-standing penchant for profits over artistic creativity, this comes as no surprise.

5. The tone of the final sentence of both passages is best described as
   (A) resigned but generally optimistic
   (B) emphatic but triumphant
   (C) objective and detached
   (D) disdainful and exasperated
   (E) indignant and perplexed

6. Both passages are concerned chiefly with
   (A) describing refreshing additions to stale schedules
   (B) tracing the decline and fall of mass entertainment in America
   (C) recommending reforms to revitalize a moribund industry
   (D) commiserating with the plight of creative writers and actors
   (E) lambasting mediocre entertainment products

7. The description of Hollywood superhero movies in Passage 2 would most likely have struck Newton Minow (line 7) as
   (A) nuanced and circumspect
   (B) needlessly provocative
   (C) ambivalent but hopeful
   (D) hyperbolic and unfair
   (E) predictable and unfortunate

8. The passages imply that entertainment executives share which assumption about how best to appeal to the viewing public?

    (A) They should heed the advice of concerned media critics.

    (B) They should pander to the public's desire for escapist fare.

    (C) They should strive to persuade skeptical viewers that social injustices must be addressed.

    (D) They should present human experiences that are dignified and inspiring.

    (E) They should earnestly attempt to promote harmony among different groups of people.

ANSWERS

5. D: The final sentences in both passages convey a negative tone. The sentence "Little has changed since" in Passage 1 refers back to Newton Minow's acid description of television as "a vast wasteland." It succinctly conveys the author's high level of contempt and frustration. The author of Passage 2 is also contemptuous of Hollywood's "long-standing penchant for profits." Both of these sentences show their authors' sense of disdain and exasperation. The correct answer is therefore (D).

6. E: Both authors lambaste or sharply criticize the mediocre products being produced by the entertainment industry. The author of Passage 1 describes the industry as "increasingly formulaic," while the author of Passage 2 denounces the industry for producing "the same stories over and over again." The correct answer is therefore (E).

7. E: Newton Minow described television as "a vast wasteland." He would therefore find the "increasingly redundant and banal" superhero movies both "predictable and unfortunate." The correct answer is therefore (E).

8. B: Reality television programs and superhero movies both provide their viewers with a chance to escape the routines of their daily lives. Since both genres are very lucrative, we can infer that the entertainment executives assume that the best way to make a profit is to "pander to the public's desire for escapist fare."

Questions 9–12 are based on the following passages.

PASSAGE 1
Line

According to a widespread but mistaken popular belief, Elizabethan London was a golden age of culture and sophistication. In reality, a small army of vagabonds and criminals prowled the city's narrow streets and preyed on unlucky residents. The city's criminal population kept its jailors and executioners very busy. Judges
5   had very little latitude in handing out punishments. London's harsh criminal code demanded that jailors cut off a thief's right ear. Executioners also had much to do. Over 200 crimes in Queen Elizabeth's London were punishable by death. Some 800 English citizens were hanged every year. The most notorious criminals and traitors were decapitated and had their heads placed on pikes at the entrance to London
10   Bridge as a grim warning to other lawbreakers.

PASSAGE 2
Line

It is quite correct to describe the Elizabethan years as throbbing with life, bold adventurers, greedy speculators, and of course great writers like Shakespeare, Bacon, and Marlow. Nevertheless, it is easy to give or obtain a warped perspective, if nothing more is written or said. The crosscurrents of economic distress and
15   prosperity; the patient quietness of those who tilled the fields and died; the political pressures that made men and women move swiftly, then and now, from the farsighted and honest to the myopic and venal—all these things, and many more, enter into the total life of any age. History is more than a section in the library.

9. In their arguments, both authors make use of
   (A) aspects of daily life
   (B) personal anecdotes
   (C) statistical data
   (D) scholarly citations
   (E) gruesome analogies

10. The description of Elizabethan London in Passage 1 would most likely strike the author of Passage 2 as
    (A) overly cryptic
    (B) exaggerated and fallacious
    (C) vivid but irrelevant
    (D) too narrowly focused
    (E) thoroughly researched

11. Unlike Passage 1, Passage 2 primarily emphasizes Elizabethan London's
    (A) corruption
    (B) heterogeneity
    (C) moral rectitude
    (D) literary geniuses
    (E) draconian laws

12. Taken together, the two passages support which of the following generalizations about Elizabethan London?

(A) Soaring nationalism and a sense of rapidly expanding horizons sparked a golden age of literature.

(B) London led the world in fashion and the arts.

(C) The city witnessed a revival of commerce and industry.

(D) The city pulsated with energy and danger.

(E) The government frequently interfered to regulate economic and social affairs.

ANSWERS

9. A: Both passages describe aspects of daily life in Elizabethan London. Passage 1 focuses on the criminal behavior, while Passage 2 notes a variety of everyday routines, including "people who tilled the fields." The correct answer is therefore (A).

10. D: The author of Passage 2 strives to avoid a "warped perspective" by focusing on "the total life of any age." He would therefore find Passage 1's exclusive focus on crime and punishment is too narrowly focused. The correct answer is therefore (D).

11. B: Passage 2 describes a variety of crosscurrents and people in Elizabethan London. This emphasis on variety leads you to "heterogeneity." The correct answer is therefore (B).

12. D: Passage 1 describes the dangers that lurked in London. In contrast, Passage 2 describes Elizabethan London as "throbbing with life." Choice (D) succinctly summarizes these twin focuses. The correct answer is therefore (D).

PRACTICE: LONG PAIRED PASSAGES

The following long paired passages are designed to give you an opportunity to practice the skill of answering comparison and contrast questions. Read each passage and circle the best answer for each question. Answers and explanations follow each passage.

Questions 13–25 are based on the following passages.
The following passages compare and contrast the political theories of and influence of Thomas Hobbes and John Locke.

PASSAGE 1

Line

John Dewey once remarked that every thinker puts "some portion of an apparently stable world in peril." Thomas Hobbes (1558–1679) was such as thinker. Hobbes's method was born of the intellectual revolution wrought by him in the field of political thought. His life bridged the turbulent age of transition from faith to science. The
5   Oxford-educated Hobbes made his living as a retainer of the feudal Cavendish family and as a pensioner of the king. His attachments were, therefore, to monarchy—but with a radical difference. He did not seek the defense of kingship and aristocracy in divine ordination, as was customary, but in reason and human nature.

The central idea in Hobbes's political thought was that government was the result
10   of human necessity rather than divine ordination. Civil society came into being not because God willed it but because humans needed it. Without government, life was intolerable and civilization impossible. In a state of nature—that is, in unorganized society—men knew neither peace nor security but only brutishness.

Crucial to Hobbes's political philosophy was his conception of human character.
15   His theory of human nature, shared by such contemporaries as Niccolo Machiavelli and Samuel Pufendorf, was based on the assumption that people were naturally wild, selfish, driven by passionate appetites, pugnacious, and prone to violence. This leads to constant conflict, each person being determined to assert his or her own pleasures, which in the end can only be restrained and controlled by strong
20   authority.

Given this state of human nature, people associate together out of sheer necessity—in order to protect each other from their ravenous appetites. In effect, they give up their personal liberty, which in a state of nature is absolute, so as to be able to attain security and order. Thus, government comes into being to avoid a "war of all
25   against all."

Hobbes's unidealized view of human nature found wide acceptance in both England and America. Whether one accepted his psychology or not, his formulations sharpened men's minds. In the critical period of the 18th century, when the American federal and state Constitutions were being shaped, one finds Hobbesian psychology
30   permeating the thinking of many leading political thinkers. Thus Alexander Hamilton,

Line

in a letter of August 27, 1782, stated: "Experience is a continual comment on the worthlessness of the human race."

Hobbesian thought underlay much of the thinking that went into the making of the Federal Constitution. His pessimistic view of human nature, while not shared by
35   everybody, was nevertheless ever-present.

PASSAGE 2

Line

Hobbes's political philosophy was important but not crucial to the American political experiment. In contrast, that of John Locke did have a direct bearing on democracy. It was Locke, not Hobbes, who provided the vital ingredients that gave stimulus to democratic development.

5   The two Lockean elements, which in essence underlay classic democratic theory, were, first, his view of human nature and secondly, his conception of natural rights. Each was a fundamental refutation of Hobbes, and both had a powerful appeal to those who were sympathetic to the democratic idea. James Madison, for example, a man not given to superlatives, classed Locke with Sir Isaac Newton as one "who
10   established immortal systems."

Locke rejected the Hobbesian view that humans were innately brutish or innately rapacious or innately anything else, saying that they were in reality what environment, opportunity, and practice—he called it experience—made them. The human being did not come into the world with a ready-made character but as species of clay to be
15   shaped by the experience of life. People, in short, were what training and education made them.

Locke's assumptions about human nature were closely linked to his political theory. In contrast, to the Hobbesian view of human beings' rapacious instincts, Locke stressed goodness and rationality. He rejected the idea that government was based
20   on force and denied the assumption that in entering civil society people surrendered their rights to the state. It made no sense, Locke argued, for people to organize government so as to escape the brutish existence of a state of nature, only to fall into the hands of an arbitrary ruler who would be no less grim.

In place of arbitrary government, where one person had all the power and the rest
25   none, Locke postulated the theory of "natural rights." People, he wrote, were born with certain basic rights—among them life, liberty, and property—which they did not surrender when they entered civil society.

Locke's optimistic view of human nature and human potential had a profound influence on leading American political thinkers. Thomas Jefferson for example,
30   proclaimed that Locke's basic theory "is perfect as far as it goes."

13. The tone of both passages is best described as
(A) urgent
(B) apologetic
(C) scholarly
(D) flippant
(E) skeptical

14. The author of Passage 2 would most likely respond to the last paragraph of Passage 1 by
(A) contending that Locke was a more brilliant political theorist than Hobbes
(B) concurring that all leading American political thinkers shared Hobbes's view of human nature
(C) suggesting that Hobbes should rethink the assumptions underlying his view of human nature
(D) agreeing that Hobbes's influence was significant, but stressing its limitations
(E) pointing out that Hobbes's view of human nature was pervasive and profound

15. The author of Passage 1 quotes John Dewey in lines 1–2 primarily in order to
(A) signal the pivotal importance of Hobbes's political ideas
(B) convey his disapproval of Hobbes's political views
(C) subtly insinuate that Dewey was more influential than Hobbes
(D) qualify his enthusiasm for Hobbes
(E) discourage anyone from questioning Hobbes's view of human nature

16. The author of Passage 1 most probably mentions Hobbes's connections to the king and the Cavendish family (lines 5–6) in order to
(A) highlight the growing rift between Hobbes and the king
(B) imply that Hobbes's support for the monarchy was linked to his financial relationship with the king and the Cavendish family
(C) underscore the originality of thought that led Hobbes to support monarchy as a form of government
(D) demonstrate the inherent flaws in Hobbes's method of thought
(E) imply that Hobbes was a secret heretic who opposed the Church of England

17. Those holding Locke's view of human nature would argue that Hamilton and Machiavelli
(A) underestimated the importance of experience in shaping character
(B) overly idealized human nature
(C) played no role in shaping American political thought
(D) ignored the dangers of unbridled patriotism
(E) supported a potentially advantageous cultural trend

18. The author of Passage 1 would most likely characterize Machiavelli and Pufendorf (lines 15–16) as
(A) skeptics who questioned the relationship between Hobbes and the Cavendish family
(B) wealthy connoisseurs who dabbled in politics
(C) sycophants who tried to flatter Hobbes
(D) prodigies who enjoyed displaying their political and literary skills
(E) theorists who shared a common political perspective with Hobbes

19. Which of the following terms would the author of Passage 1 use to describe Hobbes?
(A) aristocrat
(B) pragmatist
(C) chauvinist
(D) apologist
(E) conformist

20. Which best conveys how "human nature" is described in Passage 1 and Passage 2?
(A) harshly realistic .. malleable
(B) unalloyed idealism .. obstinate
(C) utterly selfish .. philanthropic
(D) perpetually belligerent .. peaceful
(E) unabashedly egotistical .. altruistic

21. The tone of the first paragraph (lines 34–37) of Passage 2 is best described as
(A) emphatic
(B) impartial
(C) sanguine
(D) caustic
(E) wary

22. Which of the following, if true, would most seriously undermine Locke's assumptions (lines 44–48) about human nature?
(A) Crime rates are closely linked to poverty rates.
(B) Voting patterns are closely related to a person's level of education.
(C) Political views become more conservative as income rises.
(D) Culture plays a dominant role in shaping marriage customs.
(E) Intelligence scores of children are closely related to the intelligence scores of their mothers.

23. Which of the following best describes the approach used in Passage 2?
(A) a systematic debunking of a political theory
(B) a methodical comparison and contrast
(C) a colorful, dramatic description
(D) a pointed criticism couched in sarcasm
(E) a careful presentation of a political anomaly

24. Which best describes the relationship between the two passages?
(A) They discuss antithetical philosophic approaches.
(B) They suggest how to test a historic hypothesis.
(C) They draw the same conclusion using different historic examples.
(D) They share the same view of human nature.
(E) They successfully reconcile conflicting arguments.

25. With which of the following statements would the authors of both passages be most likely to agree?
(A) Hobbes was a more original thinker than Locke.
(B) Hobbes was a more pragmatic political thinker than Locke.
(C) Hobbes and Locke were both overshadowed by the political theories of Machiavelli and Pufendorf.
(D) Hobbes's and Locke's theories were both too abstract for practical-minded Americans.
(E) Hobbes and Locke were both seminal political theorists who had a significant influence on American thought.

ANSWERS

13. C: Both passages clearly have a scholarly or serious and intellectual tone. The correct answer is therefore (C).

14. D: The author of Passage 2 does not dispute the importance of Hobbes's political theories. However, he believes that it was Locke and not Hobbes who had the greatest impact upon American political thought. The correct answer is therefore (D).

15. A: The author of Passage 1 uses Dewey's quote to identify Hobbes as a thinker who put a portion of "an apparently stable world in peril." Hobbes's political ideas must therefore have been pivotally important. The correct answer is therefore (A).

16. C: The author wants us to understand the depth of Hobbes's originality. A lesser thinker would have been influenced by his connections to aristocrats and the royal family. But Hobbes did not base his defense of monarchy upon loyalty to the crown; he based it upon "reason and human nature." The correct answer is therefore (C).

17. A: Both Hamilton and Machiavelli share Hobbes's negative view of human nature. In contrast, Locke emphasized the overriding importance of experience in shaping human character. The correct answer is therefore (A).

18. E: Both Machiavelli and Pufendorf share Hobbes's view of human nature. The correct answer is therefore (E).

19. B: The key word "unidealized" means that Hobbes was a practical or pragmatic thinker. The correct answer is therefore (B).

20. A: Hobbes's view of human nature is "harshly realistic," because he describes humans as "naturally wild, selfish, driven by passionate appetites, pugnacious, and prone to violence." In contrast, Locke viewed human nature as being "malleable" or adaptable, because human character is "shaped by the experience of life." The correct answer is therefore (A).

21. A: The author's tone is forceful and filled with conviction. This leads you to EMPHATIC (Word 54) as the correct answer. The correct answer is therefore (A).

22. E: Locke's basic assumption was that humans are entirely shaped by experience. If intelligence scores of children are closely related to the intelligence scores of their mothers, this would undermine Locke's assumption that we "are shaped by the experience of life." The correct answer is therefore (E).

23. B: The author of Passage 2 carefully compares and contrasts Hobbes's and Locke's views of human nature and political theory. The correct answer is therefore (B).

24. A: Hobbes and Locke have diametrically opposing views. The authors of the two passages thus discuss "antithetical philosophic approaches." The correct answer is therefore (A).

25. E: Both authors repeatedly emphasize that Hobbes and Locke were seminal or vitally important political theorists who had a significant impact upon American political thought. The correct answer is therefore (E).

APPENDIX:
THE TOP THIRTY SAT ROOTS

You have now learned over 600 high-frequency SAT vocabulary words. This Appendix is designed to further AUGMENT your SAT LEXICON by teaching you thirty of the most frequently used roots and 94 words derived from them. A root is a word or word element from which other words are formed. Learning roots will give you insights into unfamiliar words that will enable you to answer difficult questions. For example, one Level 4 question asked students to read the following sentence and determine how the narrator viewed Lewis' hand: "I watched his hand rather than the location, for it seemed to have power over the terrain." Knowing that the root POTEN means "power" will enable you to connect the passage word "power" with the correct answer OMNIPOTENT, meaning "all-powerful."

1. ACRI & ACER
- *Latin roots that means SHARP, VERY BITTER*
ACUTE—very sharp, as a keen insight
ACUMEN—mental sharpness, keenness
ACERBIC—characterized by a bitter, cutting tone
EXACERBATE—to make something very bitter; to worsen
ACRIMONIOUS—filled with bitterness and strong resentment; rancorous in tones

2. AMICUS
- *a Latin root meaning FRIEND*
AMICABLE—characterized by or showing friendliness
AMITY—friendly relations between people or countries
AMIABLE—good-natured and friendly; affable

3. BELLI

- *a Latin root meaning WAR*

REBELLION—an uprising that leads to war
ANTEBELLUM—before the war, especially the American Civil War
BELLIGERENT—waging war and thus inclined to fight
BELLICOSE—warlike; favoring war to settle a dispute

4. CHRON

- *a Greek root meaning TIME*

CHRONOLOGY—the story of events in time
CHRONICLE—a record of events in order of time
CHRONIC—a condition, habit, or disease that occurs all the time
ANACHRONISM—an event placed out of its proper time

5. CLUD & CLUS

- *Latin roots meaning CLOSE, SHUT*

EXCLUDE—to shut out
CONCLUSION—the close or end of a story
PRECLUDE—to exclude or shut out beforehand; to prevent because of preexisting conditions
RECLUSIVE—describes someone who prefers to shut out and therefore retire from the rest of the world

6. CRED

- *a Latin root meaning BELIEF*

CREDIBLE—capable of being believed; plausible
CREED—a formal system of beliefs
CREDIBILITY—the quality of being believable; trustworthy
CREDULOUS—disposed to believe too readily; tending to believe something with little evidence
DISCREDIT—to cause to be disbelieved or distrusted

7. DEMOS

- *a Greek root meaning PEOPLE*

DEMOGRAPHY—the study of vital statistics about people
DEMAGOGUE—a leader who uses passionate speeches to agitate the people

8. FID

- *a Latin root meaning TRUST, FAITH*

FIDELITY—to faithfully perform one's duties and obligations
CONFIDENT—a person you can trust completely
DIFFIDENT—lacking faith or confidence in oneself
PERFIDIOUS—to show disloyalty and treachery

9. FLU

- *a Latin root meaning TO FLOW*

FLUENT—able to speak readily; the words literally flow out of your mouth
CONFLUENCE—o flow together
MELLIFLUOUS—to literally flow like honey and thus to be sweet and flowing like a lullaby
SUPERFLUOUS—to flow above in the sense of exceeding what is necessary

10. GREG

- *a Latin root meaning FLOCK or HERD; in English the root GREG means GROUP*

CONGREGATE—to flock together in a group
SEGREGATE—to separate the flock into different groups
GREGARIOUS—living in flocks or herds and therefore very sociable
EGREGIOUS—standing out from the herd in the negative sense of being extraordinarily bad
AGGREGATE—to gather different groups into a whole new flock or total

11. LOQU

- *a Latin root meaning TALK*

LOQUACIOUS—very talkative
LOCUTION—a word or expression that is used by a particular person or group; a style of speaking

12. LUC & LUMEN

- *Latin roots meaning LIGHT*

LUCID—filled with light and thus very clear
ELUCIDATE—to bring into the light and thus clarify
LUMINOUS—bathed in light; glowing

13. MORI

- *a Latin root meaning TO DIE or DEATH*

MORIBUND—near death; stagnant
MOROSE—very despondent and gloomy

14. MORPH

- *a Latin root meaning SHAPE or FORM*

AMORPHOUS—lacking shape or form
ANTHROPOMORPHIC—taking human shape

15. MUT

- *a Latin root meaning CHANGE*

MUTATE—to undergo a great change
IMMUTABLE—not able to be changed

16. NOV

- *a Latin root meaning NEW*

NOVEL—new and unusual
NOVICE—a person who is new at an occupation; a beginner
INNOVATE—to introduce new ideas; methods, or products
INNOVATOR—a person who introduces new ideas, methods, or products
RENOVATE—to restore or make new again

17. ONUS

- *a Latin word meaning BURDEN*

ONEROUS—very burdensome
EXONERATE—to be freed from a burden; to be free from blame

18. PACIS

- *a Latin word meaning PEACE*

PACIFY—to bring peace to; to calm or soothe
PACIFISM—a doctrine that opposes war and the use of military force
PACIFIST—a person who opposes war or the use of physical force to settle disputes

19. PAR

- *a Latin root meaning EQUAL*

PARITY—equality in amount, value, or status
DISPARITY—an inequality in age, rank, income, or treatment
DISPARATE—entirely dissimilar; completely unequal

20. PATHOS

- *a Greek root meaning FEELING*

APATHY—to show no feeling or emotion
ANTIPATHY—to show feelings against someone or something
EMPATHY—to share strong feelings with someone; to feel as one would in another's place; great sympathy
EMPHATIC—to express very strong feelings about someone or something; great conviction

21. PLAC

- *a Latin root meaning CALM*

PLACID—to be outwardly calm and composed
PLACATE—to calm someone down, especially by appeasing or yielding concessions
COMPLACENT—to be so calm as to be self-satisfied or smug
IMPLACABLE—cannot be calmed down and therefore relentless

22. POTEN

- *a Latin root meaning POWERFUL*
OMNIPOTENT—all-powerful
POTENTATE—a very powerful person

23. PUG

- *a Latin root meaning FIST*
PUGILIST—a professional boxer
PUGNACIOUS—literally, someone who is eager to use his or her fists and therefore quick to fight; combative
IMPUGN—to use one's verbal fists, in the sense of challenging, questioning or criticizing the accuracy or honesty of someone

24. QUIESCERE

- *a Latin word meaning QUIET*
QUIESCENT—quiet and still
ACQUIESCENT—quietly accepting something

25. SCRIB

- *a Latin root meaning WRITE*
CIRCUMSCRIBE—literally, to write around, in the sense of limiting or restricting
PROSCRIBE—to write rules that forbid or prohibit an action or behavior

26. SEMIN

- *a Latin root meaning SEED*
DISSEMINATE—to spread widely, as in spreading seeds
SEMINAL—literally, an idea that is a seed for an important and original theory or new intellectual system of thought

27. SPEC & SPIC

- *Latin roots meaning to SEE or OBSERVE*
SPECTATOR—someone who sees or watches an event
PERSPECTIVE—how you see something; a point of view
CIRCUMSPECT—literally, to see around and thus to be cautious and careful
PERSPICACITY—to see through, in the sense of being very perceptive or astute

28. TEN

- *a Latin root meaning to HOLD*
TENACIOUS—to hold firmly to something; to be very persistent
TENABLE—capable of being held, defensible
TENUOUS—very thin and flimsy; difficult to hold

29. **TURB**

- *a Latin root meaning TROUBLED*
TURBULENT—very disturbed; agitated
IMPERTURBABLE—not easily troubled or disturbed
PERTURBED—to be greatly troubled and thus uneasy and anxious

30. **VIVERE**

- *a Latin root meaning to LIVE*
VIVACIOUS—full of life and therefore animated
CONVIVIAL—full in life in the sense of enjoying feasting, drinking, and good company

INDEX

A

WORD	NUMBER	PAGE	APPENDIX
Anachronism	232	72	Root 4
Analogous	37	14	
Analogy	36	14	
Anecdote	21	9	
Anguish	587	170	
Animosity	225	70	
Animus	164	58	
Anomaly	19	8	
Antebellum		316	Root 3
Antediluvian	152	54	
Anthropomorphic	401	118	Root 14
Antipathy	164	58	Root 20
Antiquated	152	54	
Antithetical	11	6	
Apathetic	72	27	Root 20
Aplomb	221	69	
Apoplectic	245	75	
Appall	489	141	
Apprehensive	595	174	
Arcane	180	60	
Archaic	152	54	
Arduous	355	105	
Artifice	289	87	
Arrest	549	159	
Assail	296	88	
Assiduously	396	116	
Assuage	588	171	
Astute	395	116	
Atypical	19	8	
Audacious	385	113	
Augment	450	131	
Auspicious	331	99	
Austerity	542	158	

WORD	NUMBER	PAGE	APPENDIX
Autocratic	397	116	
Automaton	107	38	
Autonomy	107	38	
Avarice	260	79	

B

WORD	NUMBER	PAGE	APPENDIX
Baleful	248	76	
Banal	547	159	
Bane	422	123	
Bastion	257	78	
Befuddled	320	95	
Beguile	14	6	
Belie	18	7	
Bellicose	245	75	Root 3
Belligerent		316	Root 3
Bellwether	386	113	
Bemoan	373	110	
Benefactor	87	33	
Bewilder	372	110	
Bias	48	19	
Bland	391	115	
Blithe	519	149	
Bohemian	317	94	
Bombastic	223	70	
Boon	423	123	
Boorish	121	44	
Brevity	211	67	
Broad	550	160	
Brooding	586	170	
Brusque	181	60	
Bucolic	369	109	
Bungler	110	39	
Burgeon	371	109	

C

WORD	NUMBER	PAGE	APPENDIX
Creed		316	Root 6
Crude	121	44	
Cryptic	529	152	
Criterion	49	19	
Crystallize	309	92	
Cull	389	114	
Cultivate	**579**	167	
Cupidity	260	79	
Curmudgeon	102	37	
Cursory	301	90	
Curt	182	60	
Curtail	349	104	
Cynical	64	25	

D

WORD	NUMBER	PAGE	APPENDIX
Dauntless	457	133	
Dearth	414	121	
Debacle	346	103	
Debased	114	42	
Decry	61	24	
Defunct	322	95	
Deleterious	111	41	
Demagogue	96	35	Root 7
Demarcate	363	107	
Demise	112	41	
Demography		316	Root 7
Deprecate	400	117	
Derivation	522	150	
Deride	597	175	
Despondent	113	42	
Despotic	397	116	
Destitute	418	122	
Deter	430	125	

E

F

G

H

I

WORD	NUMBER	PAGE	APPENDIX
Indignant	61	24	
Indulgent	314	93	
Ineffable	261	79	
Inept	185	61	
Inertia	513	147	
Infinite	135	47	
Infinitesimal	337	101	
Inflame	206	66	
Ingenious	464	134	
Inimical	270	82	
Innocuous	219	68	
Innovator	88	33	Root 16
Innuendo	228	71	
Inscrutable	308	91	
Insidious	220	68	
Insipid	391	115	
Instill	477	138	
Insurmountable	134	47	
Intemperate	138	48	
Interloper	83	32	
Intransigent	166	58	
Intrepid	457	133	
Intricate	504	145	
Invective	295	88	
Irascible	313	93	
Irate	245	75	
Ire	586	170	
Irony	28	11	
Irreverent	216	68	

J

WORD	NUMBER	PAGE	APPENDIX
Jaded	327	97	
Jocular	57	23	
Jovial	57	23	

WORD	NUMBER	PAGE	APPENDIX
Melancholy	497	143	
Meld	413	121	
Mellifluous	255	78	Root 9
Mendacity	344	102	
Mentor	86	32	
Mercurial	158	55	
Metaphor	24	10	
Meteoric	388	114	
Meticulous	168	58	
Milieu	431	125	
Minuscule	337	101	
Minutiae	148	53	
Misanthrope	92	34	
Miscellany	435	126	
Misnomer	414	137	
Mitigate	3	4	
Mock	481	139	
Mollify	3	4	
Moribund	143	52	Root 13
Morose		317	Root 13
Multifaceted	18	7	
Multifarious	222	69	
Mundane	469	136	
Mutate		317	Root 15
Myopic	244	75	
Myriad	141	51	

N

WORD	NUMBER	PAGE	APPENDIX
Naïve	203	66	
Narcissistic	142	51	
Nebulous	309	92	
Nefarious	156	55	
Negligent	474	137	

WORD	NUMBER	PAGE	APPENDIX
Nemesis	104	38	
Neophyte	94	35	
Nomadic	516	148	
Nonchalant	65	25	
Nonplussed	372	110	
Nostalgia	13	6	
Notorious	434	126	
Novel		318	Root 16

O

WORD	NUMBER	PAGE	APPENDIX
Obdurate	166	58	
Objective	79	29	
Obsequious	528	152	
Obstinate	166	58	
Obsolete	446	130	
Obstreperous	234	72	
Odd	551	160	
Officious	316	94	
Olfactory	524	150	
Ominous	15	7	
Omnipotent		319	Root 22
Onerous	440	127	Root 17
Opaque	424	123	
Ornate	541	157	
Orthodox	98	36	
Oscillate	442	130	
Ostentatious	596	174	
Overbearing	407	119	
Overwrought	178	60	

P

R

WORD	NUMBER	PAGE	APPENDIX
Rambling	16	7	
Rampant	412	120	
Rancid	377	111	
Rancor	418	122	
Reaffirm	375	110	
Rebuke	408	119	
Rebut	43	18	
Recalcitrant	166	58	
Reciprocate	117	43	
Reclusive		316	Root 5
Rectitude	239	74	
Reconcile	589	171	
Recondite	180	60	
Reflective	77	28	
Refractory	271	82	
Refute	44	18	
Reinvigorate	120	43	
Reiterate	270	82	
Relinquish	533	153	
Remorse	583	170	
Remuneration	426	124	
Renegade	101	37	
Renovate		318	Root 16
Reprimand	408	119	
Reprobate	82	31	
Repugnance	390	114	
Reserved	10	5	
Resignation	558	162	
Resilient	118	43	
Resolute	468	136	
Resonate	317	94	
Resplendent	340	101	
Restitution	420	122	

WORD	NUMBER	PAGE	APPENDIX
Stodgy	451	132	
Stringent	421	123	
Stymie	200	63	
Subtle	9	5	
Succinct	16	7	
Succumb	393	115	
Sumptuous	428	124	
Supercilious	198	63	
Superficial	334	100	
Superfluous	415	121	Root 9
Supine	527	151	
Surly	263	80	
Surpass	506	145	
Surreptitious	582	169	
Symbiosis	520	149	
Synthesis	258	78	

T

WORD	NUMBER	PAGE	APPENDIX
Taciturn	304	90	
Tackle	569	164	
Tactless	399	117	
Tangent	453	132	
Tasteless	575	166	
Tedious	32	12	
Temper	563	163	
Tenable		319	Root 28
Tenacious	487	140	Root 28
Tendentious	171	59	
Tenuous		319	Root 28
Tepid	540	155	
Theatrical	190	62	
Theoretical	217	68	
Thwart	199	63	
Transgression	433	126	

WORD	NUMBER	PAGE	APPENDIX
Trenchant	593	174	
Trepidation	248	76	
Trifling	148	53	
Trite	188	61	
Trivial	148	53	
Trivialize	473	137	
Truncate	281	84	
Tumult	495	143	
Turbulent		320	Root 28
Tutelage	86	32	

U

WORD	NUMBER	PAGE	APPENDIX
Ubiquitous	237	73	
Unaffected	128	45	
Unalloyed	131	41	
Unambiguous	305	91	
Unconventional	184	61	
Uncorroborated	123	44	
Uncouth	121	44	
Undaunted	125	45	
Underdog	108	39	
Undermine	45	18	
Underscore	46	18	
Understatement	31	12	
Unequivocal	294	88	
Unerring	132	46	
Unfailing	127	45	
Unfettered	122	44	
Unflappable	192	62	
Unnerved	124	44	
Unorthodox	183	61	
Unpretentious	130	46	
Unsavory	126	45	
Unscrupulous	129	46	

W

WORD	NUMBER	PAGE	APPENDIX
Watershed	236	73	
Wary	69	26	
Whimsical	74	27	
Wistful	73	27	
Wry	193	62	

Y

WORD	NUMBER	PAGE	APPENDIX
Yield	570	165	

Z

WORD	NUMBER	PAGE	APPENDIX
Zealot	100	36	
Zealous	563	163	